1939—The Year in Movies

1 9 3 9

The Year in Movies

A Comprehensive Filmography

by

Tom Flannery

McFarland & Company, Inc., Publishers
Jefferson, North Carolina, and London

British Library Cataloguing-in-Publication data are available

Library of Congress Cataloguing-in-Publication Data

Flannery, Tom.
　　1939, the year in movies : a comprehensive filmography / by Tom
Flannery.
　　　　p.　cm.
　　Includes bibliographical references.
　　Includes index.
　　ISBN 0-89950-466-3 (lib. bdg. : 50# alk. paper) ⊗
　　1. Motion pictures—United States—History.　2. Nineteen thirty-
nine, A.D.　3. Motion picture industry—United States—History.
I. Title.
PN1993.5.U6F547　1990
791.43′75′09730943—dc20　　　　　　　　　　　　　　　90-52640
　　　　　　　　　　　　　　　　　　　　　　　　　　　　CIP

Manufactured in the United States of America

McFarland & Company, Inc., Publishers
　Box 611, Jefferson, North Carolina 28640

This book is dedicated to my uncle, Gerard Flannery, in appreciation for all of the wonderful movies he introduced me to (many of which were made in 1939)

Table of Contents

vii

• —————————————— • *Acknowledgments*

The author would like to gratefully thank the following people and places: the Academy of Motion Picture Arts and Sciences, for the use of their library in researching this book; U.C.L.A., for same; Emil Reisman and his staff at Beverly Hills Videocentre, for providing me with videotapes of most of the films covered in this book — they really do have the largest selection in the West; Dwayne Sanderson, for his cooperation in the completion of this book and for his sound movie advice; and especially Anita, whose continued love and support turned my dream of this book into a reality.

Introduction

For the movies, there will never be another year like 1939.

It was a year of innocence and optimism in America. The stock market crash was past, F.D.R. was fulfilling his promise of a "New Deal" in the White House, the New York World's Fair opened in April, and the conflict that would eventually escalate into World War II was, for the time being, still "the War in Europe."

The movies of that year—like the movies of any year, really—reflected the mood of the nation. It was, after all, the year that Americans followed the Yellow Brick Road. It was the year that Garbo laughed. It was the year that Jimmy Stewart went to Washington to defend truth and justice. And, most memorably, it was the year that Clark Gable shocked a censored nation by actually saying the word "damn" in a motion picture.

It was, as any film scholar, historian, critic or aficionado would agree, the very apex of the Golden Age of Cinema.

The year 1939 was one of big stars and bigger studios. The five major studios—MGM, Warner Bros., Paramount, Twentieth Century–Fox and RKO—not only made and distributed films, but they ran their own theater chains as well. These "integrated majors" owned or controlled approximately 2,800 theaters (including nearly all of the lucrative first-run houses, where the bulk of box-office revenues came from).

With an average of four hundred new feature films flooding the marketplace each year, double-billing had become standard practice across the country. Most theaters changed their features two or three times a week just to keep up. This created a need for second-billing pictures which was filled by independent and second-rank companies, the most significant of which were Universal and Columbia (between them, they released 102 films in '39). Right behind them was United Artists, a releasing company for such hefty independent producers as David O. Selznick and Samuel Goldwyn, two men whose name above the title of a picture virtually guaranteed superior quality.

Collectively, the five major studios and these three nonintegrated outfits made up what came to be called "the Big Eight," a cartel of interdependent companies that dominated the nation's eleventh largest industry: movie-making.

Not only did they dominate the business aspect of the industry, but they also dominated the talent. Moguls like Louis B. Mayer, Jack Warner and Harry Cohn ruled their respective lairs with iron fists. In 1939, the Big Eight had a combined 590 actors, 114 directors, and 340 writers under contract, each of whom worked an eight-hour shift every weekday, half a day on Saturday, and received a weekly paycheck. It took an average of 22 days to shoot a movie, at an average cost of $300,000. And with grosses in excess of $700 million annually, they were able to guarantee bankers 4½¢ back on every dollar invested in production, which also made it easier to take a chance on "risky" or commercially untested material.

The highest-paid stars earned in excess of $400,000 a year. Short-term contracts could be even more lucrative. For example, Walter Huston once signed a contract paying him a staggering $40,000 a week (at a time when little more than 3 percent of the nation claimed taxable income). However, they were not afforded many of the luxuries that today's stars enjoy. A major star of today like Robert Redford or Dustin Hoffman not only commands a multi-million-dollar salary and a percentage of the gross, but has the luxury of choosing what material he wants to perform in, *and* wields almost exclusive control over the production of that project. The stars of '39 dutifully accepted whatever roles were offered them and worked long hours virtually year-round. If they refused, they were suspended without pay. And whereas Redford or Hoffman might decide to do one movie every two or three years, the stars of the thirties frequently worked in anywhere from four to twelve movies a year, often going literally from one set to the next. Humphrey Bogart, for instance, appeared in seven different motion pictures released in 1939.

Some stars battled the Big Eight, refusing to work in mediocre scripts and demanding better compensation. Many of them lost this battle. Others—such as James Cagney, Bette Davis, and Cary Grant—emerged victorious, thereby insuring their survival over the ensuing decades.

Clark Gable was actually punished for his protests by being loaned out to a minor studio in 1934 to star in a movie that nobody wanted to make. The studio was Columbia and the movie was *It Happened One Night,* which surprised everyone by becoming the biggest hit of the year. It also swept that year's Academy Award ceremony, winning Best Picture, Best Actress, Best Director, Best Screenplay, and a Best Actor statuette for Gable (the only one he would ever receive).

The pool of talent in Hollywood that year was quite extraordinary. Unlike today, the movie stars of '39 were not rock singers, football players, body builders, karate champions, television throw-backs, professional wrestlers, or porno queens trying to go legit. They were *stars.* They carried their own light. The list of top box-office attractions from that year reads like a veritable Who's Who of American Cinema: Clark Gable, Gary Cooper, Bette Davis, Cary Grant, Joan Crawford, Greta Garbo, James Stewart, Henry Fonda, Spencer Tracy, Katharine Hepburn, Fred Astaire, Ginger Rogers, James Cagney, Errol Flynn, Judy Garland, and Laurence

Olivier (to name but a few). Many of today's "stars" wouldn't have been able to land even a bit part if they had been around in 1939.

And the list of directors from that year is just as impressive: John Ford, Alfred Hitchcock, George Stevens, William Wyler, Carol Reed, Ernst Lubitsch, Cecil B. DeMille, Frank Capra, George Cukor, Howard Hawks, Jean Renoir, Sam Wood, and Victor Fleming all made films that were released in 1939.

Even more remarkable, perhaps, were the writers. As David Niven wisely pointed out in his book *Bring On the Empty Horses:* "Reputations and fortunes were made out of movies by producers, directors, and actors, but if they had not had good screenplays to work with, they would have sat around picking their noses." Many of the great novelists of the day, unable to support themselves writing books, had already migrated to Hollywood, where anyone who displayed even the most rudimentary talent for writing could make quick and easy money and lots of it. Ben Hecht once signed a contract guaranteeing him $15,000 a week. Even the failing F. Scott Fitzgerald—no more than a shadow of his former self—was making $1,000 a week polishing scripts in 1939, while working on a book he intended to call *The Last Tycoon.*

In May of '39, *The Day of the Locust* was published—novelist Nathanael West's searing indictment of the Hollywood studio system. However, the book sold only 1,464 copies, bringing his total earnings for his past four novels (ten years' worth of work) to a mere $1,280. Disheartened, West returned to hacking out scripts at RKO for $350 a week salary. In a letter to his publisher, he gushed: "Thank God for the movies!"

Clearly, all of their hard work paid off—not only in terms of quality, but also in box-office receipts. More than 50 million Americans went to the movies at least once a week that year, with repeat and occasional movie-goers pushing the total weekly attendance up to an incredible 80 million (roughly eight times the per capita rate of weekly attendance nowadays). The average admission price was 27 cents, for which you saw not only a double feature, but also cartoons, a newsreel and—on weekends, usually—even a thrilling serial thrown in to bring you back next weekend. Eighty percent of the nation's entertainment expenditures went towards movies. Not surprisingly, Louis B. Mayer was the highest-paid man in America for the third year running, with $1.25 million in salary and bonuses. Comparatively, Franklin Delano Roosevelt earned $75,000 that year.

At the New York World's Fair of 1939, Americans got their first look at a gadget that would ultimately put an end to the movie boom; a gadget that would capture their hearts—if not their minds—and give them less cause to leave the comfort of their living rooms in search of news and entertainment. That gadget was called television.

But in 1939, the last thing on the minds of the studio executives was television. They were too busy cranking out 365 feature films that year, in an age when sequels were rare. You never saw a *Gone with the Wind II* or a *Mr. Smith Goes Back to Washington* or a *Roaring Thirties;* when a picture said "The End," it almost always meant it, no matter how well it did commercially. Instead of the barrage of sequels and well-worn premises that is commonplace today, virtually every film released back then was an original movie idea. In fact, 329 original screenplays were written in 1939.

If the material was not original, then it was usually adapted from one of the great works of literature (Twain's *The Adventures of Huckleberry Finn*, Hugo's *The Hunchback of Notre Dame*, Brontë's *Wuthering Heights*, etc.). When Steven Spielberg accepted the prestigious Irving Thalberg Award in 1987, he urged the industry to follow Thalberg's example and return to the written word. This may seem hypocritical and trite coming from the man who directed the "Indiana Jones" trilogy and who admitted the only reason he even agreed to read *The Color Purple* was because it was such a "thin book," but nevertheless, his words rang with truth that evening.

Around the world, 1939 looked just as promising for other film industries as it did for the American cinema. After surviving a few dismal years, British cinema was clearly on the rebound in 1939, led by such promising directors as Alfred Hitchcock, Carol Reed, Michael Powell, Robert Stevenson, David MacDonald, Arthur Woods and Pen Tennyson. But the impending war would change all of that. Stevenson would leave England with his wife, the actress Anna Lee; MacDonald would never reclaim his prewar glory days; Powell would become a maverick and — although responsible for a number of great films — would fall in and out of favor with critics and audiences alike throughout his career; and neither Woods nor Tennyson would survive the war. Only Hitchcock and Reed would completely fulfill their earlier promise, each sailing for America and embarking on long and distinguished careers.

In Italy, film production was soaring, from 35 films in 1934 to 87 in 1939. Director Alessandro Blasetti made two of his best films that year: *Un'avventura di Salvator Rosa (An Adventure of Salvator Rosa)* and *Ettore Fieramosca*, with the help of a dialogue writer and assistant director who was soon to achieve world fame on his own — Renato Castellani.

Soviet cinema was growing by leaps and bounds as well. In 1938, the resolution of the Seventeenth Party Congress on the new five-year plan provided for increasing their network to 70,000 projectors. The number of sound projectors in the U.S.S.R. grew from 498 in 1934 to 15,202 in 1939, the year of the Eighteenth Communist Party. It is, however, important to note that the cinema acquired sound only on the threshold of the thirties and that most of their old theaters still ran silent pictures. In addition, film import dropped to a bare minimum during that decade. Only the premiere films were brought in from the West, including the masterpieces of John Ford, Rene Clair and Alexander Korda.

In Japan, the Motion Picture Law was passed, placing the film industry completely under government control until the end of the war in 1945. All scripts had to be passed by censors, and actors and directors had to take an examination for a license to work. Still, the country managed to produce a number of noteworthy films (the two best of which are covered in this book).

Germany, on the other hand, was too busy with its invasion of Poland to make any great contributions to world cinema in 1939.

Nineteen thirty-nine was a year of beginnings. Ingrid Bergman made her American debut, Greer Garson made her film debut, and John Wayne graduated from B-Westerns to full movie stardom. It was also a year of endings. Fred Astaire and Ginger Rogers' wonderful series of RKO musicals came to an end with the release of *The Story of Vernon and Irene Castle,* and silent movie idol Douglas Fairbanks, Sr., died of a heart attack.

But mostly it was a year of great movies — movies that are very much alive and well more than half a century later. Movies that have passed the test of time.

And that's what this book is all about.

The Adventures of Huckleberry Finn

Paramount. 92 min. Directed by Richard Thorpe.
Cast: Mickey Rooney, Walter Connolly, William Frawley, Red Ingram, Lynne Carver.

Best film version of the Twain classic, with a laid-back Rooney in fine form as Huck and Ingram giving an excellent turn as Jim. Connolly and Frawley provide laughs as the riverboat con-artists. Filmed previously in 1931 and since in 1960 and 1974 (as well as TV movies in 1975 and 1981).

Allegheny Uprising

RKO. 81 min. Directed by William Seiter.
Cast: Claire Trevor, John Wayne, George Sanders, Brian Donlevy, Wilfrid Lawson, Robert Barrat, John F. Hamilton, Moroni Olsen, Eddie Quillan, Chill Wills.

In 1939, Brian Donlevy created an array of villain roles that is unmatched by any other actor during a single year. He played the kind of guys that audiences loved to hate in *Beau Geste, Jesse James, Destry Rides Again, Union Pacific* and this picture. Here he plays an unscrupulous trader who is selling the Pennsylvania Indians liquor and firearms in colonial America 1759. John Wayne leads the local frontiersmen against him and the tyrannical British, as well, in what the Duke would later refer to as the "one cautious role of my life." This was one of many films that reteamed Wayne with his *Stagecoach* costar Claire Trevor, though none of their subsequent outings together would prove as critically or commercially successful as that classic. *Allegheny Uprising* was released in England as *The Last Rebel*.

The Arizona Kid

61 min. Directed by Joseph Kane.
Cast: Roy Rogers, George Hayes, Sally March, Stuart Hamblen, Dorothy Sebastian.

In 1938, when Gene Autry went on strike at Republic (as he had threatened to do a number of times in the past), the studio brought in a guy named Leonard Slye to replace him. Slye was a singer in a Western band called the Sons of the Pioneers, and had appeared with the group in a litany of Republic oaters. It wasn't until '38, however, and Autry's strike that he was given a starring role in his own feature, a film called *Under Western Stars*. But before that happened, the studio insisted on a change of name for their new star, so Slye was called in to confer with the top brass at Republic and come up with a suitable monicker. They settled on "Rogers" as a last name because Slye had been a lifelong admirer of Will Rogers, and when someone in the room came up with the first name of "Roy," the "King of the Cowboys" was born. His most famous sidekick was George "Gabby" Hayes, his leading lady after 1944 was wife Dale Evans, and his horse, of course, was Trigger, "the Smartest Horse in the Movies." Trigger could drink milk from a bottle, walk 150 feet on his hind legs, do simple addition and subtraction, and count to 20 as well. Roy purchased the palomino in 1938 for $2,500, a hefty sum for him at the time. Later, though, he would refer to it as "the cheapest $2,500 I ever spent." Roy Rogers would go on to make 90 features for Republic over the next 14 years, making him one of the most enduring and beloved of all American stars. In 1939, he starred in nine films including this one, which is set during the Civil War and centers on Missouri's pledge of allegiance to the North and the subsequent defection of various factions which formed outlaw gangs under the pretense of supporting the Southern cause. An interesting note is that Stuart Hamblen, who plays the villain in the movie, later made his own mark as a singer, in the country music field. Then, in 1952, he launched a brief political career by throwing his Stetson into the presidential race on the Prohibition ticket.

At the Circus

A Metro-Goldwyn-Mayer Picture. Directed by Edward Buzzell. Produced by Mervyn LeRoy. Screenplay by Irving Brecher. Photographed by Leonard M. Smith. Edited by William H. Terhune. Art direction by Cedric Gibbons; Associate, Stan Rogers. Set decorations by Edwin B. Willis. Women's costumes by Dolly Tree. Men's costumes by Valles. Sound by Douglas Shearer. Musical direction by Franz Waxman. Songs by Harold Arlen and E.Y. Harburg. Vocal and orchestra arrangements by Murray Cutter, George Bassman and Ken Darby. Dance direction by Bobby Connolly. Running time: 87 minutes.

Cast: Groucho Marx *Attorney Loophole;* Chico Marx *Antonio;* Harpo Marx *"Punchy";* Kenny Baker *Jeff Wilson;* Florence Rice *Julie Randall;* Eve Arden *Peerless Pauline;* Margaret Dumont *Mrs. Dukesbury;* Nat Pendleton *Goliath;* Fritz Feld *Jardinet;* James Burke *John Carter;* Jerry Marenghi *Little Professor Atom;* Barnett Parker *Whitcomb.*

After Thalberg's death, my interest in the movies waned. I continued to appear in them, but my heart was in the Highlands. The fun had gone out of picture-making. I was like an old pug, still going through the motions, but now doing it solely for the money. — Groucho Marx[1]

Synopsis: Though not one of the Marx Brothers' best outings, *At the Circus* is nonetheless an enjoyable picture that contains a few great scenes, the most memorable of which is Groucho's rendition of "Lydia the Tattooed Lady."

Groucho plays the fast-talking, duck-walking Attorney J. Cheever Loophole, who is brought in to help save Wilson's Wonder Circus. The owner of the circus, Jeff Wilson (Kenny Baker), owes John Carter (James Burke) ten thousand dollars, which he must pay or relinquish ownership of the circus to Carter. Assisting Attorney Loophole in the case are two circus employees, Antonio (Chico Marx) and Punchy (Harpo Marx).

Jeff raises the money with the show's receipts only to have it stolen from him aboard the train going to the next town by the circus strongman, Goliath (Nat Pendleton), and a midget named Little Professor Atom (Jerry Marenghi), two of Carter's henchmen.

At the next town, Carter passes the loot on to his girlfriend, Peerless Pauline (Eve Arden). While Attorney Loophole is grilling her, she stashes it in her bosom. "There must be some way of getting that money without getting in trouble with the Hays Office," Groucho muses.

Failing to find a way to beat the censors, he goes off to Newport to visit Jeff's wealthy aunt, Mrs. Dukesbury (Margaret Dumont). When Loophole arrives, she is in the process of organizing a major social party for that evening. He impersonates a famous maestro and cons her into paying $10,000 for Wilson's Wonder Circus.

The show is a big success, the stolen money is recovered, the bad guys are foiled, and Antonio and Punchy send the real maestro, Jardinet (Fritz Feld), and his entire orchestra floating out to sea, performing Beethoven.

Notes: By the time the Marx Brothers performed in *At the Circus* for MGM, their stock at the studio had fallen considerably. Instead of the customary staff of well-honed writers usually assigned to their projects, this time out they were given only Irving Brecher, who had never worked with the siblings before. And when Groucho was informed that he and his brothers would not be allowed to take their routines for the picture out on the road (their usual but expensive testing ground), he vowed to leave the studio as soon as his contract expired. "Why should I, at my age, let myself get upset over a movie—a movie that in three months will probably wind up on a double bill at the Oriental Theatre, with bingo and free dishes?"[2] he philosophized.

Eddie Buzzell—a former song-and-dance man who had played on the same bill as the Marx Brothers on stage many times—was given directing chores, and producer Mervyn LeRoy and songwriters Harold Arlen and

At the Circus (MGM). *Top:* **The Marx Brothers clown around.** *Bottom:* **Harpo and Chico shoot Groucho out of a cannon.**

E.Y. Harburg (all three of whom were working on *The Wizard of Oz* together that same year) were also assigned to the project.

The picture's big finale called for the services of a gorilla, and since one was not readily available, gorilla imitator Harry Gamorra was hired for the part. The only problem was, Gamorra didn't own a gorilla suit. So one was found for him to wear. On the day the scene was to be shot, two agents were present, one who represented Mr. Gamorra and one who represented the suit (valued at $5,000). Unbeknownst to Gamorra, the suit was not ventilated at all, and after only an hour or so of filming inside of it, he fainted. After recovering and shooting for another hour or so, he fainted again. When Gamorra recovered the second time, he refused to get back inside the suit until a means of ventilation was devised. While the different parties argued vehemently, Gamorra excused himself, took the suit to the studio commissary, located an ice pick and did the job himself. Then he went back to work. When shooting continued for over two consecutive hours, the agent of the suit became suspicious. No one had ever lasted more than an hour inside of it without fainting. When he examined the suit and discovered what Gamorra had done, the real fireworks began. Eventually, the agent stormed off of the soundstage in a huff, taking his mutilated, five-thousand-dollar gorilla suit with him. Another suit was later found and shooting resumed.

Florence Rice, who played Kenny Baker's love interest in the picture, was the daughter of Grantland Rice, the great sportswriter and old friend of the Marx Brothers. Also in the cast was Eve Arden, who'd been chased all over the Broadway stage by Bob Hope in *The Ziegfeld Follies of 1935*. And, of course, there was Margaret Dumont, Groucho's favorite foil. After doing her own stunt on a trapeze in this movie, she swore that she'd never work with the Marx Brothers again, under any conditions. Two years later, though, she broke that vow when she appeared in *The Big Store* with them.

At the 1973 Academy Awards, Groucho was given an honorary Oscar. In his acceptance speech, he said: "I wish Harpo and Chico were here to share this great honor. And I wish Margaret Dumont were here, too. She was a great straight woman even though she never got any of my jokes."[3]

Also worth noting is the fact that the great silent film comedian Buster Keaton — down on his luck and unable to find any work in Hollywood at the time — was hired by Harpo to provide funny visuals for the picture.

Reviews: "Between them, they whip up some passages of high hilarity, but there is no sustained comic note in their new offering. . . . What is chiefly wrong with *At the Circus* is that the brothers Marx have almost none of the split-second timing which marked their great films of the past." — Howard Barnes, *The New York Herald Tribune*

". . . a rather dispirited imitation of former Marx successes." — Frank S. Nugent, *The New York Times*

Babes in Arms

An MGM Picture. Directed by Busby Berkeley. Produced by Arthur Freed. Screenplay by Jack McGowan and Kay Van Riper. Based on the play by Richard Rodgers and Lorenz Hart. Photographed by Ray June. Edited by Frank Sullivan. Art direction by Cedric Gibbons; Associate, Merrill Pye. Set decorations by Edwin B. Willis. Wardrobe by Dolly Tree. Musical adaptation by Roger Edens. Musical director: George Stoll. Orchestral arrangements by Leo Arnaud and George Bassman. Recording director: Douglas Shearer. Running time: 97 minutes.

Songs: "Babes in Arms" and "Where or When" by Richard Rodgers and Lorenz Hart. "Good Morning" by Nacio Herb Brown and Arthur Freed. "God's Country" by Harold Arlen and E.Y. Harburg.

Cast: Mickey Rooney *Mickey Moran;* Judy Garland *Patsy Barton;* Charles Winninger *Joe Moran;* Guy Kibbee *Judge Black;* June Preisser *Rosalie Essex;* Grace Hayes *Florrie Moran;* Betty Jaynes *Molly Moran;* Douglas McPhail *Don Brice;* Rand Brooks *Jeff Steele;* Leni Lynn *Dody Martini;* John Sheffield *Bobs;* Henry Hull *Madox;* Barnett Parker *William;* Ann Shoemaker *Mrs. Barton;* Margaret Hamilton *Martha Steele;* Joseph Crehan *Mr. Essex;* George McKay *Brice;* Henry Roquemore *Shaw;* Lelah Tyler *Mrs. Brice;* Lon McCallister *Boy.*

> They had us working days and nights on end. They'd give us pep-pills to keep us on our feet long after we were exhausted. Then they'd take us to the studio hospital and knock us cold with sleeping pills—Mickey sprawled out on one bed and me on another. Then after four hours they'd wake us up and give us the pep-pills again so we could work another seventy-two hours in a row. Half of the time we were hanging from the ceiling, but it became a way of life for us.—Judy Garland[4]

Synopsis: *Babes in Arms* is a standard if energetic let's-put-on-a-show-kids vehicle, elevated from mediocrity by the teaming of Mickey Rooney, the number one box-office attraction of 1939, with Judy Garland, MGM's fastest-rising young female star, who segued directly from the set of *The Wizard of Oz* to this project. It was the first of five musicals that they would make together for the studio.

This one opens in 1921, at the venerable Palace Theatre, where veteran vaudeville comedian Joe Moran (Charles Winninger) receives word that his wife Florrie (Grace Hayes) has just given birth to a baby boy, whom they name Mickey (Mickey Rooney). The husband-and-wife team of Joe and Florrie Moran flourishes over the next decade and a half, during the glory days of vaudeville, and young Mickey is raised on a stage, performing and dreaming of someday becoming a songwriter. But in the late thirties, with the emergence of talking pictures, their fortunes change drastically, as do the fortunes of vaudeville and everyone involved in it. Even the Palace Theatre is converted into a movie house.

Mickey and Judy perform in blackface, as Al Jolson accounts for just one of Mickey's many great impersonations in *Babes in Arms* (MGM).

All of the vaudeville old-timers still living in Seaport, Long Island, decide to take a "comeback show" on the road, a last-ditch effort to revive their waning careers. Their kids — who are all now teenagers — want to be part of the show, but their parents refuse and leave them behind in Seaport. So, led by Mickey and his songstress sweetheart, Patsy Barton (Judy Garland), the kids decide to convert an old barn into an open-air theatre and put on a show of their own. They are opposed by the wicked Martha Steele (Margaret Hamilton), who would like nothing better than to foreclose on all of the actors' mortgages and have their kids put into a state work school.

The biggest obstacle facing Mickey, Patsy and all of their friends is the

Mickey as F.D.R. and Judy as Eleanor Roosevelt in *Babes in Arms* (MGM).

money needed to produce the show, but when "Baby" Rosalie Essex (June Preisser), a former child star who looks suspiciously like a teenage Shirley Temple, joins the cast, she agrees to finance the project. The one condition, however, is that she be given the female lead in the show (which Mickey has already promised to Patsy). When he breaks the news to Patsy, she is crushed, but for the good of the show and Mickey's fledgling career, she accepts the role of Rosalie's understudy. However, when she sees Mickey kissing Rosalie during one of the rehearsals, Patsy runs off in tears to join her parents in Schenectady, where the comeback show is laying an egg. Her mother (Ann Shoemaker) lectures her about the trooper spirit and convinces her to return to Seaport and to Mickey.

Prior to opening night, Rosalie's father (Joseph Crehan) arrives and totes his daughter away by her ear, forcing her to relinquish the lead and allowing Patsy to take over.

The opening of the show is ruined by a sudden hurricane, but big-time producer Harry Madox (Henry Hull) sees enough to impress him and to agree to stage it at his own theatre in New York City. Mickey reconciles with his dad, patches up his relationship with Patsy and produces a smash play that culminates with the big finale "God's Country" (a thinly veiled paean to MGM and its infamous "more stars than there are in heaven" slogan, with lyrics such as: "We've got Nelson Eddy/ Lots of others/ We've got three of the four Marx Brothers").

Notes: Richard Rodgers and Lorenz Hart's stage musical *Babes in Arms* ran for an impressive 289 performances on Broadway in 1937. The production—featuring Mitzi Green, Wynn Murray, Ray Heatherton, Alfred

Drake, Ray McDonald, and Grace McDonald—boasted a memorable score, a weak storyline, and a strong accent on youth. Lyricist Arthur Freed, who had been associate producer to Mervyn LeRoy on *The Wizard of Oz*, acquired the property for $21,000 and became a full-fledged producer when he turned it into a movie in 1939.

Freed completely overhauled the Rodgers-Hart show, retaining only the title song and "Where or When" from its score (as well as musical snippets from "The Lady Is a Tramp"). Such hit tunes as "My Funny Valentine," "Johnny One Note," "Imagine," and "I Wish I Were in Love Again" were all excised. With his songwriting partner Nacio Herb Brown, Freed wrote "Good Morning" especially for the movie version, and also threw in "I Cried for You," a song that he had written with Gus Arnheim. Harold Arlen and E.Y. Harburg, who had composed the wonderful score for *The Wizard of Oz*, contributed the big finale, "God's Country." Another Arlen-Harburg composition, "Let's Take a Walk Around the Block," was considered but ultimately rejected.

Earlier that same year, Busby Berkeley's contract had come up for renewal at Warner Bros., but the studio refused to grant him the salary increase he deserved, hoping he'd renew at the same rate. Instead, he opted to do a bit of freelancing and immediately landed an emergency assignment at MGM, creating the musical finale to *Broadway Serenade* starring Jeanette MacDonald. He came up with a surrealistic number much like the ones he had made famous while working at Warners, and it impressed studio head Louis B. Mayer so much that he subsequently assigned him full directorial chores on *Babes in Arms*. Unbeknownst to Berkeley, every director on the lot had already turned the project down, fearing it was going to be a major flop. Made for a mere $78,000 and grossing $3,335,000 in its initial release, it was anything but, and it gave Berkeley a new artistic home.

This was a perfect showcase for the talents of Judy Garland, who is young and sweet and lovely and in marvelous voice, and especially the irrepressible Mickey Rooney, who sings, dances, clowns, and does hilarious impersonations of Clark Gable, Lionel Barrymore, and Al Jolson. He was nominated for Best Actor that year for his work in this picture.

Supporting Mickey and Judy were real-life husband and wife Douglas McPhail and Betty Jaynes. In 1941, they would be divorced and McPhail would attempt suicide, unsuccessfully. Three years later, in 1944, after being discharged from the Army for being emotionally unequipped to serve, he would attempt suicide once again. This time he would succeed.

Also in the cast was Johnny Sheffield, who would join the *Tarzan* series that same year in the role of Boy.

Besides Mickey Rooney's Best Actor nod, the film was also nominated for Best Score.

Reviews: ". . . a brightly entertaining screen version of the Rodgers and Hart legit musical. Perked up by . . . Mickey's mugging and undeniable song and dance talents, and by Judy Garland's simply swell sense of swing

. . . Babes in Arms is quite a show. It moves fast, with guaranteed laughs and lots of sure-fire tunes."—Irene Thirer, *The New York Post*

"The irresistible team of Mickey Rooney and Judy Garland are currently displaying their varied talents from the Capitol screen in *Babes in Arms*. As an entertainment it has lost some of its original sophistication and the elastic snap with which it went over on the stage. But it has gained in comic interludes and serves to introduce several new screen personalities. Mickey performs with all the youthful vigor he is capable of throwing into a screen role."—*The New York Daily News*

"Mickey and Judy better than ever."—Robert Dana, *The New York Herald Tribune*

Bachelor Mother

An RKO Picture. Directed by Garson Kanin. Produced by B.G. DeSylva. Screenplay by Norman Krasna. Based upon an original story by Felix Jackson. Photographed by Robert DeGrasse. Edited by Henry Berman and Robert Wise. Art direction by Van Nest Polglase; Assistant: Carroll Clark. Set decorations by Darrell Silvera. Miss Rogers' gowns by Irene. Dances by Hermes Pan. Makeup by Mel Burns. Special effects by Vernon L. Walker. Recorded by Richard Van Hessen. Musical score by Roy Webb. Still photographer: John Miehle. Running time: 82 minutes.

Cast: Ginger Rogers *Polly Parrish;* David Niven *David Merlin;* Charles Coburn *J.B. Merlin;* Frank Albertson *Freddie Miller;* E.E. Clive *Butler;* Elbert Coplen, Jr. *Johnnie;* Ferike Boros *Mrs. Weiss;* Ernest Truex *Investigator;* Leonard Penn *Jerome Weiss;* Paul Stanton *Hargraves;* Gerald Oliver-Smith *Hennessy;* Leona Roberts *Old lady;* Dennie Moore *Mary;* June Wilkins *Louise King;* Frank M. Thomas *Doctor;* Edna Holland *Matron;* Irving Bacon *Clerk;* Reed Hadley *Dance partner;* Chester Clute and Florence Lake *Couple in park;* Barbara Pepper *Dance hall hostess;* Horace MacMahon and Charles Hall *Bouncers;* Donald Duck *Himself.*

> Do you realize that I am the director of this picture and you are the co-star, but between us we are being paid less than half what the cameraman is getting?—Garson Kanin to David Niven during the shooting of *Bachelor Mother*[5]

Synopsis: In 1939, after a string of successful musicals at RKO, Fred Astaire and Ginger Rogers amicably and mutually agreed to a professional divorce. Astaire stayed in the musical genre, dancing with just about every Hollywood beauty who didn't have two left feet. Rogers, on the other hand, branched out into light romantic comedies and even straight drama (like *Kitty Foyle,* for which she won an Oscar in 1940). The vehicle that studio head Pandro S. Berman chose to launch her post–Astaire career was

Bachelor Mother (RKO). *Top:* Ginger Rogers tries to turn a deserted baby left out on the doorstep of the foundling home over to Edna Holland and Frank M. Thomas, but they're not buying her story. *Bottom:* David Niven (seated, offering plate) and a non–English speaking Ginger Rogers celebrate New Year's Eve together.

Bachelor Mother, a charming and witty comedy that paired her with a young unknown English actor named David Niven. Rogers had doubts about the project and tried to get out of making it, but—fortunately for her—Berman convinced her to accept the role. It turned out to be one of the surprise hits of the year and launched her solo career with a bang.

Rogers plays shopgirl Polly Parrish, who is released from her duties at Merlin's Department Store the day before Christmas. On her way home after work, she sees an old lady (Leona Roberts) leaving a baby (Elbert Coplen, Jr.) at the doorstep of Atkins Foundling Home. When Polly goes to care for the child, she is mistaken for its mother by a matron (Edna Holland) who works at the foundling home. Polly tries to explain what happened, but nobody inside will believe her story.

A doctor at the facility (Frank M. Thomas) goes to Merlin's to discuss the situation with the owner's son, David Merlin (David Niven). David is a roguish playboy who has just returned from a night in the clinker. The doctor tells David that Polly has given up her baby because she couldn't afford to raise it, so David agrees to rehire her for life and give her a generous raise as well.

That night, they deliver the baby to Polly's home, but she has a date with a co-worker, Freddie Miller (Frank Albertson), and does not wish to mother a child that is not hers. So she has Freddie drive her over to the Merlin home, gives the infant to the butler (E.E. Clive)—claiming that David is "responsible"—and flees with Freddie.

David and his butler trail them to a club called the Pink Slipper, where Polly and Freddie are entered in a dance contest. David follows them inside, but gets into a skirmish with the club's bouncers (Horace MacMahon, Charles Hall) and is unceremoniously tossed out on his ear. So he finds out where Polly lives and takes the baby to her home. When she returns later that evening, David chastises her strongly for her reprehensible behavior. He also threatens to fire her, have her black-listed by every department store in town, and refuse all requests for reference requirements if she does not accept responsibility for the child and agree to raise it. Without much of a choice, Polly reluctantly complies.

Mrs. Weiss (Ferike Boros), Polly's landlady, offers to help her raise the baby and provide her with all of the necessary accessories (crib, playpen, etc.). When Mrs. Weiss asks her what the baby's name is, Polly (who doesn't even know its sex) replies, "Joanie." Mrs. Weiss (who *does* know its sex) gushes over what a nice name *Johnnie* is, and Polly suddenly realizes she has a boy on her hands.

At work, Freddie asks her to use her "influence" with David to get him a promotion to floor manager. He gets the promotion—but only because he has top seniority—and thanks Polly, marveling at how quickly she can get things done. Polly, of course, doesn't know what he's talking about.

But David does become friendly with her, and takes a paternal interest in little Johnnie's upbringing. When he finds himself without a date on New

Year's Eve at eight o'clock, he asks to take Polly out. He buys her an expensive wardrobe, escorts her to an uptown nightclub where a group of his friends are celebrating, and even gives her a brand-new identity (the daughter of a Swedish manufacturer who doesn't speak English). All of the men in David's party take turns dancing with Polly, and David is left to do the "translating." At the end of the evening, when an ex-flame of his tells David that she would have personally gone stag rather than bring Polly, Polly shoots back (in perfect English): "You could, too, with those shoulders!"

Later, in Times Square, David and Polly are separated by the throngs of people that have gathered for the annual ritual, but they reunite in time to inaugurate the new year with a long and passionate kiss. Then they sing "Auld Lang Syne" jubilantly along with their fellow New Yorkers.

Freddie, who has been ousted from his new position by David, vengefully writes a letter the next day to David's father John (Charles Coburn), the owner of Merlin's, telling him that he is a grandfather. So John follows his son to a park, where he finds him with Paula and Johnnie.

"I'd know that chin anywhere!" John exclaims when he first holds the little boy in his arms.

Back home, David finds himself in the same predicament that Polly did when his father won't believe his story. Convinced that Johnnie is his grandson, John threatens to do everything in his power to get custody of the child, even if it means taking the case to the Supreme Court.

Mrs. Weiss cajoles her son Jerome (Leonard Penn) to play the part of Polly's husband, while David offers Freddie his management position back if he will play the same part. When they show up simultaneously at John Merlin's office, it only serves to reinforce what he already strongly believes. In the confusing melee, Polly escapes undetected, planning to pack up her belongings and leave town with Johnnie. But David catches up to her at her apartment and proposes marriage. Polly accepts and they all, presumably, live happily ever after.

Notes: Written by Norman Krasna, a screenwriter whose career was marked by an obsession with comic themes of mistaken identity, this delightful comedy was originally called *Nobody's Wife* and then *Little Mother* before the filmmakers finally decided on *Bachelor Mother*.

Besides being a surprise hit in the States, the film also proved to be enormously successful in Britain, where it lightened the gloom and despair of the early days of September 1939, just before the outbreak of World War II. The film's English costar, David Niven (on loan-out from Goldwyn), was pulling all sorts of strings trying to get back to his homeland and enlist in the war effort while shooting this film.

Future director Robert Wise—who would go on to lens such classics as *West Side Story* (1961) and *The Sound of Music* (1965), among many others—worked as an editor on this picture.

Felix Jackson received an Oscar nomination for his original story, but lost to *Mr. Smith Goes to Washington*.

Bachelor Mother was remade in 1956 as a lame Debbie Reynolds–Eddie Fisher vehicle called *Bundle of Joy.*

Reviews: ". . . hits on all sixteen cylinders, becoming a powerhouse of amusement. . . . Ginger Rogers is delightful. . . . If another picture comes along to prove this department a liar, it will be a pleasure to die laughing." — Archer Winsten, *The New York Post*

"I must insist that the most timely as well as the most engaging film of the week is a little thing called *Bachelor Mother.* Any picture that could hold one's undivided attention for 82 minutes during these days, a film that could make one relax and laugh and forget everything except the moving figures on the screen is entitled to top place in a reviewer's notice and his ungrudging admiration . . . ." — *The Observer*

Beau Geste

A Paramount Picture. Produced and directed by William A. Wellman. Screenplay by Robert Carson. Based upon the novel of the same name by Percival Christopher Wren. Photographed by Theodor Sparkuhl and Archie Stout. Edited by Thomas Scott. Art direction by Hans Dreier and Robert Odell. Interior decorations by A.E. Freudeman. Musical direction by Alfred Newman. Orchestrations by Edward Powell. Sound by Hugo Grenzbach and Walter Oberst. Costumes by Edith Head. Second unit director: Richard Talmadge. Technical adviser: Louis Van Der Ecker. Running time: 114 minutes.

Cast: Gary Cooper *Beau Geste;* Ray Milland *John Geste;* Robert Preston *Digby Geste;* Brian Donlevy *Sergeant Markoff;* Susan Hayward *Isobel Rivers;* J. Carrol Naish *Rasinoff;* Albert Dekker *Schwartz;* Broderick Crawford *Hank Miller;* Charles Barton *Buddy McMonigal;* James Stephenson *Major Henri de Beaujolais;* Heather Thatcher *Lady Patricia Brandon;* G.P. Huntley, Jr. *Augustus Brandon;* James Burke *Lieutenant Dufour;* Henry Brandon *Renouf;* Arthur Aylesworth *Renault;* Harry Woods *Renoir;* Harold Huber *Voisin;* Stanley Andrews *Maris;* Donald O'Connor *Beau at 12;* Billy Cook *John at 10;* Martin Spellman *Digby at 12;* David Holt *Augustus at 12;* Ann Gillis *Isobel at 10;* Harvey Stephens *Lieutenant Martin;* Barry Macollum *Krenke;* Ronnie Rondell *Bugler;* Frank Dawson *Burdon, the butler;* George Chandler *Cordier;* Duke Green *Glock;* Thomas Jackson *Colonel in Recruiting Office;* Jerome Storm *Sergeant-Major;* Joseph Whitehead *Sergeant;* Harry Worth and Nestor Paiva *Corporals;* George Regas and Francis McDonald *Arab scouts;* Carl Voss, Joe Bernard, Robert Perry, Larry Lawson, Henry Sylvester and Joseph William Cody *Legionnaires;* Joe Colling *Trumpeter O. Leo;* Gladys Jeans *Girl in Port Said Cafe.*

> At the beginning, I ran a bus to the local house of ill-fame in Yuma, and the first couple of weeks it was packed. They were riding on top of it. But after

Beau Geste (Paramount). *Top:* Who stole the priceless Blue Water sapphire? Robert Preston, Ray Milland, Susan Hayward, Heather Thatcher, G.P. Huntley, Jr., and Gary Cooper wonder. *Bottom:* A desert tribe attacks the fort.

they had been there for two or three weeks, there was only one guy who would go there, an old stunt man. He was the only one, and he ended up burning it down. That was a rugged picture. You had to be tough. — William A. Wellman[6]

Synopsis: P.C. Wren's romantic novel about a missing gem, a debt of honor, and savagery in the French Foreign Legion was first filmed in 1926, with Ronald Colman as Beau and Noah Beery as the sadistic sergeant. Director Wellman's version was a scene-for-scene remake of that silent classic and became quite popular in its own right.

It opens as a relief column of legionnaires led by Major Henri de Beaujolais (James Stephenson) arrives at Fort Zinderneuf. Seeing no signs of life, the major dispatches a trumpeter to check the situation inside. When the trumpeter fails to return, the major himself goes into the compound. He finds all of the soldiers inside dead, and in their sergeant's hand he finds a confession note claiming that he was the one who stole the infamous "Blue Water" sapphire from Brandon Abbas. His trumpeter, meanwhile, has mysteriously disappeared. The major goes out and leads his men inside, but when they arrive, the sergeant's body and his confession have vanished. Gunshots are heard in the distance, and the relief column retreats to a nearby oasis for cover. Just as they are digging themselves in to prepare for an attack, they see Fort Zinderneuf going up in flames.

The film then flashes back fifteen years in time, to Brandon Abbas in England. The young Geste brothers, John (Billy Cook), Digby (Martin Spellman), and Beau (Donald O'Connor), are all would-be soldiers dressed in cardboard armor. Beau dreams of someday joining the Foreign Legion and of having a Viking's funeral when he dies, cremated with his weapon and a dog at his feet. His brother Digby promises to honor this request.

We learn that their guardian, Lady Patricia Brandon (Heather Thatcher), is the owner of the Blue Water sapphire, "the great-great-grandfather of all sapphires," which has a history of bringing only bad luck to those who possess it.

The film fast forwards fifteen years, and the boys have grown into dashing young men, as played by Ray Milland (John), Robert Preston (Digby), and Gary Cooper (Beau). Lady Brandon informs the boys that their benefactor, Sir Hector, has decided to sell the Blue Water. They ask to see it one last time; when she obliges, the lights go out suddenly. When they are turned back on, the jewel is gone. Lady Brandon agrees to leave its box on the table until morning in hopes that whoever took it will return it.

In the morning the jewel is still gone, and so is Beau. He leaves behind a note saying that he has stolen the Blue Water. A few hours later, Digby disappears, and leaves behind a confession note as well. John knows his brothers well enough to realize that they have gone off to join the French Foreign Legion, and he decides to go after them. He says farewell to Isobel Rivers (Susan Hayward), a young lady who grew up with the boys and with

Donald O'Connor, Billy Cook and Martin Spellman portray the Geste brothers as children; David Holt and Ann Gillis are also featured in this scene from *Beau Geste* (Paramount).

whom John has fallen madly in love. She promises to wait for him, no matter how long he is gone.

The story picks up again in Saida, where the brothers — now all legionnaires — are reunited. There they encounter the sadistic Sergeant Markoff (Brian Donlevy), who was expelled from the Siberian Penal Colonies for cruelty, joined the Legion, and has slowly risen in the ranks despite his inhumane methods. He considers his men nothing better than "scum."

Both Beau and Digby still claim to have possession of the Blue Water, so John chirps in with a confession of his own. Their flippant conversation is overheard by a Russian jewel thief, Rasinoff (J. Carrol Naish). A few nights later, Beau catches the thief searching his bed for the jewel, and a scrape ensues. Sergeant Markoff squeezes the information about the Blue Water out of Rasinoff, and devises a plan to acquire the jewel for himself.

A week later, the troop is split into two separate divisions, and Markoff seizes the opportunity to put his plan into action. He sends Digby off alone with the first regiment, and takes Beau and John with his regiment to Fort Zinderneuf. When his superior, the inexperienced Lieutenant Martin (Harvey Stephens), passes away, Markoff assumes complete control of the compound. Under his command, Zinderneuf becomes a veritable hell for the men. Schwartz (Albert Dekker) whips the other legionnaires into a mutinous frenzy. Only Beau, John, and another soldier, Maris (Stanley Andrews), refuse to participate in their planned rebellion.

Later that night, one of Markoff's informants tips him off to the mutiny. While the men are still sleeping, Markoff removes all of the rifles from the barracks and arrests all of the men, save Beau, John, and Maris. The prisoners are escorted outside, where Markoff orders Beau and John to begin executing them for treason. The brothers refuse, and Markoff counters by threatening to kill them. Just as he is about to drill the two full of holes, the fort is attacked by a wild desert tribe. The legionnaires get their rifles back and go into battle.

"Rapid fire, you scum! Rapid fire!" Markoff screams insanely.

The attacks continue throughout the night and into the next day, until only a handful of men are still alive, including John and Markoff. In the final attack, Beau is mortally wounded. When John catches Markoff rummaging through his dying brother's pockets, searching for the Blue Water, John kills the sergeant (with Beau's help). Before Beau dies, he instructs John to place a confession letter in Markoff's hand and also informs him where he can find the jewel. After leaving the confession in Markoff's hand and finding the Blue Water, John escapes on foot in the desert.

At this point, the film picks up where it began—as Major de Beaujolais' relief column is arriving at Fort Zinderneuf—and explains that mysterious episode. The trumpeter that the major sends inside is Digby Geste, and when he finds his brother's lifeless carcass among the dead, he carries him down into the barracks, lays him out on his bed with his rifle, and covers him up. Then he carries Sergeant Markoff's body down and lays him at Beau's feet, to serve as the dog. After setting the barracks on fire and fulfilling his vow to give Beau a Viking's funeral, he runs off to join his brother John.

Crossing the desert, Digby is killed in a skirmish with the wild tribe. Only John makes it back to Brandon Abbas, where he is reunited with Isobel and returns the Blue Water to Aunt Pat, along with a letter from Beau explaining that he ran off with it to protect it for her and keep her from losing it.

Notes: In 1938, Paramount announced that they would be remaking the silent 1926 adventure classic *Beau Geste*. They wanted a facsimile of the original, and they assigned the chore of shooting it to the very competent director William A. Wellman. Studio publicity sheets announced that the film would be shot in glorious Technicolor and would feature Fred Mac-Murray in the lead role. When the cameras finally rolled, however, it had already been decided that black and white photography would serve the subject better and that Gary Cooper would serve the title role much better than MacMurray.

Cooper was coming off three consecutive flops and desperately needed a box-office hit. He surprised many by backing away from the role of Rhett

Butler in *Gone with the Wind*, which he considered too irascible and sexy for his particular talents. But when Paramount offered him the lead role in *Beau Geste*, Cooper jumped at the chance. Wellman had enormous sets constructed for the picture and chose an expert cast, helping to make it the big commercial success that Cooper had been searching for. After completing the project, which was his last under contract to Paramount, the actor decided to free-lance instead of signing with any particular studio.

The cast and crew included over a thousand people. Unfortunately, of the entire cast, only Milland and Heather Thatcher were English-born and thus had the proper accents; neither Cooper nor Preston sounded the least bit English. The film contains a memorable performance by Brian Donlevy as Sergeant Markoff; the character's name (in the book as well as the original version) was actually Sergeant Lejaune, but his nationality was changed to Russian for the 1939 film, since by then there was no desire on the studio's part to offend the French with a brutally realistic depiction of a legionnaire sergeant. Nevertheless, the film was banned in France for that very depiction. Donlevy was nominated for Best Supporting Actor by the Academy for his interpretation.

The picture was shot at Buttercup Valley, in the desert near Yuma, Arizona (the same location where the original had been lensed in April and May of 1926). The flashback scenes of Brandon Abbas were shot at Busch Gardens in Pasadena, where portions of *Wings* (1927) had been filmed.

Location shooting was tough. There were frequent sand storms and constant 100°-plus heat. By the end of the month-long shoot, over twenty men had been admitted to the hospital for heat exhaustion. Tempers flared, as well, particularly when it came to Donlevy, whom everyone involved with the picture seemed to uniformly despise.

Besides Donlevy's nomination, the film received a nod for Best Art Direction, but lost in both categories.

It was remade in 1966, and spoofed by Marty Feldman in his 1977 comedy, *The Last Remake of Beau Geste*.

Reviews: "Paramount's 1939 *Beau Geste* is like meeting up with an old schoolmate who has become the town idiot. The weakness here has something to do with the heart's having gone out of a thing—characters being booted around like old tomato cans, every dramatic effect being thrown bodily into your face, and no time or concern left for such minor things as plausible motives or reason."—Otis Ferguson, *The New Republic*

"The men dote upon Mr. Cooper for his stature, his taciturnity, his gaunt countenance. The apotheosis of the manly, he is flawlessly fitted for the strong, silent, boyish heroics of *Beau Geste*. That he no longer looks quite boyish enough to play the grateful ward of a patrician lady is a captious criticism—and one the men will not tolerate.... Brian Donlevy as the horrendous Sgt. Markoff shines as the outstanding actor in the piece.... A suitable vehicle for such an aggressively he-man star as Mr. Cooper. His admirers will applaud his restraint, and the fans generally will approve Mr.

William Wellman's handsome treatment of a well-loved adventure tale." —
Bland Johaneson, *The New York Daily Mirror*

Blackwell's Island

Warner Bros. 71 min. Directed by William McGann.

Cast: Victor Jory, Rosemary Lane, John Garfield, Dick Purcell, Stanley Fields, Morgan Conway, Granville Bates, Anthony Averill, Peggy Shannon.

Based on the famous raid by Austin MacCormick on Welfare Island in 1934, this film casts John Garfield as a reporter trying to boost his own career on the fortunes of gangster Stanley Fields.

With the Warner Bros. star-making machinery in full gear behind Garfield, and the release of *They Made Me a Criminal* imminent, it was brought to Jack Warner's attention that the studio had a B-picture in the can already called *Blackwell's Island* which featured their new hot commodity in a small role. He immediately poured $100,000 into the budget of the picture and hired Michael Curtiz to direct some new scenes and reshoot some others, making *Blackwell's Island*—now an A-picture— available for release right on the heels of the successful *Criminal.*

Blind Alley

Columbia. 71 min. Directed by Charles Vidor.

Cast: Chester Morris, Ralph Bellamy, Ann Dvorak, Joan Perry, Melville Cooper, Rose Stradner, John Eldredge.

Morris plays a disturbed hoodlum who takes psychiatrist Bellamy hostage and allows himself to be psychoanalyzed. This was one of Hollywood's first attempts at portraying psychological ideas, but the film is more notable for what it tried to do than what it actually did. Remade in 1948 as *The Dark Past.*

Blue Montana Skies

56 min. Directed by B. Reeves Eason.

Cast: Gene Autry, Smiley Burnette, June Storey, Harry Woods, Tully Marshall.

The first singing cowboy of all time, quite unbelievably, was John Wayne. In a dreadful 1933 Monogram cheapie called *Riders of Destiny,* the Duke played "Singin'" Sandy Saunders, a character who would break into song at the slightest provocation. That all ended, however, when Wayne began getting requests to croon old Western favorites at his public appearances, since the singing voice used in the picture was not his. A year later, a man much better suited for the singing cowboy concept made his debut, in a Mascot feature called *In Old Santa Fe*. His name was Gene Autry and, in the film, he sang two Western ballads and delivered what few lines were given to him rather nervously and self-consciously. When he first viewed his performance at a pre-release screening, he walked out on it, hoping it was not too late to get his old radio job back and eradicate a horrible mistake. Only his wife was able to convince him that he really wasn't *that* bad and talk him into giving his new career a chance to blossom. And blossom it did. After the release of *In Old Santa Fe*, the studio received hundreds of letters from fans who adored Autry's singing voice and complained that he had too little to do in the picture. The following year, his contract was bought out by Republic Pictures, where *Tumbling Tumbleweeds* in 1935 set the pattern for the next fifty films he would star in for that studio — through 1942, when he left Hollywood for military service in World War II. Gene was the singing cowboy, his horse was Champion — billed as the "World's Wonder Horse" — and his comic sidekick was Smiley "Frog" Burnette. Autry is credited with writing the hallowed set of "Cowboy Commandments," which read as follows:

1. He must not take unfair advantage of an enemy.
2. He must never go back on his word.
3. He must always tell the truth.
4. He must be gentle with children, elderly people and animals.
5. He must not possess racially or religiously intolerant ideas.
6. He must help people in distress.
7. He must be a good worker.
8. He must respect women, parents and his nation's laws.
9. He must neither drink nor smoke.
10. He must be a patriot.

Between 1937 and 1942, Gene Autry placed first on the Motion Picture Herald Poll of Top Money-Making Western Stars, while recording many of the most popular tunes in the land. In '39, he starred in eight pictures including this one, which focused on the cowboy's battle with fur smugglers while allowing him time to croon such songs as "Rockin' in the Saddle All Day," "I Just Want You" and "'Neath the Blue Montana Sky."

The Cat and the Canary

A Paramount Picture. Directed by Elliott Nugent. Produced by Arthur Hornblow, Jr. Screenplay by Walter DeLeon and Lynn Starling. Based on the stage play by John Willard. Photographed by Charles Lang. Edited by Archie Marshek. Art direction by Hans Dreier and Robert Usher. Interior decorations by A.E. Freudeman. Sound by Philip Wisdom and Richard

The mysterious Gale Sondergaard welcomes guests Paulette Goddard and Bob Hope, as George Zucco looks on in *The Cat and the Canary* (Paramount).

Olson. Costumes by Edith Head. Music by Dr. Ernst Toch. Musical adviser: Andrea Setard. Running time: 72 minutes. Release date: Nov. 10.

Cast: Bob Hope *Wally Campbell;* Paulette Goddard *Joyce Norman;* John Beal *Fred Blythe;* Douglass Montgomery *Charlie Wilder;* Gale Sondergaard *Miss Lu;* Elizabeth Patterson *Aunt Susan;* Nydia Westman *Cicily;* George Zucco *Lawyer Crosby;* John Wray *Hendricks;* George Regas *Indian guide.*

> Young man, I've been watching the rushes of *The Cat and the Canary* every night. I want you to know that you are one of the best timers of comedy I've ever seen. — Charlie Chaplin to Bob Hope[7]

Synopsis: This entertaining version of the venerable old-dark-house chiller was played strictly for laughs and provided a perfect vehicle for a young comedian named Bob Hope, who injected the film with what would soon become known as his trademark brand of humor.

It is set at the estate of Cyrus Norman, on the tenth anniversary of the eccentric millionaire's death. His eight surviving relatives have gathered at his home — located in a bayou surrounded by swamps — to hear the reading of his last will and testament.

When Wally Campbell (Hope), a radio actor and former vaudevillian, arrives at the estate, he jokingly remarks how the whole scenario reminds him of the kind of mystery-dramas he has performed in over the years on radio. And, indeed, the setting is perfect for such a vehicle. Cyrus's house contains all of the fundamental elements for a spooky chiller: spirits on the loose, a black cat, secret passageways, human eyes peering through a portrait on the wall, sporadic electrical outages, and a housekeeper who seems to be something of an expert on the supernatural, Miss Lu (Gale Sondergaard). "Where's the leading lady?" Wally asks the room of relatives, as if that would complete the scenario. Enter the lovely young Joyce Norman (Paulette Goddard), on cue.

Just as they are all gathering around the desk of Mr. Crosby (George Zucco), Cyrus's lawyer, to hear the contents of the will, they instead hear a bell that chimes seven times. Miss Lu explains that it is a warning from the spirits, signifying how many of them will survive the night. Since there are eight present, she concludes that one of them will be dead by morning.

Crosby reads the will and proclaims Joyce the sole heiress and new mistress of the estate. However, the second part of the will states that if Joyce dies within thirty days, or if she proves to have also inherited any of the family's streak of insanity, then a second heir named in a separate envelope will be granted Cyrus's vast fortune. Only Crosby is supposed to know the identity of the alternate heir, although when he arrived at the estate he found that the envelopes had been tampered with, leading him to believe that someone else may know the name contained inside.

Along with her inheritance, Joyce is given an envelope by Miss Lu from Cyrus, containing written instructions for her to open it later that night in his master bedroom, where she will sleep (which just happens to be the same room where the old man died).

As if things weren't bad enough, a man named Hendricks (John Wray) shows up at the estate, telling everyone that he is the head guard at nearby Fairview Insane Asylum, and that one of their inmates—a maniacal killer known as "The Cat" because of his long, clawlike nails and proclivity for crawling on all fours before he strikes—has escaped and may be on the prowl in the general area.

Meanwhile, one of Joyce's former beaus, Charlie Wilder (Douglass Montgomery), tells her that he wants her back. She considers their relationship long ended and their differences irreconcilable, but promises to discuss the matter with him later.

When Crosby learns that Joyce is in grave danger, he tracks her down to the library to warn her. While they are talking, a bookcase behind him opens up and he is pulled back into a secret passageway. Joyce, who is sitting with her back to him, flipping nonchalantly through a book, doesn't see this happen. The guests search the entire house for Crosby, but to no avail. He has disappeared.

Later, when she is alone with Wally, Joyce opens the envelope that Cyrus left for her. The letter inside contains a riddle that leads to the whereabouts of a priceless necklace once owned by Cyrus which has been lost, or hidden, for many years.

The killer pulls George Zucco into his secret passageway as an unsuspecting Paulette Goddard sits in the library in *The Cat and the Canary* (Paramount).

They locate the necklace in a hidden compartment out in the garden, while someone lurking out in the weeds oversees their discovery. Joyce takes it back to her bedroom and hides it under her pillow for safety.

Later that night, while she is sleeping, a secret passageway behind Joyce's bed opens and a long, clawlike hand reaches out and grabs her. She breaks away from its grasp, screaming. When the others rush to her bedroom, they find her sprawled out on the floor unconscious. She awakes still screaming, and tells them of the hand coming out of the wall to seize her. She also discovers that the necklace has vanished.

Only Wally believes her story. The others all conveniently assume she is losing her mind. But Wally validates her story when he finds the secret passageway and Crosby's dead body comes falling out of it onto the bedroom floor.

They hear the bell once again, this time with six chimes, indicating that another death is forthcoming and — according to Miss Lu, at least — inevitable.

After everything has quieted down, Wally goes back up into the room where Crosby's body is stored to find the letter containing the name of the second heir, who he believes is the murderer. Wally is knocked unconscious from behind and, when he awakes, Crosby's body has disappeared.

While Wally is perusing the house for clues, Joyce gets trapped in the secret passageway by the killer. Hendricks — who we learn is an accomplice in all of this — is also in the passageway, but wants no part of the murder of a young girl. He is only interested in the necklace. The killer stabs him and goes after Joyce. Just as he is about to attack her, Wally arrives and exposes the killer's identity as Charlie Wilder. Charlie takes off his mask and confesses to his crimes, saying that he is the rightful heir and that Joyce has cheated him out of his inheritance. Cognizant of the fact that his name is contained in the second envelope, he tries to finish the job he started and kill Joyce. But before he can, Miss Lu arrives on the scene toting a shotgun and shoots him down.

"Oh, boy, some fun!" Wally exclaims. And indeed it has been.

Joyce gives the house to Miss Lu and goes off with Wally to be married.

Notes: Because of his success on the radio with the popular Pepsodent Show, comedian Bob Hope was upgraded from "B" pictures to an "A" picture tailored specifically for his talents by Paramount studio president Adolph Zukor. The vehicle chosen for him was this retelling of the popular John Willard play, *The Cat and the Canary*. After playing second-string to comedienne Martha Raye in films like *College Swing* (1938) and *Give Me a Sailor* (1938), this film marked the turning point in Hope's career and set him on the road to stardom. In fact, he would begin his string of enormously successful "Road" pictures with Bing Crosby the following year.

Hope's leading lady in *The Cat and the Canary* was Paulette Goddard. She had been a Ziegfeld girl at age 14 and had emigrated to Hollywood in 1931, where she met Charlie Chaplin. The two would eventually marry, but in 1939 they were living together without benefit of clergy, causing Goddard to lose out on the coveted role of Scarlett O'Hara in David O. Selznick's *Gone with the Wind*.

The Cat and the Canary became a hit and fostered an even more successful scare-comedy, *The Ghost Breakers* (1940), in which Hope and Goddard were reteamed.

There was a British remake made in 1978, sans the laughs.

Reviews: "Since mystery melodramas laid in old dark houses are mostly nonsense anyway, Paramount has had the wit and wisdom to produce a nonsense edition of John Willard's old shocker, *The Cat and the Canary*. Streamlined, screamlined and played to the hilt for comedy, the new version ... is more harebrained than hair-raising, which is at it should be.... Elliott Nugent ... has directed it smartly, taking full advantage of the standard chiller devices for frightening the susceptibles of his audience but never losing sight of his main objective—comedy. In Mr. Hope's hands and with the aid of Miss Goddard (who is getting better and better), of Elizabeth Patterson, Gale Sondergaard, Nydia Westman and the others, the objective is carried briskly and to our complete satisfaction. Good show."— Frank S. Nugent, *The New York Times*

"Retaining the basic spooky atmosphere and chiller situations of John Willard's original play, Paramount injects plenty of legitimate comedy in this one to provide good entertainment for general audiences.... *Cat and the Canary* will amply satisfy the mystery fans, and provide spine-chilling thrills...."—*Variety*

Children's Four Seasons (Kodomo No Shiki)

A Shochiku (Ofuna) Prod., Japan. Directed by Hiroshi Shimizu.

Cast: Reikichi Kawamura, Mitsuko Yoshikawa, Takeshi Sakamoto, Fumiko Okamura, Masao Hayama, Jun Yokoyama, Seiji Nishimura, Shin'ichi Himori, Teruo Furuya.

As he had done the previous year with his film *Children in the Wind,* director Shimizu again chose as the subject for his new picture the plight of children in the world, this time against the backdrop of the changing seasons. And like that film, this one was also based on a novel by Joji Tsubota and adapted for the screen by the director himself.

Code of the Secret Service

Warner Bros. 58 min. Directed by Noel Smith.

Cast: Ronald Reagan, Rosella Towne, Eddie Foy, Jr., Moroni Olsen, Edgar Edwards, Jack Mower, John Gallaudet, Joe King, Steven Darrell, Sol Gorss.

In a follow-up to an earlier 1939 Warners programmer called *Secret Service of the Air,* Reagan reprises his role of Lieutenant Brass Bancroft, this time fighting counterfeiters in America. This one was so bad that Reagan begged the studio not to release it, but they would only agree not to release it in the Los Angeles area (to spare the actor local embarrassment). The subsequent notices it received may have prompted him to think about a career in politics. Said *Variety:* "Plot structure is illogical, dialogue is strained, and futile attempts are made at comedy."

Colorado Sunset

58 min. Directed by George Sherman.

Cast: Gene Autry, Smiley Burnette, June Storey, Barbara Pepper, Larry "Buster" Crabbe.

This one concerns, of all things, a milk war, including a thrilling chase at the end involving horses, men and overturned milk wagons. A future Tarzan, "Buster" Crabbe, is featured as well.

Confessions of a Nazi Spy

A Warner Bros.–First National Picture. Directed by Anatole Litvak. Produced by Hal B. Wallis. Screenplay by Milton Krims and John Wexley. Based on material gathered by Leon Turrou. Photographed by Sol Polito. Edited by Owen Marks. Art direction by Carl Jules Weyl. Set decorations by Robert B. Lee. Costumes by Milo Anderson. Musical director: Leo F. Forbstein. Technical adviser: Leon Turrou. Narrated by John Deering. Running time: 102 minutes.

Cast: Edward G. Robinson *Edward Renard;* Francis Lederer *Schneider;* George Sanders *Schlanger;* Paul Lukas *Dr. Kassel;* Henry O'Neill *D.A. Kellogg;* Lya Lys *Erika Wolff;* Grace Stafford *Mrs. Schneider;* James Stephenson *Scotland Yard Man;* Sig Ruman *Krogman;* Fred Tozere *Phillips;* Dorothy Tree *Hilda;* Celia Sibelius *Mrs. Kassel;* Joe Sawyer *Renz;* Lionel Royce *Hintze;* Hans Von Twardowsky *Wildebrandt;* Henry Victor *Helldorf;* Frederick Vogeding *Captain Richter;* George Rosener *Klauber;* Robert Davis *Straubel;* John Voight *Westphal;* Willy Kaufman *Gruetzwald.*

> The producer of this nightmarish concoction has drawn for his material on the choicest collection of flubdub that a diseased mind could possibly pick out of the public ashcan. — May 18, 1939 issue of the *German-American Bund* newspaper

Synopsis: Before the Japanese attack on Pearl Harbor in 1941, when America was still very isolationist and people like Charles Lindbergh were traveling from coast to coast saying what a great guy Hitler was and how all he wanted was peace and happiness for everyone, the only film to emerge from Hollywood warning of the impending danger of the Nazis was this fact-based 1939 film.

The story begins in a quaint Scottish town, where a secretive woman has been receiving a huge influx of mail from all over the world. A local philatelist asks her for the foreign stamps on the envelopes she's received, but the woman vehemently refuses. Her unusual response prompts him to alert Scotland Yard, feeling that something's not right in Denmark. And, indeed, it's not. British Intelligence uncovers the fact that she is but one link in an international chain of Nazi spies.

Confessions of a Nazi Spy (Warner Bros.–First National). *Top:* A sensationalistic lobby card. *Bottom:* Edward G. Robinson and fellow agents bait a trap for Nazi Francis Lederer.

Intercepting a letter from a man named Schneider (Francis Lederer) in America, detailing a plot to kidnap an Air Force general, the United States government is alerted and tough G-man Ed Renard (Edward G. Robinson) is assigned to the case.

Schneider, a German-American with strong Nazi sympathies, turns out to be the weak link in the spy chain. He is brought in and interrogated by Renard, who persuades him to divulge the names of the Nazi ring leaders in America. They include Erika Wolff (Lya Lys), posing as a German hairdresser aboard a trans–Atlantic liner; Dr. Kassel (Paul Lukas), head of the local New York area bund; Schlanger (George Sanders), German Intelligence's liaison officer; and Hilda (Dorothy Tree), Erika's American-based accomplice.

Through diligent police work around the Western world—and with the cooperation of the various international authorities—the spy ring is broken and all of these contacts are picked up in the United States, South America and Europe.

Notes: In 1938, Jack Warner somehow learned that the F.B.I. had a number of Nazi spies under surveillance in the East. With the blessing of his good friend President Roosevelt, Warner contacted one of his contract writers, Milton Krims, and instructed him to go to New York and work with F.B.I. agent Leon Turrou. Krims had covered the Munich crisis for *Collier's* Magazine and was itching to do an anti–Nazi film.

Turrou had attended rallies of the German-American Bund, disguised as a Nazi, and he possessed a wealth of information (all of which Krims put to good use in his screenplay). The writer obtained a complete transcript of the 1937 trial in which four people were convicted of spying and based the spy characters in his script on them.

Anatole Litvak had just been replaced on the set of *The Roaring Twenties*—after only two days of work—by Raoul Walsh. "I hated it!" Litvak said later of the picture.[8] He was reassigned to *Confessions of a Nazi Spy*.

From the beginning, Krims and Litvak had two vastly different philosophies on how the picture should be made. The director wanted to infuse the film with melodramatic fiction; the writer wanted absolute realism. As always, the director won out. Krims eventually refused to work at all with Litvak, and John Wexley was brought on to provide additional dialogue.

While shooting commenced, many of the people associated with the project, including stars and studio executives, received death threats. The German consul in Los Angeles tried vehemently to have the filming stopped, but unsuccessfully. Dr. Josef Goebbels' press department in Berlin announced that the German film industry would retaliate with propaganda pictures of their own, focusing on judicial corruption and gangster activities in America. Apparently, he was unaware of the fact that Warner Bros. had been making a living off such films for years.

When *Confessions of a Nazi Spy* was released, the German-American

Bund sued Warners for half a million dollars. However, when the head of their organization (Fritz Kuhn) was brought to trial for embezzling the group's funds, the defamation suit was dropped.

Germany used its influence to have the film banned in several European and South American countries. The movie was a dud at the domestic box office, where Americans refused to believe the accusations that it boldly made and the warning that it tried to sound.

Reviews: "Hitler's pledge of non-aggression toward the Americas reached the Warners too late yesterday. They had formally declared war on the Nazis at 8:15 A.M. with the first showing of their *Confessions of a Nazi Spy* at the Strand. Hitler won't like it; neither will Goebbels; frankly, we were not too favorably impressed either, although for a different reason. We can endure just so much hissing, even when Der Fuehrer and the Gestapo are its victims. The Warners had courage in making the picture, but we should have preferred to see them pitch their battle on a higher plane."—Frank S. Nugent, *The New York Times*

"This one is a wartime propaganda picture in flavor and essence. It must stand as a living document of how little words now mean. The world is outwardly at peace. Actually there is war going on. A war of nerves, of bluff, of propaganda and counter-propaganda. The bullets may come later. Decades from now what's happening may be seen in perspective. And the historians will almost certainly take note of this daringly frank broadside from a picture company."—*Variety*

Dark Victory

A Warner Bros.–First National Picture. Directed by Edmund Goulding. Executive producer: Hal B. Wallis. Associate producer: David Lewis. Screenplay by Casey Robinson. From the play by George Emerson Brewer, Jr., and Bertram Bloch. Photographed by Ernie Haller. Edited by William Holmes. Art direction by Robert Haas. Gowns by Orry-Kelly. Music by Max Steiner. Running time: 106 minutes. Release date: April 20.

Cast: Bette Davis *Judy Traherne;* George Brent *Dr. Frederick Steele;* Humphrey Bogart *Michael O'Leary;* Geraldine Fitzgerald *Ann King;* Ronald Reagan *Alec;* Henry Travers *Dr. Parsons;* Cora Witherspoon *Carrie;* Dorothy Peterson *Miss Wainwright;* Virginia Brissac *Martha;* Charles Richman *Colonel Mantle;* Herbert Rawlinson *Dr. Carter;* Leonard Mudie *Dr. Driscoll;* Fay Helm *Miss Dodd;* Lottie Williams *Lucy.*

> Who's going to want to see a picture about a dame that goes blind and dies?—Jack Warner[9]

Synopsis: In a year dominated by big, sweeping epics and escapist fare that always ended blissfully, *Dark Victory* told the story of a young girl who

Bette Davis learns the truth about her illness and goes on a man-and-booze binge as a future United States President looks on in *Dark Victory* (Warner Bros.–First National).

dies of a brain tumor. This multi–Kleenex tear-jerker began a trend of unhappy endings in Hollywood that remained fashionable for quite some time.

It is the story of Judy Traherne (Bette Davis), a rich young socialite who loves playing bridge, throwing lavish parties, and riding her prize steed, Challenger. Her life is gay and carefree, and she insists on keeping it that way despite her persistent headaches and frequent bouts of double-vision, which she writes off as "hangovers." But when she successfully rides Challenger into a hurdle and tumbles down a flight of stairs, her personal physician, Dr. Parsons (Henry Travers), convinces her to see a specialist.

Parsons takes her to see his old friend, Dr. Frederick Steele (George Brent). Steele, a successful brain surgeon, is the antithesis of Judy. He is completely dedicated to his work, respected by his colleagues, and has little time or inclination to invest in the pursuit of pleasure.

At first, Steele refuses Parsons' plea for help; he's lost one too many patients and is giving up his lucrative practice to return to the simpler and less taxing field of brain cell research. However, when he meets Judy in the waiting room of his office, he agrees to give her a quick examination.

In what is easily one of the best-written, directed and acted scenes in the picture, Steele conducts his examination. With scarcely a word wasted, their pleasant yet combative banter cleverly reveals each one's character while still moving the story forward. Judy still wants to ignore her illness. "I'm young and strong and nothing can touch me!" she declares invincibly. But through her nervous gestures and rapid-fire delivery of her lines, Miss

Davis conveys to us the fear and vulnerability lying beneath Judy's brave facade. In lieu of the conventional static shots of two people talking, director Edmund Goulding uses these nervous gestures to show the two characters from every angle. In this cinematic way, he shows Judy and Steele—literally as well as figuratively—circling around each other. It is truly a brilliant scene.

By the time his examination is concluded, the gravity of Judy's condition has been revealed to Steele (as well as to the audience). At the last moment, he decides to postpone his planned trip to Vermont to stay and treat Judy's illness.

After spending several days with her, Steele has confirmed what he originally suspected. He tells Judy that he must operate on her brain. Initially she refuses, but because of her faith in Steele, she finally relents.

He performs the surgery but finds the tumor inoperable. According to his own diagnosis (as well as those of a dozen international specialists), Judy's case is hopeless. She will live a normal life for approximately ten months, at which time she will die, peacefully and quietly. Her only warning will be a loss of vision several hours before she passes away.

Steele insists on keeping this information from Judy and asks her best friend, Ann King (Geraldine Fitzgerald), to help him. She agrees, and Judy is told that the operation was a success and that she is completely cured.

Elated, Judy calls it her new birthday and calls for a celebration. She invites Steele, whom she has grown to respect, then to trust, and finally to love. Steele, an avowed workaholic who has never shown much interest in the opposite sex before, has suddenly and unpredictably found himself in love with her too. They plan to wed and move to Vermont together.

But while rummaging through his cluttered office one afternoon, singing his praises to his secretary, Miss Wainwright (Dorothy Peterson), Judy happens to come upon her own case file and discovers the truth.

Embittered and enraged, Judy breaks off her engagement to Steele and refuses ever to see him again. Then she embarks on a frenzied, non-stop descent into parties and men and alcohol, staying out all night drinking with her young wastrel friend named Alec (Ronald Reagan), insulting her friends and taking enormous risks to win first prize at a horse show.

Steele goes to her and implores her to meet death "beautifully and finely," not the way she has been doing it. "I'll die as I please!" she retorts. But at the end of her spiral downward, she realizes that he is right and that only with him can she find true peace and happiness in her final days. She goes to him and apologizes for her foolish behavior, then asks for his help.

They decide to marry and move to Vermont as originally planned. There, as Mrs. Steele, Judy indeed finds the peace and happiness she so desired. The two agree not to speak of her illness and act as if it didn't even exist. They live like newlyweds who have their whole lives ahead of them.

Inevitably, however, the day arrives when Judy's sight begins to fail her. She realizes that she only has a few hours left to live. Simultaneously,

Bette Davis (right) begins losing her sight, which means she has only hours to live, but implores friend Geraldine Fitzgerald not to tell her husband, George Brent. Audiences went through cases of Kleenex in 1939 during this scene from *Dark Victory* (Warner Bros.–First National).

her husband receives a telegram requesting him to present a paper detailing his research progress at a very important board meeting in New York. Because he must leave immediately—and because the meeting is so important to his career—Judy conceals the fact that she is dying and sends him off to New York.

In the famous final scene, the poignancy and beauty of which is a combined result of Goulding's sensitive direction and Bette Davis's commendably restrained performance, Judy sends Ann away, says goodbye to her dogs, climbs the staircase to her bedroom and instructs the maid, Martha (Virginia Brissac), that she is not to be disturbed. Martha pulls down the blinds, covers Judith with a quilt, and—her eyes welled with tears—leaves the room, carefully closing the door behind her. The final shot shows Judy staring blindly off into space as Max Steiner's music builds dramatically and the camera goes slowly out of focus.

Beautifully and finely, indeed.

Notes: David O. Selznick owned the rights to the film property of *Dark Victory* at first and intended to cast either Katharine Hepburn or Greta Garbo as the dying girl and Fredric March as the doctor she falls in love with. But the project never materialized, and in January of 1938, he sold the rights to Walter McEwen, head of Warner Bros.' story department, for the sum of $20,000. Warners wanted it for Kay Francis, but she turned it down.

Miss Francis was superstitious and did not want to risk playing a girl who dies of a brain tumor.

Casey Robinson, the most gifted "women's" writer in the business, had been hoping to do the movie for three years, and mentioned it to Bette Davis. He suggested Spencer Tracy for the role of the doctor, and Davis — who admired Tracy more than just about any other actor — was greatly excited by the prospect.

She fought hard to convince Jack Warner to take a chance on the project, and even after filming began, Warner maintained his doubts. Those doubts were not unfounded, either. As a Broadway play in the winter of 1934, *Dark Victory* (with Tallulah Bankhead in the lead role) had flopped, playing for a mere 51 days.

Warner reluctantly gave the project the green light, but instead of casting Tracy as the doctor, he opted to go with George Brent, who was his favorite stopgap for virtually every picture then being made without a leading man. Acquiring Tracy from MGM would have entailed difficult negotiations. And, more than that, Warner was afraid of Tracy's alcoholism.

While the movie was being shot, Bette Davis's personal life was in great turmoil. She had gone through a bitter divorce and subsequently walked out on the love of her life, William Wyler (who had directed her Oscar-winning performance in *Jezebel* a year earlier). Wyler desperately wanted her to marry him, but at the same time he was also seeing a beautiful young woman named Margaret Tallichet. One evening, upon returning home from a day on the set, Miss Davis found a hand-delivered note from Wyler on her entrance-hall table. She was too furious with him, however, to even open it. A week later, she decided to read the letter. It said that unless she agreed to marry him there and then, Wyler was going to marry Miss Tallichet on the following Wednesday. The day that she read the letter was that same Wednesday, and as soon as she finished it, the radio announcer reported that William Wyler and Margaret Tallichet had been married that morning. Bette Davis had made what she considered to be the worst mistake of her life.

Greatly upset by these events, she missed many days of shooting and even offered to relinquish the role she had fought so hard to win, feeling that she wasn't doing it justice. Producer Hal B. Wallis, who had seen all of the dailies, advised her to stay upset!

Words of wisdom, indeed, for in *Dark Victory*, Miss Davis gave what George Brent called the finest performance of her career (as it very well may be). That performance — ranging from reckless, defiant socialite to embittered hedonist to loving wife and finally resigned to brief happiness with the man she loves — was a true tour-de-force.

Coincidentally, the following year Bette Davis starred in a movie for director William Wyler. It was entitled *The Letter*.

Dark Victory was nominated for Best Picture, Actress, and Score, but lost in all three categories. It was remade in 1963 as *Stolen Hours,* starring Susan Hayward, and again as a movie for television.

Reviews: "A completely cynical appraisal would dismiss it as emotional flimflam, a heartless play upon tender hearts by a playwright and company well versed in the dramatic uses of going blind and improvising on Camille. But it is impossible to be cynical about it. The mood is too poignant, the performances too honest, the craftsmanship too expert. . . . Miss Davis is superb. More than that, she is enchanted and enchanting. Admittedly it is a great role—rangy, full-bodied, designed for a virtuosa, almost sure to invite the faint damning of 'tour-de-force.' But that must not detract from the eloquence, the tenderness, the heartbreaking sincerity with which she has played it. We do not belittle an actress to remark upon her great opportunity; what matters is that she made the utmost of it."—Frank S. Nugent, *The New York Times*

"*Dark Victory* is the kind of movie that will tear you to pieces if you give in to that sort of thing, and leave you wondering, after your emotions have calmed down, why you ever let yourself be moved by something so obviously aimed straight at your tear ducts. It does not take any long wondering to arrive at Bette Davis as the answer. It's her show, her special kind of show, all the way through. . . . The Camilleish, East Lynnish qualities are fairly well disguised by a brisk, up-to-date script and a set of characters that might have walked in from the generally accepted Long Island of smart fiction. Edmund Goulding knows how to direct such a script with slick, quick persuasiveness. . . ."—James Shelley Hamilton, *National Board of Review Magazine*

Daybreak (Le Jour se leve)

A Paris Studios Cinema Release. Directed by Marcel Carne. Produced by Brachet. Original screenplay by Jacques Viot. Adaptation and dialogue by Jacques Prevert. Photographed by Curt Courant. Edited by Rene le Henaff. Decor by Alexandre Trauner. Costumes by Boris Bilinsky. Production manager: Paul Madeux. Sound by Armand Petitjean. Assistants to the director: Pierre Blondy and Jean Fazy. Script girl: Jeanne Witta. Music composed by Maurice Jaubert. Running time: 85 minutes.

Cast: Jean Gabin *François;* Jules Berry *M. Valentin;* Jacqueline Laurent *Françoise;* Arletty *Clara;* Rene Genin *Concierge;* Mady Berry *Concierge's wife;* Bernard Blier *Gaston;* Marcel Peres *Paulo;* Jacques Baumer *The Inspector;* Rene Bergeron *The cafe proprietor;* Gabrielle Fontan *The woman on the stairs;* Arthur Devere *M. Gerbois;* Georges Douking *The blind man.*

> I wanted a set completely enclosed in order to give the impression of a man shut in, in some way walled in this room where he was passing his last night as the image of a man condemned to death in his cell.—Marcel Carne[10]

Daybreak (Le Jour se leve) (Paris Studios Cinema). *Top, left-right:* Jules Berry, Jean Gabin and Jacqueline Laurent form the love triangle. *Bottom:* The police tear-gas Jean Gabin's apartment in an attempt to force him out, but Gabin lies dead on the floor, a suicide.

Synopsis: "Poetic realism" was a popular style of filmmaking in France during the 1930s, and that style was best exemplified in Marcel Carne's classic *Le Jour se leve* (released in the United States as *Daybreak*).

The story begins and ends with a death, the first a homicide and the second a suicide.

As the movie opens, gunshots are heard coming from a third-floor apartment. A fatally wounded Valentin (Jules Berry) falls down the staircase and lands at the feet of a blind man (Georges Douking), a recurring character in the film who is trying desperately to find out what happened, but never does. Like so many people in our society, he finds that his questions all go unanswered. At the top of the staircase, we see Valentin's murderer, François (Jean Gabin).

François takes refuge in his apartment and successfully holds off the police when they arrive. Alone inside the sparsely decorated room (which during the course of the film projects more and more the look and feel of a tomb rather than an apartment), François recapitulates the series of events which led to his heinous crime.

The story unfolds through a series of flashback sequences, beginning with a lovely young girl named Françoise (Jacqueline Laurent) delivering flowers by mistake to a factory where François works as a sandblaster. The two begin talking and discover that they are both orphans, raised as wards of the state. François is immediately drawn to her.

After proposing marriage late one evening and not getting a satisfactory response, François follows her to a cafe/music hall called La Fauvette. There, Françoise meets Valentin, a small-time animal trainer working at the music hall as a performer. His assistant, Clara (Arletty), walks off during his act and befriends François, who is watching the show from the rear bar. Before long, Valentin leaves with Françoise, only to return alone and pester Clara. François warns him sternly to leave her alone.

François and Clara become lovers, even though he is still in love with Françoise and still courting her. Although he doesn't love Françoise himself, the possessive, egocentric Valentin tries to scare François off by claiming that he is her concerned father and warning him to stay away from the girl.

Françoise later insists that Valentin is not her father and gives François a brooch as a sign of her love for him. Reassured by what he sees as a touching act of faith and declaration of true love, François severs his relationship with Clara. Clara has fallen in love with him, but feigns indifference at his decision. Scornfully, though, she shows him a brooch that the lecherous Valentin gave her, a souvenir she claims he gives to all of his mistresses. A despondent François sees that it is identical to the one which Françoise presented to him so meaningfully.

Meanwhile, Françoise has severed her relationship with Valentin, refusing ever to see him again. Dejectedly, Valentin bursts into François's apartment with the intention of killing his romantic rival. The two men fight, but Valentin cannot carry out his murder plan. Instead, the sadomasochistic lover places his pistol down near François and begins to recount — detail by provocative detail — his love affair with Françoise. In a fit of jealous rage, François uncontrollably seizes the pistol and shoots Valentin, sending his lifeless body crashing down the staircase of his apartment building to land at the feet of the blind man.

In the present again, as day is breaking over the city, the riot police have arrived on the scene, and they shoot tear gas grenades into François's apartment in an attempt to force him out. As the grenades explode, a thoroughly defeated and disconsolate François aims the pistol at his heart and fires.

Just as he does, his alarm clock dutifully goes off.

Notes: This well-crafted lesson in French film noir (and the aforementioned poetic realism) benefits immeasurably from a thrilling Maurice Jaubert score, which adds greatly to the film's tension and sense of foreboding, as well as from the incredible sets constructed by Alexandre Trauner. Wrote critic Andre Bazin: "Trauner designed this small suburban square the way a painter composes his canvas. While remaining faithful to the exigencies of reality, he succeeded in giving it a delicately poetic interpretation."

In addition, the cast is roundly excellent. Jean Gabin, the greatest star in the history of French cinema, gives arguably the finest performance of his distinguished career. Jules Berry's interpretation of the odious Valentin remains his most memorable screen performance. Jacqueline Laurent delivers a compelling performance as Françoise, though she never again worked in movies.

The bulk of the credit, however, goes to director Marcel Carne and screenwriter-poet Jacques Prevert, whose numerous collaborations produced a second classic six years later, 1945's *Children of Paradise (Les Enfants du paradis)*.

Daybreak was remade, far less effectively, by Anatole Litvak in the 1947 American film *The Long Night*, with Henry Fonda in the lead role.

Reviews: "Out of the darkness of the approaching war, Carne emerged with his masterpiece. Offspring of crisis, turmoil and soul-searching, *Le Jour se leve* was a perfect example of artistic achievement." — critic Georges Sadoul

"*Le Jour se leve (Daybreak)* is another of the series of psychological studies in which French directors specialize. An otherwise excellent theme is marred by some basic errors of psychology which a more careful study of the human character would have avoided." — *Variety*

Days of Jesse James

63 min. Directed by Joseph Kane.

Cast: Roy Rogers, George Hayes, Donald Barry, Pauline Moore, Harry Woods.

This is the *other* Jesse James western made in 1939. Here, the James Boys are framed for robbery by local bank officials. It takes Roy a little over an hour to figure it all out and round up the bad guys.

Destry Rides Again

A Universal Picture. Directed by George Marshall. Asst. director: Vernon Keays. Sound by Bernard B. Brown. Produced by Joe Pasternak. Screenplay by Felix Jackson, Henry Meyers, and Gertrude Purcell. Based on Felix Jackson's screen story. Adapted from the novel of the same name by Max Brand. Photographed by Hal Mohr. Art direction by Jack Otterson. Musical direction by Charles Previn. Score by Frank Skinner. Edited by Milton Carruth. Gowns by Vera West. Running time: 94 minutes. Release date: December 8.

Songs: "Little Joe," "You've Got That Look," and "See What the Boys in the Back Room Will Have," by Frank Loesser and Frederick Hollander.

Cast: Marlene Dietrich *French;* James Stewart *Tom Destry;* Charles Winninger *Wash Dimsdale;* Mischa Auer *Boris Callahan;* Brian Donlevy *Kent;* Irene Hervey *Janice Tyndall;* Una Merkel *Lilybelle Callahan;* Allen Jenkins *Bugs Watson;* Warren Hymer *Gyp Watson;* Samuel S. Hinds *Hiram J. Slade;* Jack Carson *Jack Tyndall;* Lillian Yarbo *Clara;* Tom Fadden *Lem Claggett;* Dickie Jones *Eli Whitney Claggett;* Virginia Brissac *Ma Claggett;* Joe King *Sheriff Keough.*

I don't act. I react. — James Stewart[11]

Synopsis: A rowdy, comical western with serious overtones, *Destry Rides Again* firmly established sex and humor as vital elements of the Hollywood West.

In a crooked poker game being run at the Last Chance Saloon by Kent (Brian Donlevy) — with the aid of hostess Frenchy (Marlene Dietrich) and the consent of the mayor, Hiram J. Slade (Samuel S. Hinds) — land owners are being conned out of their property and livestock. The latest victim, Lem Claggett (Tom Fadden), loses his 3,000-acre ranch and all of his cattle in the game. When Sheriff Keough (Joe King) goes to investigate, he is shot and killed by Kent.

As a replacement, Mayor Slade appoints Washington Dimsdale (Charles Winninger), the town drunk and the person least likely to give the criminal element in the lawless town of Bottleneck any trouble. Everyone roars with laughter when his name is announced, but Wash is not amused. Professing that a man must "choose between the bottle and the badge," he chooses the badge, and vows to give the bottle up for good (which the townspeople find even funnier than his appointment).

Fond of reminiscing of his glory days as deputy to the late, great

Destry Rides Again (Universal). James Stewart incurs the wrath of Marlene Dietrich in the famous barroom brawl scene.

lawman Tom Destry, Wash also announces his intention to send for Thomas Jefferson Destry, Jr. (James Stewart), to serve as his deputy. Bragging that young Tom recently cleaned up Tombstone single-handedly, Wash guarantees that "Destry will ride again!"

The fateful day arrives and everyone goes out to meet the stage. To their amusement, Destry steps off the stage with a parasol in one hand and a parakeet in the other (fortunately, both belong to a female passenger), then ambles over to the Last Chance Saloon and orders a glass of *milk!* As if all that weren't bad enough, when Kent instigates a confrontation with him, we learn that Destry is unarmed and does not believe in using guns.

In just his first few minutes in town, Destry has become the laughingstock of Bottleneck. "I see how you cleaned up Tombstone," Frenchy tells him, handing him a broom.

In the film's classic scene, Lilybelle Callahan (Una Merkel) arrives at the saloon, furious that Frenchy won her husband's pants in a poker game and relegated him to roaming the streets in his underwear. Lilybelle accuses her of cheating, and when Frenchy replies: "You know your husband would rather be cheated by me than married to you," a raucous, tooth-and-nail cat fight breaks out between the two, with each girl giving as good as she gets. Destry allows it to continue for some time, then nonchalantly dumps a bucket of water on them. Mrs. Callahan runs out of the saloon, embarrassed. But Frenchy is not embarrassed—she's mad as hell! Having incurred her fearsome wrath, Destry does his best to evade the bottles, chairs, glasses and guitar she throws at him, and barely manages to escape.

Stewart grills Dietrich for information in the guise of a polite conversation.

Later, over at his hotel room, Wash tells him to go back to Tombstone and he'll go back to being the town drunk, feeling he's made a terrible mistake. But Destry refuses, pleading with Wash to give him (and his unconventional methods) a chance. Against his better judgment, Wash swears him in as his deputy.

Meanwhile, back at the ranch, the Claggetts (wife and child included) are defending their home against Kent and his vultures in a violent shootout. They send their son, Eli Whitney Claggett (Dickie Jones), into town for help. Eli locates Destry just as he is cooling off a gang of hotheads in town with an incredible exhibition of marksmanship that works on them as quickly and efficiently as the water did on the women. Eli explains to Destry and Wash what is happening, and they ride back to his house with him.

When Kent shows Destry the deed that Claggett signed over to him in the poker game, and Destry verifies that it's legal, he reasons the Claggetts into giving up the battle, but advises them to remain in town while he "works things out."

His next visit is to Frenchy, upon whom he has already begun to have some effect. Stewart's Destry is wearing down her tough exterior the way his Mr. Smith wore down Jean Arthur's cynicism. He cunningly deceives her into divulging information about the murder of Sheriff Keough. When she warns him to stay out of it or he's in for a lot of trouble, he declares: "Trouble is my business!"

Destry's next move is to have Wash deputize Mrs. Callahan's husband, Boris (Mischa Auer)—in exchange for a pair of pants—to help in their investigation. Then he goes over to the Last Chance Saloon and, during a "friendly" game of checkers with Mayor Slade, subtly interrogates him about the Keough murder. His interrogation is interrupted, however, by Dietrich's classic performance of "See What the Boys in the Back Room Will Have."

When the song ends, Kent reiterates Frenchy's warning about staying out of it, but Destry insinuates that he knows where Keough's missing body is, which will lead to the capture of his murderer. Kent responds by dispatching one of his boys, Gyp Watson (Warren Hymer), to check on the hidden body. But Wash and Boris follow Gyp to the secret location, and when they apprehend him with the corpse, he is arrested and jailed.

Mayor Slade, being the chief magistrate of Bottleneck, announces that he intends to try the case personally, and hand-picks his well-coached jury. He instructs them to deliberate for a reasonable amount of time before submitting a verdict of "not guilty," at which time they will be substantially rewarded.

Destry answers this by sending for a federal judge, but Boris inadvertently reveals this ploy to Kent and his gang, who naturally resort to Plan B. Frenchy invites Destry over to her place and, while she is entertaining him, Kent's boys break Gyp out of jail and shoot Wash in the back.

Destry runs to Wash's side and, in a moving death scene, reminds him that his own dad was shot in the back, too. "They didn't dare face him, either," Destry says, and Wash passes away with that comforting thought.

After Wash dies in his arms, Destry marches intently over to his hotel room and straps on the pistols his father was wearing when he was killed. Disgruntled cattleman Jack Tyndall (Jack Carson) rounds up some of the equally disgruntled townspeople down at the corral and, led by Destry, they march down to the Last Chance Saloon for a showdown with the bad guys.

The women of Bottleneck march on the saloon as well. Armed with rolling pins and brooms, they subdue Kent's gang uncontested.

Destry pursues Kent through the saloon, but it is Kent who gains the upper hand, positioning himself where he has a clear shot at Destry. Just as he squeezes the trigger, though, French throws her body in between them, taking the fatal bullet that was meant for Destry, who shoots Kent dead and kisses her goodbye in nearly one stroke.

Two major death scenes in the space of five minutes might be too much for most movies to accommodate, but not *Destry Rides Again*. This one rebounds with a recurring gag, as Boris thoroughly destroys the memory (and the portrait) of his wife's ex-husband. And Tom Destry, a leading citizen now in a civilized town, is left for good girl Janice Tyndall (Irene Hervey).

Notes: More than anything else, perhaps, *Destry Rides Again* revived the waning movie career of Marlene Dietrich. After splitting professionally

in 1935 with her mentor, director Josef von Sternberg, for whom she appeared in seven films, Dietrich had trouble finding roles suitable to the
exotic screen image with which that director had so closely identified her
in the public's eye. Her career was steadily declining, and by 1939, after appearing in the unsuccessful British venture *Knights Without Armour* in 1936
and Ernst Lubitsch's stultifying *Angel* in 1938, she was labeled "box-office
poison" and remained off the screen for two whole years.

Producer Joe Pasternak, in a big gamble, offered her a mere $75,000
to star as the brazen saloon girl Frenchy (a role originally intended for
Paulette Goddard) in the comedy–Western *Destry Rides Again*, an offer she
accepted only on the advice of von Sternberg.

It was a wise decision. The role of Frenchy allowed Dietrich to display
her considerable comedic skills, as well as her trademark singing voice
(which was clearly Mel Brooks's inspiration for the Madeline Kahn part in
his riotous 1974 Western spoof, *Blazing Saddles*). It led her to a series of
Frenchy-type roles in pictures like *Seven Sinners*, *The Spoilers*, and *Pitts-
burgh*, all of which starred John Wayne.

As for James Stewart, he had never appeared in a Western before
Destry Rides Again, but his performance in it foreshadowed the fine work
he would do in his Anthony Mann–directed Westerns of the fifties. Released only weeks after the rousing success of *Mr. Smith Goes to Washington*, this movie galvanized his career and made him a major and very bankable star. Although his role here was much more understated than that of
Mr. Smith (with his slow drawl, his analogies guised as stories of friends, his
constantly tucking Wash's shirt-tails in), it is nevertheless of the same stellar
caliber.

The casting of Stewart and Dietrich opposite each other proved to be
inspired, and their remarkable screen chemistry helped to make *Destry
Rides Again* one of the surprise box-office hits of the year.

That chemistry, it should be noted, transcended the big screen. In fact,
it is said that when Dietrich first laid eyes on Stewart, she was so impressed
by his tall, lanky frame that she exclaimed lustfully, "That's for me!"

Stewart was in love, too — but not with Dietrich. He was in love with
the comic-book hero Flash Gordon! It was all that he seemed to read, all
that commanded his attention. So Marlene had the art department at
Universal make a life-size Flash Gordon doll that was precise to the last
detail. Then she walked into Stewart's dressing room, presented it to him
and locked the three of them in there together. After that, they got along
great.

Marlene Dietrich and Una Merkel did retake after retake of their infamous barroom slugfest, with onlookers calling it the best fight since the
Tunney-Dempsey match. Afterwards, a black-and-blue Merkel entered
herself into a hospital for several days of observation.

Destry Rides Again proves director George Marshall to be adept at
handling both comedy and action extremely well. He successfully fought

the censors to retain the scene where Dietrich drops some change into her cleavage, although the accompanying line was omitted: "There's gold in them thar hills!" The film deserves its place among 1939's best offerings for many reasons, not the least of which is the way it combined drama, humor, action, musical numbers and a love story all in a Western and remained unerringly consistent throughout.

It was remade as a vehicle for Audie Murphy in 1954, entitled simply *Destry*, but like all of the remakes of films from '39, it suffers by comparison.

Reviews: "*Destry Rides Again* might be the Western to end all Westerns—God forbid! It sums up so sophisticatedly so much of the incident and quality of Westerns, with almost a faint tone of parody that never, however, drowns out the essential character and excitement of its story, that in the end it can be taken as a delightful joke, or a knowing commentary on one of the oldest and most persistent types of the movie. Or simply, as it will be taken for the most part, as a rattling good picture...."—James Shelley Hamilton, *National Board of Review Magazine*

"*Destry Rides Again* is anything but a super-western. It's just plain, good entertainment, primed with action and laughs and human sentiment, with a cast that should not only react well from the marquee but ingratiate itself heartily all the way up and down the family age line."—*Variety*

Dodge City

A Warner Bros. Picture. Directed by Michael Curtiz. Produced by Hal B. Wallis. Original screenplay by Robert Buckner. Photographed by Sol Polito; Associate: Ray Rennahan. For the Technicolor Company: Color director, Natalie Kalmus; Associate, Morgan Padelford. Edited by George Amy. Art direction by Ted Smith. Special effects by Byron Haskin and Rex Wimpy. Sound by Oliver S. Garretson. Costumes by Milo Anderson. Makeup by Perc Westmore. Dialogue director: Jo Graham. Music by Max Steiner. Musical director: Leo F. Forbstein. Running time: 104 minutes.

Cast: Errol Flynn *Wade Hatton;* Olivia de Havilland *Abbie Irving;* Ann Sheridan *Ruby Gilman;* Bruce Cabot *Jeff Surrett;* Frank McHugh *Joe Clemens;* Alan Hale *Rusty Hart;* John Litel *Matt Cole;* Henry Travers *Mr. Irving;* Henry O'Neill *Colonel Dodge;* Victor Jory *Yancey;* William Lundigan *Lee Irving;* Guinn "Big Boy" Williams *Tex Baird;* Bobs Watson *Harry Cole;* Gloria Holden *Mrs. Cole;* Douglas Fowley *Munger;* Georgia Caine *Mrs. Irving;* Charles Halton *Surrett's lawyer;* Ward Bond *Bud Taylor;* Cora Witherspoon *Mrs. McCoy;* Russell Simpson *Orth;* Monte Blue *Barlow;* Nat Carr *Crocker;* Clem Bevans *Barber;* Joseph Crehan *Hammond;* Thurston Hall *Twitchell;* Chester Clute *Coggins.*

I want to get swords and horses the hell out of my life![12]—Errol Flynn

Errol Flynn romances Olivia de Havilland in *Dodge City* (Warner Bros.).

Synopsis: *Dodge City* is a colorful and action-packed Western that puts much of the Warner Bros. stock company to good use and contains the definitive barroom brawl scene. It was also Mel Brooks's principal inspiration for his hilarious 1974 Western spoof, *Blazing Saddles* (except for the Madeline Kahn musical number, which harks back to Marlene Dietrich in *Destry Rides Again*).

It begins in 1872, as cattleman Wade Hatton (Errol Flynn) leads a wagon train into Dodge City, a lawless mecca of gambling, liquor and murder. During the trek, he becomes infatuated with Abbie Irving (Olivia de Havilland), but she wrongly blames him for the death of her careless kid brother (William Lundigan) and is not interested in listening to any explanations.

Wade and his saddle pals, Rusty and Tex (Alan Hale and Guinn "Big Boy" Williams), find Dodge City in the clutches of Jeff Surrett (Bruce Cabot), an old nemesis of Wade's. Surrett is in the business of cheating cattlemen out of their livestock and killing anyone who gets in his way. He and his gang have also run the last few sheriffs out of town.

The city townspeople offer the vacancy to Wade, confident that he can clean up the town, but he still has a herd of cattle to unload, so he politely declines. However, when a group of children are caught in a crossfire on Dodge's main street and one young boy (Bobs Watson) is killed, Wade changes his mind and accepts the town's tin star.

He deputizes Rusty and Tex, and together they stop the street shooting and the mob lynchings, creating a new law on handgun confiscation and putting a curfew on gambling. Before long, the jail house is filled to capacity and the streets are uncharacteristically peaceful and quiet. New settlers begin pouring into the suddenly civilized town, and Abbie finds herself succumbing to Wade's charms.

Together, the couple teams with crusading newspaperman Joe Clemens (Frank McHugh) to gather enough evidence to convict Surrett of murder, but the night before the story hits the press, Clemens is murdered and his evidence stolen by one of Surrett's henchmen, Yancey (Victor Jory). Wade arrests Yancey and arranges to get Abbie—the prosecution's key witness—safely out of town. He and Rusty are forced to take Yancey out of town on the same train when a vigilante mob made up mostly of Joe Clemens' friends threatens to take the law into their own hands. The train is crawling with Surrett and his boys, who are plotting to kill Wade and rescue Yancey. There is a shoot-out on the train (as well as a fire when a gas lamp is smashed) during which Surrett gets Yancey out and leaves Wade, Rusty and Abbie behind to burn in the conflagration. They escape, however, and gun down Surrett and Yancey as they are trying to make their getaway.

With matters settled in Dodge, Wade is asked to tackle Virginia City next, a town reputedly even wilder than Dodge was at its worst. Again, he politely declines, this time because of his impending marriage and honeymoon plans with Abbie. Rusty and Tex, itching for some more action, are very disappointed by his decision. But Abbie enters the room, after overhearing the gist of the conversation, and asks Wade when they're leaving for Virginia City, giving him and his two old compadres a second reason to celebrate.

Notes: In 1938, Jack Warner had the bright idea of casting the English swashbuckler, Errol Flynn, in a Western. Some months later, *Dodge City* was released. The movie explained his unmistakable accent by giving him a pedigree that included Irish origins and an incurable case of wanderlust. It didn't matter. Audiences accepted him so readily in this kind of outdoor adventure yarn that they never even questioned what an Englishman might be doing cleaning up the Old West. The film became so popular that it

Olivia de Havilland, Errol Flynn and Alan Hale are trapped in a train car that's on fire in *Dodge City* (Warner Bros.).

made an unlikely Western star of Errol Flynn, who would go on to make seven more of them over the next eleven years. But Warners never again bothered to try and explain the origins of any of the cowboy characters that he portrayed. Still, Flynn was fond of claiming (either jokingly or mistakenly) that there were two lines of dialogue which appeared in every Western he ever made:

HEAVY: Where you from, pardner?
FLYNN: I happen to come from Ireland, but I'm as American as you are!

Flynn—who yearned to play serious, dramatic roles that challenged him as an actor—was embarrassed by the Westerns he made, feeling he was grossly miscast. To its credit, though, *Dodge City* was one of the best. What it lacked in story, it more than made up for with beautiful Technicolor, a memorable score by the great Max Steiner, a wonderful cast (which included Ann Sheridan, the "Oomph Girl," and Alan Hale, a favorite of Flynn's despite his reputation as a notorious scene-stealer), and the ultimate barroom brawl scene.

Once again, Flynn found himself working with two people who were major sources of frustration for him (albeit for vastly different reasons): director Michael Curtiz and actress Olivia de Havilland. Flynn felt that

Curtiz (with whom he made ten movies) worked him too hard and demanded far too much. He also blamed the director for the death of a close friend of his during the shooting of *The Charge of the Light Brigade* (1936). Flynn was in love with de Havilland (with whom he co-starred in nine films), but his unwillingness to court her in a traditional manner—compounded by the fact that he was married at the time—forestalled any conceivable consummation between the two.

On April 1, a conspicuously clean-shaven audience showed up for the film's premiere in Dodge City, Kansas. The local men had been growing beards to honor their ancestors until it was discovered that in the Old West, only the danged sheepherders sported facial hair!

In 1951, Warners reissued a black-and-white print of *Dodge City* on a double bill with another Flynn Western, *Virginia City* (1940), in line with a current Civil War Western film cycle. The double feature did exceptionally well.

Reviews: "Michael Curtiz's direction has been flawless part by part, but, as a whole, it has failed to fuse his film into anything approaching dramatic unity. It has become merely an exciting thriller for the kiddies, or for grown folk with an appetite for the wild and woolly. . . . The supporting cast . . . seemed competent enough. Of course, it was hard to tell sometimes, with all that gunsmoke and dust about."—Frank S. Nugent, *The New York Times*

Drums Along the Mohawk

A Twentieth Century–Fox Film. Directed by John Ford. Executive producer: Darryl F. Zanuck. Associate producer: Raymond Griffith. Screenplay by Lamar Trotti and Sonya Levien. Based on the novel by Walter D. Edmonds. Photographed by Bert Glennon and Ray Rennahan. Technicolor director, Natalie Kalmus; Assistant, Henri Jaffa. Edited by Robert Simpson. Art direction by Richard Day and Mark-Lee Kirk. Set decorations by Thomas Little. Costumes by Gwen Wakeling. Sound by E. Clayton Ward and Roger Heman. Music by Alfred Newman. Running time: 103 minutes. Release date: November 3.

Cast: Claudette Colbert *Lana Magdelana Martin;* Henry Fonda *Gilbert Martin;* Edna May Oliver *Mrs. McKlennar;* Eddie Collins *Christian Reall;* John Carradine *Caldwell;* Dorris Bowdon *Mary Reall;* Jessie Ralph *Mrs. Weaver;* Arthur Shields *Reverend Rosenkrantz;* Robert Lowery *John Weaver;* Roger Imhof *General Nicholas Herkimer;* Francis Ford *Joe Boleo;* Ward Bond *Adam Hartman;* Kay Linaker *Mrs. Demooth;* Russell Simpson *Dr. Petry;* Spencer Charters *Innkeeper;* Si Jenks *Jacob Small;* J. Ronald Pennick *Amos Hartman;* Arthur Aylesworth *George Weaver* Chief Big Tree *Blue Back;* Charles Tannen *Dr. Robert Johnson;* Paul McVey *Captain Mark Demooth;* Elizabeth Jones *Mrs. Reall;* Beulah Hall Jones *Daisy;* Edwin

Maxwell *Reverend Daniel Gros;* Robert Greig *Mr. Borst;* Clara Blandick *Mrs. Borst.*

> It was like being a child again at camp. — John Ford, on the shooting of *Drums Along the Mohawk*[13]

Synopsis: In the twelve-month period between March 2, 1939, and March 15, 1940, four films directed by John Ford were released: *Stagecoach, Young Mr. Lincoln, The Grapes of Wrath,* and *Drums Along the Mohawk.* The general consensus among film scholars and historians is that *Drums* does not compare to the astonishing creativity of the other three, but it is not a film without significant merit. Based on the popular 1936 novel, it vividly depicted events in upstate New York's Mohawk Valley from 1776–1781, and how the Revolutionary War affected its farmers and residents. Very few films have dealt with this crucial period in our nation's history and — for that reason alone — *Drums* is a worthwhile cinematic experience.

It begins in Albany, at the wedding of Gil Martin (Henry Fonda) and Lana Magdelana (Claudette Colbert). After the ceremony, the newlyweds leave immediately for Gil's farm in the rugged Mohawk Valley. Frontier life in 1776 is tougher than Lana had anticipated, and upon arriving at Gil's crude log cabin and encountering his Indian friend Blue Back (Chief Big Tree) inside, she wants to return home and call the whole thing off. But as time goes by, Lana becomes acclimated to their home and learns how to be a farmer's wife.

The nearest settlement to their farm is a fort at German Flats, and Gil introduces Lana to all of their neighbors there. They also take the opportunity to announce to everyone that Lana is expecting a child.

Thus far, their homeland has been untouched by the ongoing Revolutionary War, but word has spread that the British are inciting the Indians in their valley to war upon the settlers. To prepare for any attack, the men are training under General Herkimer (Roger Imhof). He warns all his neighbors that if they ever hear the fort's cannon go off, or the bell ring, to "come running."

From miles around, all of their neighbors in the valley come to help Gil and Lana clear their land (one of the many traditions of that era). While they are working, Blue Back arrives with news of an Indian attack and everyone races off for the fort. Reluctantly, the Martins leave their home and all of their worldly possessions (including their cow) behind.

The Indians arrive soon after and burn everything to the ground, led by Caldwell (John Carradine), a one-eyed British officer. They also attack the caravan of settlers en route to the fort, but are repelled. In all of the excitement, Lana passes out and, due to complications, miscarries her baby.

Things quiet down in the valley, and over the winter, Gil and Lana take

Drums Along the Mohawk (Twentieth Century–Fox). *Top:* Henry Fonda, Claudette Colbert and Edna May Oliver dance a reel. *Bottom:* Fonda, Colbert and settlers flee from an Indian uprising.

jobs as hired hands on the farm of Mrs. McKlennar (Edna May Oliver), a crusty old widow. They hope to earn enough money to rebuild their own farm someday.

One Sunday in church, Reverend Rosenkrantz (Arthur Shields) announces that General Washington has sent word that a regiment made up of British soldiers and Indian savages is on its way into the Mohawk Valley. He calls for all men between the ages of sixteen and sixty to report for military duty the following day. After saying goodbye to Lana, Gil leaves her with Mrs. McKlennar and goes off to battle with the other draftees.

Time passes, and the waiting becomes unbearable for Lana. Finally, the day comes when the men return. They have won their battle, but it was a costly victory. Of the six hundred men who went off to fight, only two hundred and forty have come back. A wounded Gil is among them. Lana informs him that they are going to have another baby.

Things quiet down in the valley again and, several months later, Lana gives birth to a healthy baby boy. The subsequent two years are very peaceful ones, and Lana prays that it will remain that way forever, but her prayer is not answered. The warning bell sounds at the fort one day, signifying another Indian uprising.

The settlers all gather inside the fort and can do nothing but watch as all of their homes and farms are burned to the ground by Caldwell and his band of more than one thousand Indians.

After destroying everything in their path, the savages siege the fort with bows and arrows, muskets and ladders to scale its high walls. During the first attack, Mrs. McKlennar is hit by an arrow and passes away, calling out her late husband's name. Before dying, though, she wills her land and property to Gil and Lana, who are the closest thing she has to "kin."

Low on ammunition, the settlers decide that someone must try to make it to Fort Dayton on foot for help. Joe Boleo (Francis Ford) volunteers, but he is captured outside the fort and burned alive by the Indians.

Gil volunteers next, confident that if he can make the woods, there isn't an Indian alive who can outrun him. He makes it out to the woods, but three Indians see him and go after him on foot. They chase him the entire night and most of the next day before finally giving in to exhaustion. Gil, having outpaced his pursuers, continues on to Fort Dayton. He makes it back to German Flats with a regiment of men just in time, as the Indians are smashing through the walls of the church, where the valley's women and children have been barricaded.

Caldwell and his savages are slaughtered and, with Cornwallis's surrender to Washington in 1781, peace comes at last to the Mohawk Valley.

Notes: Darryl Zanuck bought the rights to Walter Edmonds' novel even before it was published in 1936. Still, before committing himself to such a lavish production, he waited to see how the book sold. Not until 1939—when the book was in its thirty-first printing and had been a perennial on the best-seller list—did Zanuck finally decide to finance *Drums Along the Mohawk*. He personally supervised several treatments of the script (including one by William Faulkner) and brought on John Ford as director.

Drums was Ford's first film in color, and the results are beautiful. Credit for this must be shared with his expert cinematographers, Bert Glennon and Ray Rennahan, who did a superb job. The acute attention paid to period detail also contributed greatly to the film's authentic look and feel.

The movie was shot on location in Utah's Wasatch Mountains, where weather conditions caused enormous delays and difficulties. And the director's brother Francis, who had minor roles in many of Ford's films, makes an appearance here as Joe Boleo.

This was the first of Henry Fonda's movies that his young children, Peter and Jane, were allowed to see. They watched in terror as the three Indians chased after Fonda for nearly two days, fearing for their father's life. "It was the longest movie of my life," Jane would later be quoted as saying.[14]

Fonda's most memorable scene in the picture, in which he recounts the battle with the British and Indians to Colbert, was actually pure improvisation between him and Ford. Zanuck had ordered the director to shoot a massive battle scene, which Ford believed was unnecessary. Instead, he leaned Fonda against a wall and interrogated him with questions like: "How did the battle begin?" "What happened to this guy?" "What happened then?" "What about that guy?", etc. Later, Ford's voice was removed and all of Fonda's answers ended up in the final cut, where the battle scene was supposed to be.

Drums Along the Mohawk was nominated for Best Supporting Actress (Oliver) and Best Color Cinematography by the Academy, but lost in both categories to *Gone with the Wind*.

Reviews: "*Drums Along the Mohawk* was tailored to Mr. Ford's measure. It deals with a colorful period. It is romantic enough for any adventure-story lover. It has its humor, its sentiment, its full complement of blood and thunder. About the only Ford staple we miss is a fog scene. Rain, gun smoke and stockade burnings have had to compensate. The fusion of them all has made a first-rate historical film, as rich atmospherically as it is in action."—Frank S. Nugent, *The New York Times*

"Having great sweep and colorful backgrounding, with the photography unusually good, the picture is an outdoor spectacle which highly pleases the eye even if the story, on occasion, gets a bit slow and some incidents fail to excite."—*Variety*

Dust Be My Destiny

Warner Bros. 88 min. Directed by Lewis Seiler.
Cast: John Garfield, Priscilla Lane, Stanley Ridges, Alan Hale, Billy

Halop, Charlie Grapewin, Frank McHugh, Henry Armetta, John Litel, Bobby Jordan, Moroni Olsen, Victor Killian, Ward Bond.

Garfield is ideally cast here as a misfit trying to find himself. In so doing, he meets soul mate Lane and falls in love with her. But when her disapproving father attacks the young man and suffers a stroke, Garfield is blamed for killing him. He and Lane live the lives of fugitives for a while, but she soon realizes the futility of their existence and turns him in. At the trial, he is cleared of the murder charge and goes off with Lane to make the best of his second chance at life. The script, which bore some resemblance to the real life escapades of Bonnie and Clyde, called for the two to be shot to death at the end (like the famous Depression-era gangsters). But because a tragic finale had been the commercial undoing of a recent and similar picture, Fritz Lang's *You Only Live Once* (1937), the studio opted for the cheerier conclusion. Garfield tried to get a New York actress friend named Margot Stevenson the role opposite him in this film, but although Warners obligingly signed her to a contract, they put her to work in another picture and gave Priscilla Lane the lead female role in this one (fearful that the married Garfield's interest in Miss Stevenson was more than professional).

Each Dawn I Die

A Warner Bros. Picture. Directed by William Keighley. Executive producer: Hal B. Wallis. Associate producer: David Lewis. Screenplay by Norman Reilly Raine and Warren Duff. Based on the novel by Jerome Odlum. Photography by Arthur Edeson. Edited by Thomas Richards. Art direction by Max Parker. Gowns by Howard Shoup. Sound by E.A. Brown. Musical score by Max Steiner. Musical director: Leo F. Forbstein. Makeup by Perc Westmore. Assistant director: Frank Heath. Technical adviser: William Buckley. Narrated by John Conte. Running time: 92 minutes.

Cast: James Cagney *Frank Ross;* George Raft *Hood Stacey;* Jane Bryan *Joyce Conover;* George Bancroft *Warden John Armstrong;* Maxie Rosenbloom *Fargo Red;* Stanley Ridges *Mueller;* Alan Baxter *Pole Cat Carlisle;* Victor Jory *W.J. Grayce;* John Wray *Pete Kassock;* Edward Pawley *Dale;* Willard Robertson *Lang;* Emma Dunn *Mrs. Ross;* Paul Hurst *Garsky;* Louis Jean Heydt *Joe Lassiter;* Joe Downing *Limpy Julien;* Thurston Hall *D.A. Jesse Hanley;* William Davidson *Bill Mason;* Clay Clement *Stacey's attorney;* Charles Trowbridge *Judge;* Harry Cording *Temple;* John Harron *Lew Keller;* John Ridgely *Jerry Poague;* Selmer Jackson *Patterson;* Robert Homans *Mac;* Abner Biberman *Shake Edwards;* Napoleon Simpson *Mose.*

I was at the New York City's World Far in 1939 with Charles Boyer... And Boyer was a bigger star than I was, a great actor; but no one spoke to him. I had just made *Each Dawn I Die*, a prison picture with Cagney, and the crowd was yelling, "Hi, George" or "Hi, Stacey"—as if I was in the prison

James Cagney (left) and George Raft (center) are brought before warden George Bancroft in *Each Dawn I Die* (Warner Bros.).

yard with Cagney—"How are you?"... The average guy identified with me. It would have sounded funny for them to yell "Hi, Charlie" to Boyer.— George Raft[15]

Synopsis: "Cagney meets a Raft of trouble!" the ads screamed for this assembly-line prison picture from Warners, elevated somewhat by the impressive performances of the aforementioned actors.

Frank Ross (James Cagney), a hard-nosed reporter for the *Banton Record*, uncovers a scandal at the town's construction company which involves—among others—prominent district attorney Jesse Hadley (Thurston Hall), who is seeking election as governor.

To thwart his investigation, several of Hadley's henchmen knock Frank unconscious one evening, douse him with alcohol, and send him off in a speeding car that crashes into another vehicle in a busy intersection and kills three innocent people. Frank survives the crash only to be charged with drunk driving, found guilty of manslaughter and sentenced to a maximum twenty years hard labor at Rocky Point Prison.

On the train en route to Rocky Point, Frank has a run-in with tough-guy "Hood" Stacey (George Raft), who is serving a 199-year sentence courtesy of the state. However, when they get to the prison and Frank aids Stacey in a scrape with "Limpy" Julien (Joe Downing)—a ruthless killer who got his handicap and his nickname from Stacey when he ratted on him and spoiled one of his biggest jobs—and a power-mad "screw" named Pete Kassock (John Wray), the two men become allies.

While the convicts are all being treated to a movie one night, someone tosses a shiv into Limpy's back, killing the stoolie. Although Stacey is the

Cons James Cagney and George Raft (under table) set their sights on stool pigeon Joe Downing (foreground) in *Each Dawn I Die* (Warner Bros.).

prime suspect, there is no proof to charge him with the crime (which carries a punishment of life in "the hole").

Stacey has been planning a departure, but not by breaking out from the prison itself; he realizes that's impossible. His only chance is to escape from a courtroom. He persuades Frank to go to Warden Armstrong (George Bancroft) and tell him that he witnessed Stacey throwing the knife into Limpy's back (even though it was another convict who committed the crime). In exchange, Stacey promises to use his vast resources on the outside to clear Frank's name and get him freed from prison.

At the inquiry into Limpy's murder, Stacey jumps out of the courtroom window into a mattress-filled truck positioned several flights below and makes a clean getaway. Before he makes his dramatic escape, though, he spots several of Frank's newspaper cohorts in the courtroom taking his picture and feels that he has been sold out by a man he thought was his friend.

Frank, meanwhile, is given a beating by Pete and some of the other prison guards, in an effort to extract information on Stacey's whereabouts from him. When that fails, Warden Armstrong throws him into the hole for an indefinite amount of time. There, Frank becomes a changed man. He goes from serving "good time" to being the most problematical convict in the prison.

The only person who hasn't given up on him is Joyce Conover (Jane Bryan), his girlfriend and former co-worker at the *Banton Record.* She goes to see Stacey's attorney (Clay Clement) and arranges a meeting with the fugitive. He dispatches his boys to find "Shake" Edwards (Abner Biberman), Stacey's only lead in Frank's manslaughter case.

Next, Joyce visits Warden Armstrong and convinces him to show Frank mercy. He releases Frank from the hole and promises that if he goes back to serving good time, his tarnished record at Rocky Point will be cleaned and he will be given another chance before the parole board. Frank gratefully agrees.

When he is returned to general pop, Frank learns that his buddies are planning a break-out. He tries to dissuade them, but to no avail. Even when his request for parole is turned down, he refuses to throw in with them.

Stacey, meanwhile, catches up to Shake Edwards and squeezes the name of the man who framed Ross out of him. Edwards fingers "Pole Cat" Carlisle (Alan Baxter), an old friend of Limpy Julien's who is currently doing time at Rocky Point.

On the day of the planned break-out, Stacey arrives at the prison door in a cab, attired nattily in a new suit. He hands the hack a hefty stack of bills and turns himself in.

The cons brutally murder prison guard Pete Kassock in the jute mill and begin to riot. They eventually get trapped in the solitary confinement area, with the warden as their hostage. As most of the other cons are being slaughtered in a hopeless battle with the well-armed prison security forces, Stacey finds Pole Cat Carlisle and forces a confession out of him in front of Warden Armstrong. Having accomplished what he set out to do, Stacey is killed in a blaze of gunfire.

Frank Ross is set free to fight crime his own way once again. District Attorney Hadley and his accomplices are all indicted.

Notes: James Cagney and George Raft first became friends during their vaudeville days in Manhattan in the 1920s, when they were both aspiring dancers. In 1932, Cagney got Raft a small part dancing with him in the Warners release *Taxi*. Seven years later, they were teamed for the first time as co-stars of nearly equal stature in this film, and it was their close friendship that may have saved Cagney's life during the production (or at least spared him serious bodily harm).

Willie Bioff was a ruthless gangster turned union racketeer who was extorting huge sums of money from Hollywood producers and industry leaders. Along with his partner, George Brown, Bioff controlled the International Alliance of Theatrical Stage Employees union. They threatened work stoppages and numerous other more serious problems if their demands were not met. Whenever payments were late, thugs would be imported from Chicago and "accidents" would happen on the sets of films. When Warner Bros. refused to pay up, such an accident was planned for James Cagney on the set of *Each Dawn I Die*. But when Bioff learned that his old friend Raft was also in the cast, and that he was a personal friend of Cagney's, these plans were nixed.

Not long after this episode, Bioff retired as a labor organizer and moved to Arizona, where—under an assumed name—he went into the grocery business. On the morning of November 4, 1955, when he turned the ignition key in his pick-up truck, the vehicle exploded and Bioff was killed instantly. No one ever found out who put all those sticks of dynamite under his hood.

Cagney had originally been offered the role of "Hood" Stacey in the film, but rejected it in favor of the more demanding character role of Frank Ross (which in one scene called for him to break down in tears helplessly before a parole board). John Garfield and Fred MacMurray were both said to have been subsequently set for the Stacey part, but when George Raft was released from his contract at Paramount, he was immediately given the role. After the film became a solid box-office hit and Raft earned critical raves, he was rewarded with a $5,000-a-week contract by the studio.

Jane Bryan replaced Ann Sheridan in the supporting role of Ross's vigilant, crusading girlfriend Joyce. Miss Bryan was one of Warners' most promising young actresses, but retired early in her film career.

Scenes from another 1939 Warner Bros. film, *Wings of the Navy*, were also used in the picture (uncoincidentally).

Reviews: "The men will rejoice to welcome as lusty a melodrama as *Each Dawn I Die*, which divests itself of glamour from its first shot and pursues the course of blood-thirsty and ruthless hatreds from its opening sequence. It is rich in horror and brutality, qualities which invariably charm the men. And the Messrs. Raft and Cagney never have been better."—Bland Johaneson, *The New York Daily Mirror*

"Director William Keighley covers up the numerous threadbare spots in the story with a patchwork of Raft-Cagney sequences that contain some of the best acting of the season. Warner Brothers, in teaming Cagney and Raft, have hit on a combination that will go far and win wide audiences. However, the danger that melodrama may prove a destructive vehicle for these fine stars is always present and their superb work in *Each Dawn I Die* serves notice that they are meant for better things."—Howard Rushmore, *The Daily Worker*

Earth (Tsuchi)

A Nikkatsu (Tokyo) Picture. Directed by Tomu Uchida. Screen adaptations by Ryuichiro Yagi and Tsutomu Kitamura. Based on the novel by Takashi Nagatsuka. Photographed by Michio Midorikawa. Music by Akihiro Norimatsu.

Cast: Isamu Kosugi *Kanji;* Kaichi Yakamoto *Uhei;* Akiko Kazami *O-Tsugi;* Donguri Boya *Yokichi;* Bontaro Miake *Heizo;* Chiyeko Murata *Wife of the land-owner.*

Synopsis: The 1939 *Cinema Yearbook of Japan* called *Earth* "the finest picture yet made in Japan." It is the story of a farmer who loses his inheritance, is driven to poverty and despair, then manages to find new faith in the end.

It begins with the passing of winter, telling the story of what happened on the farm during the ensuing year. The principal characters are Kanji (Isamu Kosugi), his daughter O-Tsugi (Akiko Kazami), and his father-in-law Uhei (Kaichi Yakamoto). In marrying Uhei's daughter, Kanji has been adopted as the family heir. After the death of his wife—who had been a great help on the farm—his daughter pitches in to help him wrest a living from the soil. But the soil is poor, and no matter how hard the two work, they can do nothing but eke out a hand-to-mouth existence. An argument with Uhei only convinces the old man that his son-in-law is a failure and a good-for-nothing, and he disinherits Kanji.

In the end, it is O-Tsugi who brings the two back together and helps them iron out their differences.

Notes: When the Nikkatsu Studio chiefs heard that director Tomu Uchida wanted to make *Earth*, they were vehemently against it. Though recovering slowly from the losses it had recently incurred, the studio was in no position to finance a film as experimental as this one. Because Uchida insisted on chronicling the changing of the seasons and how they affected life on the farm, the film would take an entire year to shoot, making it a very costly prospect. But even if the head office was opposed to the project, the studio people were behind it 100 percent, and they helped Uchida to make the film in secret. Facilities, money, film and materials were slipped to the *Earth* production unit. In the meantime, Uchida was dashing back from location shooting—he also insisted on making it in the very region described in the novel upon which the script was based—to the Tokyo studios, where he continued to churn out more commercial, money-making films, such as *A Thousand and One Nights in Tokyo (Tokyo Senichi-ya)*.

When the finished film was delivered to Nikkatsu, the studio chiefs were very annoyed, but grudgingly released it. To their complete surprise, *Earth* became a major hit and won the Kinema Jumpo "Best One" award for the year. Since no costs were ever recorded by the unit, the film also earned an absolutely unprecedented return on its investment.

The End of the Day *(La Fin du jour)*

Filmsonor, France. 106 min. Directed by Julien Duvivier.

Cast: Michel Simon, Louis Jouvet, Victor Francen, Gabrielle Dorziat, Madeleine Ozeray, Sylvie.

Tensions mount at a home for retired actors, giving three fine French actors (Simon, Jouvet and Francen) a perfect opportunity to play off each other. This excellent French film came about when director Duvivier and screenwriter Charles Spaak were driving past a home for retired actors in France. Spaak, pointing at the facility, remarked that there was a film to be made there, and the director agreed.

First Love

Universal. 84 min. Directed by Henry Koster.

Cast: Deanna Durbin, Robert Stack, Helen Parrish, Eugene Pallette, Leatrice Joy, Marcia Mae Jones, Frank Jenks.

Delightful Cinderella story of orphaned girl Durbin going to live with snobbish relatives and falling for local bigwig Stack (in his film debut). Her first screen kiss (courtesy of the newcomer) made headlines around the world. In July of '39, Universal signed Miss Durbin to a contract that guaranteed her $3,750 a week for five years, and this film was undoubtedly the studio's attempt to introduce their child star to adult audiences.

It was nominated for Best Black & White Cinematography, Best Interior Decoration and Best Score.

The Flying Deuces

RKO. 67 min. Directed by Edward Sutherland.

Cast: Stan Laurel and Oliver Hardy, Jean Parker, Reginald Gardiner, Charles Middleton, James Finlayson, Jean Del Val, Clem Wilenchick.

Jilted by the girl he loves, Hardy decides to kill himself by jumping into the Seine. Laurel is willing to help him, but not so willing to accompany him. A Foreign Legionnaire convinces them to enlist instead, but when his wife turns out to be the same woman who jilted Hardy, the usual hijinks ensue. Film highlights (of which there are precious few, unfortunately) include Stan "playing" a prison bed spring like a harp and the boys doing a song-and-dance routine to "Shine On, Harvest Moon." The suicide sequence was pulled from an unused portion of the script for their earlier comedy *The Live Ghost.* Many years after *The Flying Deuces* was released, director Sutherland confessed: "I didn't want to do it, I didn't like doing it and I hated the finished film."[16]

The Four Feathers

Denham, United Artists. 115 min. Directed by Zoltan Korda.

Cast: Ralph Richardson, C. Aubrey Smith, June Duprez, Clive Baxter, John Clements, Jack Allen, Donald Gray.

A.E.W. Mason's novel of the old empire, with heroism and cowardice in the Sudan after General Gordon's death, was magnificently produced by

Alexander Korda (who produced earlier versions in 1921 and 1928, as well). Zoltan Korda directed another remake in 1955, entitled *Storm Over the Nile,* which was stretched into CinemaScope and used much of the same footage used in this film. Even so, the '39 version remains the best of the lot. It was released in England at 130 minutes. Nominated for Best Color Photography.

Frontier Marshal

Twentieth Century–Fox. 70 min. Directed by Allan Dwan.

Cast: Randolph Scott, Nancy Kelly, Cesar Romero, Binnie Barnes, John Carradine, Edward Norris, Lon Chaney, Jr., Ward Bond, Chris-Pin Martin.

A good Western with Scott playing Wyatt Earp, the infamous marshal of Tombstone, Arizona. In this romanticized account of his life, Earp cleans up the town and faces the bad guys in a showdown at the O.K. Corral. Eddie Foy, Jr., appears in the picture as his own father, who historically did perform in Tombstone (and throughout the Wild West) at the time.

Frontier Pony Express

58 min. Directed by Joseph Kane.

Cast: Roy Rogers, Mary Hart, Raymond Hatton, Edward Keane, Noble Johnson.

Roy tangles with a Confederate spy and a Southern politician as Yankee and Rebel forces vie for the allegiance of California in the Civil War.

Gaslight

British National, England. 84 min. Directed by Thorold Dickinson.

Cast: Anton Walbrook, Diana Wynyard, Frank Pettingell, Cathleen Cordell, Robert Newton, Jimmy Hanley.

Patrick Hamilton's stage shocker about a Victorian wife being deliberately driven insane by her husband in an attempt to conceal a past murder and discover a fortune in jewels was filmed perfectly in 1939. In 1943, Louis B. Mayer bought and remade it, with Charles Boyer, Ingrid Bergman and Joseph Cotten in the leads and George Cukor directing. Mayer also summarily destroyed the negative of the original film and tried to have all other copies of it obliterated as well (to save his own MGM remake from being compared to a clearly superior product). Fortunately, though, some prints did manage to survive and have been shown in America as *Angel Street.* What it lacks in budget, this version more than compensates for with electrifying atmosphere, delicious performances, and a sense of madness and evil lurking beneath the surface of the ostensibly mundane.

Golden Boy

A Columbia Picture. Directed by Rouben Mamoulian. Produced by William Perlberg. Screenplay by Lewis Meltzer, Daniel Taradash, Sarah Y. Mason, and Victor Heerman. Based on the play by Clifford Odets. Photographed by Nick Musuraca and Karl Freund. Edited by Otto Meyer. Art direction by Lionel Banks. Sound by George Cooper. Music by Victor Young. Musical director: Morris W. Stoloff. Orchestrations by Leo Shuken. Montage effects by Donald W. Starling. Assistant director: Eugene Anderson. Costumes by Kalloch. Miss Stanwyck's hairdresser: Hollis Donahue. Technical adviser: Abe Roth. Running time: 99 min. Release date: September 15.

Cast: Barbara Stanwyck *Lorna Moon;* Adolphe Menjou *Tom Moody;* William Holden *Joe Bonaparte;* Lee J. Cobb *Mr. Bonaparte;* Joseph Calleia *Eddie Fuseli;* Sam Levene *Siggie;* Edward S. Brophy *Roxy Lewis;* Beatrice Blinn *Anna;* William H. Strauss *Mr. Carp;* Don Beddoe *Borneo;* Frank Jenks *Pepper White;* James "Cannonball" Green *"Chocolate Drop";* Thomas Garland *fighter;* Charles Lane *Drake;* Harry Tyler *Mickey;* Stanley Andrews *Driscoll;* Robert Sterling *elevator boy.*

> The picture industry will gain a new and vital personality out of *Golden Boy.* The result can't help but create a new film star. — Robert Mamoulian[17]

> I don't think anybody had as much determination and ambition as I had the day I started making this movie. Then, one day, I went to the opening of *Golden Boy* and saw my name up on the marquee. There was my name in lights, and I suddenly knew that it didn't mean a damn thing to me. — William Holden[18]

Synopsis: It would be many years before William Holden would achieve the stardom and critical recognition (not to mention an Academy Award) he proved to deserve, but it was *Golden Boy* in 1939 that rescued him from years of bit parts and gave him his first big break.

As the movie opens, boxing manager Tom Moody (Adolphe Menjou) is desperately trying to raise enough money to divorce his estranged wife and marry Lorna Moon (Barbara Stanwyck), "a dame from Newark." Moody's fighter — and main source of revenue — "Lucky" Nelson breaks his hand before a big match. Enter Joe Bonaparte (Holden), who wants to take Nelson's place in the ring. Moody just laughs at the kid and at his last name. But when he gets to the gym and learns that it was Joe who broke Nelson's hand, he gives him a try-out. Joe passes with flying colors, and Moody takes him on.

Golden Boy (Columbia). *Top:* Father and son clash: William Holden (left) wants to be a prize fighter for the money, while Lee J. Cobb wants him to be true to his gift and become a violinist. *Bottom:* William Holden fights for the prize money.

Through his father (Lee J. Cobb), we learn that Joe does other things with his hands just as well. He has studied and practiced playing the violin since he was a child and has become something of a virtuoso. His talent has earned him a music scholarship.

Joe takes "Lucky" Nelson's place in the ring and wins the match convincingly, for which he is paid one hundred dollars. When Joe's father hears this news, he is broken-hearted. He has lofty ambitions for his son as a classical musician. But Joe is more interested in financial riches than spiritual ones, and prize fighting is his fastest track to fame and fortune.

Despite the fact that Joe considers boxing an "insult to man's soul," he agrees to go on the road with Moody and Lorna, where he wins one fight after another and collects one big paycheck after another. His father, however, will accept none of his money. He wants no part of Joe's new profession.

Joe and Lorna fall in love with each other, but before she'll leave Moody for him, she wants Joe to give up the fight game and return to music. But when Eddie Fuseli (Joseph Calleia), an underworld figure who strikes fear into the hearts of anyone who knows his reputation, gets Joe a big fight at Madison Square Garden, Joe cuts him in on a piece of the action. At that point, Lorna agrees to marry Moody, who sells all of his interest in Joe to Fuseli.

Before long, Joe gets a shot at the number one contender in the middle-weight division, "Chocolate Drop" (James "Cannonball" Green). Joe beats Chocolate Drop to a pulp (smashing his own right hand in the process) and, after the bout, learns that he has killed the boxer.

When Lorna hears the news, she rushes back to him. Joe gives up the fight game for good, and goes off to start a new life with Lorna.

Notes: Clifford Odets' allegorical stage play *Golden Boy* was originally produced by the Group Theatre in New York City. Harry Cohn paid $75,000 for the film rights to the property. When his studio, Columbia, first announced their newest acquisition, it seemed a strange choice. They did not usually cultivate dramas of strong social significance. So it was not at all surprising when Cohn hired four top writers to adapt Odets' play and the scenarists subsequently eliminated some of the play's controversial characters, excised the playwright's capital-labor arguments, built up the romance between Joe and Lorna, downplayed Joe's neuroticism, simplified his conflict, and changed the ending (in the play, Joe dies at the end). Still, despite the changes, the resulting screenplay was a relatively faithful adaptation.

The toughest part of making the movie was in casting the lead role. Cohn had acquired the property for John Garfield (who had played a supporting role in the stage play), but by the time filming began, Cohn was feuding with Garfield's boss, Jack Warner, so someone else had to be found. Director Rouben Mamoulian tested some 65 youthful actors, stars as well as unknowns, but managed to find fault with every one of them. But when he tested an unknown 21-year-old named William Holden, who had done very little in films, both Mamoulian and Stanwyck went to bat for the kid. Against his better judgment, Cohn signed him (at twenty-five dollars a week), and William Holden received his first starring role.

Mamoulian found in Holden an indefinable quality that made his projection of the character an honest and living thing. He was also impressed by the actor's drive to excel. Holden worked arduously at a gym on his boxing, memorized the correct fingering for the violin, studied words and phrases meticulously with a dialogue coach, and was always willing to retake a scene over and over again to get it right. Several weeks into production, all this work finally caught up to the actor. He suffered a nervous breakdown and was forced to miss a couple of days of shooting. Several crew members had already been replaced on the somewhat chaotic set, and consideration was given to dropping Holden as well. But Stanwyck stepped in, convinced the studio to stick with him, and coached him through the remainder of the shoot.

At the 1977 Academy Awards ceremony, Stanwyck and Holden were called upon to give away the Oscar for Best Sound. When they stepped up to the podium, Holden said: "Before Barbara and I present this next award, I'd like to say something. Thirty-nine years ago this month, we were working in a film together called *Golden Boy*. It wasn't going well, and I was going to be replaced. . . . But due to this lovely human being and her interest and understanding and her professional integrity and encouragement and, above all, her generosity, I'm here tonight."[19] Stanwyck, totally unprepared for his remarks, could only mutter, "Oh, Bill!" And the two old friends embraced warmly.

Jean Arthur was actually first announced for the role of Lorna Moon, and then Ann Sheridan, who (like Garfield) worked for Jack Warner, before the plum part created on the Broadway stage by Frances Farmer was finally given to Miss Stanwyck.

Shortly before filming was completed on the project, the actress married actor Robert Taylor.

Golden Boy was nominated for an Oscar for Victor Young's original score.

Reviews: "Skillfully directed by Rouben Mamoulian, *Golden Boy* is a ring saga with a difference — a balanced blend of the usual pug pyrotechnics and a poignant family-and-love interest. The excellence of the cast contributes greatly to the film's effectiveness. . . . In the film's title role, dominating Barbara Stanwyck's Lorna and Menjou's Moody, William Holden is both personable and surprisingly capable." — *Newsweek*

"An interesting, entertaining, dramatic but scarcely first-rate motion picture. While it has changed the ending of the Odets allegory, it remains on the whole a sincere, adult and faithful translation of his work. Perhaps that fidelity is the picture's chief fault, or there is such a thing as being too true to an original, too conscious of a drama's stage-bound pattern. . . . It

is the sort of film we can endorse heartily in spite of its shortcomings."—
Frank S. Nugent, *The New York Times*

Gone with the Wind

A Metro-Goldwyn-Mayer release of a Selznick International Picture.
Directed by Victor Fleming and (uncredited) William Cameron Menzies,
George Cukor and Sam Wood. Produced by David O. Selznick. Second-
unit direction by Reeves Eason. Screenplay by Sidney Howard and (un-
credited) Ben Hecht, F. Scott Fitzgerald, John van Druten, Oliver H.P.
Garrett and Jo Swerling. Based on the novel by Margaret Mitchell.
Photographed in Technicolor by Ernest Haller and Ray Rennahan. Edited
by Hal C. Kern and James E. Newcom. Production design by William
Cameron Menzies. Interiors by Joseph B. Platt. Art direction by Lyle
Wheeler. Interior decoration by Edward G. Boyle. Costumes by Walter
Plunkett. Music by Max Steiner. Special effects by Jack Cosgrove and Lee
Zavitz. Technical advisers: Susan Myrick and Will Price. Sound by Thomas
T. Moulton. Dance directors: Frank Floyd and Eddie Prinz. Running time:
222 minutes. Release date: December 15.

Cast: Clark Gable *Rhett Butler;* Vivien Leigh *Scarlett O'Hara;* Leslie
Howard *Ashley Wilkes;* Olivia de Havilland *Melanie Hamilton;* Hattie
McDaniel *Mammy;* Thomas Mitchell *Gerald O'Hara;* Barbara O'Neil *Ellen
O'Hara;* Carroll Nye *Frank Kennedy;* Laura Hope Crews *Aunt Pittypat
Hamilton;* Harry Davenport *Dr. Meade;* Rand Brooks *Charles Hamilton;*
Ona Munson *Belle Watling;* Ann Rutherford *Careen O'Hara;* Oscar Polk
Pork; Butterfly McQueen *Prissy;* Evelyn Keyes *Suellen O'Hara;* Victor Jory
Jonas Wilkerson; Isabel Jewell *Emmy Slattery;* Cammie King *Bonnie Blue
Butler;* Jane Darwell *Dolly Meriwether;* Ward Bond *Tom, a Yankee captain;*
George Reeves *Brent Tarleton;* Fred Crane *Stuart Tarleton;* Paul Hurst
a Yankee deserter; Mickey Kuhn *Beau Wilkes.*

> Don't do it, Louis. No Civil War picture ever made a nickel!—Irving
> Thalberg to Louis B. Mayer, 1936[20]

> Don't be a damn fool, David. This picture is going to be one of the biggest
> white elephants of all time.—Victor Fleming to David O. Selznick, 1939[21]

Synopsis: On December 15, in Atlanta, Georgia, the culminating
cinematic event of the decade was unveiled: *Gone with the Wind.* It was the
most highly publicized film in the annals of Hollywood. For three years
gossip columns had been filled with every conceivable detail about the production of the picture, and in 1939 a Gallup Poll indicated that 56.5 million
people were looking forward to it. Perhaps the most amazing of all of
GWTW's many achievements was that it actually lived up to all of that
publicity.

The film is set in the Old South, with the first half devoted to the Civil War and the second half to the Reconstruction period that followed. It opens at Tara, the plantation of Irish immigrant Gerald O'Hara (Thomas Mitchell). The Tarleton Twins (George Reeves, better known as television's Superman, and Fred Crane) have come to call on Gerald's eldest daughter, the enticingly beautiful Scarlett O'Hara (Vivien Leigh). All the boys want to talk about is the impending war with the North, but such talk bores Scarlett. She would much rather discuss the barbecue and ball being held the following day at Twelve Oaks, plantation of the Wilkes Family. When the boys happen to mention the fact that Ashley Wilkes (Leslie Howard) intends to announce his engagement to Melanie Hamilton (Olivia de Havilland) at the ball, Scarlett reacts like a jilted lover. "But Ashley loves me!" she tells herself.

At Twelve Oaks the next day, Scarlett finds Ashley and confesses her love for him. But he only confirms the rumors she's heard, telling her that he plans to wed the virtuous Melanie. Scarlett insults Melanie and bitterly accuses Ashley of leading her on.

The same day, she meets the visitor from Charleston with the bad reputation, Rhett Butler (Clark Gable), who takes odds with the other men at the ball when they boast of how quickly and efficiently the South will dispose of the North if the differences between the two do indeed escalate into a war. When Rhett first catches sight of Scarlett, gliding up a staircase, she remarks to another girl that he's staring at her as if he can see right through her dress. But Rhett can see through more than her clothing. He can see through to her black heart and empty soul, right down to the wickedness that is the core of her being. He knows precisely who she is, and loves her for it.

War is declared and the men rejoice, running off gung-ho to enlist in the army. Before leaving, one of Scarlett's many suitors, Charles Hamilton (Rand Brooks), Melanie's brother, asks for her hand in marriage. Although Scarlett doesn't love him, she accepts his proposal, only to spite Ashley Wilkes. The two are married the day after Ashley and Melanie are.

Their marriage is a short and unconsummated one, as Charles dies of pneumonia shortly after going off to war. Scarlett becomes a reluctant widow. She doesn't want to dress in black and stay home in mourning; she would much prefer to dress in bright colors and attend all of the social functions.

Scarlett is so heartsick that her mother decides to send her to Atlanta, to stay with Melanie. Scarlett heartily agrees to go, seeing it as an opportunity to be there when Ashley returns from the war. She raises lots of eyebrows in Atlanta, appearing in public at dances and the like, not proper etiquette for a recent widow.

To raise desperately needed funds for war effort, an auction is held at one of the dances, with the men bidding for the privilege of dancing with the lady of their choice. Rhett Butler is there and bids a hefty $150 in gold for Scarlett O'Hara. The crowd is shocked by this bid; they are even more shocked when Scarlett accepts.

While they are dancing, Rhett tells Scarlett that his goal is to one day hear her say the words he overheard her say to Ashley Wilkes back at Twelve Oaks: "I love you." Scarlett assures him that he'll never hear those words come out of her mouth.

After the Battle of Gettysburg, the hopes of the South are crushed. Ashley survives the battle and, for meritorious service, is given a Christmas furlough, which he spends in Atlanta with Melanie and Scarlett. Before returning to duty, Ashley makes Scarlett promise him that she'll always look after the weaker and more vulnerable Melanie in his absence. Then he rides off, as Scarlett whispers hopefully to herself: "When the war's over, Ashley. When the war's over."

Panic hits Atlanta with the first of Sherman's shells. Melanie and Scarlett work tirelessly as nurses at the Military Hospital, but the casualties are endless and the operating conditions barbaric. Scarlett wants to return home to Tara, but Melanie is pregnant and due to give birth soon, and Scarlett will not break the vow she made to Ashley to look after her.

A few weeks later, with the Yankee arrival imminent and the whole town being evacuated, Melanie goes into labor. Scarlett is forced to deliver the baby herself, with only the aid of a "simpleminded darkie," Prissy (Butterfly McQueen). When the child is born, Scarlett sends Prissy to find Rhett Butler, who arrives in a stolen buggy shortly thereafter and leads them all through explosions, a scavenger attack and a burning munitions dump out of Atlanta.

They return to Tara, but before arriving there, Rhett leaves them to go back and join the Confederacy. He is ashamed of himself and wants to be there for the last stand of the South. Scarlett begs him not to go, but he kisses her goodbye passionately and departs, after telling her how much he loves her.

When they reach Tara, the house is still standing, but Scarlett's mother is dead and her father has lost his mind. There is no food and no money, but as she walks out on the grounds of her family's plantation, Scarlett defiantly swears that never again will she or any of her kin know another hungry day, no matter what she has to do to guarantee it.

She soon proves it when a Yankee deserter arrives at their house with the intention of plundering and Scarlett shoots him point-blank in the face, killing him.

Lee surrenders at Appomattox, the war ends, and Ashley returns home. Scarlett wants him to take her away, but although he claims to love her, he will not desert his wife and child. Scarlett insists that there is nothing to keep them at Tara.

"Nothing but honor," Ashley replies.

Scarlett's father is killed when he is thrown from a horse while chasing carpetbaggers off of his land, and she is left to raise $300 to pay the property

Gone with the Wind (MGM). *Top:* Rhett Butler (Clark Gable) and Scarlett O'Hara (Vivien Leigh) flee the Northern army along with a bunch of beaten and tired Southern soldiers. *Bottom:* The ineffectual Ashley Wilkes (Leslie Howard) struggles with himself and with Scarlett's pursuit of him.

taxes or lose Tara. But still Scarlett refuses to surrender. She makes a dress from her parlor drapes and wears it into town, where she meets one of her sister's old beaux, Frank Kennedy (Carroll Nye). Since the end of the war, Frank has built a stable business and saved some money in hopes of marrying Scarlett's sister Suellen (Evelyn Keyes). But Scarlett seduces and subsequently marries Frank, thereby acquiring the tax money necessary to save Tara.

Frank is shot and killed in a skirmish with some forest renegades and, once again, Scarlett is a reluctant widow. She accepts a marriage proposal from Rhett Butler, another man she doesn't love but who is now enormously wealthy. She spends his money renovating Tara and gives him a daughter, Bonnie Blue (Cammie King). Their marriage of convenience soon turns sour, though, and Rhett asks her for a divorce. She informs him that she's pregnant again, but loses the baby when she swings at him, misses, and tumbles down a staircase.

When Bonnie Blue, Rhett's pride and joy, is killed in a horseback-riding accident, Rhett is devastated. He locks himself alone in a room with his little girl's lifeless body and refuses to allow her to be buried. Only Melanie can finally convince him otherwise, after which she herself succumbs to illness and exhaustion. When Melanie dies, it clears the way for Ashley and Scarlett to consummate a lifelong passion. But when Ashley confesses that he truly loves Melanie, that she is in fact the only woman he has ever loved, Scarlett realizes that it doesn't matter to her, that the only thing that really matters is Rhett, whom she's always truly loved though she never before realized it.

She rushes back to their house, where she finds Rhett packing his belongings. She does her best to convince him of her feelings, but he will have none of it. When she asks what she will do and where she will go without him, he replies squarely: "Frankly, my dear, I don't give a damn."

Rhett leaves her, but she is determined to win him back. She decides to return to Tara, where she can think clearly and devise another way to do it.

She tells herself hopefully: "Tomorrow is another day...."

Notes: In 1926, Margaret Mitchell Marsh, recovering from a sprained ankle, began writing a novel about the Civil War. The heroine was to be named Pansy O'Hara and the title of the book was to be *Tomorrow Is Another Day.* She worked tirelessly on it for nine years and it was published in May of 1936, after the publisher suggested a change of name for Miss Pansy and a different title for the book. It quickly became an unprecedented best seller, selling over one million copies by Christmas of that same year.

A month after its publication, producer David O. Selznick bought the screen rights for $50,000, at that time the highest sum ever paid for a novel. His initial problem was adapting the 1,037-page book to the screen. To photograph the novel literally would have yielded a film that exceeded eight

The burning of Atlanta. If that looks like Clark Gable and Vivien Leigh to you, guess again. This was the first scene that was shot for *Gone with the Wind* (MGM). Vivien Leigh hadn't even been cast yet, and the guy in the white suit is a stand-in for Gable.

hours in length; rearrangement of the story and characters was mandatory. For this task, he chose Sidney Howard, whom he called "a great constructionist." Before and during the shooting of *GWTW*, various writers would have a hand in working on the script (among them Ben Hecht, Oliver H.P. Garrett, John van Druten, Jo Swerling, and the novelist F. Scott Fitzgerald), but it was essentially Howard's script that Selznick ended up using.

As stated, changes were inevitably made in the passage from book to film. Scarlett's first two children were eliminated; Rhett's candid confessions of his blockade activities were minimized; the book's prostitute character, Belle Watling, was cleaned up; all references to the Ku Klux Klan were dropped; love scenes, particularly the so-called "Orchard Love Scene" or "paddock scene," were toned down; and, of course, some of the characters were either dropped or fused and many of the scenes and events were eliminated. Still, Margaret Mitchell's book remained relatively intact and the final product is, remarkably, quite a faithful one.

Another problem that confronted Selznick was the casting of the picture. Never before had he worked on a story that had so recently been emblazoned on the mind of the public.

When he asked Miss Mitchell whom she envisioned in the role of Rhett Butler, she suggested Groucho Marx. (Her actual choice was Basil Rathbone, who genuinely pictured himself in the heroic role and desired it greatly.) But the public demanded Clark Gable. At first, however,

Selznick balked at this idea. He had left his highly regarded position as a producer at MGM to free himself from the tyranny of Louis B. Mayer, who was then his father-in-law. The split had not been an amicable one and Selznick knew that Mayer would never let him have Gable without some MGM strings attached, so he decided to shop around. He tried Gary Cooper, but his friend Sam Goldwyn, who had Cooper signed to an exclusive contract, didn't extend his friendship to loaning out such a valuable property for another producer's profit. He then made plans with Warner Bros. to obtain Errol Flynn and Bette Davis for the main roles, but David refused ever to work with Flynn again after her experience with him on *The Private Lives of Elizabeth and Essex*. But the public would not be compromised. It had to be Gable! Reluctantly, Selznick went to Mayer and gave MGM exclusive distribution rights and 50 percent of the profits for the services of "The King."

When Mayer and Selznick approached Gable about playing Rhett Butler, he said he had never read the book and didn't know what they were talking about. He took the novel home with him and raced through it during a nerve-wracking weekend. When he returned to the studio with his verdict, both Selznick and Mayer were astounded. "I don't want the part for money, chalk, or marbles,"[22] he told them. He considered Rhett a Ronald Colman role and had no desire or intention of doing it.

But there was another matter to be considered: love. Gable had fallen in love with the actress Carole Lombard, and his estranged wife, Rhea Langham, refused to give him a divorce unless she received a cash settlement of over a quarter of a million dollars. Mayer cajoled the star with a $100,000 bonus, and Gable agreed.

Selznick had to wait a whole year for him, though, while the actor fulfilled his prior commitments. He used the time wisely, launching a campaign to find an actress to play opposite Gable in the role of Scarlett O'Hara. That star search has not been equaled to this day. Over $92,000 was spent on the monumental talent hunt; 1,400 women were interviewed before the cameras; 149,000 feet of black-and-white film and 13,000 feet of Technicolor were shot; and $10,000 was spent to audition 59 candidates. It lasted from September 1936 to December 1938 and eventually 31 women were actually screen-tested (unknowns as well as established stars).

Among the first tested was Tallulah Bankhead, who was too old, too flamboyant and stagy, and surely too acid. Even a telegram from the governor of Alabama failed to convince Selznick that Miss Bankhead was appropriate for the role.

George Cukor, who had been chosen to direct *GWTW*, wanted Katharine Hepburn for the part and personally made a test of her for Selznick. Hepburn told Selznick: "The part was practically written for me. I *am* Scarlett O'Hara." Selznick replied, rather bluntly: "I can't imagine Rhett Butler chasing you for ten years."

An unknown New York model named Edythe Marrener was tested.

She failed, and changed her name to Susan Hayward. Also said to be in the front-running were Frances Dee, Joel McCrea's wife, and Margaret Tallichet, Carole Lombard's discovery.

Finally, Selznick announced his decision. Scarlett O'Hara would be played by the vivacious Paulette Goddard, Charlie Chaplin's protégée and lover. But when she couldn't produce a marriage license to prove she was married to Chaplin, the search continued.

Shooting had already begun on the film when Selznick's brother, Myron, introduced him to British actress Vivien Leigh, who was in Hollywood visiting her husband and Myron's client, Laurence Olivier. "David," Myron said to his brother, "I'd like you to meet Scarlett O'Hara." Miss Leigh was signed shortly thereafter.

For the part of Melanie Hamilton, director Cukor asked Joan Fontaine to read for it. Fontaine wasn't interested in the role, but suggested her sister, Olivia de Havilland. Miss de Havilland was *very* interested in the role and pleaded with her boss, Jack Warner, to allow her to do it.

"You don't want to be in *Gone with the Wind*," he told her. "It's going to be the biggest bust ever."[23]

But de Havilland would not be dissuaded, and enlisted the aid of Warner's wife, who intervened successfully on behalf of the actress.

For the part of Ashley, Leslie Howard had been considered early, but Selznick's main concern was that he was considerably older than the young man in his twenties depicted in the novel. Melvyn Douglas gave what Selznick described as "the first intelligent reading of Ashley we've had," but Selznick considered him the wrong type for the role. Ray Milland, Robert Young, Douglas Fairbanks, Jr., Jeffrey Lynn, and Lew Ayres were also considered for the part.

When Selznick finally decided on Leslie Howard and offered him the role, Howard told him: "I haven't the slightest intention of playing another weak, watery character such as Ashley Wilkes. I've played enough ineffectual characters already."[24] But when Selznick promised Howard an associate producer's function on his other production of that year, *Intermezzo,* he accepted.

Selznick had wanted Mae West for the role of Belle Watling, Rhett's prostitute friend. But when the actress agreed to do it only if she could write her own dialogue, Selznick found someone else.

On December 18, 1938, the burning of Atlanta was filmed on the old Pathé lot in Culver City, where old film scenery (including the gates of the native village from Selznick's *King Kong,* 1933) represented the burning city. On January 26, 1939, principal shooting began; 140 days later (Gable worked 71 days, Leigh 125 days), on July 1, 1939, it ended with a retake of the opening scene, which was later discarded. In between, there were temper tantrums, nervous breakdowns, at least one suicide attempt, walkouts, and endless in-fighting.

Three weeks into shooting, Cukor was replaced as director by Victor

Fleming on Gable's recommendation. The reason Gable gave was Cukor's preoccupation and fastidiousness over the roles of Scarlett and Melanie, and his reputation as being a "woman's director." However, in his book *Hollywood Babylon II*, Kenneth Angers asserts that the reason for Gable's dissatisfaction with Cukor was altogether different. Angers claims that, as a struggling young actor, Gable had given sexual favors to a male cowboy star, who was a friend of the notoriously homosexual Cukor. Although words were never exchanged between the actor and director, Gable knew that Cukor was cognizant of what he had done, and couldn't stand the thought of taking direction from him every day for such a prolonged period of time.

In any case, the women (Leigh and de Havilland) were furious over Cukor's dismissal and protested it, to no avail. They even met with the director at night and on the sly to receive coaching from him. Gable, meanwhile, had the steadying influence of his hunting companion Fleming, a director he trusted implicitly, on the set.

There were still quarrels between the two leading stars, though. Although Gable admired Leigh's salty vocabulary (one of her favorite expressions was, "What are you fucking about for?"), he was put off by her intellect and her dedication to work. Leigh, in turn, was put off by Gable's bad breath, caused by his dentures, and complained each time they were supposed to kiss.

Something had to give under the weight of all this strain, and it was Fleming's nerves. He suffered a nervous breakdown and was replaced for the final weeks of shooting by Sam Wood, another director that Gable liked.

The whole shoot had been a hellish one for Gable, whose insecurity reached its nadir when he was asked to break down and cry in one scene. He had done this only once before on screen (in the film *Hold Your Man*, 1933) and it had turned out disastrously. He had sworn that he would never do it again. He locked himself in Olivia de Havilland's dressing room and refused to come out for hours, until she finally convinced him to give it a try (the same way her character talks Rhett Butler out of the room in which he has locked himself with his daughter's corpse). When he did, he was so wrought up that it took only one take to shoot. The scene remains one of the finest and most memorable of Gable's entire career.

When first previewed, *GWTW* ran for 4 hours and 20 minutes. It was later edited down to 3 hours and 24 minutes. The final cost was $3,957,000. A mere twenty years later, the same film would have cost an estimated $40 million!

After several months of editing, effects cinematography, retakes, and scoring, *GWTW* had its world premiere in Atlanta, Georgia, on December 15, 1939. Clark Gable had grown to dislike Selznick so much that he threatened to skip the premiere. He felt that Selznick's nit-picking had taken a year off Fleming's life and also objected to the fact Selznick was publicly crediting all three directors who had worked on the film for the quality of the finished product, instead of just Fleming. But Carole Lombard, who was Gable's wife by this time, convinced him that Rhett Butler had to attend the premiere. His reception in Atlanta was overwhelming, even by Hollywood's standards. "The second coming of the great prophet couldn't match the first coming of Gable," wrote *The Hollywood Reporter.* "Lindbergh's arrival after his flight is the nearest thing to it."

The success of the film was even greater than anyone had anticipated. Unanimously hailed by critics, it was nominated for a then-record 13 Academy Awards and won a then-record 8, and quickly became the biggest blockbuster of all time. By July of 1943, it had tallied a domestic gross of $32 million (*Snow White and the Seven Dwarfs,* 1938, placed a very distant second at the time with $8 million).

In 1942, David O. Selznick sold all interest to the picture, not anticipating the further financial successes the film would reap from re-issues in America in 1947, 1954, 1961, and 1967. For the '54 reissue, *GWTW* was released in a remasked, widescreen version with "Perspecta" stereophonic sound. In '61, for the Civil War centennial, it was given a spectacular gala in Atlanta. Vivient Leigh, Olivia de Havilland, David O. Selznick, and Stephens Mitchell (brother of the author, who died in 1949) were among the notables in attendance. In '67, an "adapted" negative was made for showing in 70mm; it was successful financially if not aesthetically.

In November of 1976, the film made its television debut on NBC, and drew the largest audience of any program shown on one network in the history of the medium. In 1978, CBS paid $35 million for the television rights to the film for twenty years.

In 1977, the classic was dubbed, by an official tabulation of the voting members of the American Film Institute, "The Greatest Film Ever Made."

GWTW has never been remade, despite constant hearsay, but the Margaret Mitchell estate did recently commission an author to write a long-awaited sequel to the novel, which means that a movie sequel is probably not too far off in the future.

Like any film, *GWTW* was the result of a lot of combined talents. Without question, though, the dominant force behind it and the man most deserving of the credit for its success is producer David O. Selznick. He was involved in every single detail of the production, from start to finish, and it is still the leading example of a creative producer's work. Selznick still believed what he had told his bosses at Paramount eight years earlier: that a motion picture was like a painting, and it had to be painted and signed by one artist. *Gone with the Wind* is his painting, and it bears his signature.

Reviews: "Understatement has its uses too, so this morning's report on the event of last night will begin with the casual notation that it was a great show. . . . You will leave it, not with the feeling you have undergone a profound emotional experience, but with the warm and grateful remembrance of an interesting story beautifully told. Is it the greatest motion picture ever made? Probably not, although it is the greatest motion mural we have seen and the most ambitious film-making venture in Hollywood's spectacular history.

"Miss Leigh's Scarlett has vindicated the absurd talent quest that indirectly turned her up. She is so perfectly designed for the part by art and nature that any other actress in the role would be inconceivable. . . .

"Olivia de Havilland's Melanie is a gracious, dignified, tender gem of characterization. Mr. Gable's Rhett Butler (although there is the fine flavor of the smokehouse in a scene or two) is almost as perfect as the grandstand quarterbacks thought he would be. Leslie Howard's Ashley Wilkes is anything but a pallid characterization of a pallid character. Best of all, perhaps, next to Miss Leigh, is Hattie McDaniel's Mammy. . . .

"*It* has arrived at last, and we cannot get over the shock of not being disappointed; we had almost been looking forward to that." — Frank S. Nugent, *The New York Times*

Goodbye Mr. Chips

An MGM Picture. Directed by Sam Wood. Produced by Victor Saville. Screenplay by R.C. Sherriff, Claudine West, and Eric Maschwitz. From the book of the same name by James Hilton. Photographed by F.A. Young. Edited by Charles Frend. Art direction by Alfred Junge. Production manager: Harold Boxall. Music by Louis Levy. Sound by A.W. Watkins. Running time 115 minutes. Release date: June 19.

Cast: Robert Donat *Mr. Chips;* Greer Garson *Katherine;* Terry Kilburn *John Colley/Peter Colley I/Peter Colley II/Peter Colley III;* John Mills *Peter Colley (as a young man);* Paul von Henried *Staefel;* Judith Farse *Flora;* Lyn Harding *Wetherby;* Milton Rosmer *Chatteris;* Frederick Leister *Marsham;* Louise Hampton *Mrs. Wickett;* Austin Trevor *Ralston;* David Tree *Jackson;* Edmond Breon *Colonel Morgan;* Jill Furse *Helen Colley;* Scott Sanderland *Sir John Colley.*

> Every screen actor in the world should go and study Robert Donat as Mr. Chips. There is something so magnificent in this character study and performance that it seems almost a miracle that it could happen. — James Stewart

> May I say without reservation that your Mr. Chips is the finest performance I have ever seen on the screen. I should like someday to give one remotely approaching it. — Spencer Tracy[25]

Synopsis: *Goodbye Mr. Chips* is the beautiful and endearing story of a dull, unpopular schoolmaster who — through the love of a good woman and his loss of her — becomes a benevolent and legendary old man.

Goodbye, Mr. Chips (MGM). *Top:* Robert Donat (Mr. Chippings) instructs his students. *Bottom:* Mr. Chippings' colleagues are pleasantly surprised by how lovely and charming his new bride (Greer Garson) is.

The film is set almost entirely at Brookfield, a very old and very traditional boys' school modeled after Leys School in Cambridge. It begins on
the first day of a new semester, at the general assembly. The headmaster
apologizes for the unavoidable absence of Mr. Chippings (Robert Donat),
who is bedridden with a cold. It is the first opening-day assembly that the
83-year-old man has missed in 58 years of teaching.

Even as the head is making this statement, "Chips" is en route, scurry-
ing across the school grounds, fully intent on keeping his perfect record un-
tarnished. When he arrives, the boys give him a hearty welcome. He seems
to know each one of them personally, as well as all of their ancestors.

Listening to the school song being played, mouthing the words to it
wistfully, Chips begins to reminisce about Brookfield and the many years
that he has spent there. The movie flashes back to his youth, over half a century earlier, to the very first day he arrived and began his tenure. Only
minutes after stepping off of the Brookfield Express—the train that
transports teachers, or "heads," and students alike to the facility—Chips
takes an immediate liking to his new school and speaks of one day becoming
headmaster.

In the faculty lounge, he is warned by his colleagues that a new head
is considered little more than blood sport by the pupils, a warning that
proves well-founded when he arrives in his assigned classroom and is summarily sieged.

Despite a rather shaky start, Chips settles in at Brookfield and conducts his life there as quietly and unobtrusively as possible. He is almost
like a spirit passing through a material world. The days pass into weeks, the
weeks into months, the months into years, the years into decades. The film
cleverly bridges this time span by collaging roll calls of new semesters and
listening in on the conversations of some of the boys, who discuss famous
historical events that date them, such as the "English chap" crossing the
Channel or the death of a queen.

When the story resumes, Chips is a moustached middle-aged man. His
life is staid and uneventful. Being a shy and docile man who is diffident with
women, he has never married and is terribly lonely. School has just recessed
for a holiday vacation, but Chips is more concerned about a housemaster
vacancy he expects to be appointed to. Even his vacations have become dull
and regimental. When he is informed that he has been passed over for the
promotion in favor of a less-qualified head, he submissively accepts the
news.

His friend Staefel (Paul von Henried) invites him to join him on a walking tour through Austria to Vienna and Chips decides to go. While
mountain-climbing there, Chips gets stuck alone up high in a thick mist. He
hears a woman calling out and, assuming she's in danger, climbs a perilous
rock with the intention of saving her. At the summit, he meets a beautiful
young woman named Katherine (Greer Garson, in her screen debut), who
is quite safe. They wait together for the mist to clear, talking and laughing

and eating ham sandwiches. When the mist finally lifts, they both seem almost disappointed.

At the inn where they are staying, a celebration is thrown in honor of Chips, "the hero of the mist." But the guest of honor retires early, despite protests from the others. The following morning, Katherine and her friend Flora (Judith Farse) leave early on their bicycles, which they are pedaling across Austria.

For the remainder of his trip, Chips cannot put Katherine out of his mind. When he mets her again in Vienna, the night before she is scheduled to return home to London by train, they attend a formal dance together and waltz the night away.

At the train station the next day, Chips proposes to her, awkwardly but sincerely. Just as the train is pulling out of the station, she accepts, and they are subsequently wed.

Back at Brookfield, Chips' colleagues read about his marriage in the social pages and assume that his bride must be old and ugly. When he introduces her to them, they are all nonplussed. The new Mrs. Chippings wins them over easily with her beguiling charm and beauty.

Next she encounters some of Chips' students, and invites them over for a Sunday tea party (which quickly becomes a weekly ritual with the boys). As host of the party, Katherine charms the youngsters in her inimitable way.

She revolutionizes Chips' life, encouraging him to tell jokes in class and open up more, which he does with tremendous results. And because of this dramatic metamorphosis, Chips finally receives the promotion to housemaster at Brookfield that seemed so elusive for such a long time. The man that everyone barely knew existed for nearly twenty years has, suddenly and unexpectedly, become the most popular man on campus among staff and students alike (with emphasis on the latter faction).

Katherine becomes pregnant by Chips but dies of complications, along with the baby. Chips is devastated, but insists on conducting his class that day. His students — unaware of what has happened — have prepared an April Fools Day prank for him. When they spring it, they are surprised by his somber reaction. Then a boy arrives with the tragic news and the mood in the classroom quickly changes, from laughter to tears. As one of the boys recites Latin verse, the pupils all share in Chips' grief. It is a simple and tender scene that is one of the saddest and most moving of any ever filmed.

More years pass and Chips — an old man now — finally retires. The boys at Brookfield present him with a memorial cake holder, in honor of his infamous Sunday tea parties. But when World War I suddenly erupts, and many of the heads leave for active duty, Chips is asked to return to Brookfield to serve as the temporary headmaster, until the conflict has ended. He accepts, and finally realizes his life's ambition.

The war eventually ends, Chips retires for good and thereafter passes away. Before he dies, however, he hears someone remark what a pity it was he never had any children.

"But you're wrong," Chips corrects sternly. "I have. Thousands of them. And all boys."

Notes: In 1939, the list of nominees for the Best Actor statuette at the Academy Awards included Clark Gable for his fiery Rhett Butler, James Stewart for his impassioned Mr. Smith, and Laurence Olivier for his tormented Heathcliff (three of the most popular male performances of all time). But when the envelope was opened, the name inside was that of English actor Robert Donat, for his brilliant and unforgettable portrayal of the benevolent schoolmaster, Mr. Chips.

The genesis of *Goodbye Mr. Chips* occurred in 1937, when a London magazine commissioned writer James Hilton to prepare a piece of fiction for its Christmas edition. Hilton submitted a 20,000-word story about a professor in an English boys' school. He later denied that the story's protagonist was based on his own father, an aged schoolmaster. When the novelette was published in the United States, its success convinced Irving Thalberg to purchase the screen rights for MGM.

To enhance the film's realism, it was shot in England, partly at MGM's studio in Denham (at the time, the biggest sets for any British-made film were constructed there) and on location at Repton College, where many of the students and some faculty members acted as extras.

The foremost problem was in casting the all-important lead role, which required an actor to age from twenty-four to eighty. Charles Laughton and Wallace Beery were among the potential candidates, but in the end, MGM decided to utilize the services of Robert Donat, whom they had signed to a six-picture deal.

Donat had suffered from chronic asthma all of his life and always worked with an oxygen tank nearby. Because of his condition, he was forced to turn down the leading role in scores of other films, including *Captain Blood, The Adventures of Robin Hood, A Double Life,* and *How Green Was My Valley.* Still, by the late 1930s, he had solidly established himself as a heroic leading man in films such as Hitchcock's *The 39 Steps* (1935) and Metro's *The Citadel* (1938), and he was strongly advised not to go against type in the timid role of Mr. Chips. Fortunately, Donat didn't listen and accepted the role for which he would always be remembered and which earned him his only Oscar.

Former child star Terry Kilburn remembered him fondly: "(Donat) made a deep impression on me by always remaining in character as the old Mr. Chips, even when he was off-camera. Many people thought that this was rather affected of him, but it was a deep dedication he felt toward the role and I thought it was splendid."[26]

Robert Donat died at 53, an immeasurable loss to the film industry.

Greer Garson was an accomplished West End leading lady in roles such as the heroine in *Accent on Youth* and had been under contract to

MGM for over a year before making her screen debut in *Chips*. Legend has it that she had given up and actually had her bags packed to return home to London when Hollywood finally called. The film's success launched her career as one of MGM's leading stars.

Also in the cast was Paul von Henried, who played the German master. Later he would go to Hollywood, simplify his name to Henried and win acclaim for his performances in *Casablanca* (1942) and *Now Voyager* (1942).

Donat's Oscar was the only one the film received, but it was also nominated for Best Picture, Supporting Actress (Garson), Director, Screenplay, Sound Recording and Film Editing.

It was remade under the same title in 1969, with Peter O'Toole in the title role, but that one (a musical) was overlong and lifeless.

Reviews: "... No unlikelier book for screening comes easily to mind, so little story had it, so gentle and uneventful Mr. Hilton's fond sketch of an insightful little English schoolmaster. That it made a motion picture which so many people find engrossing is something of a movie-maker's triumph....

"Robert Donat ... is the very essence of great-uncles who live forever. It is really a remarkable character creation....

"It is so downright refreshing to come across a face and voice and manner like Greer Garson's, all so radiantly new, that she seems like a vigorous breeze blowing into a musty room.... Brief as her time in the picture is she is the character who gives the plot its one step forward, the one bright, positive person in the long years, to be gratefully and delightedly remembered."—James Shelley Hamilton, *National Board of Review Magazine*

"*Goodbye Mr. Chips* will appeal to others more than me, for while there is no run and life to it as a movie and a general air of stagnant sentiment, there are certain qualities of kindness and wisdom, loneliness and enduring faith in the figure of this spry and gentle soul. (Robert Donat does wonderfully well against the handicap of having to be a young actor in an octogeneric wig and twinkle; but even so the part as written for him is actually pretty straight type, monotonous in incident.) I thought the emphasis given in writing and direction to the old-school stuff made it less recreative of an attitude than silly...."—Otis Ferguson, *The New Republic*

The Great Man Votes

RKO. 72 min. Directed by Garson Kanin.

Cast: John Barrymore, Peter Holden, Virginia Weidler, Katharine Alexander, Donald MacBride, Bennie Bartlett, Brandon Tynan, Elizabeth Risdon, Granville Bates, Luis Alberni, J.M. Kerrigan, William Demarest.

John Barrymore plays a Prohibition drunk who is regenerated when he learns that he is the lone voter in a precinct vital to an upcoming election. RKO studio chief Pandro Berman didn't want any part of Barrymore after firing the alcoholic actor from a project called *Hat, Coat and Glove,* but director Kanin convinced him that Barrymore was the perfect choice for the part. Barrymore proved worthy of Kanin's trust by delivering a warm, touching and delightfully funny performance. As an enthusiastic campaign manager, William Demarest displayed the energy and humor that would make his services invaluable to writer-director Preston Sturges over the ensuing years.

The Great Victor Herbert

Paramount. 91 min. Directed by Andrew L. Stone.
Cast: Walter Connolly, Allan Jones, Mary Martin, Susanna Foster, Lee Bowman, Jerome Cowan.
Paramount billed this one as "the grandest of love stories told to the tunes of the grandest musical score ever written!" Well, the love story wasn't so grand, but the musical score ("March of the Toys," "Ah Sweet Mystery of Life," and others) certainly was. The film was nominated for Best Score and Best Sound Recording, but lost in both categories.

Gulliver's Travels

A Paramount Picture. Directed by Dave Fleischer. Produced by Max Fleischer. Story adaptation by Edmond Seward. Screenplay by Dan Gordon, Cal Howard, Ted Pierce, I. Sparber, and Edmond Seward. Based upon the story by Jonathan Swift. Music and lyrics by Ralph Rainger and Leo Robin. Atmospheric music created and conducted by Victor Young. Scenics: Erich Schenk, Robert Little, Louis Jambor, and Shane Miller. Photographed by Charles Schettler. Technical adviser: Johnny Burks. Directors of animation: Seymour Kneitel, Willard Bowsky, Tom Palmer, Grim Natwick, William Henning, Roland Crandall, Tom Johnson, Robert Leffingwell, Frank Kelling, Winfield Hoskins, and Orestes Calpini. Animators: Graham Place, Arnold Gillespie, Nicholas Tafuri, Alfred Eugster, James Culhane, David Tendlar, George Germanetti, Joseph Digalo, Nelson Demorest, Reuben Grossman, Abner Kneitel, Frank Endres, Otto Feuer, Joseph Oriolo, Harold Walker, Lod Rossner, Joe Miller, Frank Smith, Edwin Rehberg, Ben Clopton, James Davis, Stephen Muffatti, Irving Spector, Sam Stimson, George Moreno, Ted Dubois, William Sturm, Lou Zukor, Bill Nolan, Stan Quackenbush, Robert Bentley, Edward Smith, Thurston Harper, and Tony Pabian. Running time: 77 min. Release date: December 18.
Song: "It's a Hap Hap Happy Day" by Sammy Timberg, Al Neiburg, and Winston Sharples.

Singing Voices: Jessica Dragonette *Princess Glory;* Lanny Ross *Prince David.*

> It shows the smallness of human beings regardless of how great they think they are. — Max Fleischer[27]

Synopsis: The success of Walt Disney's *Snow White and the Seven Dwarfs* (1937) inspired the renowned Fleischer Brothers to make a feature-length animated film of their own, *Gulliver's Travels,* based on the immortal tale by Jonathan Swift. Neither the animation nor the music compares to Disney's work, but nevertheless this film remains a favorite of children.

It begins as a shipwrecked sailor named Lemuel Gulliver crawls up onto the beach of an uncharted island and falls into a deep sleep. He has landed in the kingdom of Lilliput, inhabited by a race of tiny people (the tallest of whom is no more than six inches high).

King Little of Lilliput is in the process of making final arrangements with King Bombo of Blefuscu for the wedding of their children, Princess Glory (Little's daughter) and Prince David (Bombo's son). King Little insists that his country's song, "Faithful," be played at the wedding; King Bombo demands that his country's song, "Forever," be the song. When the two cannot agree, King Bombo lividly declares war on Lilliput and leaves in a huff with his son, Prince David.

At about the same time, one of Lilliput's citizens, Gabby, runs into the village with the news of having found a giant on the beach. He rings the village bell furiously, awakening all of Lilliput.

The citizens all march down to the beach, led by Gabby, but do not find any sign of a giant. They suspect Gabby of hallucinating and chide him mercilessly. Suddenly, though, one of them hears a heartbeat, followed by deep breathing, and they realize that they're walking on the giant's chest. They scatter quickly.

Working en masse, with diligence and great ingenuity, they build a rolling cart and load Gulliver onto it. Then they bind his arms, legs, body and hair down to the cart. Pulled by a pack of horses, the cart is wheeled slowly across the beach and up into their village.

King Little is awakened and informed that the giant has been captured. He steps outside and, when he sees the enormous size of Gulliver, nearly kills himself racing back into his castle and under his bed sheets.

The Lilliputians search their prisoner, finding a watch, a telescope and a pistol, which accidentally goes off and blows one of their buildings to pieces. It also awakens the sleeping giant. Gulliver effortlessly breaks free from the ropes they have bound him with and picks Gabby up into the air by his shirt tails.

"I won't taste good! I'll give you indigestion! I've got a wife and kids . . . millions of kids!" Gabby pleads.

Just as the palace guards are about to fire upon Gulliver, their kingdom

Gulliver's Travels (Paramount). *Top:* Gulliver is captured by the citizens of Lilliput. *Bottom:* King Little wants "Faithful" to be the song played at the wedding of Prince David and Princess Glory, while King Bombo argues for the song "Forever." This disagreement leads to war between the two countries and cancellation of the wedding plans of their two children.

is attacked by Bombo's fleet. However, when the warring king catches sight of Gulliver, he turns his ships around and returns to Blefescu with all haste.

The kingdom of Lilliput realizes that Gulliver is a friendly giant—not to mention a valuable ally—and they parade jubilantly through the streets, proclaiming victory over Bombo's mighty navy. It's a hap hap happy day for all of Lilliput, save Princess Glory, who mourns the loss of her betrothed.

Bombo sends a message to his spies in Lilliput, warning them to dispose of the giant or face the consequences of their failure. They find his pistol—marked "Gulliver's Thunder Machine"—and select that as their weapon of choice.

The heartsick Prince David returns to Lilliput alone, serenading Princess Glory with the song "Forever." When King Little hears the song, he dispatches his guards. As David is fighting them off single-handedly, Gulliver intervenes, moving the two young lovers away to a safer area. Discussing the problem that separates their respective kingdoms, Gulliver gets the idea to sing "Faithful" and "Forever" together, as one song.

Meanwhile, Bombo's spies send word to the king that plans are afoot to assassinate the giant. Bombo returns word that he will attack at dawn, but Gabby intercepts the message and warns all of the villagers. They rush down to the beach to meet Bombo's attack and defend their homeland.

Gulliver captures Bombo's fleet single-handedly and totes the ships to shore. When David spots Bombo's spies setting the "thunder machine" up to kill Gulliver, he attacks them speedily on his white stallion, deflecting the bullet and nearly getting killed himself in the process. Prince David and Princess Glory sing "Faithful Forever" together, and their duet reunites the opposing kingdoms, as everyone joins in and sings along.

Wedding plans are resumed. To repay Gulliver for bringing peace to their little worlds, the people build him a new ship and he sails away, leaving behind many friends who will be faithful forever to his memory.

Notes: When Paramount Pictures commissioned a feature-length animated film from the Fleischer Brothers, Max and Dave, they took nearly six months to choose a subject, finally deciding on Jonathan Swift's *Gulliver's Travels* (one of Max's favorite books). However, because the scope of the Swift novel was so gargantuan—in the book, Gulliver travels to several different lands and has a variety of adventures—they opted to pare the story down and concentrate exclusively on his visit to the strange little kingdom of Lilliput. Instead of the war with Blefuscu being over which side of an egg is the appropriate one to crack, they had the kings arguing over their respective national anthems, and original songs were written. They also added the characters of Prince David and Princess Glory (based not too loosely on Disney's Snow White and Prince Charming characters).

Gulliver's Travels turned out to be a massive undertaking. It took 700 artists a year and a half to complete the job; more than 12 tons of paint were brushed on half a million celluloids and backgrounds that made up the 115,700 composite scenes; approximately 16 tons of drawing paper were used in the process; and the final script measured out to be 27 miles, 385 yards long.

After its world premiere at the Sheridan Theatre in Miami, Florida, on December 18, 1939, it opened four days later in general release. By the end of its first week at the Paramount Theatre in New York City, it broke that house's all-time attendance record by playing to 13,758 people before 3:00 p.m. on one day. By the second week, 264,798 people had come to see the picture (79,927 of whom were children). When more than 3,000 people attended the theatre before 3:00 p.m. on five consecutive days, a new 8:30 A.M. opening time was established at the Paramount for the duration of the film's run.

Gulliver's Travels was nominated for Best Original Score and for Best Song ("Faithful Forever," by Rainger and Robin), but *The Wizard of Oz* was taking home the statuettes for music in '39; it won for its score and "Over the Rainbow" was selected as the Best Song.

Gulliver was remade twenty years later as *The Three Worlds of Gulliver* (a Ray Harryhausen stop-motion animation special), and as a live-action film with Richard Harris in the seventies.

Reviews: "By any other standards than those of the juvenile audience the film is so far beneath the level of Mr. Disney's famous fantasy that out of charity we wish we did not have to make the comparisons demanded by professional responsibility. If it were only possible to soften the blow by suggesting that the second cartoon feature automatically loses the novelty value of the first we should be cushioning our typewriter with the excuse right now. But it is far more than novelty that Gulliver lacks: it is the wit, the freshness, the gaiety and sparkle, the subtlety, the characterization and for that matter the good drawing that are the trademarks of the Disney factory."—Frank S. Nugent, *The New York Times*

"All in all *Gulliver's Travels* possesses the appeal of a superior cartoon well drawn as to the scenery and people, utilizing the fantastic size contrasts of the Jonathan Swift classic for all they're worth. The musical and Disney additions further enhance the production. Let's don't be stuffy about borrowing. Nothing is really original or at least it's very rare."—Archer Winsten, *The New York Post*

Gunga Din

An RKO Picture. Produced and directed by George Stevens. Executive producer: Pandro S. Berman. Screenplay by Joel Sayre and Fred Guiol. Story by Ben Hecht and Charles MacArthur and (uncredited) William Faulkner. Suggested by the Rudyard Kipling poem. Photographed by Joseph

H. August. Edited by Henry Berman and John Lockert. Art direction by Van Nest Polglase and Perry Ferguson. Set decoration by Darrell Silvera. Gowns by Edward Stevenson. Technical advisers: Cpt. Clive Morgan, Sgt.-Maj. William Briers, and Sir Robert Erskine Holland. Special effects by Vernon L. Walker. Music by Alfred Newman. Sound by John E. Tribly and James Stewart. Running time: 117 minutes. Release date: January 27.

Cast: Cary Grant *Cutter;* Victor McLaglen *MacChesney;* Douglas Fairbanks, Jr. *Ballantine;* Sam Jaffe *Gunga Din;* Eduardo Ciannelli *Guru;* Joan Fontaine *Emmy Stebins;* Montagu Love *Colonel Weed;* Robert Coote *Higginbotham;* Abner Biberman *Chota;* Lumsden Hare *Maj. Mitchell;* Cecil Kellaway *Mr. Stebbins;* Reginald Sheffield *Kipling;* Ann Evers, Audrey Manners, and Fay McKenzie *Girls at Party;* Roland Varno *Lt. Markham.*

> Though I've belted you and flayed you
> By the living Gawd that made you
> You're a better man than I am, Gunga Din!
> — Rudyard Kipling

Synopsis: Writers Ben Hecht and Charles MacArthur (with uncredited assistance from the novelist William Faulkner) took the title, the setting and these last three lines from Kipling's "Barrack Room Ballad," and turned them into a rollicking, red-blooded adventure yarn filled with spectacular heroics, down-to-earth humor and tongue-in-cheek melodrama.

While professing to be the story of a lowly Indian water boy who dreams of becoming a soldier, the plot revolves primarily around the escapades of three Imperial Lancers: the clowning Cutter (Cary Grant), the bullish MacChesney (Victor McLaglen), and the dashing Ballantine (Douglas Fairbanks, Jr.). They are the British Empire's answer to "The Three Musketeers."

In fact, when we first meet them, they are in the middle of a knockdown-dragout brawl that they instigated over a treasure map which Cutter—an incorrigible fortune hunter—somehow acquired. This scene could have been used as a worthy climax for a lesser adventure film, but these boys are just getting started.

From there, director George Stevens cuts immediately to the chase. We learn that the Thuggees, a sect of murderous fanatics who worship Kali, the Goddess of Blood, and perform ritualistic ceremonies like digging the graves of their victims before going into battle, have risen again after years of inactivity. Led by their Guru (Eduardo Ciannelli), they have vowed to rid their country of the colonial British. Their first target is the village of Tantrapur, which they overrun easily.

Cutter, MacChesney and Ballantine are dispatched along with a regiment of Lancers to investigate. When they reach Tantrapur, they are ambushed by the Thugs in one of the most exciting, elaborate, and impeccably choreographed action sequences ever captured on celluloid. Stevens—

Cary Grant, Douglas Fairbanks, Jr., and Victor McLaglen as the dashing Imperial Lancers in *Gunga Din* (RKO).

shooting on location at Lone Pine, near California's Mount Whitney—pulls out all of the stops for this one, in what he called "cavalry style improvisation." He even reaches back to his days as a cameraman for Laurel and Hardy for a few old tricks. Dynamite blasts and fistfights and gunfire and daring leaps from one building to another and even a little swordplay are thrown in for good measure. It is a rollercoaster ride of a sequence that finally stops when our heroes plunge off of a cliff and into a river far below.[28]

After this narrow escape, Cutter and MacChesney are presented with a much more serious matter: Ballantine announces that he is leaving the service to get married and go into the tea business.

"Married!" MacChesney growls.

"Tea business!" Cutter screams.

They can hardly believe their ears.

At a formal later that evening, their grief is only compounded when they encounter Ballantine's proposed replacement, Bertie Higginbotham—as strait-laced and humorless as his name might infer. They proceed to get him deliriously drunk on spiked punch, forcing Ballantine to accompany them on one last expedition. He does so grudgingly.

During their trek, Cutter gets word of a temple of gold said to be located in the nearby region and rides off on MacChesney's pet elephant, Annie, to claim his fortune. To serve as a guide, he brings along Gunga Din (played by the great character actor Sam Jaffe). When they reach the temple, they discover that it is actually the headquarters for the bloodthirsty

Thugs. After overhearing their plan to massacre the British troops, Cutter allows himself to be captured so that Din can escape and return to warn the regiment. "The colonel's got to know!" Cutter proclaims urgently, and Din reacts with the relish of a soldier who has just been given his first order.

Din returns and relays all of this to MacChesney, who prepares to ride off and rescue Cutter single-handedly. Ballantine insists on going with him, but MacChesney refuses to take "a civilian" along on a military operation. To circumvent regulations, Ballantine agrees to sign a reenlistment form (which MacChesney just happens to have handy), explaining to his frustrated bride-to-be (Joan Fontaine): "I hate the blasted army, but friendship, well, that's something else." Then he, MacChesney and Din ride off to save Cutter.

They arrive at the temple but, instead of saving Cutter, are captured as well.

"Where's the troops?" demands Cutter.

"Another fine mess you've gotten us into," MacChesney retorts—another throw-back to Stevens' Laurel and Hardy days.

The sergeants improbably manage to take the Guru prisoner and lock his followers outside the temple. They take him to the summit of the temple, where for some time things remain stalemated. The Lancers will not release the Guru and the Guru will not call off his men. He is their "shield," but they are his "bait," being unwittingly used to lure the entire regiment into his valley, where the groundwork has already been laid for their annihilation.

Soon the bagpipes can be heard, signaling the approach of the regiment, but the Thugs will not proceed while their Guru's life is in jeopardy. To break this impasse, the Guru runs back down into the temple and throws himself into a pit of poisonous snakes. This last act of martyrdom propels his troops forward and sets his plan back into motion.

Ballantine and MacChesney are recaptured; Cutter and Din are stabbed and left for dead. But before the regiment marches to their certain death, Din reappears, climbing to the peak of the temple, enlisting the aid of a bugle and blowing a warning call. He is shot down and killed, but not before saving the lives of the entire regiment, as well as those of his three comrades.

The good guys prevail, of course; Ballantine reenlists; and Gunga Din is buried with full honors, as a corporal in Her Majesty's Army. As the colonel recites Kipling's famous last verse, Din's face is superimposed over the screen. He is dressed in full regimental regalia and smiling proudly.

Notes: Executive producer Pandro S. Berman had tried to get this project off the ground in 1936, with Howard Hawks to direct and Ronald Colman and Spencer Tracy playing two of the almost equal three male leads, but it never materialized.

Two years later, he tried again. This time around there was a new cast, but Howard Hawks was still set to direct. However, when Hawks ran

Douglas Fairbanks, Jr. (far left), Victor McLaglen (second from left), Sam Jaffe (right of center), and Cary Grant (far right) hold Eduardo Ciannelli (center) hostage in *Gunga Din* (RKO).

overbudget and overlong on *Bringing Up Baby* (1938), Berman opted to go with George Stevens instead, primarily because he had a reputation for being quick and economical. He certainly didn't have any action credentials to his credit. Up until '39, Stevens had dabbled mostly in light comedies (such as *Alice Adams*) and musicals (such as *Swing Time*). So imagine Berman's chagrin when Stevens turned out to be more painstaking and costly than Hawks ever could have been, running the budget up to nearly two million dollars and making *Gunga Din* the most expensive film in RKO's history!

The end product was worth the wait. Shooting without a completed script (just as Curtiz did with *Casablanca*) and using much improvisation (including the famous final scene between Grant and Jaffe), Stevens created a timeless classic which can arguably be called the greatest adventure film of all time. It was also the second highest grossing film of the year, surpassed only by *Jesse James*.

Cary Grant was initially cast in the lead role of Ballantine, but after shooting began, he went to Berman and Stevens and asked if he could switch roles with Fairbanks, feeling himself better suited for the second lead role of Cutter. He also talked them into changing Cutter's first name to Archibald, as a sort of inside joke. (Grant's real name was Archibald Leach.)

In the film, Grant finally got the chance to emulate his idol, Douglas

Fairbanks, Sr., leaping through the air, performing somersaults, and brandishing a sword against the foe of Her Majesty's Empire. In fact, he cheated Fairbanks, Jr., out of one of the most memorable moments in the picture. In a rooftop scene, the younger Fairbanks had to wrestle with a native adversary, pick him up and hurl him into the street below. Grant coveted the bit himself, so he told his co-star: "Doug, you really shouldn't do this. It looks like you've killed the guy. It wouldn't help your image. And you know your father never would have done such a thing on the screen."[29]

Convinced that Grant was right, the worried Fairbanks begged Stevens to assign the chore to someone else. When Stevens agreed, Grant jumped forward and said: "George, I'll do it!"[30]

The production values are uniformly excellent. Henry Berman's and John Lockert's magnificent editing (especially of the action sequences), Alfred Newman's rousing musical score and Joseph H. August's indispensable panoramic skills all contribute greatly to the finished product.

And credit must also be given to a very energetic and enthusiastic cast, who obviously had a lot of fun making this picture. Stand-outs are Ciannelli, maniacally evil as the Guru, and Grant, whose boyish charm and impetuosity have rarely been put to better use.

On the night that this movie opened, it received a free plug on national radio. Asked on an NBC quiz show how the title character of the poem dies, humorist Oscar Levant quipped: "In an RKO picture."

Gunga Din was remade as *Soldiers Three* in 1951 and as a vehicle for the Rat Pack (Frank, Dean and Sammy) 11 years later in *Sergeants Three*. A third remake is currently in production.

Reviews: "George Stevens has taken this gaily irresponsible script and directed it for all it's worth, and made an excellent job of it. The glories of the old days when movies moved instead of talking are here notably revived.... Everybody concerned with putting *Gunga Din* on the screen did his technical best (including a remarkably good composer of the musical score), and to excellent effect. If as a whole it can't be taken very seriously it's because its authors seem to have been indulging in a little swing session on Kipling themes, improvising with more gusto than intention, with really nothing to say."—James Shelley Hamilton, *National Board of Review Magazine*

"Three Black Shirts could not indulge in an orgy of brutality with more gusto than do the three Khaki Shirts (Cary Grant, Victor McLaglen, Douglas Fairbanks, Jr.), who dash laughingly across the screen killing right and left and exhibiting themselves as practically bullet-proof by nature. The picture is ghastly and disgusting to one who knows what war really looks like. But you are expected to leave your better feelings and your brain at home. That such a picture should be produced in the greatest and freest democracy of the world and with the approval of the Hays Office and the state boards of censorship, which protect us from the sight of a baby being born but have nothing against the inspiring influence of wholesale massacres, may be only a symptom of the cultural level on which the great industry and its mentors operate. Provided it is hypocritically disguised, the appeal to the lowest instincts is still legitimate business."—Franz Hoellering, *The Nation*

Hell's Kitchen

Warner Bros. Directed by Lewis Seiler and E.A. Dupont.

Cast: Billy Halop, Bobby Jordan, Leo Gorcey, Huntz Hall, Gabriel Dell, Bernard Punsley, Frankie Burke, Margaret Lindsay, Ronald Reagan, Stanley Fields, Grant Mitchell.

For Ronald Reagan, the title of this picture might have sounded like the shooting location when Warner Bros. cast him along with the young hellions of the studio lot, the Dead End Kids. He later described the experience as "similar to going over Niagara Falls the hard way—upstream."[31] Before reporting to the set, though, he consulted actor James Cagney, who not only worked with the Kids a year earlier in *Angels with Dirty Faces,* but was himself a product of the same New York area that spawned them. Cagney advised him: "Just tell them you look forward to working with them but you'll slap hell out of them if they do one thing out of line."[32] The storyline has the Kids graduating from reform school and being sent to a "Boys Town"–type shelter, where they encounter crooked superintendent Mitchell and his assistant, ex-racketeer Fields. Reagan portrays a social worker at the shelter whose romance with Lindsay is helped along by the boys. Co-produced by Mark Hellinger of *The Roaring Twenties* fame.

Hollywood Cavalcade

Twentieth Century–Fox. 96 min. Directed by Irving Cummings.

Cast: Don Ameche, Alice Faye, J. Edward Bromberg, Alan Curtis, Stuart Erwin, Jed Prouty, Buster Keaton, Donald Meek, Al Jolson, Mack Sennett, Rin-Tin-Tin, Jr., and the original Keystone Kops.

The first half of this film is terrific, as producer Ameche brings singer Faye out to Hollywood, where hilarious re-staging of silent slapstick comedies by some of the masters (Keaton *et al.*) unfortunately gives way to heavy-handed personal melodrama. The story is based more than loosely on the lives of producer Mack Sennett (who actually appears in the picture!) and actress Mabel Normand.

Home on the Prairie

58 min. Directed by Jack Townley.

Cast: Gene Autry, Smiley Burnette, June Storey, George Cleveland, Jack Mulhall.

Gene plays a border inspector forced to quarantine the area when a hoof-and-mouth disease erupts. He also tangles with some ruthless cattlemen who try and take their diseased cattle to market. This is one of the few Autry oaters which contains more action than song.

The Hound of the Baskervilles

A Twentieth Century–Fox Film. Directed by Sidney Lanfield. Screenplay by Ernest Pascal. Based upon the novel of the same name by Sir Arthur Conan Doyle. Associate producer: Gene Markey. Photographed by Pervell Marley. In Charge of Production: Darryl F. Zanuck. Art direction by Richard Day and Hans Peters. Edited by Robert Simpson. Music by Cyril J. Mockridge. Costumes by Gwen Wakeling. Set decoration by Thomas Little. Sound by W.P. Flick and Roger Herman. Running time: 80 minutes. Release date: March 31.

Cast: Basil Rathbone *Sherlock Holmes;* Nigel Bruce *Dr. Watson;* Richard Greene *Sir Henry Baskerville;* Wendy Barrie *Beryl Stapleton;* Lionel Atwill *Dr. Mortimer;* John Carradine *Barryman;* Barlowe Borland *Frankland;* Beryl Mercer *Mrs. Jennifer Mortimer;* Morton Lowry *John Stapleton;* Ralph Forbes *Sir Hugo Baskerville;* E.E. Clive *Cabby (John Clayton);* Eily Malyon *Mrs. Barryman;* Nigel DeBrulier *Convict (Selden);* Mary Gordon *Mrs. Hudson;* Peter Willes *Roderick;* Ivan Simpson *Shepherd;* Ian Maclaren *Sir Charles Baskerville;* John Burton *Bruce;* Dennis Greene *Jon;* Evan Thomas *Edwin;* Lionel Pape *Coroner.*

> Murdstone has haunted me. It's closed instead of opened doors to me.—
> Basil Rathbone in 1936, on being typecast because of his portrayal of the
> wicked Murdstone in *David Copperfield* (1935)[33]

Synopsis: In March of 1939, this first in an incredibly popular series of Sherlock Holmes mysteries starring the quintessential team of Basil Rathbone and Nigel Bruce was released.

The story opens at Dartmoor in Devonshire, a fog-enshrouded heath filled with treacherous quicksand pits, where a man is running in a panic away from a howl similar to that of a wolf. The man is Sir Charles Baskerville (Ian Maclaren) and, while running, he succumbs to a heart attack and dies. At a formal inquiry investigating his death, the coroner (Lionel Pape) concludes and officially rules that he died of heart failure. But at least one man present at the hearing is not satisfied. Mr. Frankland (Barlowe Borland) cries out that Sir Charles was murdered and claims that there are nameless others in the room who know he speaks the truth.

Next we go to London, specifically 221-B Baker Street, address of the celebrated sleuth Sherlock Holmes (Rathbone). We are immediately given an exhibition of Holmes's brilliant deductive skills when he constructs the

The Hound of the Baskervilles (Twentieth Century–Fox). *Top, left-right:* Lionel Atwill, Basil Rathbone, Nigel Bruce and Richard Greene discuss the perplexities of
the case. *Bottom:* "The game is afoot!" Sherlock Holmes (Basil Rathbone, standing)
and Dr. Watson (Nigel Bruce, second from right) are on the case.

personality of a man, Dr. Mortimer (Lionel Atwill), simply by examining a walking cane that Mortimer left behind at his office. As always, Holmes's companion and biographer, Dr. Watson (Bruce) is thoroughly impressed. Mortimer soon returns to 221-B Baker Street and confesses to Holmes that he is concerned about the life of another Baskerville, Sir Henry (Richard Greene), who is next in line to inherit the family fortune. Holmes has already deduced, while reading a newspaper account of Sir Henry's impending visit to London, that the young man's life is in jeopardy. He instructs Mortimer to bring Sir Henry to him as soon as he arrives in London.

Then Sir Hugo tells Holmes and Watson the tale of the Baskerville hound, a giant predatory beast that has stalked the family for generations, dating all the way back to the evil Sir Hugo (Ralph Forbes), who was torn to shreds by the supernatural beast. He informs them that the footprints of the hound were discovered near Sir Charles's body and shows them a document which traces the ancient curse back in Baskerville lineage to Hugo in the mid-1600s.

Mortimer meets Henry at the dock when his cruise ship pulls in, as ordered, but on the way back to their hotel, a rock is thrown through the window of their carriage with a note attached. The note is addressed to Sir Henry, warning him to stay away from Baskerville Hall, the estate in Devonshire he has inherited and plans to make his home.

Back at 221-B Baker Street, Mortimer recounts the incident to Holmes. When the detective asks Henry if there have been any other strange occurrences recently, Henry tells him that, inexplicably, one of his brand-new boots was stolen during the cruise, while the matching boot was left behind.

When Mortimer and Henry leave Holmes's residence, the detective and Watson follow them out onto the foggy London streets, remaining a comfortable distance behind them and watching closely. Just as Holmes anticipated, an attempt is made upon Sir Henry's life, which Holmes manages to foil. The would-be assassin escapes, however, in a horse-drawn cab.

Later, at Sir Henry's hotel room, he discovers that someone has returned his new boot and taken an old hiking boot in its place, once again leaving the matching boot behind. But despite all of the bizarre events of the day, Henry fearlessly announces that he intends to return to Baskerville Hall and considers the tale of the hound and the supposed curse upon his family name pure nonsense. Holmes decides to send Watson back to Devonshire with him, as a precaution, while he remains behind in London.

Watson, Mortimer and Sir Henry travel back to Baskerville Hall together, where they meet Henry's servants, the suspicious-looking and -acting Barrymans (John Carradine and Eily Malyon). Late one night, out on the moors, Watson and Henry hear the same eerie howl that Sir Charles heard just before he died. In a letter to Holmes he pens the following day, Watson ponders: "The wind? . . . A bird? . . . Or the hound?"

During an afternoon venture, they encounter two of Henry's neighbors, the affable John Stapleton (Morton Lowry) and his lovely stepsister Beryl (Wendy Barrie). Henry is very grateful to Beryl when she stops him from walking into one of the moor's quicksand pits, and becomes instantly smitten with her. When the Stapletons invite them for dinner the following evening, Watson and Henry graciously accept.

At the dinner, Dr. Mortimer's wife (Beryl Mercer) agrees to perform a séance in an attempt to contact the ghost of Sir Charles. As she calls out Sir Charles's name, the howling begins again out on the moors, and each of the dinner guests seems to have his own theory about the source of the noise.

Sir Henry and Beryl begin seeing a great deal of each other, horseback-riding out on the moors each day together. One day, accompanied by Dr. Watson, they are accosted by an old codger with a rheumatic cough who tries to sell them a whistle. Oddly enough, the man limps on one foot when he approaches them and on the other one when he leaves.

An unsigned note is left at Baskerville Hall for Watson, requesting a rendezvous with him in a secluded cave out on the moors. When he arrives at the cave—pistol in tow—he is dismayed to find the old codger waiting there for him. However, when this "old codger" rips off his fake moustache and beard, revealing himself as Sherlock Holmes in one of his clever disguises, Watson is pleasantly shocked. Incognito, Holmes has been free to roam the moors at will and investigate Sir Charles's death undisturbed. He tells Watson that he is close to solving the case.

The two witness the hound's sudden attack on a man they believe to be Sir Henry up on a cliff. The hound knocks him down onto the rocks below, and they run to his aid, only to discover that the victim isn't Sir Henry, but a stranger dressed in his clothing. Holmes identifies the man as the notorious "Notting Hill Murderer," an escaped convict. He later exposes the fact that the convict was Mrs. Barryman's brother and that she was the one who supplied him with the clothes.

Holmes suspects that the convict died because the hound had been trained to stalk Sir Henry by scent, which would also explain the mystery of the boots. However, back at Baskerville Hall, he announces that the killer is dead and therefore he and Watson must depart on the train for London the next day. Henry makes an announcement as well. He and Beryl have decided to wed, and a dinner party is being thrown the following evening to celebrate their engagement, after which the two young lovers will go off to be married and spend their honeymoon together. Holmes apologizes for not being able to stay for this celebration.

As scheduled, Holmes and Watson leave on the morning train. A few miles out of Devonshire, though, Holmes admits to Dr. Watson that Sir Henry's life is still in danger and their departure is merely a ruse intended to smoke out the real killer. They switch trains and head back to Devonshire.

The dinner party is thrown, and afterwards Henry decides to walk home alone across the moors. The carriage of Holmes and Dr. Watson, meanwhile, loses a wheel en route to Baskerville Hall, and they are forced to continue on foot.

It is here that we learn the true identity of the killer. After putting his sister to bed, John Stapleton removes a pair of gloves and Henry's stolen boot from one of his cabinets and unleashes a mad dog onto Sir Henry's trail. The dog catches Henry and attacks him viciously, but Holmes arrives in the nick of time, shooting the dog and saving Henry's life. Watson carries a mauled Henry on to Baskerville Hall and attends to his wounds. Holmes remains behind to investigate further and locates the pit in which the animal was caged. Stapleton manages to lock him in the pit and goes to Baskerville Hall. When he gets there, he tells Dr. Watson that Holmes needs him urgently out on the moors. As soon as Watson is gone, he mixes a drink laced with arsenic and gives it to Henry. Before he drinks it, though, Sherlock Holmes arrives, exposing Stapleton as the killer and the next in line to the Baskerville fortune, who concocted the entire scheme to claim that inheritance. Stapleton escapes, but Holmes has stationed constables in the nearby region, so we're assured he won't get far.

Holmes accepts the gratitude and thanks of all, then exits hurriedly. But not before reminding his friend: "Oh, Watson, the needle." The line referred to his cocaine addiction and is quite shocking considering the year in which the film was made.

Notes: According to the popular version of the story, Darryl Zanuck of Twentieth Century–Fox, actor/director Gregory Ratoff and writer Gene Markey were all at a Hollywood party one night when Ratoff remarked: "Somebody should turn Conan Doyle's Sherlock Holmes into a movie series."

The other two men liked the idea. After some discussion, Zanuck queried: "Yes, but who would play Sherlock Holmes?"

"Who else but Basil Rathbone?" replied Markey.

A week after the party, Zanuck (in a brilliant stroke of casting) had signed Rathbone to play the fictitious London sleuth, Sherlock Holmes, and veteran British character actor Nigel Bruce to play his loyal associate and biographer, Dr. Watson. Their definitive portrayals of the pair would provide the heart and soul of the most popular movie series ever made up until the time Sean Connery said the words, "Bond, James Bond," and ordered his drinks shaken, not stirred.

Rathbone had always considered himself a logical choice for the role of Holmes, as he felt he bore a striking resemblance to actor Frederic Dorr-Steele's portrait of the character. More than that, he bore a striking resemblance to the *character*, whom creator Conan Doyle described as being "over six feet tall, excessively lean, with penetrating eyes and a hawk-like nose."

Basil Rathbone became Sherlock Holmes. So associated was he with the role in the mind of the public that when he walked down the street people commonly referred to him as "Mr. Holmes" (and requested he sign autographs as such). All of his Shakespearean training, his years on the English stage, even his two Oscar nominations, couldn't change that. He portrayed Holmes in 14 movies, on television, on stage, and in over 200 radio performances, and his acting career never recovered from it. The loss of his own identity inevitably led to his indifference toward the role, and the quality of the films suffered because of it. After hanging up his magnifying glass and violin, Rathbone never again played a major role in a major movie. Eventually, he wound up in such ignoble things as *Ghost in the Invisible Bikini* and *Hillbillies in a Haunted House,* a tragic end to an illustrious career.

The Hound of the Baskervilles was Rathbone's favorite of the series, and although it wasn't the best one (that honor would have to go to *The Adventures of Sherlock Holmes,* which would be released later that same year), it runs a close second. *Hound* skillfully incorporates every aspect of the great detective: the ever-present pipe, his scratchy violin performances, his hunting cap and cape, and his secretive ways and boundless nervous energy. There is even a reference to his drug addiction—quite a coup in the Hays Office era.

And credit must surely be given to Nigel Bruce, who was cast in the role of Watson primarily because he was Rathbone's personal selection. Millions of fans approved of the choice. Although Bruce's interpretation is far from the character Conan Doyle originally created, future Watsons seemed to be patterning their performances upon him and not upon the literary character. His good humor, his bumbling antics, and most importantly, his fierce devotion to Holmes, made him an integral factor in the popularity of the series. It should also be noted that long after Rathbone began walking through the episodes, Bruce seemed as content and amused as ever with his role.

The Hound of the Baskervilles has been remade several times, but without the Rathbone-Bruce team, the others are all just pretenders to the throne.

Reviews: "The cinema has never yet done justice to Sherlock Holmes . . . atmosphere of unmechanised Edwardian flurry is well caught; the villain bowls recklessly along Baker Street in a hansom and our hero discusses plans of action in a four-wheeler. The genuine Holmes London, too, is neatly touched in through the cab windows. . . . Dartmoor is a rather gothic landscape. . . . What is wrong, surely, is Mr. Rathbone's reading of the Great Character: the good humor . . . and the general air of brisk good health . . . the deductions are reduced to a bare minimum and the plot is swollen. . . . What we really need in a Holmes picture is far more dialogue and far less action. Let us be presented in a series of close-ups, as poor Dr. Watson was, with all the materials for deduction, and let the toothmarks on a walking stick, the mud on a pair of boots, the stained fingernail be the chief characters in a Holmes film."—Graham Greene, *The Spectator*

"Putting its straightest face upon the matter and being so weird as all get-out, the film succeeds rather well in reproducing Sir Arthur's macabre detective story along forthright cinema lines. The technicians have whipped up a moor at least twice as desolate as any ghost-story moor has need to be, the mist swirls steadily, the savage howl of the Baskerville hound is heard at all the melodramatically appropriate intervals and Mr. Holmes himself, with hunting cap, calabash and omniscience, whispers from time to time, 'It's murder, Watson, murder!'"—Frank S. Nugent, *The New York Times*

The Hunchback of Notre Dame

An RKO-Radio Picture. Produced by Pandro S. Berman. Directed by William Dieterle. Screenplay by Sonya Levien. Based upon Bruno Frank's adaptation of the novel *Notre-Dame de Paris,* by Victor Hugo. Photographed by Joseph H. August. Edited by William Hamilton and Robert Wise. Art direction by Van Nest Polglase. Interior decoration by Darrell Silvera. Special effects by Vernon L. Walker. Make-up by Perc Westmore. Costumes by Walter Plunkett. Music by Alfred Newman. Sound by John Aalberg. Running time: 114 minutes. Release date: December 29.

Cast: Charles Laughton *Quasimodo;* Maureen O'Hara *Esmerelda;* Sir Cedric Hardwicke *Dom Claude Frollo;* Thomas Mitchell *Clopin;* Edmond O'Brien *Pierre Gringoire;* Harry Davenport *King Louis XI;* Walter Hampden *Archbishop;* Alan Marshal *Phoebus de Chateaupers;* George Zucco *Procurator;* George Tobias *Beggar;* Rod La Rocque *Phillipo;* Fritz Leiber *Old nobleman.*

> When Laughton acted the scene on the wheel, enduring the terrible torture, he was not the poor, crippled creature, expecting compassion from the mob, but rather oppressed and enslaved mankind, suffering injustice. —William Dieterle[34]

Synopsis: There have been three film versions of *The Hunchback of Notre Dame* and one television production. In addition to the 1939 film there was a 1923 silent version directed by Wallace Worsley and starring Lon Chaney as Quasimodo and Patty Ruth Miller as Esmerelda; and a 1957 French version (which suffered from the dubbing in of its English-language release), featuring Anthony Quinn and Gina Lollabrigida in the lead roles. The B.B.C. produced the television version shown in the United States in 1977, with Warren Clarke in the title role; it was well acted but had conspicuously low-budget production values. Although some scholars prefer the Chaney version, the critical and moviegoing consensus is that the finest and most memorable film of Victor Hugo's 1831 novel was made in 1939 by RKO, under the direction of William Dieterle and starring Charles Laughton as Quasimodo.

The story opens in 1482, during the reign of Louis XI. It is both Epiphany Sunday and the Feast of Fools, and the streets are packed with Parisians who have braved beggars and thieves alike to join in the celebration. Despite a city ordinance banning gypsies, a beautiful young gypsy dancing girl, Esmerelda (Maureen O'Hara), manages to slip inside along with some other festival-goers, hoping to plead with the king for mercy for her people. Not far away, Pierre Gringoire (Edmond O'Brien), a poet and playwright, is trying to produce an allegorical masque of death and retribution, but the mob pays little attention to the play and eventually hoots him down. They want to elect a Pope of Fools—an honor bestowed upon the person who can display the ugliest countenance. Numerous contestants are quickly discarded, but suddenly the crowd gasps with horror and falls silent upon seeing the grotesque face of Quasimodo (Charles Laughton), the bellringer of the Notre Dame cathedral. He is instantly proclaimed Pope of Fools and crowned with a jester's cap and bells. Hitherto, Quasimodo— with his immense hunchback, misshapen face, and twisted limbs—has been a figure of horror in the city, and now he is delighted to be the center of attention and ostensibly of admiration. The festivities are soon disrupted, though, by the stern priest, Dom Claude Frollo (Sir Cedric Hardwicke), who has adopted Quasimodo and now orders him back to the cathedral.

Though a priest who has taken a vow of chastity, the seemingly ascetic Frollo is a repressed sensualist who lusts for the gypsy girl, Esmerelda. He dispatches Quasimodo to abduct her. When the hunchback seizes her in the street, she is rescued by a handsome gallant, Captain Phoebus de Chateaupers (Alan Marshal), who with his guardsmen also captures Quasimodo.

Meanwhile, Gringoire, the discouraged playwright, with no money and no sleeping quarters for the evening, wanders unwittingly into the Parisian underworld, where he is taken prisoner and brought before the king of the beggars, Clopin (Thomas Mitchell). Although intruders are ordinarily put to death, Clopin gives Gringoire a chance: if he can successfully pick the pocket of a mannequin spangled with bells and hanging from a rope, his life will be spared and he can join the band of thieves. Gringoire fails the test clumsily, but just as Clopin is about to sentence him to death, Esmerelda takes pity on Gringoire and saves his life by taking him in marriage. Gringoire is enchanted, but she intends the marriage to be in name only, for she has become infatuated with Captain Phoebus.

Quasimodo, meanwhile, has been taken before a deaf judge. Deafened himself by the tolling of Notre Dame's enormous bells, Quasimodo does not understand the judge's questions. Thinking the hunchback is mocking him, the judge sentences him to be bound to a wheel before Notre Dame, flogged, and left in chains at the mercy of the sun and the mob. Frollo refuses to intervene, and Quasimodo is tortured. Esmerelda, passing by, takes pity on him, braving the hostile crowd to bring him water. In his inarticulate way, he looks at her with adoration.

The Hunchback of Notre Dame (RKO-Radio). *Top:* Charles Laughton as the hunchbacked Quasimodo prepares to kidnap Esmerelda (Maureen O'Hara). *Bottom:* Quasimodo prepares a fiery liquid to pour down on his attackers.

Frollo continues to burn for Esmerelda, and when he finds her in the arms of Phoebus, he stabs the captain in a jealous rage. Esmerelda is arrested for the murder and, because part of her dancing act includes magic tricks with a goat, she is tried as a witch. Frollo's frustrated desire has turned to fear and hatred, and he becomes her chief prosecutor. When Esmerelda confesses under torture, she is sentenced to be hanged in the square before the cathedral, as Gringoire stands by observing in helpless agony. From one of the cathedral towers, though, Quasimodo is also observing.

As the hangman is about to carry out the sentence, Quasimodo grabs a rope from the construction, swings down, seizes Esmerelda, and before the startled crowd can stop him, swings back with her into the tower, crying his infamous cry of "Sanctuary!"

For the time being, Esmerelda is safe; she finds the grotesque hunchback to be a gentle, sensitive soul who protects her and respects her person. Although deaf, he can speak in a halting fashion, and she comes to sympathize with his loneliness and deformity.

In the meantime, Clopin has assembled an army of beggars and marches on the city to rescue Esmerelda. When they try to force the gates of the cathedral open, Quasimodo thinks that they have come to harm her, and he battles them single-handedly, hurling down a deadly rain of building stones and timbers from construction upon them. Undaunted, Clopin orders his motley band to pick up one massive timber and use it as a battering ram against the barred doors of the cathedral. When it looks as though the beggars will succeed, Quasimodo lights fires under the cauldrons of lead intended to repair the roof and pours the molten metal into the rain gutters. It runs through the rainspout mouths of gargoyles and drenches the attackers in a lethal downpour, killing Clopin and defeating his army. At this point, the king's troops arrive, and Quasimodo realizes to his despair that he has fought the wrong side. Fortunately, though, an appeal that Gringoire has sent to the king has been granted by Louis, ensuring Esmerelda's safety.

Soon Quasimodo hears the bell that he has told Esmerelda to ring to penetrate his deafness if she is ever in danger. He rushes to her and discovers Frollo pursuing her. Turning against his master, Quasimodo lifts the priest high up over the battlements and hurls him to his death.

In the end, realizing that it is Gringoire whom she truly loves, Esmerelda goes off with him, as the forlorn hunchback sits alone among the gargoyles. He embraces one and says: "If only I had been made of stone, like you."

Notes: It was originally Irving Thalberg's idea to refilm Victor Hugo's classic novel (which Lon Chaney had had his greatest success with in the 1923 version), but it was eventually Pandro S. Berman, the head of RKO, who brought it to the screen. RKO actually used sets from the 1923 version, but in every other respect, it was intended to be, and indeed was, totally different.

To direct, Berman chose German expatriate William Dieterle, whose only eccentricity seemed to be his habit of wearing white gloves while directing. Dieterle claimed that in his days in the Berlin theatre, when he was acting or directing, he would often be called upon to move the furniture, and because he had a neurotic fear of dirtying his hands, he adopted the white gloves. He was coming fresh from a string of outstanding film biographies starring Paul Muni: *The Story of Louis Pasteur* (1936), *The Life of Emile Zola* (1937), and the less successful *Juarez* (1939).

Cast in the lead was Charles Laughton, who four years earlier had played a memorable Javert in Hugo's *Les Misérables*. His make-up, that famous mask of mangled features, took months to evolve, under Laughton's personal direction. Jack Warner loaned the inventor and perfector of modern movie make-up, Perc Westmore, to RKO for $50,000, and he produced version after version for Laughton, only to have them rejected after a moment's consideration. The actor knew what he wanted, and he finally got it.

Westmore covered the left side of Laughton's face with a sheet of sponge rubber, concealing his own eye and creating an artificial eye socket further down on the cheek. And to make Quasimodo's deafness more believable, Laughton's ears were plugged with wax so he would not show the slightest reaction to any sudden loud noises on the set.

As for the hunchback's costume, Laughton knew what he wanted there, as well: pain. He felt it was an integral part of the role. And, once again, the actor got what he wanted. The hump itself was made of foam rubber and weighed four pounds; in addition, his clothing was heavily padded and his body covered in rubber to give the impression of enormous muscular power. In the scene where he is lashed on the wheel, while the crowd was jeering, Laughton asked the make-up assistant to twist his foot off-camera: "More, more!" he screamed. "Twist it more!"

Although a stand-in did most of the acrobatic scenes, Laughton's performance was a demandingly physical one: he had to swing on cathedral bells, haul heavy chains, and move with a twisted, deformed gait. To complicate matters, the burning sun that summer broke all existing records, averaging 100°F each day. Laughton perspired so heavily at times that his make-up was washed away.

The awareness of events in Europe so far, far away hung heavily over the making of the film. The day that England officially declared war on Germany, Dieterle was shooting the scene in the bell tower, which was supposed to be a sort of love scene between Quasimodo and Esmerelda. But instead, Laughton, moved by the events of the day, went on ringing and ringing the bells until he collapsed, completely exhausted. Everyone on the set was incredibly moved. Later, in his dressing room, Laughton said: "I couldn't think of Esmerelda in that scene at all. I could only think of the poor people out there, going in to fight that bloody, bloody war! To arouse the world, to stop that terrible butchery! Awake! Awake! That's what I felt when I was ringing the bells!"[35]

Nineteen-year-old Maureen O'Hara made her American debut in the film. A year earlier, she had appeared with Laughton in the British production *Jamaica Inn* (1939), directed by Alfred Hitchcock. Both Laughton and his wife, Elsa Lancaster, had taken a liking to the young actress and had arranged for her to get the part of Esmerelda.

Making his Hollywood debut as Gringoire was Edmond O'Brien (looking younger than he has ever looked), whose previous work had been on the stage with the Mercury Theatre.

The film was nominated for Best Sound Recording and Best Score, but lost in both categories. A fourth film version is currently in production, with Willem Dafoe in the lead role.

Reviews: "The Music Hall is the last place in the world where we should expect to find a freak show, but *The Hunchback of Notre Dame* is that and little more. . . . Maybe we are an exception to the rule laid down by one of the film's characters that ugliness is fascinating. It has never fascinated us. We prefer to avert our eyes when a monstrosity appears, even when we know he's a synthetic monster, compounded of sponge rubber, greasepaint and artifice. Horror films have their followings, but children should not be among them. The Music Hall is no place for the youngsters this week. Take warning!"—Frank S. Nugent, *The New York Times*

"*The Hunchback of Notre Dame*, all expense and care and dramatic possibilities considered, is my candidate for the worst-made class-A film of the year. Charles Laughton is effective as usual; the spectacles are spectacular and the sets are good; the main belfry and mob-scene stuff is so near foolproof that it could be crippled only by a super-scrupulous application to ham theatricals. But they went at it scrupulously; a junior Errol Flynn combines the Villon legend, John Reed, and Frank Merriwell; a 'gypsy' girl suffers endlessly in what she apparently takes to be the diction of Katharine Cornell; a nice mix-up with *A Tale of Two Cities* flushed a rogues' gallery of types that they made up and photographed in exact character for *A Night in the Bastille* with the Marx Brothers. They practically spelled the final 'e' in Sir Cedric Hardwicke with trick lighting effects and conquered Thomas Mitchell long before Alamodo had bounced a rock as big as a coffin off his shoulder like a basketball, making him feel almost too sick to speak his last lines fifteen minutes later. The excitement was exciting when they got to it at last—but the audience was already too limp and damp to rise to anything, except go home."—Otis Ferguson, *The New Republic*

Idiot's Delight

MGM. 105 min. Directed by Clarence Brown.

Cast: Clark Gable, Norma Shearer, Edward Arnold, Charles Coburn, Joseph Schildkraut, Burgess Meredith, Laura Hope Crews, Skeets Gallagher.

Robert E. Sherwood's acclaimed pacifist play about a fake Russian countess and the hoofer who was once her lover meeting on the eve of war at a hotel on the Swiss border was originated on the stage by Alfred Lunt and Lynn Fontanne. But when MGM purchased the film rights to the property, they did so for two of their top stars, Clark Gable and Norma Shearer. It was the first time since 1932's *Strange Interlude* that the two had been paired together on screen, and it worked just as well this time around as it had the first.

In Name Only

RKO. 92 min. Directed by John Cromwell.
Cast: Carole Lombard, Cary Grant, Kay Francis, Charles Coburn, Helen Vinson, Katharine Alexander, Jonathan Hale, Maurice Moscovich.
Grant plays an unhappily married man who falls in love with Lombard and wants to marry her. However, his venomous wife (played by Kay Francis), who married him for his money and social position, refuses to divorce him. This beautifully acted soaper all works out in the end.

In Old Caliente

55 min. Directed by Joseph Kane.
Cast: Roy Rogers, Mary Hart, George Hayes, Jack LaRue, Katherine DeMille.
Half-breed LaRue tries to pin a robbery on some of the peaceful settlers who have been migrating to California in search of a better life. Roy takes up the settlers' cause and, with his usual blend of flying fists, hard riding and smoking guns, turns the tables on LaRue and his henchmen.

In Old Monterey

Directed by Joseph Kane.
Cast: Gene Autry, Smiley Burnette, June Storey, George Hayes, Hoosier Hot Shots.
As an example of just how modern Gene's Westerns could be, this one casts the cowboy as an army attaché trying to secure land for bombing exercises in preparation for American involvement in the war that was raging in Europe in 1939. Supporting performances by George "Gabby" Hayes and a host of radio stars make what would otherwise be a below-average entry a respectable one.

Intermezzo (A Love Story)

A Selznick International Production released by United Artists. Directed by Gregory Ratoff. Produced by David O. Selznick. Associate producer: Leslie Howard. Screenplay by George O'Neil. Based upon the original Swedish screen scenario by Gosta Stevens and Gustaf Molander. Photographed by Gregg Toland. Edited by Hal C. Kern and Francis D. Lyon. Art direction by Lyle Wheeler. Special effects by Jack Cosgrove. Miss Bergman's costumes by Irene Travis Banton. Musical director: Lou Forbes. Running time: 70 minutes. Release date: October 5.

Cast: Leslie Howard *Holger Brandt;* Ingrid Bergman *Anita Hoffman;* Edna Best *Margit Brandt;* Ann Todd *Ann Marie Brandt;* Douglas Scott *Eric Brandt;* John Halliday *Thomas Stenborg;* Enid Bennett *Greta Stenborg;* Cecil Kellaway *Charles Moler;* Eleanor Wesselhoeft *Emma;* Maria Flynn *Marianne.*

> Vy don' you spik English! Say it like I do! — Russian director Gregory Ratoff to Swedish star Ingrid Bergman, during the shooting of *Intermezzo*[36]

Synopsis: As sweet and lilting as the violins which permeate the film, *Intermezzo* is best remembered today as the movie that introduced the astonishingly beautiful Swedish actress Ingrid Bergman to American audiences.

After a triumphant concert tour, famed violinist Holger Brandt (Leslie Howard) returns to his home in Sweden. He is greeted at the train station by his wife, Margit (Edna Best), and their two children, Eric (Douglas Scott) and Ann Marie (Ann Todd). Later that same day, Holger meets his daughter's piano teacher, Anita Hoffman (Bergman). At first, he doesn't pay her much mind, but a few nights later—at Ann Marie's eighth birthday party—he hears her play a piano piece and becomes enraptured with her. They play a duet together passionately, their music building to an orgasmic climax. Holger is so impressed by Anita's talent that he offers her the job of accompanist to him, a position recently vacated by his good friend Thomas Stenborg (John Halliday). Anita, however, is interested only in pursuing her studies and earning a music scholarship in Paris, so she politely declines.

After a chance encounter one evening at a recital, the two go off together to a local cafe for a glass of wine. Later that evening, as Holger is walking her home, Anita tipsily but boldly declares: "Tonight I would dare anything!" And, together, they do. Before long, their encounters have become anything but coincidental, as they steal time in dark corners and sparsely lit, out-of-the-way places.

They try to end it gracefully, but to no avail. They have fallen too completely in love with each other. Holger leaves his family and runs away with Anita. She becomes his accompanist and they embark on a concert tour together.

Anita soon receives word from Stenborg that she has been granted her music scholarship in Paris, but decides to turn it down and stay with Holger instead.

After the tour ends, Stenborg tracks them down to a small seaside village where they are vacationing. He brings along the final divorce papers for Holger to sign. But despite his passion for Anita, Holger procrastinates; he is not as eager as he thought to break completely away from his roots and his past.

Guilt-ridden and hopelessly cognizant of the fact that Holger belongs with his wife and children, Anita accepts the music scholarship after all and runs away to Paris one afternoon, leaving behind a farewell note for Holger explaining her decision.

Holger returns home to Sweden and drives out to the local schoolyard to visit Ann Marie. When she spots her father, the little girl bolts blindly out into the street traffic towards him and is struck down by a car.

The child recovers and Holger is reunited for good with his long-suffering wife, who is most willing to forgive all of his transgressions.

Notes: In 1937, two of producer David O. Selznick's personally supervised productions placed among the top box-office successes of the year: *Nothing Sacred* and *The Prisoner of Zenda*. By the summer of '38, he had already launched production of *The Adventures of Huckleberry Finn* and was well under way with his mammoth plans of filming Margaret Mitchell's best-seller *Gone with the Wind*. When his New York–based chief story editor, Kay Brown, recommended a Swedish film called *Intermezzo* to him as an idea for an American remake, Selznick decided to see the film for himself. When he did, the producer found himself as much taken with its female lead—a young Swedish actress named Ingrid Bergman—as with its romantic storyline. He immediately dispatched Miss Brown to go to Stockholm and persuade Bergman to come to Hollywood and star in an English-language version of the film.

As it turned out, Bergman was married to a dentist and medical student named Peter Lindstrom, by whom she had a daughter named Pia. Because of Peter's intensive studies, it was impossible for him to make such a trip, and Bergman was reluctant to leave her family. But when Selznick offered her a one-picture deal (in lieu of the standard seven-year agreement), she accepted, feeling that if the movie was successful, she could then bring her family over to America, and if it was not, she could return to Sweden no worse for wear. Thus, in the spring of 1939, Ingrid Bergman arrived alone in Hollywood, ready for work.

In the beginning, Selznick had second thoughts about the casting of

Opposite: Intermezzo (A Love Story) (United Artists). *Top:* Violinist Holger Brandt (Leslie Howard) is with his wife Margit (Edna Best) in this picture, but thinking about and longing for his mistress, Anita (Ingrid Bergman). *Bottom:* Leslie Howard and Ingrid Bergman—making her American debut.

Bergman, and seriously considered recasting the picture with Loretta Young (among other possibilities). He also considered changing the Swedish beauty's name to Ingrid Lindstrom, but decided that it was not sufficiently memorable.

However, as filming proceeded, Bergman's proficiency improved dramatically, as did her stock with Selznick. The producer was pleased and impressed by her total and unselfish commitment to the success of the picture and her willingness to invest many long, hard days to achieve that goal. And under the tutelage of Ruth Roberts (an MGM language coach who had recently drilled Hedy Lamarr), she learned English quickly and fluently, proving herself to have a natural flair for languages.

When *Intermezzo* opened in October of '39, it was a resounding success, and Ingrid Bergman became an international star overnight. Selznick rewarded her with a seven-year contract and she enjoyed a flourishing career as one of Hollywood's leading actresses until 1948, when she bore an illegitimate child by Italian director Roberto Rossellini. The international scandal forced a return to Europe, where she worked in a number of inferior films. In 1956, Hollywood's door opened up to her again, and she received the Academy Award for Best Actress that year for her performance in *Anastasia*.

Intermezzo (A Love Story) was nominated for Best Musical Score and Best Black-and-White Cinematography. Although cameraman Gregg Toland lost for his work on this film, he still managed to win the latter category. He was awarded the Oscar for his work on *Wuthering Heights*.

Reviews: "The film is most worth seeing for the new star, Miss Ingrid Bergman, who is as natural as her name. What star before has made her first appearance on the international screen with a highlight gleaming on her nose tip? That gleam is typical of a performance that doesn't give the effect of acting at all, but of living—without make-up."—Graham Greene, *The Spectator*

"Sweden's Ingrid Bergman is so lovely a person and so gracious an actress that we are rather glad David O. Selznick selected the quiet *Intermezzo—A Love Story* for her Hollywood debut instead of some more bravura drama, which, while it might not have overwhelmed its star, might have overwhelmed us, and made us less conscious of the freshness, the simplicity and the natural dignity that are Miss Bergman's pleasant gifts to our screen.... There is that incandescence about Miss Bergman, that spiritual spark which makes us believe that Selznick has found another great lady of the screen.

...*Intermezzo* is not exactly a dramatic thunderbolt, nothing the glamour-conscious will be inflamed about. But we found it a mature, an eloquent, and a sensitive film and we recommend it to you."—Frank S. Nugent, *The New York Times*

Invisible Stripes

Warner Bros. 105 min. Directed by Lloyd Bacon.

Cast: George Raft, Jane Bryan, William Holden, Flora Robson, Humphrey Bogart, Paul Kelly, Moroni Olsen, Tully Marshall.

Standard Warners crime drama, crisply directed by Bacon, about parolee Raft trying to go straight and protect kid brother Holden from gangster Bogart. Newcomer Holden received billing over veteran Bogart, which enraged Bogie to no end. During filming, Bogart constantly chided and antagonized the young actor; Holden, in turn, was constantly challenging him to a fistfight. By the time shooting was wrapped, the two men despised each other. Fifteen years later, Bogart would accept an offer to perform in Billy Wilder's romantic comedy *Sabrina* (an unlikely genre for him) only because he was guaranteed top billing over co-star Holden, and their bickering resumed on the set of that delightful picture.

Jamaica Inn

Mayflower Prod., England. 98 min. Directed by Alfred Hitchcock.

Cast: Charles Laughton, Horace Hodges, Hay Petrie, Frederick Piper, Leslie Banks, Marie Ney, Maureen O'Hara, Robert Newton.

Laughton plays the leader of a band of plundering pirates in this adventure yarn based upon Daphne du Maurier's soapy gothic novel. He was originally cast as a licentious parson but, because of a possible run-in with the Hays Office, was switched to the squire role. A ravishingly beautiful but unknown 18-year-old named Maureen O'Hara was cast in the female lead and made her screen debut in it. In an interview before the picture opened, Laughton commented: "I told them [the other cast members] we must all get behind Maureen and help. If we all tried, we could get her through it some way. Two days later, we were fighting for our scenes. That child was stealing the picture from us. She's not just an actress. She's a fine actress."[37] Also in the cast were playwright Emlyn Williams, who had written *The Corn Is Green* and *Night Must Fall,* and Basil Radford, who had charmed audiences the previous year in Hitchcock's *The Lady Vanishes.* This was to be the last film that Hitchcock would make in pre-war England. After production was completed, he set sail for America, where he was destined to make his greatest mark as a director.

Jeepers Creepers

69 min. Directed by Frank McDonald.

Cast: Leon Weaver, Frank Weaver, Elviry, Roy Rogers, Maris Wrixon.

This is a Weaver Brothers feature all the way, with Roy relegated to a minor supporting role. His best moment in the film is when he sings the popular title song to Maris Wrixon. This was one that Roy was contractually obliged to appear in, but it is safe to assume it was not a chore he relished.

Jesse James

A Twentieth Century–Fox Film. Directed by Henry King. Produced by Darryl F. Zanuck. Associate producer: Nunnally Johnson. Screenplay by Nunnally Johnson. Based on historical data assembled by Rosalind Shaffer and Jo Frances James. Photographed by George Barnes. Technicolor camera: W. Howard Greene. Technical directors: Natalie Kalmus and Henri Jaffa. Edited by Barbara McLean. Art direction by William Darling and George Dudley. Set decoration by Thomas Little. Music by Louis Silvers. Costumes by Royer. Sound by Arthur Von Kirbach and Roger Herman. Running time 110 minutes. Release date: January 13.

Cast: Tyrone Power *Jesse James;* Henry Fonda *Frank James;* Nancy Kelly *Zerelda "Zee" Cobb;* Randolph Scott *Will Wright;* Henry Hull *Major Rufus Cobb;* Slim Summerville *Jailer;* J. Edward Bromberg *George Runyan;* Brian Donlevy *Barshee;* John Carradine *Bob Ford;* Donald Meek *McCoy;* Jane Darwell *Mrs. Samuels;* John Russell *Jesse James, Jr.;* Charles Tannen *Charlie Ford;* Ernest Whitman *Pinky Washington;* Harold Goodwin *Bill;* Arthur Aylesworth *Tom Colson;* Claire Dubrey *Mrs. Bob Ford;* Willard Robertson *Clark;* Paul Sutton *Lynch;* George Chandler *Roy;* Spencer Charters *Preacher;* Paul Burns *Hank;* Charles Halton *Heywood the banker;* Erville Alderson *Old marshal;* Harry Tyler *farmer;* Eddie Waller *deputy;* Virginia Brissac *Boy's mother;* George Breakstone *Farmer's boy;* Lon Chaney, Jr. *James Gang member;* Wylie Grant and Ethan Laidlaw *Barshee's henchmen.*

> About the only connection the film had with fact was that there was once a man named James and he did ride a horse. — Jo Frances James, descendant of Jesse James[38]

Synopsis: Surprisingly enough, with all of the elaborate costume dramas, star-packed dramas, and sparkling comedies, it was a Western, *Jesse James,* that outgrossed all other motion pictures at the box office in 1939.

The villain of the film is not young Jesse at all, but an evil agent for the St. Louis Midland Railroad named Barshee (Brian Donlevy). Determined to snare the farmers' land for the railroad at the cutthroat price of one dollar per acre, Barshee gleefully bullies the farmers. In one instance, he punches a teenage boy in the face and then turns him over to his men for further punishment in an effort to coerce the boy's hysterical mother into signing

Jesse James (Twentieth Century–Fox). *Top:* Tyrone Power (center) and Henry Fonda (right), as the James Brothers, make their getaway after robbing a bank. *Bottom:* Tyrone Power is wounded in a shoot-out.

over her farm. Barshee and his boys also apply pressure on the James clan—Jesse (Tyrone Power), his brother Frank (Henry Fonda), and their mother, Mrs. Samuels (Jane Darwell)—but they refuse to be intimidated. Frank punches Barshee, and Barshee retaliates by trying to decapitate him with a sickle. Jesse stops Barshee by shooting him in the hand.

Later that evening, as the James Boys are taking refuge in a secluded cave, Barshee returns to their farm and blows it up with a bomb, killing Mrs. Samuels in the explosion. When Jesse hears what has happened, he goes directly to the town saloon and guns down the quivering Barshee, then vows bloody vengeance against the St. Louis Midland Railroad.

Jesse becomes a folk hero, but his escapades are not looked upon with pride by his sweetheart, Zee (Nancy Kelly). She refuses to marry him unless he gives himself up to United States Marshal Will Wright (Randolph Scott), an unsuccessful suitor of Zee's, who has been promised by the railroad that it will go easy on Jesse if he surrenders. Jesse reluctantly agrees and, after he and Zee are married, gives himself up. Once he is incarcerated, however, railroad president McCoy (Donald Meek) goes back on his word and prepares to prosecute Jesse to the full extent of the law.

"By the Almighty, he is going to hang!" McCoy announces.

"Suppose Jesse don't *want* to be hanged?" Wright queries.

That night, predictably, Frank and the other members of Jesse's gang bust him out of jail, but not before Jesse forces McCoy to eat his promise . . . *literally.*

While an embittered Jesse's criminal career becomes increasingly wild and reckless, he and Zee grow further and further apart. He is away when his son is born, and a heartbroken Zee—tended by the loyal Wright— moves back with her uncle, Rufus Cobb (Henry Hull).

Meanwhile, the governor offers amnesty and a monetary reward to any member of the James gang who will assassinate Jesse, and it's an offer too good for Bob Ford (John Carradine) to pass up. He informs Pinkerton Detective Runyon (J. Edward Bromberg) of Jesse's plan to rob the First National Bank in Northfield, Minnesota. In the scene's most memorable sequence, the James gang is ambushed at Northfield. A wild chase ensues after Frank and a wounded Jesse, which culminates with Frank guiding his own horse and Jesse's over a cliff and into a river far below. (This stunt inspired awed applause from moviegoing audiences in 1939, but unfortunately resulted in the death of a horse.) Frank escapes and is presumed drowned; Jesse makes his way back home, where his faithful wife and son are keeping watch for him.

Jesse makes plans to move his family to California and leave his desperado lifestyle behind. But on the day of their departure, Bob Ford and his brother Charlie (Charles Tannen) show up. As Jesse is removing a "God Bless Our Home" sampler from the wall, a cowardly, perspiring Bob Ford, his hand trembling uncontrollably, shoots the outlaw in the back.

At Jesse's funeral—as Zee and Wright listen—Rufus Cobb eulogizes the notorious renegade, then unveils and reads the infamous words of the grave marker: "In Loving Remembrance—Jesse W. James. . . . Murdered by a traitor and coward whose name is not worthy to appear here."

Notes: Darryl Zanuck, the head of Twentieth Century–Fox, initially opposed a production about the life of Jesse James, feeling it would generate only regional appeal in the South. But director Henry King—who had directed such Fox triumphs as *Lloyds of London* (1936), *In Old Chicago* (1938), and *Alexander's Ragtime Band* (1938)—convinced him otherwise. The producer approved location shooting in the Ozarks, where King flew his plane over miles of countryside to find a proper locale after it was determined that Liberty, the James brothers' hometown, had become "too civilized" over the years. The director eventually chose Pineville, Missouri, where the cast and crew were lodged in houses rented by the studio and townspeople were recruited as extras.

After proving his versatility to Zanuck, drop-dead good-looking Tyrone Power was given the lead role. Although critics felt he was miscast, audiences loved him as Jesse, and it remains arguably the actor's most famous part. It propelled him from tenth place in the 1938 box-office polls to second place in 1939. Interestingly, Henry Fonda was cast as his brother Frank only at King's insistence; Zanuck considered him "a lousy actor."

So popular was this film with audiences that many of the actors found themselves mistaken for their on-screen counterparts in real life. Not long after the release of the film, John Carradine rode in a Hollywood parade and was booed and pelted with garbage for two miles by "fans," many of whom squealed: "There's the sneak who shot Jesse James!" And years later, when Henry Fonda caught a taxi cab in New York, the driver addressed him as "Frank."

The enormous success of the film also spawned a sequel the following year, "Fox's *The Return of Frank James,* in which Fonda, Hull, Carradine, Bromberg, Tannen, Ernest Whitman, and George Chandler reprised their original roles.

Nunnally Johnson's script went out of its way to build sympathy for Jesse and paint him as a hero of the Old West, and in so doing it completely rewrote history. In fact, the film never even mentioned any of Jesse's bloody exploits with Quantrell. Critics blasted the film roundly for its historical inaccuracy, but nevertheless it remains to this day the definitive screen chronicle of the notorious outlaw, and by far the most entertaining.

It was remade in 1957 by Fox as *The True Story of Jesse James,* sans all of the fictional elements. In that one, Robert Wagner and Jeffrey Hunter played Jesse and Frank, respectively.

Reviews: "Handsomely produced by Messrs. Darryl Zanuck and Nunnally Johnson, stirringly directed by Henry King, beautifully acted by its cast . . . an authentic American panorama."—B.R. Crisler, *The New York Times*

"Notable victim of past miscasting, Power is miscast again—this time as the almost legendary badman. . . . Compensation for moviegoers who may not appreciate Tyrone Power's wrestling with a difficult role is the Technicolor photography of the film's Ozark background, the authenticity of its Americana, and the general excellence of its actors."—*Newsweek*

Juarez

A Warner Bros. Picture. Directed by William Dieterle. Produced by Hal B. Wallis. Associate producer: Henry Blanke. Screenplay by John Huston, Aeneas MacKenzie and Wolfgang Reinhardt. Based on the play *Juarez and Maximilian* by Franz Werfel, and on the novel *The Phantom Crown* by Bertita Harding. Photographed by Tony Gaudio. Edited by Warren Low. Art direction by Anton Grot. Music by Erich Wolfgang Korngold. Orchestral arrangements by Hugo Friedhofer and Milan Roder. Musical director: Leo F. Forbstein. Sound by C.A. Riggs and G.W. Alexander. Make-up by Perc Westmore. Costumes by Orry-Kelly. Technical adviser: Ernesto Romero. Dialogue director: Irving Rapper. Running time: 132 min. Release date: June 10.

Cast: Paul Muni *Benito Pablo Juarez;* Bette Davis *Empress Carlota von Habsburg;* Brian Aherne *Emperor Maximilian von Habsburg;* Claude Rains *Louis Napoleon;* John Garfield *Porfirio Diaz;* Donald Crisp *Marechal Bazaine;* Gale Sondergaard *Empress Eugenie;* Joseph Calleia *Alejandro Uradi;* Gilbert Roland *Colonel Miguel Lopez;* Henry O'Neill *Miguel Miramon;* Pedro de Cordoba *Riva Palacio;* Montagu Love *Jose de Montares;* Harry Davenport *Dr. Samuel Basch;* Walter Fenner *Achille Fould;* Alex Leftwich *Drouyn de Lhuys;* Robert Warwick *Major DuPont;* John Miljan *Mariano Escobedo;* Irving Pichel *Carbajal;* Walter Kingsford *Prince Metternich;* Monte Blue *Lerdo de Tejada;* Louis Calhern *LeMarc;* Vladimir Sokoloff *Camilo;* Georgia Caine *Countess Battenberg.*

> I first made a picture with Dieterle called *Fog Over Frisco,* his first film at Warners. Then Muni found him, and Dieterle gave up his identity to Mr. Muni, and that was Dieterle's funeral. . . . Dieterle could have been one of the most important directors in Hollywood. —Bette Davis[39]

Synopsis: Though heavy-handed and overlong, *Juarez* is still remembered fondly by movie buffs as one of the premiere films of 1939. It's not a great film, but it is a good one, and it provided Warner Bros. with another topic for their series of historical dramas that starred Paul Muni and were directed by William Dieterle.

It is the story of Benito Pablo Juarez (Muni), the phlegmatic Zapotecan Indian who was elected President of Mexico, deposed by the scheming Napoleon III of France (Claude Rains), and went on to become one of Mexico's great liberators, eventually establishing a democratic system in that country.

**Paul Muni (second from right) as Juarez listens to counsel from his advisors in
Juarez (Warner Bros.).**

Napoleon has undertaken this war in an effort to rob Mexican peons
of their rich land and divide it among a handful of wealthy statesmen.
However, his illegal actions have all been predicated on the notion that the
South will be victorious in its fight against the North in the American Civil
War, which is going on at the same time. When Napoleon receives word
that General Lee's army has been defeated at Gettysburg and that Northern
victory is imminent and unavoidable, he is furious. He blames everything
on his Minister of War, whom he feels is responsible because of his poor
advice.

Napoleon's wife, Empress Eugenie (Gale Sondergaard), suggests that
he appoint a monarch to Mexico, which could conceivably protect France
from violating America's Monroe Doctrine and incurring that powerful and
resourceful nation's wrath. Napoleon agrees, and Maximilian von Habsburg
of Austria (Brian Aherne) is duped into believing that he has been elected
Emperor of Mexico.

En route to Vera Cruz—while traveling along the same path that Cor-
tez took in his conquest of Mexico—the new emperor and his wife, Carlota
(Bette Davis), find a letter in their coach which claims that the election
responsible for making him emperor was a fraud and advising him to leave
Mexico immediately and never return. The letter is signed by Benito
Juarez.

Maximilian is shocked when he learns that the United States still
recognizes Juarez as the President of Mexico, and that the situation in his

country is not—as he had previously thought—pacified. Interested only in ruling peacefully, and by no means a militarist, the emperor instructs that negotiations begin with Juarez.

Marechal Bazaine (Donald Crisp), a definite militarist, tells Maximilian not to concern himself with Juarez. Napoleon has reinforced Bazaine's army with fifty thousand men and complete munitions for a final offensive, which he launches ferociously on all fronts. "Within thirty days, the Indian will be dead, captured or driven out of the country!" Bazaine proclaims confidently.

The sudden offensive drives Juarez into retreat, but not out of the country. He disbands his army and creates a "capital on wheels." With the apparent if illusory victory, Maximilian is presented with a bill that would give the land confiscated by Juarez to the wealthy French statesmen. The emperor refuses to sign it, and many of his council members summarily resign.

The Civil War ends and Juarez hides out in the hills, awaiting news from Abraham Lincoln, who has promised him aid once the War Between the States is over. But the news Juarez receives from America is disheartening: Lincoln has been assassinated by John Wilkes Booth at Ford's Theatre. Juarez orders that all flags be flown at half mast and his officers wear black arm bands, to mourn the loss of a friend.

A young shepherd arrives at his camp with news that the disbanded army is ready to fight, as soon as they are provided with arms and ammunition. When the shepherd tells Juarez the story of how his pack of sheep dogs fought and killed a dangerous wolf, Juarez ponders the story heavily. "Yes, Pepe," he tells the young shepherd, commenting on the strategy of the dogs. "That is the right way to fight the wolf."

Juarez implements the same strategy against the French, striking quickly and ferociously across the land.

When Maximilian refuses to sign a document calling for the immediate execution of all citizens bearing arms unlawfully, he is informed by Bazaine that the election which made him emperor was indeed a fraud and that the vast majority of those who voted for him were ignorant peons who understood not what or whom they were voting for. He is advised to crush the rebellious uprising mercilessly or risk being in violation of the Monroe Doctrine.

Maximilian informs Carlota that they are both the unwitting pawns of Napoleon and that everything Juarez wrote in his letter was true. He wants to abdicate, but she convinces him to stay on and try to deliver Mexico from the hands of its enemies. Inspired, Maximilian visits one of Juarez's captured soldiers, General Porfirio Diaz (a very miscast John Garfield), in prison and tells him that he wants the same things for Mexico that Juarez wants, but explains that a king is better suited to provide those things than a president is, for various reasons. He asks Diaz to bring a message to Juarez, offering him the position of Prime Minister of Mexico.

Colonel Lopez (Gilbert Roland, standing left on stairs) looks on as Emperor Maximilian (Brian Aherne) and Empress Carlota (Bette Davis) have their adopted son coronated prince of Mexico, thereby making the boy a successor to their throne, in *Juarez* (Warner Bros.).

When Juarez receives Maximilian's offer from Diaz, he wants no part of it. "When a monarch misrules, he changes the people," he tells his general. "When a president misrules, the people change him." Though only the word "democracy" stands between the two leaders, it is — in Juarez's mind, at least — an unbridgeable gap.

Because Carlota cannot bear children, she and Maximilian decide to adopt a child of royal blood and train him for the throne, thereby providing a successor for the monarchy. At a ceremony proclaiming their new son the crown prince of Mexico, Juarez has a French munitions cache destroyed. Maximilian angrily signs the decree and, across the land, hundreds are executed.

America intervenes on behalf of Mexico, supplying them with arms and munitions to enforce the Monroe Doctrine, and Napoleon orders all French soldiers to withdraw from Mexico. At about the same time, one of Juarez's compadres, Alejandro Uradi (Joseph Calleia) — who has long eyed the presidency for himself — breaks from Juarez with a faction of of his forces. He also manages to confiscate the American arms.

Juarez travels to his rival's camp alone and denounces Uradi as a traitor. Uradi orders his men to kill Juarez, but they refuse. Instead, Uradi is shot by one of his own cohorts, and the Mexican forces are once again unified.

Carlota sails off to France and implores Napoleon to keep his forces in Mexico. When he denies her impassioned plea, Carlota slowly begins to lose her mind.

From the fortified city of Queretaro, Maximilian's dwindling army makes reserved strikes at each of Juarez's four converging armies, waiting and hoping all the while for the prompt arrival of Miramon (Henry O'Neill) and his army from the south. Miramon does arrive, but only after being ambushed by General Diaz's forces and losing most of his command.

Maximilian is captured and executed by the Mexican forces. Reinstated as president, Benito Juarez pays tribute to the slain monarch, who he realizes was a dedicated leader that, like himself, wanted peace and freedom for the people of Mexico.

Notes: As early as 1935, producer Hal B. Wallis had talked about the idea of making a film about Maximilian, Carlota, and Juarez. When he eventually got around to putting together a package for such a film, William Dieterle was chosen to direct. Wallis conducted some discussions with Luther Adler about playing the part of Juarez, but opted to go with Paul Muni instead, who had been very successful in two other biographies directed by Dieterle, *The Story of Louis Pasteur* (1936) and *The Life of Emile Zola* (1937). To appease the star, Wallis agreed to change the film's working title from *The Phantom Crown* to *Juarez*.

Prior to the start of filming, Muni and Dieterle conducted a six-week tour of Mexico, visiting every place where a new piece of information on Benito Juarez might be found. The research department also provided the pair with 372 books, documents, letters, and albums of rare photographs. In addition, Warners budgeted the film at $1,750,000, the most money the studio had ever spent on one picture. An entire Mexican village was constructed from scratch on the Warner Bros. ranch, 7,360 blueprints were required for the sets, and 54 actors had speaking roles, to cite only a few of this film's amazing statistics.

Since the antagonists never meet in *Juarez*, the picture was shot virtually as two separate entities, with the Maximilian-Carlota sequences going before the cameras first. When Muni viewed the already edited footage, he presented some fifty pages of additional dialogue to the producers that he wished added to his role. Because he was the most important star on the Warners lot at the time, this demand was met.

On October 12, 1938, while they were making *Dark Victory*, Wallis offered the role of Carlota to Bette Davis. It was a small part, but she had been fighting Jack Warner tooth-and-nail for more character roles, so she accepted (if only to play the challenging scene where the Empress goes mad). But Davis was furious when she learned that many of her scenes with Brian Aherne had been excised in order to make room for Muni's additional fifty pages. She would always maintain that it was this self-aggrandizing action on Muni's part that prevented a good film from being a great one.

But behind-the-scenes machinations were not restricted to Muni alone. The production was also affected — somewhat strangely — by Dieterle's wife, Charlotte, whose acute superstitiousness pervaded the shooting of the picture. She loved the film's title because it contained six letters, a lucky omen. She insisted that this magic number be reversed for the title alone and not wasted during her husband's direction with six-letter words like "Camera!" and "Action!" Her husband concurred, and every direction he gave consisted of eight letters: "Here . . . we . . . GO!" She also decreed that the picture could not begin on the scheduled start date of November 15, 1938, so her husband obligingly shot one insert of a poster being ripped from a wall on October 29th of that year.

A private screening of *Juarez* was arranged for the President of Mexico, Lazaro Cardenas, who loved the picture and requested that its premiere be held at Mexico's National Theater in the Palace of Fine Arts. It was the first time that a film was ever shown in this great hall — reserved for symphonic concerts and classic works of drama. Though it proved a rousing success there, *Juarez* was neither a critical nor a commercial success when released in the States.

"We made our mistake by dividing the action between Juarez and the Maximilian/Carlota relationship," explained associate producer Henry Blanke. "If we had followed the Franz Werfel play more closely, we would have had a much stronger film. Juarez never appears in the play."[40]

The screenwriting triumvirate included a young John Huston, who was still two years away from making his directorial debut with *The Maltese Falcon*. Irving Pichel, an actor-director who had a minor role in *Juarez*, would go on to direct Paul Muni the following year in *Hudson's Bay*.

Juarez earned Academy Award nominations for Best Supporting Actor (Aherne) and Best Black-and-White Cinematography, but lost in both categories.

Reviews: "To the list of distinguished characters whom he has created in films, Paul Muni now adds a portrait of Benito Pablo Juarez, Mexico's patriot and liberator. With the aid of Bette Davis, co-starring in the tragic role of Carlota, of Brian Aherne giving an excellent performance as the ill-fated Maximilian, and a story that points up the parallels of conflicting political thought of today and three-quarters of a century ago, Muni again commands attention from the trade and public in a documentary picture. It's among the best that has been produced by Warners." — *Variety*

"When a movie so sincere and handsome and expansive as *Juarez* comes along, done with such patent good intentions and good taste, it is disappointing not to be able to burst into involuntary and unreserved applause. . . . It is almost an ungracious thing to say, in spite of its earnest and painstaking excellencies, that *Juarez* is more of a duty than a pleasure." — James Shelley Hamilton, *National Board of Review Magazine*

Lady of the Tropics

MGM. Directed by Jack Conway.

Cast: Robert Taylor, Hedy Lamarr, Joseph Schildkraut, Gloria Franklin, Ernest Cossart, Mary Taylor, Charles Trowbridge.

Hedy Lamarr had been brought to America in 1937 as one of Louis B. Mayer's highly touted protégées. He had discovered her during a visit to London to launch *A Yank at Oxford* (where he would also discover Greer Garson). Lamarr was a dreadful actress who had made a big splash in a 1931 Czech film called *Ecstasy* (which featured her in an infamous nude swimming scene). Mayer changed her last name from Kiesler to Lamarr (after silent screen beauty Barbara LaMarr) and set about making her a star in America. It was no easy task. After a somnambulistic performance opposite Charles Boyer in *Algiers* (1938), she was teamed with MGM's most respected actor, Spencer Tracy, in *I Take This Woman.* That project turned into a fiasco quickly and became the laughingstock of the industry. After a succession of script, director and cast problems, it was being called *I Re-Take This Woman.* It was temporarily shelved and released in 1940. Robert Taylor inherited her next, and the dismal *Lady of the Tropics* was the result. This was only one of three bad pictures that Taylor would make in '39, while waiting for that one good picture that would change the course of his faltering career. That picture, *Waterloo Bridge,* was still a year away. Meanwhile, he and Lamarr were both so strikingly beautiful that the word on the set of this film was to "keep them staring at each other and looking absolutely lovely for the camera, and we might sneak by on visual appeal if nothing else."[41]

Let Us Live

Columbia. 66 min. Directed by John Brahm.

Cast: Maureen O'Sullivan, Henry Fonda, Ralph Bellamy, Alan Baxter, Stanley Ridges, Henry Kolker, Peter Lynn, George Douglas, Philip Trent.

As he had been in *You Only Live Once* (1937) and as he would be again, many years later, in *The Wrong Man* (1956), Fonda was cast as an innocent man who is accused and imprisoned. This story was based on an actual event that occurred in Lynn, Massachusetts, five years earlier in which two taxi drivers were identified by several witnesses as the men responsible for robbing a local theater and killing a man while making their getaway. In the third week of their trial, as the evidence piled up against the cabbies, the real culprits were apprehended, thwarting a near miscarriage of justice. The filmmakers took that incident and dramatically extended it for this movie. When the Commonwealth of Massachusetts threatened legal action if the movie too closely paralleled the Lynn case, the studio edited the final cut down to a mere 66 minutes, making it the shortest of all Henry Fonda's movies.

The Light That Failed

A Paramount Picture. Produced and directed by William A. Wellman. Screenplay by Robert Carson. Based on the novel by Rudyard Kipling. Photographed by Theodor Sparkuhl. Edited by Thomas Scott. Art direction by Hans Dreier and Robert Odell. Interior decorations by A.E. Freudeman. Sound by Hugo Grenzbach and Walter Oberst. Music score by Victor Young. Second unit director: Joseph C. Youngerman. Running time: 98 minutes.

Cast: Ronald Colman *Dick Heldar;* Walter Huston *Torpenhow;* Muriel Angelus *Maisie;* Ida Lupino *Bessie;* Dudley Digges *The Nilghai;* Ernest Cossart *Beeton;* Ferike Boros *Madame Binat;* Pedro De Cordoba *Monsieur Binat;* Colin Tapley *Gardoner;* Fay Helm *Red-haired girl;* Ronald Sinclair *Dick (as a boy);* Sarita Wooten *Maisie (as a girl);* Halliwell Hobbes *Doctor;* Charles Irwin *Soldier model;* Francis McDonald *George;* George Regas *Cassavetti;* Wilfred Roberts *Barton.*

> He didn't like me; I didn't like him—the only two things we fully agreed upon.—William A. Wellman, on his relationship with Ronald Colman[42]

Synopsis: In 1939, Bette Davis did not play the only character to go blind and die. Ronald Colman's character suffered the same fate in the Rudyard Kipling tale *The Light That Failed.*

Colman plays Richard Heldar, a soldier in the British Army and an aspiring artist who is serving in the Sudan. During a battle with the fuzzie-wuzzies, a band of Arab natives on the warpath, Dick is slashed in the face with a blade while saving the life of his good friend Torpenhow (Walter Huston). He recovers and begins to travel the world in search of new people and places to sketch.

His work eventually pays off. Dick is recalled to London, where his Sudan Campaign sketches are garnering widespread attention and acclaim. Back home, he is reunited with Torpenhow—with whom he shares a spacious house—and is courted by all of the local papers. In a very short time, he becomes a noted and well-paid commercial artist.

One day, while walking in the park, Dick recognizes a pretty young lady as his childhood sweetheart, Maisie (Muriel Angelus). She is also a local artist, although much more a novice. They begin spending their Sunday afternoons together and Dick falls in love with her, but his love is not reciprocated. She wishes to remain merely friends and tells him one day that she is leaving for Paris to continue her painting and studies.

Torpenhow takes in a barmaid and girl of the streets named Bessie (Ida Lupino) whom he finds passed out on the street one evening, and it is not long before the two become romantically involved. Dick is intrigued by the girl's face and pays her to sit for him occasionally, but he disapproves of Torpenhow's affair with her. He sends his friend away on an extended

The Light That Failed (Paramount). *Top:* Torpenhow (Walter Huston) tends to Richard Heldar (Ronald Colman), who has been wounded in battle. *Bottom:* On the verge of blindness, Heldar completes his masterpiece. His subject is Ida Lupino.

vacation, thereby putting an abrupt end to it. Bessie, in turn, vows to get even one day.

When his vision starts becoming blurry and confused, Dick decides to see an eye specialist. The oculist (Halliwell Hobbes) he consults tells him that he is showing the early signs of complete degeneration and offers him little hope. The condition is due to pressure on his optic nerve caused by the slash he suffered all those years ago in the Sudan.

At first, Dick drowns his sorrows in alcohol, more devastated by the impending loss of his painting career than of his eyesight. But, before long, he becomes possessed with creating a final masterpiece in what little time he has left, a portrait of Bessie into which he wants to pour all of his heart and soul. He wants to capture the melancholia of mankind on his canvas.

Torpenhow returns from his vacation to find Bessie driven to the brink of insanity by Dick's possessiveness. Dick goes to sleep, having completed his masterpiece, and Bessie approaches Torpenhow one more time, only to be rejected and sent away. Before she goes, however, she avenges herself by destroying Dick's painting.

When Dick awakes, his sight is completely gone. "I'm blind, and the darkness won't go away!" he cries out.

Torpenhow finds Maisie and tells her about Dick's predicament. She returns to London with the intention of marrying Dick and taking care of him, but he realizes it's out of pity, not love, and sends her away.

He convinces Torpenhow that Maisie and he are going to be married, freeing his friend for service in the Sudan. Torpenhow leaves with some army buddies one day, and Dick's life becomes common and serene. Following a chance encounter with Bessie in the park, he learns for the first time that she destroyed his masterpiece on the day that he finished it. Devastated by the loss of Maisie, his profession and his great final portrait, Dick follows Torpenhow down to the Sudan, where he successfully carries out a suicide mission by riding determinedly into battle with his British comrades. As an act of mercy, Torpenhow aids Dick in his ultimate endeavor, as any good friend and true Kipling character would.

Notes: Rudyard Kipling's first novel, *The Light That Failed,* was published in 1890, when the author was in his mid-twenties. In it, the story's protagonist, Richard Heldar, is killed in action by a "kindly bullet" after losing his eyesight and his childhood sweetheart. However, his publisher favored a happier ending, in which Heldar would marry Maisie and live happily ever after with her. Kipling eventually won out, but when the book was first made into a motion picture (in 1916) and then remade (in 1923), the happy ending was chosen. Unfortunately, Kipling didn't live long enough to see the most faithful version of his book produced (in 1939), which used not only the original tragic ending, but also contained long stretches of his own dialogue from the book (which scenarist Robert Carson incorporated into his screenplay).

Director William Wellman, the perfect choice for this material, and leading man Ronald Colman—who delivered one of his finest, most poignant performances—got off on the wrong foot together, and things only went downhill from there. Initially, they clashed over the casting of the part of Bessie, the London slut. Colman wanted Vivien Leigh for the role, and as much as personally promised it to her. However, Wellman had already selected a girl named Ida Lupino when she burst into his office one day and declared that she was born to play Bessie, then gave a reading that convinced the director she was right.

In addition, Wellman was from the one-take school of direction, which conflicted with Colman's painstaking perfectionism. At one point, Colman went to the front office at Paramount and threatened to quit the picture if Wellman was not immediately replaced, but the studio stood by their director of choice. Colman was forced to bite his tongue and return to work, but years later—when he starred in a television show called *The Halls of Ivy*—the heavy was named "Wellman," a blatant reference to his experiences making *The Light That Failed*.

Like Wellman's previous film, *Beau Geste,* much of this picture was shot on location in the desert (in this instance, near Santa Fe, New Mexico). And like *Beau Geste,* the shooting was plagued by intense heat and frequent sandstorms. One dust devil picked up a portable dressing room that housed costars Walter Huston and Dudley Digges and carried it for nearly forty feet. Although the dressing room was smashed to pieces, Huston and Digges were fortunately unscathed.

Also worth noting is that when Wellman asked composer Victor Young for some "authentic Hindu music" to use in the picture, Young responded with a piece that was, essentially, "Yankee Doodle Dandy" played backwards. When Wellman heard it, he was delighted with the "Hindu music" and used it as part of the score.

The Light That Failed made a star of Ida Lupino, who later moved on to Warner Bros. and enjoyed a very substantial career.

Reviews: "Letter-perfect. . . . There is a fine tweedy, tobacco-ey, stout-booted air to it; a directness of approach and clarity of thought which we like to describe . . . as masculine; the comforting impression that the characters, good fellows all, will never concede that it's a woman's world they're living in. Oh, they're chivalrous enough, even in their dealings with the ungrateful hussy who preferred immorality to immortality; but *The Light That Failed* is essentially the last defiant blaze of the torch of man's freedom from woman. (Naturally it fails, but it's none the less gallant for a' that.)"—Frank S. Nugent, *The New York Times*

The Little Princess

A Twentieth Century–Fox Film. Directed by Walter Lang. Executive producer: Darryl F. Zanuck. Associate producer: Gene Markey. Screenplay by Ethel Hill and Walter Ferris. Based on the novel by Frances Hodgson Burnett. Photographed in Technicolor by Arthur Miller and William Skall. Technicolor color director: Natalie Kalmus; Associate: Morgan Padelford. Edited by Louis Loeffler. Art direction by Bernard Herzbrum and Hans Peters. Set decorations by Thomas Little. Dances staged by Nicholas Castle and Geneva Sawyer. "The Fantasy": words and music by Walter Bullock and Samuel Pokrass; ballet staged by Ernest Belcher; settings by Richard Day. Costumes by Gwen Wakeling. Sound by E. Clayton Ward and Roger Heman. Music by Louis Silvers. Running time 91 minutes. Release date: March 17.

Cast: Shirley Temple *Sara Crewe;* Richard Greene *Goeffrey Hamilton;* Anita Louise *Rose;* Ian Hunter *Captain Crewe;* Cesar Romero *Ram Dass;* Arthur Treacher *Bertie Minchin;* Mary Nash *Amanda Minchin;* Sybil Jason *Becky;* Miles Mander *Lord Wickham;* Marcia Mae Jones *Lavinia;* Beryl Mercer *Queen Victoria;* Deidre Gale *Jessie;* Ira Stevens *Ermengarde;* E.E. Clive *Mr. Barrows;* Eily Malyon *Cook;* Clyde Cook *Attendant;* Keith Kenneth *Bobbie;* Will Stanton and Harry Allen *Grooms;* Holmes Herbert, Evan Thomas and Guy Bellis *Doctors;* Kenneth Hunter *General;* Lionel Braham *Colonel Gordon.*

> There must be a lot of trouble in the world. Everyone else has problems. When do I get to have some? — Shirley Temple to her mother, during filming of *The Little Princess*[43]

Synopsis: *The Little Princess* was a lavishly mounted production that provided child phenomenon Shirley Temple with a film that many considered to be her best. It was also, coincidentally, her first picture in Technicolor.

The story is set in Victorian England, at the turn of the century. Captain Crewe (Ian Hunter) has been drafted for service in the Boer War and must leave immediately for Africa. He enrolls his daughter Sara (Temple) at a prestigious girls' school run by the cross-looking Miss Minchin (Mary Nash) and her much more affable brother, Bertie (Arthur Treacher), a former stage song-and-dance man.

Because of her father's wealth and social position, Sara is given special treatment at Miss Minchin's Seminary and quickly earns the monicker of "the little princess." Still, her winning personality earns her several quick friends at the school: Rose (Anita Louise), one of her instructors; Goeffrey Hamilton (Richard Greene), a stable worker at the school whom Rose has been seeing on the sly (away from the disapproving eyes of Miss Minchin); Ram Dass (Cesar Romero), an Indian servant who works at the estate next door for a crusty old man named Lord Wickham (Miles Mander); and Becky (Sybil Jason), a servant at the school who is about her own age and treats Sara like true royalty.

News arrives that her father's regiment has been cut off and surrounded

Goeffrey Hamilton (Richard Greene) and Sara Crewe (Shirley Temple) in *The Little Princess* (Twentieth Century–Fox).

by the Boers in Africa, so volunteers are called on to form a relief column. One afternoon, Goeffrey arrives to take Sara riding, but she is too concerned about her father's plight to ride. Instead, they sit out on the front stoop and talk. Goeffrey tells her that he has enlisted for volunteer duty and also divulges the fact that he and Rose plan to be married before he leaves. He asks for Sara's help in outwitting Miss Minchin, and the little girl is only too glad to oblige.

While they are talking together, they run into Lord Wickham, who Sara learns is Goeffrey's grandfather. He has disowned his grandson over a long-past argument, and still resents the boy for his independence and self-sufficiency. When Goeffrey informs him that he is working at the school as a common stable boy, Lord Wickham is outraged.

Goeffrey and Rose are secretly married before he leaves for Africa. Some time passes, and Captain Crewe's regiment is relieved. They return home, beaten and bruised, but still alive, on what just happens to be Sara's birthday. To celebrate, she throws a party for the school and buys gifts for everyone as a way to express her gratitude. Miss Minchin finances the whole affair, expecting to be reimbursed by Captain Crewe when he arrives.

However, Mr. Barrows (E.E. Clive) arrives with the news that Captain Crewe was killed in the action and all of his property and cash were confiscated by the enemy, making Sara suddenly a pauper. Miss Minchin is furious. She calls an abrupt halt to the party, takes back all of the girls and orders Rose to break the news to Sara.

Rose reluctantly complies, and the little girl breaks down in tears, refusing to believe that her father is dead. When she has regained herself, Miss Minchin moves her from the luxurious room she has been staying in to a cold and drab servants' quarter, explaining that from now on the girl will have to work at the school until she has paid off her father's indebtedness. In addition, Miss Minchin sells off all of Sara's clothes and belongings.

When she intercepts a letter containing money addressed to Rose from Goeffrey, she summarily fires the teacher and evicts her from the premises. Her brother Bertie volunteers for service, preferring "the less painful horrors of the battlefield" to his sister's shameful treatment of Sara and Rose. To add insult to injury, he also threatens to reprise his song-and-dance act.

Bertie doesn't get very far. In fact, he makes it only to the local military hospital, where he gets a maintenance job. Eventually, Sara arrives there, searching among the wounded for her father. One day, news arrives of 1,200 men being shipped there from the battle lines, and she is sure her father is among them. Because of her duties at the school, however, she gets there past visiting hours and is turned away. She promises to return the following morning.

In fact, Captain Crewe is among the men. He is delirious from malaria and has lost his papers, so no one can identify him. His doctors (Holmes Herbert, Evan Thomas and Guy Bellis) all agree that an operation is needed, and they make plans to have him shipped out the next day to a brain specialist. The only thing he will say, over and over again, is "Sara."

Sara goes to sleep that night and dreams that she is queen of a land in which stealing kisses is against the law. Goeffrey and Rose appear in her court, charged with the crime by the evil, meddling Miss Minchin. When the couple kiss for Sara, they are acquitted and Miss Minchin is banished from the kingdom. This ruling is followed by a small ballet.

When Sara awakes, her room has been transformed. It's as if she is still in her wonderful dream, and neither she nor her friend Becky can believe their eyes. The room has been furnished with lovely furniture, a fire has been started, a buffet of food has been set up and expensive clothing is there. It has all been provided by Lord Wickham, who prefers to remain anonymous.

When Miss Minchin enters the room, she accuses the girls of stealing it all. She locks them in their room and runs off to call the police. While she is gone, the girls climb out on the ledge and over to Lord Wickham's house, where they make their escape.

A policeman chases them through the streets, catching Becky, but Sara gets away. Miss Minchin and the policeman go down to the hospital to capture her. Visitors are not allowed on this morning, but Sara breaks in and encounters Queen Victoria (Beryl Mercer), who instructs Colonel Gordon (Lionel Braham) to escort the little girl through all of the wards. The search proves fruitless, but she does run into Goeffrey and Rose, who have no information for her.

Shirley Temple and Arthur Treacher in a sequence from *The Little Princess* (Twentieth Century–Fox).

While she is evading Miss Minchin and the policeman, though, she rushes into the hospital's waiting room and finds her father. When Captain Crewe lays eyes on his daughter, he comes to his senses, and they jump into each other's arms.

As the queen leaves the hospital, Sara and her dad promise each other that they will never be separated again.

Notes: From 1934 to 1938, Shirley Temple reigned as the nation's number one box-office draw. Her films grossed a combined $20 million-plus. But *The Little Princess* was destined to be Shirley's last great success as a child star. Fox provided her with a healthy $1.3 million budget, Technicolor, a very capable song-and-dance partner in the person of Arthur

Treacher, an attractive pair of costars (Richard Greene and Anita Louise) and—because of their success using Abraham Lincoln in *The Littlest Rebel* (1935)—the brief appearance of Queen Victoria (played by Beryl Mercer). Still, although the picture was a critical success, it was not a financial one.

The following year, Darryl Zanuck stuck her in a musical fantasy called *The Blue Bird*. It was Fox's answer to *The Wizard of Oz*, but it was a true stinker (and the first Shirley Temple film to *lose* money). It marked, for all intents and purposes, the final and irreconcilable divorce between the child star and her legions of fans. Never again would she command such a stronghold of the nation's heart (or pocketbooks).

Reviews: "While the picture is excellently acted and directed, it's from a general production standpoint that it excels most. In addition to the Temple draw, the story's natural appeal, and the color processing, 20th-Fox made certain that all factors of production were given top attention. There are a number of big production scenes and casting throughout is excellent." — *Variety*

Love Affair

An RKO-Radio Picture. Produced and directed by Leo McCarey. Screenplay by Delmer Daves and Donald Ogden Stewart. From an original story by Mildred Cram and Leo McCarey. Photographed by Rudolph Mate. Edited by Edward Dmytryk and George Hirely. Art direction by Van Nest Polglase. Set decorations by Darrell Silvera. Special effects by Vernon L. Walker. Montage by Douglas Travers. Gowns by Howard Greer and Edward Stevenson. Musical score by Roy Webb. Running time: 89 minutes. Release date: March 16.

Songs: "Wishing," music and lyrics by Buddy De Sylva; "Sing My Heart," music by Harold Arlen, lyrics by Ted Koehler.

Cast: Irene Dunne *Terry McKay*; Charles Boyer *Michel Marnet*; Maria Ouspenskaya *Grandmother*; Lee Bowman *Kenneth Bradley*; Astrid Allwyn *Lois Clarke*; Maurice Moscovich *Maurice Coubert*.

> For what it was, it was almost perfectly executed. It came closer than any of my other pictures to being exactly what it had hoped to be. — Charles Boyer[44]

Synopsis: 1939 was a year of great screen couples: Clark Gable and Vivien Leigh, Laurence Olivier and Merle Oberon, Leslie Howard and Ingrid Bergman. But perhaps no screen couple of that watershed year generated as much chemistry, charisma, or sensuality as Charles Boyer and Irene Dunne in the wonderful comedy-drama *Love Affair*.

Aboard a luxury liner bound for America, international playboy Michel Marnet (Boyer) meets small-town Kansas girl Terry McKay (Dunne). He is

Irene Dunne and Charles Boyer meet on a cruise and fall in love with each other in *Love Affair* (RKO-Radio).

crossing the Atlantic to wed millionairess Lois Clarke (Astrid Allwyn), she to wed her boss, Kenneth Bradley (Lee Bowman). But, despite their impending marriages, the attraction between the two is undeniable. That attraction soon manifests itself in flirting, innuendo, and sexual playfulness.

For the sake of her reputation, Terry suggests that they stay away from each other for the remaining eight days of the cruise. But when their paths inadvertently cross at the bar, over two chilled glasses of pink champagne, it is only the first in a series of chance encounters. Before long, the whole ship is talking.

When the luxury liner makes an afternoon stop at Porto Santo in Madeira, Michel takes Terry to visit his grandmother (Maria Ouspenskaya), and they spend the day together at her villa. Terry is deeply moved by the spirituality of the place and by the warmth and wisdom of Michel's grandmother, who confesses her concern to Terry that one day Michel may be presented with an enormous bill for a life in which everything has come so easily. She feels, though, that with the right girl he would be safe, and smiles at Terry as if she were that girl.

"Anything can happen on a boat," the grandmother says.

Back on the ship, on the eve before they dock, Michel confesses to Terry that he has never done an honest day's work in his life. He asks for six months to try and make a life for them, and the following morning, after tossing and turning on it, she agrees. They plan to meet six months from that day — assuming everything has worked out for both parties — at the top of the Empire State Building.

When Terry reads that Michel has broken off his engagement with Lois Clarke, she leaves Kenneth and takes a singing job in a nightclub, agreeing to only a six-month contract. Michel, meanwhile, begins painting again, after years of inactivity, and sells his first canvas.

The fateful day arrives, but Terry is hit by a car rushing into the busy midday traffic on her way to their rendezvous. While Michel waits anxiously up above, we can hear the ambulance siren 122 floors below. After spending the whole day and most of the stormy night waiting, Michel finally gives up, leaving a very disappointed man.

At the hospital, Terry learns that she may never walk again, and won't know for sure for another six months. Until it is certain, she insists that Michel not know about the accident or about her condition.

Michel's grandmother dies and he is left heartbroken and alone. The old woman's tragic prophecy has come to pass.

Terry gets along so fabulously with the children at the hospital where she is recuperating that she is offered a job there once she has recovered, which she gratefully accepts.

Michel, a successful artist now, has sold all of his paintings, with the exception of one he painted of Terry kneeling in prayer at his grandmother's chapel, which he refuses to accept money for. He eventually agrees to part with it, though, when his agent, Maurice Coubert (Maurice Moscovich), informs him that a poor, crippled woman who comes into his shop adores the painting, and Michel tells him to give it to her.

He soon begins stepping out on the town again, and one night he runs into Kenneth and Terry at the theatre. She is sitting down, and though Kenneth wants to tell Michel the truth, Terry will not allow it. So when she is taken out of the theatre in a wheelchair, Michel is not there to witness it. He goes home early that evening, no longer content to live the life of a playboy.

On Christmas Eve, Michel goes to visit Terry, telling her that he never made it to their rendezvous. She is obviously heartbroken by this revelation, but does her best to conceal it. They chat politely and, as a Christmas present, he gives her his grandmother's shawl.

Just as he is preparing to leave, Michel catches sight of the painting — the one of Terry in the chapel — in a mirror reflection, and only then learns the truth of her paralysis. The lovers are reunited at last, and Terry exclaims jubilantly: "If you can paint, I can walk!"

Notes: Leo McCarey was primarily a comedy director who had made an initial reputation supervising some of the most memorable silent films of Laurel and Hardy, and who later guided the Marx Brothers in one of their best films, *Duck Soup* (1933). In subsequent outings, McCarey never lost his talent for whimsical improvisation, but he also developed a flare for sentiment that enriched such classics as *Ruggles of Red Gap* (1935) and *The Awful Truth* (1937), while *Make Way for Tomorrow* (1937) is an unexpected and fully realized tragedy of a man and wife cruelly separated in their twilight years. These varied earlier films give a context for the balance between romantic comedy and melodrama that McCarey so successfully achieved in *Love Affair*.

Throughout most of 1938, McCarey was involved (or was supposed to be involved) in *The Cowboy and the Lady*. He had sold the idea to Samuel Goldwyn for $50,000 without so much as a script, primarily because it seemed a likely bet for bringing together Goldwyn's two contract stars, Gary Cooper and Merle Oberon. McCarey was the intended writer-director but excused himself from both functions after he lost his enthusiasm for the project, although he was screen-credited for an original story that he never actually wrote. *The Cowboy and the Lady* (1938) eventually employed over a score of writers and became a minor scandal in the industry. No doubt Boyer—who had a nodding acquaintance with McCarey from when they worked at Paramount Studio at the same time—had heard all the gossip and was probably cautious when McCarey initiated discussions about a story he was writing especially for him and Irene Dunne. But when the three were brought together socially to talk about the project, Boyer elected to cancel his half-made plans to work for Paramount or Columbia or both, and go with McCarey and Dunne instead. By the time *Love Affair* went before the cameras for RKO in the fall of '38, they were all very good friends, and Boyer's rapport with Dunne already rated as extraordinary.

Boyer was a methodical actor, given to early memorization of all his dialogue, but McCarey advised him against memorizing a script that wouldn't be used. McCarey liked to improvise. That wasn't Boyer's style, but both the actor and director agreed that there were fundamental problems with the shooting script. The original story had been written by McCarey himself (along with Mildred Cram); Delmer Daves had developed a scenario from it; and later, the redoubtable Donald Ogden Stewart was hired to supply additional dialogue (mainly light banter for the shipboard sequences). But still, after shooting began, McCarey told his actors: "I don't think it will work, not with this script." The change of mood from light and playful to dark and serious was too quick, so Boyer suggested that they turn the minor scene with Maria Ouspenskaya into a substantial midpicture sequence. As played, it became the pivotal scene that made all of *Love Affair* work.

They continued making changes daily, embellishing parts of the script while abandoning whole chunks and devising new material.

Although McCarey's directing style often seems relatively simple, he does manage to find certain images which have a direct visual effectiveness. And his work on *Love Affair* is no exception. The scene of Terry and Michel in the chapel, for instance, which was beautifully lit by Rudolph Mate, conveys a warm and exquisite empathy between the characters as they kneel in wordless communion. Another example, the most powerful in the film, is when Michel opens the door of Terry's bedroom in the final sequence and the camera shoots over to a mirror reflecting the painting, causing the audience to share the shock and sadness of Michel's realization of Terry's paralysis.

Love Affair also benefits immeasurably from three wonderful songs, each of which expresses some aspect of the film's meaning. The first, the haunting "Plaisir d'Amour," poignantly foreshadows the feasibility of tragedy at a time when it seems the movie will be played for laughs all the way through. The second, which Terry sings during an audition for a nightclub job, is "Sing My Heart," and it assures us to expect (despite sudden, tragic events) "that happy ending" which Hollywood is so famous for. The third and final, the beautiful "Wishing," expresses what the audience wants to believe and what the film insists is the truth, that "wishing will make it so."

When a rough cut of the film was screened in January of '39, they all felt they had a winner on their hands. Two months later, when it was released, *Love Affair* surpassed even their own lofty expectations. Its box-office endorsement was commensurate with its critical acclaim.

Charles Boyer and Irene Dunne, hoping to capitalize on a good thing, segued directly into *When Tomorrow Comes* (which was also released in 1939), but this endeavor received none of *Love Affair*'s glowing reviews or financial rewards.

In 1977, when Irene Dunne appeared before a glittering audience in Washington's Kennedy Center following an American Film Institute screening of *Love Affair,* she refused to name a "favorite leading man" of her film career, but narrowed it to a contest between Boyer and Cary Grant, with each of whom she made three pictures. She claimed that they were as different as two men can possibly be: Cary was a mischievous scamp, and to make a picture with him wasn't work but play; whereas Boyer's dedication meant that working with him was a demanding if agreeable challenge. She called Boyer "the perfect gentleman," and for many years it was the consensus of the film community that Irene Dunne was herself the perfect lady.

Love Affair was nominated for five Academy Awards: for Best Picture, Irene Dunne for Best Actress, Maria Ouspenskaya (formerly of Stanislavsky's legendary Moscow Art Theater) for Best Supporting Actress, for Best Original Story, and for Best Song (Buddy De Sylva's "Wishing," which became the most popular song in the nation during the summer of '39).

It was remade by the same director some two decades later, retitled *An Affair to Remember* and starring Cary Grant and Deborah Kerr.

Reviews: "Nothing could be simpler, or even more machine-made and threadbare, than the plot of *Love Affair* . . . . But a plot by the time it reaches the screen can be quite a bit more than he plus she plus the things that make them they, and Leo McCarey enters largely and predominantly into the sum total of *Love Affair.* He must have had good help from the men who wrote the dialogue, but as part author, as well as producer and director, he must himself have been chiefly responsible for as fine a piece of movie-making as any made-for-the-customers thing of this sort is likely to be in this or any other year."—James Shelley Hamilton, *National Board of Review Magazine*

"Leo McCarey has created another extraordinarily fine film in *Love Affair.* In a sense, this film is a triumph of indirection—for it does one thing while seeming to do another. Its immediate effect is comedy; its after-glow is that of a bitter-sweet romance. Mr. McCarey has balanced his ingredients skillfully and has merged them into a glowing and memorable picture. A less capable director, with a less competent cast, must have erred one way or the other—either on the side of treacle or on that of whimsy. Like other McCarey pictures, this one has the surface appearance of comedy and the inner strength of a hauntingly sorrowful romance."—Frank S. Nugent, *The New York Times*

Made for Each Other

United Artists. 90 min. Directed by John Cromwell.

Cast: Carole Lombard, James Stewart, Charles Coburn, Lucile Watson, Harry Davenport, Ruth Weston, Donald Briggs, Eddie Quillan, Esther Dale, Rene Orsell.

By today's standards, this David O. Selznick production is over-dramatic and dated. But in 1939, it was a highly regarded effort, even being selected by the *New York Times* as one of the ten best films of the year. It chronicles the struggles of a young married couple and their eventual triumph.

The Man in the Iron Mask

A United Artists Picture. Directed by James Whale. Produced by Edward Small. Screenplay by George Bruce. Based on the novel by Alexandre Dumas. Photographed by Robert Planck. Edited by Grant Whytock. Art direction by John Du Casse Schulze. Music by Lucien Moraweck. Musical director: Lud Gluskin. Sound by W.H. Wilmarth. Costumes by Bridgehouse. Makeup by Paul A. Stanhope. Special effects by Howard Anderson. Fencing director: Fred Cavens. Production manager: Val Paul. Second unit director: Cullen Tate. Assistant director: Edgar Anderson. Running time: 111 minutes.

Cast: Louis Hayward *Louis XIV/Philippe of Gascony;* Joan Bennett *Maria Theresa;* Warren William *D'Artagnan;* Joseph Schildkraut *Fouquet;* Alan Hale *Porthos;* Walter Kingsford *Colbert;* Miles Mander *Aramis;* Bert

Roach *Athos;* Marian Martin *Mlle. de la Valliere;* Montagu Love *Spanish Ambassador;* Doris Kenyon *Queen Anne;* Albert Dekker *Louis XIII;* Nigel de Brulier *Cardinal Richelieu;* William Royle *Commandant of Bastille;* Boyd Irwin *Lord High Constable of France;* Howard Brooks *Cardinal;* Reginald Barlowe *Jean Paul;* Lane Chandler *Captain of Fouquet's Guards;* Wyndham Standing *Doctor;* Dorothy Vaughan *Midwife;* Sheila Darcy *Maria Theresa's maid;* Robert Milasch *Torturer;* Darcy Corrigan *Tortured prisoner;* Peter Cushing *Second officer;* Emmett King *King's Chamberlain; and the St. Brendan Choir.*

> Small had a thing against directors. He was on the set a lot and would interfere. He'd stand at the back of the stage and yell, 'That's not right!' He was never happy. — Louis Hayward[45]

Synopsis: In the 1930s and 1940s, with the studio system at the peak of its power, there was little room for the independent producer. The most successful of the lot, by far, was David O. Selznick. But another one who achieved considerable success was Edward Small. Although later in his career he would branch out into different genres, Small made his bones with a series of well-crafted costume adventures. After scoring a major hit with *The Count of Monte Cristo* in 1934, he produced *The Last of the Mohicans* (1936), *the Son of Monte Cristo* (1940), and *The Corsican Brothers* (1941) over the following seven years. His contribution to 1939 was *The Man in the Iron Mask,* based on Alexandre Dumas's most venerable tale.

In it, Queen Anne of Austria (Doris Kenyon) gives birth to a son, the crown prince and heir to the throne of France. A few minutes later, though, she gives birth to an identical twin of the boy. Fearing a conflict for supremacy—even civil war—between his sons when they come of age, Louis XIII (Albert Dekker) arranges for his good friend D'Artagnan (Warren William) to take the second son away to Gascony and raise him. Only the wily messenger Fouquet (Joseph Schildkraut) uncovers this plot, but he decides to hold his tongue until he can use the information most advantageously.

A generation passes and the first son becomes King Louis XIV (Louis Hayward, who also plays the second son, Philippe of Gascony). Louis is a decadent and unworthy monarch who is crippling the people of France with his heavy taxes and tyrannical rule. Philippe, on the other hand, has been reared a dashing swordsman by D'Artagnan and the three musketeers: Athos (Bert Roach), Porthos (Alan Hale), and Aramis (Miles Mander).

When the king's tax agents come to collect a particularly confiscatory tax, the musketeers insist, rightly, that Louis XIII personally made them exempt. The royal troops disregard this and try to apprehend the musketeers. Along with Philippe, they nearly fight off the entire regiment, but are eventually subdued and taken as prisoners to Paris.

Louis has learned of a plot to assassinate him and, when he sees how much Philippe looks like him, asks the prisoner to take his place. Knowing nothing of the deadly conspiracy, Philippe agrees in an effort to save his friends from execution.

Philippe shaves his moustache, dons a wig, and on his first venture as the King of France, his coach is attacked by an angry mob. He jumps out, sword in hand, and fights off the mob single-handedly. But instead of punishing them, Philippe promises redress of their wrongs, and he is cheered roundly by his would-be assassins.

When Philippe first meets the Spanish princess Maria Theresa (Joan Bennett), with whom a marriage has been arranged for Louis, he is struck immediately by her beauty and charm, and he woos her gallantly. She has been treated only with contempt by Louis—who even flaunts his affair with Mme. de la Valliere (Marian Martin) before her eyes—and is pleasantly surprised and enchanted by what she perceives as a sudden and unexpected about-face by the king. The two fall quickly and effortlessly in love with each other.

Colbert (Walter Kingsford), who was as close and loyal to Louis XIII as D'Artagnan, plots to use Philippe to consecrate this marriage while Louis is away temporarily with Valliere in Fontainebleau. This plot is foiled, however, when his arch-rival Fouquet sends a messenger to Fontainebleau telling the king what is happening in France. But while Philippe is impersonating his brother, he takes the opportunity to free D'Artagnan and the musketeers. They flee to a prearranged rendezvous point, where Philippe agrees to meet them soon.

Louis returns hastily from his retreat, and when he learns that Philippe is actually his twin brother, he orders his sibling imprisoned for life in the gloomy dungeon of the Bastille and his face forever locked in an iron mask, to hide his royal countenance. This mask is the instrument of a hideous torture, for as the prisoner's beard grows, it will slowly suffocate him to death. Thus, there is an urgent need to rescue Philippe before it is too late.

When he doesn't show up at the rendezvous as planned, the musketeers return for him, using the secret passageways of the king's castle that D'Artagnan knows like the back of his hand. They enlist the aid of Colbert and of Maria Theresa, who discovers her love's true identity and his horrible fate at the hands of the man she is engaged to marry. She steals the key to the mask from Louis when he returns in a drunken stupor from an evening with Valliere, and takes it back to the musketeers. They use it to rescue Philippe from the Bastille and the mask, which they force Louis into. Then they take him down to the Bastille via the secret passageways and leave him locked in Philippe's dungeon cell.

Philippe resumes his impersonation of the king and proceeds with his plans to marry Maria Theresa. He also uses his newfound power to rescind all of his brother's taxes. Louis, meanwhile, manages to scrawl a note on a pewter plate containing instructions for its finder to bring it to Fouquet in exchange for a generous reward, then tosses the plate out of the dungeon

The Man in the Iron Mask (United Artists). *Top:* Louis XIV (Louis Hayward, far right) and Fouquet (Joseph Schildkraut, second from right) look on as the iron mask is prepared for the king's brother. *Bottom:* Maria Theresa (Joan Bennett) solicits the aid of the Three Musketeers to free Philippe from the dungeon and presents them with the key.

window. When Fouquet receives the message it contains, he interrupts Philippe's wedding and denounces him as an imposter. Then he shoots Valliere and flees. He rejoins Louis, who is being escorted by a group of his soldiers to Fontainebleau, where he can reclaim his throne.

Their coach is intercepted by Philippe and the musketeers, who battle the king's men. The musketeers are killed in the scrape, but not before helping D'Artagnan and Philippe kill Louis and Fouquet. D'Artagnan is wounded in the fight — a wound that proves fatal when he collapses on the altar as Philippe and Maria Theresa recite their final vows. But his job is done: France is in the hands of a great king, and France's king is in the arms of a great woman.

Notes: Edward Small, an actor and agent turned independent producer, entered into a three-picture deal with the troubled United Artists in 1938. That same year, he delivered the first two pictures of that pact, *The Duke of West Point* and *The King of the Turf.* They were both small and inexpensive productions that were written by George Bruce and directed by Alfred E. Green, and neither film made much of a splash at the box office. The third and final picture, however, was a massive undertaking, with a detailed and wordy screenplay by Bruce based upon the Alexandre Dumas classic *The Man in the Iron Mask.* Swashbucklers were bigger than ever, as evidenced by Warners' *The Adventures of Robin Hood* (1938), and Small's production cashed in on this very lucrative genre.

Small was so pleased with Bruce's adaptation of the Dumas classic that he steadfastly made him a writer-producer and gave him *Kit Carson, Adventurer* (1940) to work on. But the man whom Small chose to direct *The Man in the Iron Mask,* James Whale, was far less satisfied with the overlong and overwritten script. Whale was best known for his horror classics: *Frankenstein* (1931), *The Bride of Frankenstein* (1935), *The Invisible Man* (1933), and *The Old Dark House* (1932). He had a flair for the macabre, but Small's insistence on backing Bruce and even some of the actors in disagreements prevented him from making *The Man in the Iron Mask* as stylishly unique a film as he might have. In fact, Whale was fired from the production by Small before it was completed, and Bruce was allowed to personally direct nine days of retakes.

Still, for his services, Whale was paid his usual fee as well as a percentage of the profits. So, although his interest would wane greatly while he shot the film on over 47 sets built at the General Service Studios in Hollywood during the last week in February of '39, he was richly compensated when the picture became a surprise commercial hit.

The following year, Small reteamed Louis Hayward and Joan Bennett in *The Son of Monte Cristo.* Hayward then went on to star in a number of swashbucklers, but the scripts and productions declined steadily in quality. He ended up portraying D'Artagnan in a second-rate production called *The Lady in the Iron Mask* (1952).

The Man in the Iron Mask was nominated for Best Original Score. It was remade in the late 1970s as a movie for television with Richard Chamberlain in the dual roles.

Reviews: . . . "Moderately entertaining costume piece which matches the Dumas novel in its length, if not in its effectiveness. Its running time is one hour and fifty-one minutes, of which far too much has been devoted to the Bennett sighs, the Joseph Schildkraut simpers, the artless (and rather hopeless) attempt of night club's Marian Martin to play that famous courtesan, la Valliere. By the time the Three Musketeers are rushed to the rescue of plot as well as princeling, the film is teetering on the edge of dullness. . . . Told directly, with a deal of steel-clashing and merely the trace of gallant vaporing, it could have served a romance as blithe as *Prisoner of Zenda.* But told in the Hollywood-Dumas manner, with no guard against repetition, with pauses for tableaux and well-rehearsed speeches, with an overfondness for pageantry and stiff heroics, it emerges as something considerably less tolerable." — Frank S. Nugent, *The New York Times*

The Man They Could Not Hang

A Columbia Picture. Directed by Nick Grinde. Produced by Wallace MacDonald. Screenplay by Karl Brown. Based on a story by Leslie T. White and George W. Sayre. Photographed by Benjamin Kline. Edited by William Lyon. Art direction by Lionel Banks. Musical direction by Morris W. Stoloff. Running time: 72 minutes.

Cast: Boris Karloff *Dr. Henryk Savaard;* Lorna Gray *Janet Savaard;* Robert Wilcox *"Scoop" Foley;* Roger Pryor *District Attorney Drake;* Don Beddoe *Lieutenant Shane;* Ann Doran *Betty Crawford;* Joseph De Stefani *Dr. Stoddard;* Charles Trowbridge *Judge Bowman;* Byron Foulger *Lang;* Dick Curtis *Kearney;* James Craig *Watkins;* John Tyrrell *Sutton.*

> Being a bogeyman — like baggage-smashing and truck driving — is apt to be a rather exhausting occupation. I know, because I've tried all three. On the whole I think I would prefer truck driving to house haunting. — Boris Karloff[46]

Synopsis: Although 1939 will always be remembered for the extraordinary number of high-cost and equally high-quality epics, it had its share of "B" movies as well, and *The Man They Could Not Hang* was the best of the bunch.

In it, Boris Karloff plays Dr. Henryk Savaard, a world-renowned scientist who has been conducting radical experiments with a mechanical heart. The device has proven successful in every other form of animal, so one of Savaard's medical students volunteers to be the first human guinea pig. Savaard puts him into a "state of death" using special gases which don't poison body tissue, then—with his assistant Lang (Byron Foulger)—prepares to bring him back to life. In the meantime, however, the student's girlfriend, Betty Crawford (Ann Doran), runs down to the police station and informs them that Savaard is in the process of murdering one of his students. When she returns with Lieutenant Shane (Don Beddoe) and some other officers, Savaard gets Lang out of the lab safely and then prepares to confront them. They burst in during the middle of his experiment and find the student dead. Savaard begs for one hour to revive the boy, but instead he is arrested and charged with murder, and an autopsy is performed on the student.

During his trial, Savaard pleads passionately and eloquently in his own defense, but his words fall on deaf ears. He is found guilty and sentenced to hang. Before being taken away, though, he addresses the courtroom, vowing revenge on Judge Bowman (Charles Trowbridge), District Attorney Drake (Roger Pryor), the jury members, Betty and Lieutenant Shane. "I offered you life and you gave me death!" he says.

Before being executed, Savaard signs his body over to medical research—in the form of Lang. As soon as he is hanged, Lang uses Savaard's own mechanical heart to resuscitate the doctor. However, Savaard is no longer interested in furthering the human race through scientific research. Now he is interested only in vengeance.

Several months pass and, during that short period, six members of the Savaard jury are found hanged to death, apparent suicides. Reporter "Scoop" Foley (Robert Wilcox)—who has become romantically involved with Savaard's daughter Janet (Lorna Gray)—assumes that a vigilante is at work and tenaciously gets on the case. In trying to contact the surviving members of the jury, he learns that they have all been summoned by Judge Bowman to Savaard's house. Janet, however, tells him that her father's house is locked up, and only she has the keys. Suspecting foul play, Scoop heads out to the house himself.

He runs into Judge Bowman, who claims not to have summoned anyone to the house but to have been summoned himself by Janet Savaard. Inside, they find the other jury members, Lieutenant Shane and Betty, all of whom have wires forged with Bowman's signature requesting their presence.

When Doctor Savaard enters the room, they are all shocked. He leads them into the dining room, where places have already been set for everyone, and informs them that they will all systematically be murdered that evening, beginning with Judge Bowman at seven o'clock. The others will be killed one at a time in fifteen-minute intervals after Bowman, he says.

With seven o'clock only two minutes away, the judge bolts for the door. But when he tries to open the gates which enclose the living room, he is electrocuted to death. The others rush to his side and, in the hysteria, Savaard disappears.

They search for a way out of the building, only to discover that they are

Boris Karloff hosts a deadly party in *The Man They Could Not Hang* (Columbia).

trapped. All of the exits have been sealed and the telephone lines are dead. In addition, the clock is ticking. Kearney (Dick Curtis), the foreman of the jury who worked so diligently during their 60-hour deliberation for Savaard's death, is next in line. Suddenly, though, the phone rings, and Kearney's business partner is supposedly on the other line. Hoping to get help sent to the house, Kearney picks up the receiver, which is rigged to shoot a poison-dipped blade through his skull. Kearney is killed instantly.

Just as the clock is ticking down to Betty's execution, Janet arrives at the house. She finds her father upstairs and pleads with him to give up his homicidal cause and release the others, but to no avail. She realizes quickly that her father is not the man he once was; whereas he once wanted life, he now wants only blood.

Savaard sends her away, but instead of leaving, she tries to free the others by opening the living room gates. Janet is electrocuted to death and, when her father rushes downstairs to her side, he is shot and wounded by Shane.

They all take her body upstairs, where Savaard successfully resuscitates her heart with his machine. But before dying, he uses his gun to destroy the invention into which he once poured his heart and soul, denying a cruel and superstitious world its wonders.

Notes: The storyline of *The Man They Could Not Hang* was inspired by actual experiments conducted by Dr. Robert Cornish. The biochemist attracted publicity during the 1930s by restoring dogs to life after killing them with nitrogen gas. Dr. Cornish also tried to obtain permission to restore life to executed convicts in order to further test his theories, but permission was denied.

The film's success encouraged Columbia to sign Karloff for several more films which used the same theme (*The Man with Nine Lives, The Devil Commands,* etc.), launching the actor onto his second "crazed scientist" cycle. It lasted until early 1941, when Karloff returned to the stage.

Ironically, the experiments that Karloff conducted in the film — restoring life to the dead with a mechanical heart — precipitated similar medical advances in real life. More than twenty-five years later, human lives were successfully prolonged by surgical heart transplants.

Reviews: "Boris Karloff looks less menacing than he has been in the past, but while he is a complacent, kindly type of character part of the way . . . he ends up on a rather sinister note. . . . Plot is inconsistent with the deep interest of Karloff in promoting life by his discovery to deliberately turn murderer in the end. The unexpected and implausible revenge doesn't jell, but Karloff turns in his usual good performance." — *Variety*

Mexicali Rose

58 min. Directed by George Sherman.

Cast: Gene Autry, Smiley Burnette, Noah Beery, Luana Walters, William Farnum.

Gene aids poor Mexican children while defending their land from swindling oil land developers. "You're the Only Star in My Blue Heaven," one of the songs he sings in this film, became a big hit with his fans.

Midnight

A Paramount Picture. Directed by Mitchell Leisen. Produced by Arthur Hornblow, Jr. Screenplay by Charles Brackett and Billy Wilder. Based upon a story by Justus Mayer and Franz Schulz. Photographed by Charles Lang. Edited by Doane Harrison. Gowns by Irene. Asst. director: Hal Walker. Music by Frederick Hollander. Art direction by Hans Dreier and Robert Usher. Special effects by Farciot Edouart. Running time: 92 minutes. Release date: April 5.

Cast: Claudette Colbert *Eve Peabody;* Don Ameche *Tibor Czerny;* John Barrymore *Georges Flammarion;* Francis Lederer *Jacques Picoin;* Mary Astor *Helene Flammarion;* Elaine Barrie *Simone;* Hedda Hopper *Stephanie;* Rex O'Malley *Marcel;* Monty Woolley *Judge;* Armand Kaliz *Lebon;* Lionel Pape *Edouart;* Ferdinand Munier and Gennaro Curci *the majordomos.*

One of the authentic delights of the '30's! — Pauline Kael[47]

Claudette Colbert makes a point to John Barrymore in *Midnight* (Paramount).

Synopsis: "Every Cinderella has her midnight," Claudette Colbert's character says at one point, giving the title to this delightful screwball comedy from the brilliant screenwriting team of Charles Brackett and Billy Wilder, who wrote *Ninotchka* for Ernst Lubitsch that same year, and the underrated director Mitchell Leisen.

The film begins on a rainy night in Paris, where showgirl and would-be gold digger Eve Peabody (Colbert) arrives via train, with nothing to her name but the gold lamé gown on her back. All of her other belongings were lost on a roulette wheel back in Monte Carlo.

She cajoles a Parisian cab driver named Tibor Czerny (Don Ameche) into chauffeuring her around the city in search of a job, promising him twice the meter reading once she has found one. But after auditioning unsuccessfully at every nightclub in the city, she ditches Czerny, who has already begun to care for her, and crashes a high society soirée.

There, she is invited to join in on a game of bridge, with Georges Flammarion (John Barrymore), his beautiful wife Helene (Mary Astor), and her lover, playboy Jacques Picoin (Francis Lederer), where she loses a substantial amount of money. Flammarion, who has been on to her little charade for some time already, slips enough money into her purse to pay her gambling debt.

Before the evening is through, he also sets her up in a luxurious suite at a posh hotel, provides her with a chic wardrobe and a bank account of

$50,000 to draw from, all under the alias of the "Countess Czerny." In return for his kindness, Flammarion requests that she attend a weekend retreat at his country estate, where he wants her to use all of her beguiling charms to seduce Jacques away from his wife. Eve, not a girl who would ever ask opportunity to knock a second time, heartily accepts his offer, figuring she can land the well-off Jacques in the process.

Meanwhile, Tibor has enlisted the aid of every cab driver in the city to find Eve. When he learns her whereabouts, he drives out to the country estate masquerading as Eve's royal-blooded husband, the Hungarian Count Czerny.

When they are alone together, Tibor proposes to Eve, but she doesn't want to live the life of a working-class housewife. So although she loves Tibor, Eve turns him down. And before he can convince their hosts that they are both imposters, she convinces them that he is insane and given to bouts of schizophrenia. Thus, when he shows up in his cab, wearing his dirty uniform, and announces that he is a common hack and Eve a former showgirl, and that neither of them has even a trace of royal blood in their veins, they all humor him patiently.

Eve accepts a marriage proposal from Jacques, which sends an affronted Helene back into the grateful arms of husband Georges. But before the marriage can take place, Eve must first get a "divorce" from Tibor, to whom she is not even married. But when Tibor gives the impression of someone who is mentally unstable in court, the judge (Monty Woolley) remembers the existence of an old French law under which an insane man or woman cannot be legally divorced from their spouse. He tells Eve that she is stuck with Tibor.

The lovers reconcile, and this time when Tibor proposes, Eve accepts; Georges and Helene have rediscovered their own love, and they walk off arm-in-arm; and Jacques, a man who earns a "superior income from an inferior champagne," takes his loss in stride.

When the judge leaves his chambers and sees Tibor and Eve walking off together, he asks, "Where are you going now?"

"To get married!" Tibor responds euphorically, leaving the judge a very confused and perplexed man.

Notes: Director Mitchell Leisen, a man of many talents, received his original training as an architect. He worked in interior design, and his first screen credits came as a costume designer for Cecil B. DeMille and Douglas Fairbanks. In fact, he designed Claudette Colbert's costumes for *The Sign of the Cross* (1932). He was soon promoted to assistant director, and in 1933 Paramount gave him his big break with his first directorial assignment. He soon proved himself particularly talented at directing fun-loving glimpses of high life, in films such as *Easy Living* (1937) and *Hands Across the Table* (1935), and with *Midnight* he reached his zenith as a filmmaker.

His star, Claudette Colbert, had a crazy notion that her nose was crooked on the right side of her face, so there is hardly a shot in the whole film where you see her "bad side." The sets had been constructed and camera angles planned in advance to make sure of that. This led certain members of the cast and crew to refer to the right side of Miss Colbert's face as "the other side of the moon," because nobody ever saw it.

John Barrymore was in his declining years and his health was wasting away, but his performing style was still fresh and professional. He did, however, require cue cards (very large ones) containing his dialogue, which crew members displayed just beyond camera range.

Said Leisen, "He'd read one speech over Claudette's left shoulder, then she'd say her lines, then he'd get the next speech over Claudette's right shoulder. It was always funny the ways he could find to stall in a scene while he was trying to find the cards with his next speech." Said Barrymore, "Why should I remember this stuff when I'll only have to forget it tomorrow?" He offered, instead, to recite Shakespeare's *Hamlet*.[48]

Mitchell Leisen, perhaps because of his early technical training, always had a tendency to be more concerned about how his film looked than what it said or how it said it. Still, he was a professional craftsman and a commercial one, and *Midnight* was the first in a string of successful features that he directed. In fact, it was such a successful venture that a mere six years later he remade the film as *Masquerade in Mexico,* which was neither as successful nor as funny as *Midnight.*

Reviews: "The ice went out of the river at the Paramount yesterday, and Spring came laughing in with *Midnight,* one of the liveliest, gayest, wittiest and naughtiest comedies of a long hard season. Its direction, by Mitchell Leisen, is strikingly reminiscent of that of the old Lubitsch. Its cast . . . is in the best of spirits. Its script . . . is a model of deft phrasing and glib narrative joinery; and its production, while handsome, never has been permitted to bulk larger than its players. The call is for three cheers and a tiger: the Paramount is back on Broadway again."—Frank S. Nugent, *The New York Times*

"Despite lavish production and substantial outlay, story itself does not measure up to other ingredients which went into the making. However, principals turn in individual performances far superior to the material provided. Result is a rather amusing and light comedy. . . ."—*Variety*

The Mikado

GFD, England. 91 min. Directed by Victor Schertzinger.

Cast: Kenny Baker, John Barclay, Martyn Green, Jean Colin, Constance Wills, Sydney Granville, Gregory Stroud, Elisabeth Paynter.

In Japan, a timid official is appointed Lord High Executioner, only to learn that his first intended victim is the Emperor's son, traveling incognito. Fine version of the Gilbert and Sullivan comic opera, with all of the show's wonderful tunes intact. Released in the States by Universal, it was their first all-color endeavor. The film was nominated for Best Color Photography.

Mr. Smith Goes to Washington

A Columbia Picture. Produced and directed by Frank Capra. Assistant director: Arthur S. Black. 2nd Unit Director: King Vidor. Screenplay by Sidney Buchman. Based on the story *The Gentleman from Montana* by Lewis R. Foster. Photographed by Joseph Walker. Edited by Gene Havlick and Al Clark. Art direction by Lionel Banks. Music by Dimitri Tiomkin. Gowns by Kalloch. Montage effects by Slavko Vorkapich. Technical adviser: Jim Preston. Running time: 125 minutes. Release date: October 16.

Cast: Jean Arthur *Clarissa Saunders;* James Stewart *Jefferson Smith;* Claude Rains *Sen. Joseph Paine;* Edward Arnold *Jim Taylor;* Guy Kibbee *Gov. Hubert Hopper;* Thomas Mitchell *Diz Moore;* Eugene Pallette *Chick McGann;* Beulah Bondi *Ma Smith;* H.B. Warner *Sen. Agnew;* Harry Carey *President of the Senate;* Astrid Allwyn *Susan Paine;* Ruth Donnelly *Emma Hopper;* Grant Mitchell *Sen. MacPherson;* Porter Hall *Sen. Monroe;* Pierre Watkin *Sen. Barnes;* Charles Lane *Nosey;* William Demarest *Bill Griffith;* Dick Elliott *Carl Cook;* H.V. Kaltenborn *Broadcaster;* Jack Carson *Sweeney;* Joe King *Summers;* Paul Stanton *Flood;* Russell Simpson *Allen;* Stanley Andrews *Sen. Hodges;* Walter Soderling *Sen. Pickett;* Byron Foulger *Hopper's secretary;* Dickie Jones *Page;* Allan Cavan *Ragner;* Maurice Costello *Diggs;* Ann Doran and Helen Jerome Eddy *Paine's secretaries.*

> More fun, even, than the Senate itself.—Frank S. Nugent[49]

Synopsis: The second and best of Frank Capra's "right overcoming might" trilogy (the other two were *Mr. Deeds Goes to Town* in 1936 and *Meet John Doe* in 1941), this red-white-and-blue commentary on American idealism and political chicanery deftly combines comedy with drama and amusingly naïve heroes with corrupt, power-hungry villains.

When the senator from an unnamed state dies suddenly, a new one must be appointed in his place. James Taylor (Edward Arnold), the boss of a corrupt political machine, wants one of his stooges to be appointed, mainly because the bill for a land-grabbing scheme he has been working on for years now is finally being presented to the Senate, and he doesn't want anything to stand in the way of its ratification. Public outcry, however, forces the governor of the state, Hubert Hopper (Guy Kibbee), to instead appoint a man of the people, namely one Jefferson Smith (James Stewart). Smith doesn't have a single day's political experience under his belt, but he is a very popular leader of the "Boy Rangers" and can quote Lincoln and Washington verbatim. His greatest accomplishment seems to have been putting out a forest fire single-handedly (not exactly leading credentials for nomination to the United States Senate).

The other senator from the unnamed state, the highly respected Joseph Paine (Claude Rains), has been in Taylor's pocket for all of his political career. When he learns that Smith is the son of an old and dear friend, he takes the young man paternally under his wing.

On the train to Washington, we learn through a conversation between Smith and Paine that Smith's father was a vigilant crusader who took on a powerful mining syndicate with his little "four-page newspaper" over the constitutional rights of one miner, and when bribery and intimidation failed to dissaude him, he died a martyr at the hands of that syndicate.

"I suppose, Mr. Paine, when a fella bucks up against a big organization like that, one man by himself can't get very far, can he?" Smith reasons.

"No," Paine firmly concurs.

When they reach Washington, Smith slips away for an impromptu five-hour tour of the nation's capital. In a montage sequence prepared by Slavko Vorkapich (who was a master at such things), we see the Washington Monument, the Liberty Bell ringing, the signing of the Declaration of Independence, the Tomb of the Unknown Soldier, and the Lincoln Memorial, where a small boy is reading Lincoln's Gettysburg Address. Considering that Americans have grown up with all of these symbols, learned about them in school, read about them in history books, seen them dramatized in movies and teleplays, it is amazing how effectively stirring this sequence is for an American audience, even after seeing the film several times.

Clarissa Saunders (Jean Arthur), a jaded reporter whose hard-won cynicism is eventually worn down by Smith's idealism, allows the vultures of the Washington Press Corps to get their hands on Smith, and they have a field day with him. His picture shows up in all of the papers the next morning, embarrassing himself as well as the governing body he now represents. When he is shown these unflattering pictures, he travels around town, punching out all the responsible parties.

When some reporters accuse him of being a "Christmas tiger," another yes-man sitting in a painted chair, Smith is cut to the quick and decides to learn more about the laws he is being asked to vote upon. This is, needless to say, the last thing that the Taylor Machine wants. To divert him, Paine suggests that he draw up a bill proposing the creation of a boys' camp in his home state, which Smith had earlier discussed wanting to accomplish during his term. This diversion backfires, however, when Smith enthusiastically draws this bill overnight (with the aid of Saunders) and chooses as its proposed site Willet Creek—the very land Taylor has planned to build his water dam on.

The services of Paine's enticing daughter Susan (Astrid Allwyn), whom Smith is infatuated with, are employed to lure him away from his Senate seat on the day that Taylor's Deficiency Bill is proposed on the floor. Smith is flabbergasted by her invitation and readily accepts. But Saunders, who has been growing increasingly fonder of Jeff, tells him about Taylor's plan and shows him the paperwork on the project as proof.

Once again, Smith is flabbergasted. He cannot believe that Joseph Paine, a man he has respected and revered all of his life, whom his father called "the finest man he ever knew," could be involved in such graft. When Taylor informs him that he has "told Joe Paine what to do for twenty years," Smith calls him a liar.

It isn't until Paine himself explains the facts of life to Smith that he finally realizes just how malignant the cancer of corruption in his home state government really is. Paine tells him that he has been living in a boy's world, and advises him to stay there. "This is a man's world," he tells him. "You've got to check your ideals at the door along with your rubbers."

After bribery and intimidation fail to dissuade Smith, Paine accuses him the next morning on the Senate floor of owning the land proposed for his boys' camp and drawing up the bill to line his own pockets with the dimes and nickels of Boy Rangers all across the country. Smith tries to respond but is quieted by a round of boos.

Paine submits falsified documents to support his charges, and Taylor enlists all of his cronies to rise up and testify against Smith at his hearing. As the evidence piles up against him, Smith walks out on the proceedings, determined to leave Washington and his lofty ideals far behind. On the steps of the Lincoln Memorial, though, Saunders returns to his side and urges him to fight the Taylor Machine, inspiring new life in him.

Smith arrives on the Senate floor the following morning just in time for the roll call, and when the issue of his expulsion is introduced, he seizes the floor, demanding to be heard.

Paine asks him to yield the floor, but Smith refuses, fully cognizant of the fact that as long as he doesn't yield, sit down, leave the chamber or cease talking, he can control the floor and command the attention of his fellow senators for as long as he likes.

With seasoned coaching from veteran Saunders, who is sitting in the visitors' gallery up above the floor, he tells his side of the story, but his impassioned plea only encourages his fellow senators to walk out on him en masse, led by Paine. When they are all forced to return, Smith pulls out his thermos and his lunch and from Daniel Webster's desk conducts a rousing campaign on his own behalf. And from his own desk, James Taylor conducts his campaign, lining his whole machine up against the lone crusader.

In this great filibuster sequence, Smith reads from the Constitution and the Bible and intermittently stops to argue his case with the other senators, until finally, after nearly twenty-four consecutive hours of this, he collapses. Paine rushes out of the Senate chamber and tries to kill himself with a gun. Failing this, he bursts back into the chamber and purges his soul, confessing that everything Smith said was true and that he and Taylor were the true villains, not Smith. Saunders, who has already declared her love for Smith, runs to his aid and is relieved to find that he is all right.

Jefferson Smith has proven, to himself as much as anyone else, that one fella can buck a big organization and win.

Top: Edward Arnold and several of his stooges try to explain the rules of Washington politics to James Stewart, but the young Senator will hear none of it, in *Mr. Smith Goes to Washington* (Columbia). *Bottom:* Smith confronts Senator Paine (Claude Rains) on the Senate floor with accusations of impropriety.

Notes: Between 1932 and 1939, director Frank Capra made six movies that were nominated for the Academy Award for Best Picture. The first of his Columbia comedy series was the enormously successful sleeper *It Happened One Night* (1934), which won all five major Oscars that year (Best Picture, Actor, Actress, Director and Screenplay) and remained the only film to do so until *One Flew Over the Cuckoo's Nest* in 1975. The last in this series was *Mr. Smith Goes to Washington,* which was nominated for 11 Academy Awards. But in an Oscar race dominated by *Gone with the Wind,* it won only one of those, for Lewis R. Foster's Original Story.

In bringing *Mr. Smith* to the screen, Capra was faced with a key decision right at the very beginning: whom to cast in the pivotal role of Jefferson Smith. General consensus had it that Gary Cooper would get the call, based on his success in *Mr. Deeds Goes to Town* (1936), the film that was clearly *Mr. Smith's* cinematic predecessor. But for the role of Jefferson Smith, Capra needed an idealistic innocent, someone who could convincingly gawk at all of the Washington landmarks and later, when the battle lines were drawn, take on the big, corrupt political machine with guts and determination. For these qualities, he chose James Stewart, and a wise decision it turned out to be.

Mr. Smith Goes to Washington reveals James Stewart at the peak of his power as a populist actor. It is arguably the finest performance of his long and very distinguished career, and one that deserved Academy recognition. But in a year of exceptionally fine acting, it was Mr. Chips (Robert Donat) who took home the coveted statuette, not Mr. Smith. Stewart was compensated to some degree when the New York Film Critics chose him, over Donat, as Best Actor of the Year. And it is relatively safe to assume that the Oscar he took home a year later for *The Philadelphia Story*—over such heady competition as Henry Fonda in *The Grapes of Wrath* and Laurence Olivier in *Rebecca*—was to make up for the one he actually deserved for *Mr. Smith.*

It is interesting to note that one day on the set, after rehearsing the memorable filibuster, Capra walked over to Stewart and told him simply that he didn't believe the sequence—that Stewart didn't sound like he'd been talking continuously for twenty-four hours. And then he walked away.

Stewart, a disciplined professional who deeply respected Capra, was unnerved by this remark. So on the way home from the studio that night, he stopped at a throat specialist's office and asked the doctor if he would give him a sore throat. The doctor, who thought he'd heard it all from Hollywood types, was amazed anew—but he proceeded to give Stewart the sorest throat he had ever had in his life. Over the next few days, while he filmed the filibuster sequence, Stewart's throat was painted three times daily to keep it properly sore and froggy.

Mr. Smith Goes to Washington is not Stewart's triumph alone, however. He is supported by a stellar cast of character actors such as Claude Rains, Thomas Mitchell, William Demarest, Jack Carson, Edward Arnold, Eugene

Pallette, and—in a brilliant, nearly pantomimic cameo role—Harry Carey as the President of the Senate. And the wonderful Jean Arthur is quite endearing playing the girl Friday role she created in *Mr. Deeds.*

An additional bonus is the meticulous attention Capra paid to detail in bringing *Mr. Smith* to the screen. Columbia Studios created a perfect duplication of the Senate floor, and James B. Preston, former superintendent of the Senate press gallery, was hired as technical adviser on legislative procedure.

Although by today's standards this film may seem the essence of "Capra-corn," with its blend of sentiment, pathos, and flag-waving patriotism, for its time it caused quite a stir. After a highly publicized premiere in Washington's Constitution Hall, Senator Alben Barkley condemned it as being a "grotesque distortion" of the truth. Ambassador to Great Britain Joseph Kennedy claimed that it damaged America's reputation abroad and played into the hands of Hitler's propaganda machine. There was even punitive legislation threatened against Hollywood. Fearing industry-wide censorship, the other Hollywood studios offered to repay all production costs to Columbia (approximately two million dollars) to have the film withdrawn.

These charges, then and now, are utterly ridiculous. If anything, *Mr. Smith Goes to Washington* is a portrait of democracy in action, and to the audiences who loved it, James Stewart's impassioned rhetoric seemed to impart a new optimism about their country and the basically decent principles for which it stood. In fact, in 1942, when the Nazis banned all American films from France, *Mr. Smith* was purposely the last one shown (for 30 straight days) and it was cheered roundly.

Mr. Smith was remade, more or less, in the seventies as the ridiculous *Billy Jack Goes to Washington.*

Reviews: "Frank Capra has gone after the greatest game of all, the Senate, in *Mr. Smith Goes to Washington*. . . . In doing so, he is operating, of course, under the protection of that unwritten clause in the Bill of Rights entitling every voting citizen to at least one free swing at the Senate. Mr. Capra's swing is from the floor and in the best of humor. . . . Capra, like the juggler who performed at the Virgin's shrine, has had to employ the only medium he knows. And his comedy has become, in consequence, not merely a brilliant jest, but a stirring and even inspiring testament to liberty and freedom, to simplicity and honesty and to the innate dignity of just the average man."—Frank S. Nugent, *The New York Times*

"Many films of the past ten years . . . have revealed the bitter conviction of everyday people that they are being betrayed by the "men higher up" whom they have entrusted with the reins of power. And they are forced by their own logic to conclude that the only way to set things right again is to replace the corrupt leaders with idealists who, magically, will retain their ideals in the face of the world, the flesh, and the devil. . . . Individual idealism is no solution for any practical problem, but it is the totem people worship when every other way out cuts across their thinking habits. A film which embodies this phenomenon enjoys, to my mind, an importance beyond itself. It is to be evaluated less as a mirror of life than as a document of human psychology, an index to the temper of the popular mind. *Mr. Smith Goes to Washington* is such a film, and the classic example of its type."—Richard Griffith, *National Board of Review Magazine*

Mountain Rhythm

57 min. Directed by B. Reeves Eason.
Cast: Gene Autry, Smiley Burnette, June Storey, Maude Eburne, Ferris Taylor.
Gene fights land speculators and sings, among other songs, "It Makes No Difference Now" in this rather inferior tumbleweed saga.

Naughty but Nice

Warner Bros. Directed by Ray Enright.
Cast: Dick Powell, Gale Page, Ann Sheridan, Helen Broderick, Allen Jenkins, Zasu Pitts, Ronald Reagan, Maxie Rosenbloom.
By the summer of 1938, after seven years and twenty-seven musicals for the studio, Dick Powell wanted out of his contract at Warner Bros. Unlike the classics he had made there in the early '30s, the films he was lately being assigned to had steadily declined in quality. This one—his last for the studio—was no exception. In it, he plays a music professor who unwittingly writes a hit song called "Hooray for Spinach." The songs in the film were adapted from such composers as Wagner, Liszt, Mozart and Bach.

Never Say Die

Paramount. 80 min. Directed by Elliott Nugent.
Cast: Martha Raye, Bob Hope, Andy Devine, Gale Sondergaard, Sig Ruman, Alan Mowbray, Monty Woolley.
Hope—before *The Cat and the Canary* set him on the road to screen stardom (not to mention the *Road* series, which began the following year)—weds Raye at the Swiss spa of Bad Gaswasser, believing he has only two weeks left to live. This lively, amusing romp was co-written by former businessman, inventor and playwright Preston Sturges, who one year later would make his stellar debut as writer-director at the studio with *The Great McGinty.*

Ninotchka

An MGM Picture. Produced and directed by Ernst Lubitsch. Screenplay by Charles Brackett, Billy Wilder, and Walter Reisch. From an original story by Melchior Lengyel. Photographed by William Daniels. Edited by Gene Ruggiero. Art direction by Cedric Gibbons, Randall Duel, and Edwin B. Willis. Costumes by Adrian. Music by Werner R. Heymann. Hairstyles for Miss Claire by Sydney Guilaroff. Sound by Douglas Shearer and Conrad Kahn. Makeup by Jack Dawn. Asst. director: Horace Hough. Running time 110 minutes. Release date: November 3.

Cast: Greta Garbo *Ninotchka;* Melvyn Douglas *Leon D'Arbott;* Ina Claire *Grand Duchess Swana;* Bela Lugosi *Razini;* Sig Ruman *Iranoff;* Felix Bressart *Buljanoff;* Alexander Granach *Kopalski;* Gregory Gaye *Rakonin;* Rolfe Sedan *Hotel manager;* Edwin Maxwell *Mercier;* Richard Carle *Gaston.*

I've been to Paris France and I've been to Paris Paramount. Paris Paramount is better. — Ernst Lubitsch[50]

Synopsis: Though by no means a comedienne, Greta Garbo found the ideal role for herself in Ernst Lubitsch's witty and urbane spoof of Communism, *Ninotchka,* which ranks as the finest comedy from 1939.

Three Russian emissaries — Iranoff (Sig Ruman), Buljanoff (Felix Bressart), and Kopalski (Alexander Granach), the most lovable rogues since the Seven Dwarfs — are sent to Paris on a mission to sell some czarist jewels. Upon arrival in Gay Paris, though, the comrades are immediately seduced by the virtues of capitalism, choosing to stay in the Royal Suite of a luxurious French hotel rather than the "people's hotel" where their government made reservations for them. There, they wholeheartedly begin living it up, like men who have been imprisoned for years and are given a weekend pardon.

The jewels were confiscated by their government from the Grand Duchess Swana (Ina Claire), the deposed wife of the former czar. Swana is currently living in Paris, and when she learns that her jewels are in the city, she sends her gigolo lover, Leon D'Arbout (Melvyn Douglas), to present the Russian emissaries with an injunction forbidding the sale or removal of the jewels. Leon is a suave, fast-talking con-man who depends on the favors of the Grand Duchess for his livelihood. He serves the papers, thereby dissuading a potential buyer, and then proceeds to wine and dine his comrades, as well as provide them with pretty French maids to dance with. Leon also writes an angry letter to their superior, Razini (horror film star Bela Lugosi), explaining to him what has happened to the jewels.

Razini sends an even angrier letter back to his subjects, revoking their power in the matter and cancelling all sale negotiations. He tells them that an envoy extraordinaire is being sent to take control of the situation.

The three comrades panic, fearing they are in jeopardy of being exiled to Siberia . . . or worse. They quickly move their belongings out of the Royal Suite and into the smallest, most unassuming suite in the hotel.

When they go to the train station to meet the envoy they assume will be a man, they instead meet Ninotchka (Garbo), a cold, distant, and businesslike woman. She warns them that there may be serious repercussions because of their un–Partylike behavior.

Later that night, Ninotchka decides to take a tour of the city, to study the technical advances and make a detailed report for her government. At a crosswalk, she meets Leon, who is instantly intrigued by her beauty. When he learns her nationality, Leon speaks of his fondness for the Russian people and culture. "I've been fascinated by your Five-Year-Plan for fifteen years now," he quips.

Ninotchka is unamused and continues about her business. But Leon follows her and unpredictably manages to get her alone back at his apartment. He tries to seduce her, but she overhears a telephone conversation he has with one of her comrades and realizes that Leon is in the enemy camp. Although she doesn't find his general appearance distasteful — as she tells him — she leaves his apartment and prepares to go to court over the custody of the jewels.

Leon and Ninotchka meet again, however, at a working-class restaurant. He asks her to smile, but she refuses. He, in turn, refuses to leave the restaurant until he has made her laugh. He tells a few of his best jokes, sending many of the other patrons into hysterics, but Ninotchka remains unmoved. It is not until Leon leans too far back on his chair and accidentally tumbles over that she breaks into rapturous, uncontrolled laughter.

Following this incident, Ninotchka undergoes a dramatic metamorphosis. She becomes romantically involved with Leon, dresses herself in the latest French fashions, and is still laughing while going over the court case with her lawyers. She has fallen in love, an emotion she never even knew existed before.

The Grand Duchess learns of their affair and possessively seeks to destroy it. One evening, after the lovers get a little too drunk on champagne, Swana has the jewels stolen from Ninotchka, and uses them to blackmail her into leaving Paris immediately. Ninotchka and her three subordinates glumly fly back to Russia. Leon tries to obtain a visa to go after her, but he is turned down.

Back in the U.S.S.R., Ninotchka and her comrades have a small, intimate party at her crowded apartment, where they reminisce wistfully about Paris. She receives a letter from Leon, but breaks into tears when she finds that it has been censored by the government.

"They can't censor our memories, can they?" Kopalski consoles her.

Ninotchka throws herself unsparingly into her work, but when Razini calls her in and informs her that Iranoff, Buljanoff and Kopalski have gotten themselves into trouble again — this time in Constantinople — and that she

Ninotchka (MGM). *Top:* One of the most heralded moments in motion picture history: Garbo laughs, at Melvyn Douglas's expense. *Bottom:* Greta Garbo, Melvyn Douglas and Ina Claire in a pleasantly combative scene.

must again bail them out, she pleads with him to send someone else. But he orders her to go.

When she arrives in Constantinople, her friends greet her at the airport with flowers and take her back to their lavish hotel suite. They tell her that they have decided against returning to Russia and have opened up a restaurant together. When she asks who has put them up to all of this, Leon enters the room from out on the terrace, and the lovers are reunited for good.

In the final scene, Kopalski is outside of the restaurant he co-owns, striking against his partners, in a flagrant and unashamed exhibition of democracy.

Notes: "Garbo laughs!" the ads proclaimed, giving as much weight to the advancement of her career as "Garbo talks!" had done in 1930 when she had made her first talkie, *Anna Christie*. Actually, the famous slogan was concocted even before there was a finished script, as part of a campaign to remove Garbo from her aristocratic perch and make her more accessible in the eyes of the public. The same had already been done with Katharine Hepburn and Marlene Dietrich, in order for their careers to survive. In fact, the character of Ninotchka—rigid, humorless, unaccostable—was tailored to fit Garbo's public image, and the overwhelming success of this picture boosted her career and her image immeasurably.

However, because of its overwhelming success, MGM decided to reteam Garbo and Melvyn Douglas in another social comedy, the disastrous *Two-Faced Woman,* and assigned George Cukor to direct it. Cukor disliked the title, the script, the plot, and the theme, but felt he had to obey orders. Midway through the film, he realized that he was confronted with a complete disaster, a film so ragged, repetitive and incoherent that it would have been better if everyone involved just stopped working and went home.

Garbo felt that MGM, for some unimaginable reason, had embarked upon a conspiracy to destroy her career, and she was devastated by the whole experience. The film was released shortly after Pearl Harbor and was damned by critics and moviegoers alike. To this day, it remains one of the most horrible films ever produced in the Golden Age of Cinema.

Two-Faced Woman was not intended to be Garbo's last film. She didn't think so and neither did the studio. There were always interesting comeback vehicles being discussed, among them *Madame Curie,* which the studio purchased for her but ended up starring Greer Garson. Never again would Greta Garbo return to Hollywood, despite many lucrative offers.

For the part of Leon D'Arbout in *Ninotchka,* Lubitsch originally wanted Cary Grant, and Grant (feeling it was the perfect vehicle for him) very much wanted to do it. In fact, the director was so eager to team him with Greta Garbo that his writers, Charles Brackett and Billy Wilder, were standing ready to tailor the role to the actor's exact specifications. But Grant owed his next picture after *Gunga Din* to Columbia and Harry Cohn. Since Columbia didn't own theatres as the bigger studios did, it depended on revenues from advance block bookings to cover production costs. Since exhibitors had already been promised "a Cary Grant picture," Columbia was bound by contract to deliver. Melvyn Douglas got the part of Leon, and Grant reported to Columbia to make *Plane Number Four*. (The title was later changed to *Only Angels Have Wings*.)

On September 1, about a month before *Ninotchka*'s premiere, Germany invaded Poland, prompting a declaration of war from England and France on September 3. There is a joke of mistaken identity in the film which, after its completion, was given a particularly bitter shading by the subsequent turn of events. The three members of the Russian Board of Trade, at the train station awaiting the arrival of the "envoy extraordinaire" (whom they have never met), spot a man in distinctly non–Parisian attire and assume that he's their man. Just as they are about to accost him, the man is greeted by a woman who exchanges a Nazi salute and a "Heil Hitler!" with him.

"No, that's not him," Iranoff says.

"Positively not!" Buljanoff concurs.

The intended meaning of mistaking an enemy for a comrade was given a perverse twist in which the erstwhile enemy did in fact become a comrade when in August—after the film's completion but before its release—the Soviet Union and Germany signed a non-aggression pact which, in effect, brought an end to the Popular Front.

For over a decade after its release, *Ninotchka* was the object of censorship efforts in various countries because of its unflattering portrayal of Communism. And when MGM rereleased the film in 1947—during the House Un-American Activities hearings—many witnesses in the probe hearings cited it as proof that the industry was not overridden with subversive elements, based on the movie's treatment of Communists.

Ninotchka was nominated for Best Picture, Actress and Screenplay, but lost in all three categories to *Gone with the Wind*. In the Best Original Story category, it was bested by *Mr. Smith Goes to Washington*. In the fifties, it was remade as a Fred Astaire musical called *Silk Stockings*.

Reviews: ". . . One of the sprightliest comedies of the year, a gay and impertinent and malicious show which never pulls its punch lines (no matter how far below the belt they may land) and finds the screen's austere first lady of drama playing a dead-pan comedy role with the assurance of a Buster Keaton. . . . Ernst Lubitsch . . . finally has brought the screen around to a humorist's view of those sober-sided folk who have read Marx but never the funny page. . . . In poking a derisive finger into these sober-sides, Mr. Lubitsch hasn't been entirely honest. But, then, what humorist is? He has created, instead, an amusing panel of caricatures, has read them a jocular script, has expressed—through it all—that people are much the same wherever you find them and decent enough at heart. What more could any one ask?"—Frank S. Nugent, *The New York Times*

"Probably nobody but Ernst Lubitsch could have directed this sort of comedy so lightly and skillfully. He has never in all his years of directing done anything better. His unique and clever way of handling an incident in fresh visual terms, his cinematic tropes which with loftier material would have to be called poetic (such as the masterly indirection by which he suggests the whole by showing only a part, as when we are made completely aware of what goes on behind the doors of the royal suite merely by seeing the servants in the hall outside)—this element of style which has become commonly known as the *Lubitsch touch* has never flourished so richly before."—James Shelley Hamilton—*National Board of Review Magazine*

Nurse Edith Cavell

RKO. 98 min. Directed by Herbert Wilcox.
Cast: Anna Neagle, George Sanders, May Robson, Edna May Oliver, Alan Marshal, ZaSu Pitts, H.B. Warner, Robert Coote.

Neagle gives a fine performance as the dedicated World War I nurse who was executed as a spy. Filmed previously in 1930 as *Dawn,* with Sybil Thorndike in the lead role. Anthony Collins' original score was nominated for an Academy Award.

Of Mice and Men

A United Artists Film. Produced and directed by Lewis Milestone. Screenplay by Eugene Solow. Based upon the novel and stage play by John Steinbeck. Photographed by Norbert Brodine. Edited by Bert Jordan. Art direction by Nicholai Ramisoff. Special effects by Roy Seawright. Sound by Elmer Raguse. Music by Aaron Copland. Running time: 107 minutes. Release date: December.
Cast: Burgess Meredith *George Milton;* Lon Chaney, Jr. *Lennie Small;* Betty Field *Mae;* Bob Steele *Curley;* Charles Bickford *Slim;* Roman Bohnen *Candy;* Leigh Whipper *Crooks;* Noah Beery, Jr. *Whit;* Oscar O'Shea *Jackson;* Granville Bates *Carlson;* Helen Lynd *Susie.*

> It is a beautiful job. Here Milestone has done a curious lyrical thing. It hangs together. — John Steinbeck, in a letter to his agents, upon viewing *Of Mice and Men*[51]

Synopsis: *Of Mice and Men* is the faithful screen adaptation of John Steinbeck's morality tale about a gentle but homicidal giant who has to be killed by his best friend.

It was the first film ever to employ a pre-title sequence, during which two drifters narrowly escape a sheriff's posse by hopping a freight train. The two men are George Milton (Burgess Meredith), a pint-sized man with brains, and Lennie Small (Lon Chaney, Jr.), a simpleminded giant whose fondness for soft things like rabbits can turn fatal because of his uncontrollable brute strength. Though well-meaning, Lennie has never recovered mentally from being kicked in the head by a horse years ago, and George has taken it upon himself to care for and protect the volatile child-man.

The title and credits roll as the train speeds off towards the San Joaquin Valley. En route to a barley ranch there, they spend the night in a thicket near the Salinas River. It is a safe haven, and George tells Lennie to return there if he is ever in serious danger. Lennie, meanwhile, promises not to cause any trouble for them this time.

At Lennie's insistence, George talks at length about the dream they share. Their hearts are set on settling down one day, saving their money and buying a little ranch of their own. They even have a piece of property picked out, but the $600 price tag is still way out of their range.

The following morning, the two men report for work. Their boss becomes suspicious when George does the talking for both of them. George explains that, although Lennie is not very bright, he is exceptionally strong (which Lennie proves by lifting a cart into the air while George hangs from one of its wheels). This incredible feat of strength lays all of their boss's worries to rest. It does not, however, appease his son Curley (Bob Steele), an amateur boxer who hates big guys and regularly picks fights with them.

Curley's lovely wife, Mae (Betty Field), hates her dull and unfulfilling life on the ranch. She also hates her mean, obsessively jealous husband. The only enjoyment she seems to get is in teasing and flirting with all of the ranch hands. Curley, meanwhile, is more than ready to use the leather gloves he wears on any man who responds to her sexual availability.

"She's purty," Lennie remarks after watching some of her provocative posing.

"Let her be," George warns firmly. He realizes all too well the explosiveness of the situation.

The only man on the ranch that George comes to trust is Slim (Charles Bickford), to whom he confides a bit of Lennie's history. It is during this conversation we learn that their trouble at the last ranch was caused when Lennie frightened a young girl by wanting to stroke her dress, and she accused him of attacking her sexually.

When another one of their coworkers, a one-armed swamper named Candy (Roman Bohnen), hears George and Lennie talking about their dream place, he offers to contribute the three hundred dollars he's been able to save and the fifty more he has coming in wages if they'll let him join in. Combined with their own salaries, that would make George and Lennie's dream a reality in little more than a month. They readily accept Candy's offer.

At this point, Curley comes barging into the bunkhouse, demanding to know where his wife is. Slim tells him off, and the other men join in ridiculing him. Afraid to take on any of the others, Curley lashes out furiously at Lennie, battering his face with punches.

Curley (Bob Steele) picks a fight with Lennie (Lon Chaney, Jr.) as Slim (Charles Bickford) looks on in *Of Mice and Men* (United Artists).

"Get 'im, Lennie!" George screams, and the giant responds awesomely, grabbing Curley's fist and crushing it in his enormous hand, as if it were nothing more than one of his former pets. Slim persuades Curley to claim that he caught his hand in a machine, and Lennie is safe for the time being.

Unfortunately, that time doesn't last very long. Mae realizes it was Lennie who broke her husband's hand, and she goes to him admiringly. Lennie remembers George's warning and excuses himself to go out and play in the barn with a puppy that was given to him by Slim. Mae follows him out there relentlessly and finds him with the dead puppy. He lies and tells her that the puppy tried to bite him and he in turn smacked it a little too hard. Mae consoles him, but before long she is pouring out her dreams to Lennie. She wants to leave her husband later that night, when it gets dark. Her destination is Hollywood, where she hopes to make it as a movie star. Lennie, meanwhile, is pontificating about the dream he shares with George, the ranch they're going to have and all of the rabbits. It is a hauntingly sad scene in which—through a series of insightful close-ups showing them both talking, neither one really paying attention to the other—we see the separate loneliness of their respective characters.

Mae eventually comes around to asking Lennie why he likes rabbits so much. He tells her that he likes to pet soft things. Mae responds by putting

Lennie (Lon Chaney, Jr.) and George (Burgess Meredith), with a posse on their trail, in *Of Mice and Men* (United Artists).

his hand on her hair and, though reluctant at first, Lennie begins stroking it softly, like one of his pets. When she tells him to stop or he will mess it up, he panics, and when she screams, he puts his hand over her mouth to quiet her. When he takes his hand away, Mae is dead.

Realizing the seriousness of his act, Lennie goes to the thicket near the Salinas River to hide. After borrowing a pistol from Carlson (Granville Bates), another ranch hand, George goes there as well. He arrives before the vigilante mob which has formed to hunt down and kill the giant. Instead of appearing angry, George recounts their dream to Lennie one final time, which soothes him tremendously and assuages their fears. George tells him to just look across the river and he will be able to see their place. When Lennie does so, George shoots him in the back of the head, sparing him the misery which surely awaited him.

Notes: Though tame by today's standards, John Steinbeck's *Of Mice and Men* was considered shocking material in the late 1930s, due to its language and adult subject matter. Despite the fact that it was the novelist's first big success—the book sold over 300,000 copies and the play won the New York Drama Critics' Circle Award—there were many in Hollywood who questioned whether it could be made into a movie (especially considering the rigidity of the Hays Office). In fact, Harry Cohn of Columbia had taken out an option on the property, but had let it expire because he feared the censors.

Nevertheless, director Lewis Milestone and screenwriter Eugene Solow felt that the film *had* to be made, and they did a remarkable job in bringing it to the screen. They wrote the script on "spec" (i.e., on speculation that someone would buy it from them) in only six weeks, got the daring material okayed by the Hays Office, won Steinbeck's approval, and somehow convinced Hal Roach — best known for his Laurel and Hardy films and Our Gang series — to back them financially. And this dynamic duo was just getting warmed up. They shot the film in record time (variously reported as 39 to 42 days) on a minuscule budget pegged at roughly a quarter of a million dollars. It boasted no major stars; Spencer Tracy, James Cagney and John Garfield were all eager to play the role of George, but all were unable due to prior commitments. The role eventually went to Burgess Meredith, an actor who had appeared in Broadway in a number of Maxwell Anderson plays. Lon Chaney, Jr., won the lead role over twenty-five other actors, including Broderick Crawford (who had played Lennie on the stage), and he delivered the finest performance of his career.

Milestone wanted to shoot the exteriors at the actual ranch in the Salinas Valley that Steinbeck had used as a model while writing his book. But when they found it hopelessly run down, the director had a replica built on the Hearst Agoura ranch, which was rented for $25 a day.

Steinbeck, by the by, contributed some additional dialogue to the script, which Solow later said was some of the most beautiful dialogue he had ever read. And when the author saw the finished product, he was enormously pleased with Milestone's translation.

Among the cast of "unknowns" was Bob Steele, the former B-Western star, who played the neurotic, malevolent Curley.

In 1949, Milestone, Steinbeck and composer Aaron Copland reunited to tackle the author's *The Red Pony*, with considerably less success.

Of Mice and Men was nominated for Best Picture, Best Sound Recording and Best Musical Score, but lost in all categories. Like many of the films of 1939, if it had been released in a less spectacular year, it certainly would have fared much better.

In 1981, Robert Blake fulfilled a lifetime dream by producing and starring in a remake of the film, which was made for television. The role of Lennie was played by Randy Quaid.

Reviews: "His biographers report that John Steinbeck's pet aversions are Hollywood and New York. Happily the feeling is not reciprocated. Hollywood, which brought his *The Grapes of Wrath* so magnificently to the screen, has been no less reverent toward the strangely dramatic and compassionate tale that Steinbeck called *Of Mice and Men*.... The pictures have little in common as narrative, but they have much in common as art: the same deft handling of their material, the same understanding of people, the same ability to focus interest sharply and reward it with honest craftsmanship and skill." — Frank S. Nugent, *The New York Times*

"First a novel, then a play, *Of Mice and Men* might have been written with the stage in mind: it naturally falls into scene divisions, with a lot of its drama presented in dialogue. That Lewis Milestone has broken that almost inevitable mold, rehandled the material and made it move in the flow-eddy-flow style of the screen and yet kept the essentials of events and characters true to their author's conception, is in itself a director's triumph. But he has done more than that—he has put an intensity into it, a tragic sense of doom, and a prevailing, understanding compassion, that Steinbeck, with all his violent sympathy with his creations, never quite achieved.... Steinbeck's tragedy was theatrical, Milestone and Eugene Solow's script has given it dignity, inevitability and an unusual strain of excitement. If what happens to the people is outside the universal to the point of being bizarre, the people themselves are universal in their humanness."—James Shelley Hamilton, *National Board of Review Magazine*

The Oklahoma Kid

Warner Bros. 80 min. Directed by Lloyd Bacon.

Cast: James Cagney, Humphrey Bogart, Rosemary Lane, Donald Crisp, Harvey Stephens, Hugh Sothern, Charles Middleton, Edward Pawley, Ward Bond, Lew Harvey.

Warner stock gangster cast is relocated to, of all places, the Old West. Cagney is given a ten-gallon hat and a pair of six-shooters for the journey. The studio spared no expense in bringing this one to the screen, stocking it with top-notch technical people as well as a fine cast: director Bacon (working on his ninth Cagney picture in six years), cinematographer James Wong Howe, composer Max Steiner. Although it's hard to get used to Cagney and Bogart and the others in Western garb, the film is fast-paced and contains strong performances. Cagney sings "I Don't Want to Play in Your Yard"—a number interrupted by gunfire—and "Rockabye Baby" in Spanish to an infant.

The Old Maid

A Warner Bros. Picture. Directed by Edmund Goulding. Executive producer: Hal B. Wallis. Associate producer: Henry Blanke. Screenplay by Casey Robinson. Based on the play by Zoe Akins and the novel by Edith Wharton. Photographed by Tony Gaudio. Edited by George Amy. Art direction by Robert Haas. Costumes by Orry-Kelly. Makeup by Perc Westmore. Sound by C.A. Riggs. Music by Max Steiner. Orchestral arrangements by Hugo Friedhofer. Musical director: Leo F. Forbstein. Running time: 96 minutes.

Cast: Bette Davis *Charlotte Lovell;* Miriam Hopkins *Delia Lovell;* George Brent *Clem Spender;* Jane Bryan *Tina;* Donald Crisp *Dr. Lanskell;*

Louise Fazenda *Dora;* James Stephenson *Jim Ralston;* Jerome Cowan *Joe Ralston;* William Lundigan *Lanning Halsey;* Cecilia Loftus *Grandmother Lovell;* Rand Brooks *Jim;* Janet Shaw *Dee;* DeWolf Hopper *John.*

> Miriam is a perfectly charming woman, socially. Working with her is another story. — Bette Davis, on costar Miriam Hopkins[52]

Synopsis: On the day of her wedding to wealthy socialite Jim Ralston (James Stephenson), Delia Lovell (Miriam Hopkins) receives word that her former fiancé, Clem Spender (George Brent) — who knows nothing of her impending marriage — has returned after two years of trying to make a name for himself to claim her hand. Delia's cousin Charlotte (Bette Davis) goes off to meet Clem at the train station and break the news to him.

He agrees to "behave like a gentleman," but nevertheless he is heartbroken. Charlotte slips away from Delia's wedding procession, and in her arms, Clem finds comfort. Afterwards, he joins the Union Army and goes off to fight in the Civil War, where he is killed in battle.

The story resumes four years later, in the Reconstruction period. Following a trip out West "for her health," Charlotte returns home and opens a nursery, where she cares single-handedly for stray, orphaned children. She is planning to marry Joe Ralston (Jerome Cowan), Jim's brother, who — like everyone else — wants her to give up the nursery and devote all of her time to being his wife and bearing his children. Charlotte adamantly refuses.

On the day of their wedding, Charlotte confesses the truth privately to Delia, telling her that one of the children in the nursery, a foundling named Tina, is actually her daughter, fathered by Clem Spender and born out of wedlock.

Delia's compassion turns to outrage when she learns who the father was, and she threatens to tell Joe the truth. Instead, however, she tells him that Charlotte has fallen seriously ill and therefore cannot be expected to fulfill the duties of a wife. He calls off the wedding, and Charlotte assumes that her cousin has carried out her threat.

Charlotte gives up the nursery and retreats to a solitary existence, taking only Tina with her. Several months later, though, she returns upon learning that Jim has been hurt very badly in a horseback riding accident and is near death. She is reunited with Joe, who is now married, and discovers for the first time that Delia never told him about Tina at all, but instead destroyed her only chance for happiness with a conniving lie.

Jim dies, and Charlotte and Tina eventually move into Delia's home.

Opposite: *The Old Maid* (Warner Bros.). *Top:* Charlotte (Bette Davis) and Clem (George Brent) return after stealing away to make love. *Bottom:* Delia (Miriam Hopkins, right) learns for the first time who the father of Charlotte's illegitimate daughter is, and she is outraged.

Over time, Tina begins referring to Delia as "mommy" and to her true mother as "Aunt Charlotte." The years pass, and she grows into a lovely but spoiled young woman (played by Jane Bryan). She cannot hide her contempt for Charlotte, whom she considers a bitter old maid who's never been young, never danced, and never known the love of a man.

Tina and Lanning Halsey (William Lundigan) are in love and want to be married, but his parents object fiercely to the idea. They have money and social position and do not wish to see their son marry a foundling whose heritage is a complete mystery. After Charlotte threatens to take Tina away with her and begin a new life somewhere else, Delia offers to adopt her legally and give her the influential Ralston name, making her unassailable in the eyes of society. Charlotte agrees to this, and Tina and Lanning are married.

After the ceremony, before leaving on their honeymoon together, Tina jumps down from her carriage to give her Aunt Charlotte an affectionate kiss goodbye. Then she rides off with her husband, never to know the truth about "the old maid."

Notes: In the early part of the twentieth century, Edith Wharton wrote four novellas, each of which represented a different decade of life in the nineteenth century. The real tear-jerker of the tetralogy was *The Old Maid*, the story of how two women fight a lifetime for the love of a child. In 1935, playwright Zoe Akins dramatized the story in a full-length play, which was presented at the Empire Theater in New York and won the prestigious Pulitzer Prize for Best Drama of that year. Shortly thereafter, it was purchased as a film idea by Paramount Studios. However, when they couldn't find two suitable female stars among their stable of actresses to play the lead roles, they sold the property to Hal B. Wallis of Warner Bros., who felt that it would be perfect for his studio's greatest star, Bette Davis.

For the costarring role, Miriam Hopkins was selected. Interestingly, Miss Hopkins had played the lead female role in the stage version of *Jezebel*, which had flopped on Broadway (the same role Miss Davis played in the 1938 screen version and for which she won her second Academy Award). Whether for this or more personal reasons, Hopkins hated Davis, and the first day of principal photography set the tone for the entire shoot. Hopkins showed up wearing a costume which Davis had worn in *Jezebel*, and the battle lines were drawn.

From that point on, Hopkins did everything she could to unnerve Davis. She constantly complained about her dialogue, forcing Casey Robinson to return from a desert vacation for rewrites; she purposely ruined many of Davis's best takes; and she seemed to have a new trick up her sleeve every day designed solely to rattle the star. Things got so bad that, at one point, when a spotlight accidentally fell from a catwalk and missed hitting Bette Davis by a few inches, she glared accusingly at Hopkins. A pale Hopkins retorted, "I didn't do that!"

When filming was finally completed, Davis swore that she would never work with the problematical actress again, a vow she would break in 1943 when the two were reteamed in *Old Acquaintance.*

For the part of Clem Spender, the romantic hero, Humphrey Bogart was chosen. However, after only two days of shooting, he looked so thin, pale and thoroughly unromantic that Jack Warner demanded he be fired from the project. Director Goulding and producer Wallis got the dirty job of breaking the news to Bogie, who merely shrugged and walked off the set when told. George Brent was brought in to take his place.

Reviews: "The reproduction of the atmosphere and manners and morals of its genteel period is just about perfect, and inherent in that perfection is a quietness, even drabness, strikingly out of time with what usually constitutes entertainment these days."—James Shelley Hamilton, *National Board of Review Magazine*

"Once again Bette Davis has to suffer, but it's suffering in an entirely good cause, for *The Old Maid* is most decidedly going to be one of the best pictures. ... This is one of Bette Davis' outstanding performances."— Lionel Collier, *Picturegoer*

On Borrowed Time

MGM. 99 min. Directed by Harold S. Bucquet.

Cast: Lionel Barrymore, Sir Cedric Hardwicke, Beulah Bondi, Una Merkel, Bobs Watson, Nat Pendleton, Henry Travers, Grant Mitchell, Eily Malyon.

By the late 1930s, Lionel Barrymore's inflammatory rheumatism had reduced him to living and working from a wheelchair. He performed in almost constant pain, especially in the scenes in which he was required to stand. In order to keep him working steadily and reduce some of the pain, he was regularly administered cocaine at the studio infirmary. And whenever the dosage exceeded legal limits, Louis B. Mayer saw to it that an adequate supply was obtained, with the studio absorbing the cost. In 1939, MGM publicity announced that Barrymore would walk in his upcoming picture, *On Borrowed Time.* In fact, the actor was able to stand for only one scene, the final one in the picture, while a moving backdrop created the illusion of walking. In the rather hokey and dated film, Barrymore plays an old man who chases Death (in the form of Sir Cedric Hardwicke) up a tree and keeps him there, hoping to prolong the inevitable. Though confined to the wheelchair for most of the movie, he was still able to deliver one of his finest and most sensitive screen portrayals.

Only Angels Have Wings

A Columbia Picture. Produced and directed by Howard Hawks. Screenplay by Jules Furthman. From an original story by Howard Hawks.

Photographed by Joseph Walker. Aerial photography by Elmer Dyer. Edited by Viola Lawrence. Special effects by Roy Davidson and Edwin C. Hahn. Music by Dmitri Tiomkin. Art direction by Lionel Banks. Costumes by Kalloch. Technical adviser and chief pilot: Paul Mantz. Running time: 121 minutes. Release date: May 25.

Cast: Cary Grant *Jeff Carter;* Jean Arthur *Bonnie Lee;* Richard Barthelmess *Bat McPherson;* Rita Hayworth *Judith;* Thomas Mitchell *Kid Dabb;* Sig Ruman *Dutchman;* Victor Kilian *Sparks;* John Carrol *Gent Shelton;* Allyn Joslyn *Les Peters;* Donald Barry *Tex Gordon;* Noah Beery, Jr. *Joe Souther;* Melissa Sierra *Lily;* Lucio Villegas *Dr. Lagorio;* Forbes Murray *Hartwood;* Maciste *The Singer;* Pat Flaherty *Mike;* Pedro Regas *Pancho;* Pat West *Baldy.*

> I knew every character in the picture. I knew how they thought and how they talked. Some critics said I went too far in the film, but there wasn't a single scene in the whole film that wasn't real.—Howard Hawks[53]

Synopsis: If director Howard Hawks' original story for *Only Angels Have Wings* was one former aviator's homage to the good old days, then the resulting film is, or seems to be, his personal view on the way life *should* be. It is a two-fisted morality tale filled with real men engaged in a dangerous and demanding task (no quiche here, strictly meat and potatoes), beautiful but headstrong women, and the director's trademark three-cushion dialogue. Everyone is noble, everyone heroic, and even when they go astray, they invariably make the right decision in the end.

The movie takes place in Barranca, a "port of call for the South American banana boats." As it opens, one of these boats is pulling in to dock, where Les Peters (Allyn Joslyn) and Joe Souther (Noah Beery, Jr.) are waiting expectantly for new females to conquer.

When Brooklynite Bonnie Lee (Jean Arthur) walks down the plank, they are both captivated by her quirky beauty. After trailing her through the streets of Barranca for some time, they introduce themselves, and when she learns that they are fellow Americans, she agrees to go to the local bar with them and have a drink.

At the bar, Les and Joe good-naturedly compete for Bonnie Lee's attention and affections. They tell her that they're both mail fliers and that one of them must go up in the inclement weather that evening. They toss a coin to determine who has to fly the mail out and who gets to stay and buy Bonnie Lee a steak dinner. Joe wins and gleefully orders the steaks.

But when their boss, Jeff Carter (Cary Grant), arrives on the scene, all of their plans are altered. He orders Joe up and sends Les out on an all-night job.

"When did you decide that?" Les demands to know.

"Just now," Jeff retorts, eyeing Bonnie Lee lasciviously.

Shortly after takeoff, Joe encounters a thick fog bank and is forced

When Jeff Carter (Cary Grant) and fellow pilots joke and laugh together after one . of their friends has been killed, they are confronted by an angry Bonnie Lee (Jean Arthur) in *Only Angels Have Wings* (Columbia).

to turn around and return to Barranca. He tries to land but, unable to see the runway, scrapes some treetops and nearly crashes. Jeff—who is trying to talk him down—orders him to forget about attempting a second pass at the runway and remain in the sky until the fog lifts. But Joe is determined to have that steak dinner with Bonnie, so he disobeys Jeff's order and, on his next try, crashes and dies.

A few minutes later, back in the bar, Bonnie is appalled when Jeff and some of the other fliers are laughing and joking and pretending that they never knew anyone named Joe.

When she bursts into tears and runs off crying, Jeff follows her and explains that they all feel much worse about Joe's death than she does, but all of the mourning in the world isn't going to bring him back.

Bonnie is already becoming attached to Jeff, but The Kid (Thomas Mitchell), a flier for twenty-two years and Jeff's best friend, warns her off, claiming that he's nothing but trouble for the fainthearted fairer sex.

She eventually returns to the bar and joins in on the party being thrown there. Later that night, alone with her in the bar, Jeff tells her about the girl from his past who left him because of his high-risk profession and broke his heart. He is doing the same thing that The Kid tried to do: warn her off. But she's not buying.

The fog lifts and, when The Kid informs him that it's still "nobody's picnic," Jeff kisses Bonnie farewell, wishes her a safe trip back to America, and departs.

"Say, things happen awful fast around here!" Bonnie Lee observes.

When Jeff returns the following day, he is surprised to find Bonnie waiting for him in the bar where he left her, having breakfast. He tells her that he doesn't want to get burned in the same place twice and orders her to be on the next boat home, which leaves in another week.

A new flier arrives, introducing himself as Bat McPherson (Richard Barthelmess), but Jeff recognizes him as Bat Kilgallon, a flier who bailed out of his plane and left his mechanic behind to die. The mechanic who perished in that crash was The Kid's younger brother, and when McPherson returns from a flight, The Kid warns him to stay out of his way.

When McPherson introduces his wife, Judith (Rita Hayworth), to the other men, they treat her respectfully and mention nothing about her husband's reputation.

Despite protests from his fliers, Jeff gives McPherson an assignment. It is a treacherous trip up into the mountains, taking a doctor up to a secluded mine to attend to a boy who has been badly hurt, but McPherson—eager for work—readily accepts.

While he is gone, he confronts Judy, who we learn (as does Bonnie) is the woman from his past, though unbeknownst to her husband. He also gives The Kid an eye examination, which confirms what he has suspected for some time: that The Kid is losing his eyesight. Jeff grounds him permanently, but promises that there will always be office work for him to do.

Desperately short of pilots, and with an important contract and subsidy hanging in the balance, Jeff officially hires McPherson upon his return, promising him all of the most difficult and dangerous assignments. Claiming he'd have it no other way, McPherson signs on. He soon learns that Jeff wasn't kidding about the clause in his contract when he is ordered to fly a planeload of nitroglycerin up into the mountains.

After he leaves, Judy goes to Jeff and implores to know why her husband is always given such perilous jobs and why the other pilots refuse to socialize with him. Through Jeff, she comes to realize that her husband's past doesn't really matter to her (no more than hers matters to him); all that matters is that they love each other and can be together.

A few days later, Jeff prepares to take an untested plane up into a heavy storm, and The Kid cajoles him into letting him serve as his copilot. But Bonnie, in a desperate act of passion, steals Jeff's gun from him and tries to stop him from going, unsuccessfully. She stops him *successfully*, though, when she throws the gun down and it accidentally goes off, hitting Jeff in the shoulder.

McPherson volunteers to replace Jeff, and he and The Kid take the plane up together. When a bird crashes through their windshield and immobilizes The Kid, he exhorts McPherson to bail out while he has the chance.

"Not this time!" McPherson says.

He lands the burning plane, suffering third-degree burns on his face

Former flame Judith (Rita Hayworth, left) and current one Bonnie Lee (Jean Arthur) vie for the attention of Jeff Carter (Cary Grant) in *Only Angels Have Wings* (Columbia).

and hands. The Kid, however, is not so fortunate. His neck is broken and—after asking Jeff to buy McPherson a drink for him—he passes away.

McPherson gets accepted by the other fliers, Bonnie Lee gets Jeff, and life goes on frenziedly in the little republic of Barranca.

Notes: After finishing his *Gunga Din* duties, Cary Grant had his heart set on playing opposite Greta Garbo in Ernst Lubitsch's Communism spoof, *Ninotchka*. However, he contractually owed his next picture to Harry Cohn at Columbia, so he was forced instead to report to the set of what was then titled *Plane Number Four*, which sounded suspiciously like another of those aviation programmers from his Paramount days. Whatever doubts and fears he harbored, though, were put to rest when he learned that Howard Hawks (who had directed him the year before in *Bringing Up Baby* and would direct him the following year in *His Girl Friday*), would be running the show.

Plane Number Four—which would soon be renamed *Only Angels Have Wings*—was based on Hawks' own experience as a flier. He had known a pilot who parachuted from a burning plane, leaving his copilot behind to die in the ensuing crash. Spending the rest of his life shunned by other pilots, the man was finally killed in an attempt to redeem himself.

This film was an important showcase for Harry Cohn's latest discovery, a stunningly beautiful unknown named Rita Hayworth. Hawks had developed a reputation for being very helpful to new actresses, so Cohn cast her in the picture's second female lead, as a woman bored with her husband, and told Hawks to "make her a star." This was no simple task. At this point in her career, Miss Hayworth was extremely self-conscious, not at all spontaneous, and—worst of all—not a particularly good actress. So Hawks and Grant did the only thing they could do: they improvised.

For one interior scene, Hayworth was supposed to cry, but it just wasn't happening. A lunch break was called during which the two men conferred. When shooting resumed, the scene was moved outdoors and a rain machine was brought in. Hayworth was so soaking wet, you couldn't tell if it was tears or rain on her face.

In another scene, Hawks couldn't get the right reaction from Hayworth, so once again he and his star conferred. They decided that Grant should suddenly pour a jug of iced water over Hayworth's head without telling her they were going to do it. Hawks got the reaction he wanted.

On another occasion, Hayworth was supposed to be drunk, but she couldn't get her lines right. Finally, Grant suggested that she simply sag down and he would in effect do his lines and hers, too. It worked. Critics later gave her kudos for playing a great drunk scene and Cohn gave Hawks the keys to a brand-new car, as a token of his appreciation. "He gave me a car and I gave him a star,"[54] Hawks commented.

As for Cary Grant, it's easy to see why Sidney Sheldon, when accepting the Academy Award for his original screenplay of *The Bachelor and the Bobby Soxer* (1947), said that Grant had won more Oscars for other people than any actor in the history of the medium.

Only Angels Have Wings was nominated for Best Cinematography (in black-and-white) and Best Special Effects, for the spectacular aerial footage, but it lost in both categories. There was a proposed remake in 1949, to be titled *Count Three and Pray*—with an all-girl cast!—but fortunately it never materialized.

Reviews: "This year's output of aviation films subtracts none of the vigor and little of the freshness from *Only Angels Have Wings*. More than a year in production, and coming at the tail end of an overworked screen cycle, this Columbia film easily outranks most of its plane-crashing, sky-spectacular predecessors."—*Newsweek*

"Howard Hawks has had an uneven if successful career, but he directed the best of all airplane movies, *Ceiling Zero*, and it is too bad he and an above-average cast had to be wasted on a story of *Only Angels Have Wings*. . . . The atmosphere was right to start with . . . . In the minor things, where the ridiculous or the stereotype didn't intrude, there was a swell realization of their personalities, of friendship and banter and weariness and trouble. Howard Hawks can be faultless in a sense of how to speed up a situation, or make it flexible and easy with the right emphasis, grouping, understatement. In fact, all these people did the best they could with what they were given—but look at it. The battle with mechanics and the elements, in this as in other art films, provides suspense all right; but so does hanging."—Otis Ferguson, *The New Republic*

Paris Honeymoon

Paramount. 92 min. Directed by Frank Tuttle.
Cast: Bing Crosby, Franciska Gaal, Shirley Ross, Akim Tamiroff, Edward Everett Horton, Ben Blue, Rafaela Ottiano, Gregory Gaye, Alex Melesh.

In this agreeable Bing Crosby outing, the crooner plays a Texas millionaire who travels to Europe to marry the equally wealthy countess Ross, but along the way falls for beautiful peasant girl Gaal. Songs include "I Have Eyes," "Joobalai" and "The Maiden by the Brook."

The Private Lives of Elizabeth and Essex

A Warner Bros. Picture. Directed by Michael Curtiz. Executive producer: Hal B. Wallis. Associate producer: Robert Lord. Screenplay by Norman Reilly Raine and Aeneas MacKenzie. From the stage play by Maxwell Anderson (as produced by The Theatre Guild, Inc.). Photographed by Sol Polito; Associate: W. Howard Greene. Edited by Owen Marks. Art direction by Anton Grot. Makeup by Perc Westmore. Music by Erich Wolfgang Korngold. Musical director: Leo F. Forbstein. Orchestrations by Hugo Friedhofer and Milan Roder. Sound by C.A. Riggs. Costumes by Orry-Kelly. Dialogue director: Stanley Logan. Special effects by Byron Haskin and H.E. Koenekamp. For the Technicolor Company: Natalie Kalmus, Color Director; Morgan Padelford, Associate. Assistant director: Sherry Shrouds. Technical adviser: Ali Hubert. Sound by Nathan Levinson. Running time: 106 minutes.

Cast: Bette Davis *Queen Elizabeth;* Errol Flynn *Robert Devereux, Earl of Essex;* Olivia de Havilland *Lady Penelope Gray;* Donald Crisp *Francis Bacon;* Alan Hale *Earl of Tyrone;* Vincent Price *Sir Walter Raleigh;* Henry Stephenson *Lord Burghley;* Henry Daniell *Sir Robert Cecil;* James Stephenson *Sir Thomas Egerton;* Nanette Fabares (later changed to Nanette Fabray) *Mistress Margaret Radcliffe;* Ralph Forbes *Lord Knollys;* Robert Warwick *Lord Mountjoy;* Leo G. Carroll *Sir Edward Coke.*

It wasn't a very pleasant picture to make.—Errol Flynn[55]

Synopsis: The year 1939 was not without its turkeys, and the expensive, colorful and ambitious costume drama *The Private Lives of Elizabeth and Essex* was certainly—and quite unfortunately—among them.

The Earl of Essex (Errol Flynn) defends himself from accusers as Queen Elizabeth (Bette Davis) looks on interestedly in *The Private Lives of Elizabeth and Essex* (Warner Bros.).

It concerns the aging Queen Elizabeth (Bette Davis) and her love for the dashing young Earl of Essex (Errol Flynn). When Essex returns from defeating the Spanish at Cadiz, he is hailed as a hero. But Elizabeth — outraged that he chose personal glory over the security of Spain's treasures, which were sunk by the Spanish themselves during the battle — rebukes Essex in front of her whole court at Whitehall Palace. And then, to add insult to injury, she promotes Sir Walter Raleigh (Vincent Price), an old enemy of Essex, to Commander of the Guard. Essex returns insult for insult, calling Elizabeth a "king in petticoats" and storming furiously out of the palace.

He retreats to Wanstead, his ancestral home northeast of London, where he remains until the queen orders him back and appoints him Master of the Ordinance in England's war with Ireland and the rebellious Earl of Tyrone (Alan Hale). It's a post that will keep him in London and out of combat, but Essex is duped at a council meeting into boasting that he can defeat Tyrone, and nothing Elizabeth says or does can stop him from leaving for Ireland.

While at war, Essex sends letter after letter back to Elizabeth, pleading urgently for her to send more men and supplies. But a conspiracy within the palace has stopped all correspondence from reaching the queen.

Essex is defeated by Tyrone, a loss he blames entirely on Elizabeth. He assembles a new army and seizes Whitehall Palace, determined to depose the queen and claim the throne for himself. Elizabeth pretends to comply with his revolt, the volatile lovers reconcile again, and Essex disbands his forces. As soon as he does, Elizabeth has him arrested for treason, tried and sentenced to death.

Before his execution, though, she offers to spare his life if he'll agree to share the throne with her. But that's not good enough for the stubborn Essex, who wants all of England for himself or nothing. He is taken directly from her chambers to the chopping block, where the sound of rolling drums turns into a moment of silence, and a heartbroken Elizabeth knows that the executioner's axe has fallen upon her beloved.

Notes: In 1938, Errol Flynn had a major hit with *The Adventures of Robin Hood* and was quickly establishing himself as Hollywood's premiere swashbuckler. Jack Warner—always ready to capitalize on a popular trend—was looking for another costume piece to put him in. That same year, Bette Davis won an Academy Award for her performance in *Jezebel.* She had been fighting bitterly with Warner for better roles and scripts, hoping to do a serious character study in lieu of straight drama. Thus, the ideal vehicle for both seemed to be an adaptation of Maxwell Anderson's *Elizabeth the Queen*, the first in his trio of Tudor plays (the other two were *Mary of Scotland* and *Anne of a Thousand Days*).

However, the relationship between Davis and Flynn was anything but ideal. He considered her arrogant, she considered him flighty and unprofessional, and they clashed frequently and furiously during the making of the picture.

It began in pre-production, when Flynn suggested that the title of the film be changed from *Elizabeth the Queen* to something which acknowledged his half of the story. When the studio came up with *The Knight and the Lady,* he was elated, but Miss Davis threatened to walk off the picture. To appease all parties involved, *The Private Lives of Elizabeth and Essex* was finally chosen.

The feud carried over to the shooting of the film. Davis nearly broke Flynn's jaw in a scene in which she strikes him with a fist full of heavy rings; he retaliated by slapping her on the fanny during one of their love scenes and, according to his own account, lifting her several feet off the ground.

When David O. Selznick was trying to cast his epic *Gone with the Wind,* he at one point took it to Warner Bros. as part of a package that would include Bette Davis and Errol Flynn as Scarlett and Rhett. However, the deal fell through because Davis refused ever to work with Flynn again after her experiences making *The Private Lives of Elizabeth and Essex.*

This ongoing battle did not deter Miss Davis from preparing for the role she was to play. To be convincing as the middle-aged queen, she had her hairline shaved back three inches, her eyebrows completely removed and replaced by thinly penciled lines, her lips made to seem fuller, her features covered by a pasty white makeup base, and pouches drawn under her eyes. Flynn, on the other hand, could not devote himself so thoroughly

Queen Elizabeth (Bette Davis) and the Earl of Essex (Errol Flynn) clown around together in *The Private Lives of Elizabeth and Essex* (Warner Bros.). Behind the scenes, things weren't quite so jovial.

to a picture (and a costar) for which he could not conceal his distaste. He simply walks through the picture. And in one scene in which he must declare his eternal love for Elizabeth, it seems all he can do from breaking into hysterics is smirk with disbelief at his own words. Accordingly, Bette Davis's performance was uniformly hailed by critics upon release of the movie, and Flynn's was uniformly panned.

The Private Lives of Elizabeth and Essex was nominated for Best Color Photography, Interior Decoration, Sound Recording, Musical Score, and Special Effects, but lost in all categories.

Reviews: "It's Queen Bette's picture just as surely as Mr. Flynn is a good-looking young man who should be asked to do no more in pictures than flash an even-toothed smile and present a firm jaw-line. His Essex lacked a head long before the headsman got around to him. . . . It is a good film, one well worth seeing; how much better it might have been with an Essex worthy of Miss Davis's Elizabeth we can only surmise."—Frank S. Nugent, *The New York Times*

"Productionally, picture is important, rating with the best historical film documents turned out by Warners. . . . [It] has its slow spots, particularly the excursion of Essex to Ireland to subdue Tyrone. At times the dialog becomes brittle, and direction grooves into stagey passages that could have been lightened by greater movement allowed by the camera. Minor shortcomings, however, in the general excellence of the production."—*Variety*

Q Planes

Harefield, London Films, England. 82 min. Directed by Tim Whelan. Cast: Laurence Olivier, Ralph Richardson, Valerie Hobson, George Curzon, George Merritt, Gus McNaughton, David Tree, Sandra Storme, Hay Petrie, Frank Fox.

Olivier plays a test pilot at an airplane factory where planes have been mysteriously disappearing in this delightful tongue-in-cheek espionage yarn. Curzon plays the confidential secretary to the factory manager, who is responsible for secreting the planes onto a ship during their proving flights. And Richardson is a standout as the easy-going alcoholic inspector who cracks the case in the end. Released in America as *Clouds Over Europe*.

Raffles

Samuel Goldwyn Co. 72 min. Directed by Sam Wood and William Wyler.

Cast: David Niven, Olivia de Havilland, Dame May Whitty, Dudley Digges, Douglas Walton, Lionel Pape, E.E. Clive, Peter Godfrey, Margaret Seddon, Gilbert Emery.

This story, which tells of an aristocratic cricket player who by night is a notorious safecracker and thief, was a virtual scene-for-scene remake of a 1930 Goldwyn production that featured Ronald Colman in the title role. Earlier versions included one in 1917 starring John Barrymore and another in 1925 starring House Peters. It was a part that David Niven desperately wanted to play and, with the actor's contract coming up for renewal, one which Goldwyn dangled teasingly before his eyes. Niven settled his differences with his autocratic boss and signed a new contract with him. Not long after starring in *Raffles*, though, Niven was off for his homeland of England and service in World War II, putting his acting career on indefinite hold.

The Rains Came

A Twentieth Century–Fox Picture. Directed by Clarence Brown. Executive producer: Darryl F. Zanuck. Associate producer: Harry Joe Brown. Screenplay by Philip Dunne and Julien Josephson. Based on the novel by Louis Bromfield. Photographed by Arthur Miller. Edited by Barbara McLean. Art direction by William Darling and George Dudley. Set decorations by Thomas Little. Special effects by E.H. Hansen and Fred Sersen. Costumes by Gwen Wakeling. Music by Alfred Newman. Title song by Mack Gordon and Harry Revel. Sound by E.H. Hansen, Alfred Bruzlin and Roger Heman. Running time: 103 minutes.

Cast: Myrna Loy *Lady Edwina Esketh;* Tyrone Power *Major Rama Safti;* George Brent *Tom Ransome;* Brenda Joyce *Fern Simon;* Maria Ouspenskaya *Maharani;* Nigel Bruce *Lord Albert Esketh;* Joseph Schildkraut *Mr. Bannerjee;* Mary Nash *Miss McDaid;* Jane Darwell *Aunt Phoebe Smiley;* Marjorie Rambeau *Mrs. Simon;* Henry Travers *Rev. Homer Smiley;* H.B. Warner *Maharajah;* Laura Hope Crews *Lily Hoggett-Egbury;* William Royle *Raschid Ali Kahn;* Montague Shaw *General Keith;* Harry Hayden *Rev. Elmer Simon;* Herbert Evans *Bates;* Abner Biberman *John the Baptist;* Mara Alexander *Mrs. Bannerjee;* William Edmunds *Mr. Das.*

> I loved him, but he was married to that damn Frenchwoman! — Myrna Loy on costar Tyrone Power[56]

Synopsis: Like David O. Selznick, Darryl Zanuck was sparing no expense in bringing an epic best-seller to the screen in 1939. Zanuck's choice was Louis Bromfield's mammoth 1937 novel *The Rains Came*, which told the story of a love affair played against the backdrop of an earthquake, flood, fire and plague. It wasn't the runaway blockbuster that *Gone with the Wind* turned out to be, but it does contain one of the most incredible natural disaster scenes ever captured on celluloid.

A tinted-skinned Tyrone Power stars as American-educated Hindu surgeon Rama Safti, who has been raised by the Maharajah of Ranchipur (H.B. Warner) and his wife, the Maharani (Maria Ouspenskaya), both as a son and as a future leader of India. Upon returning home from America, Rama opens a clinic and works indefatigably for the impoverished people of his country. An old friend, wastrel Tom Ransome (George Brent), has settled in Ranchipur as well, where he continues his life of drinking and cavorting. He spurns the affections of lovely young Fern Simon (Brenda Joyce), a missionary's daughter who — at the behest of her social-climbing mother (Marjorie Rambeau) — has thrown herself shamelessly at him, and instead makes a play for his old flame, Lady Edwina Esketh (Myrna Loy). The callous Lady Edwina has married Lord Esketh (Nigel Bruce), a wealthy industrialist, solely for his money and has been involved in an endless series of meaningless affairs. She now has her sights on the charismatic Rama Safti, and before long, the two are involved in a passionate love affair. At first, she views Rama as just another sexual conquest, but as time passes, she becomes consumed by the doctor's integrity and devotion to his work. The two end up falling madly in love with each other.

Mother Nature herself disrupts all of the foreplay and interplay when an earthquake and flood wreak havoc on Ranchipur, killing thousands of people. Among the casualties are Lord Esketh and the Maharajah.

In the wake of the destruction, an outbreak of malaria sweeps across the land, killing people just as indiscriminately as the natural disasters did. A reformed Lady Edwina works tirelessly as a nurse at Rama's clinic, doing whatever she can to help. The Maharani, aware that Rama will be chosen to

The Rains Came (Twentieth Century–Fox). *Top:* The flood and earthquake sequence that won the 1939 Academy Award for Best Special Effects. *Bottom:* Rama Safti (Tyrone Power) and Lady Edwina Esketh (Myrna Loy) work at the hospital together, but still find the time for romance.

replace her deceased husband as the leader of India, tries to enlist Tom's aid in sending Edwina away. She also tries to arrange a marriage between her son and Fern Simon.

Edwina refuses to leave Ranchipur, more determined than ever to marry Rama. At the clinic, though, she inadvertently drinks from a malaria victim's glass, falls ill and dies. Before passing away, she learns to her joy that the love she feels for Rama is reciprocated.

In the end, Rama marries Fern and assumes his rightful place as the leader of his people.

Notes: By the time that *The Rains Came* was released, Tyrone Power was the second biggest box-office draw in the country, trailing only "Andy Hardy" himself, Mickey Rooney, in popularity. Darryl Zanuck bought Louis Bromfield's book and, though the film was shot entirely within Fox's studio walls, still invested $2 million in the project just to provide his fast-rising young star with a suitable vehicle. Shortly before filming began, Power married French-born actress Annabella—his costar from *Suez* (1938)—and as soon as final retakes were completed, the two went on a long-delayed honeymoon.

A slew of Hollywood leading ladies campaigned for the role of Lady Edwina, but Zanuck ended up borrowing Myrna Loy from MGM for the part. Zanuck had fired Miss Loy years earlier after casting her as a vamp in a series of trivial Fox pictures. She went to MGM and became the most popular leading leady in the country as the very domesticated Mrs. Charles in the immensely popular *Thin Man* series. Despite her perfect wife image, Zanuck once again cast her as the vamp.

Miss Loy insisted that "her director," Clarence Brown, be borrowed as well from Metro, and Zanuck obliged.

For the second female lead role of Fern Simon, Zanuck considered and tested several of his studio's budding starlets, including at one point Lana Turner, but passed them all over in favor of Brenda Joyce, who made her film debut in the movie. Ironically, Lana Turner would be cast in the lead female role of Lady Edwina in 1955 when Fox remade the film as *The Rains of Ranchipur*.

The Rains Came was nominated for Best Score, Art Direction, Editing, Sound, and Special Effects. The only Oscar it captured was the last, for the film's extraordinary earthquake and flood sequences.

Reviews: "As entertainment, *The Rains Came* suffers from the fact that it uses its salvo of disasters not to solve the problems of its characters but to heighten them. Since these characters to begin with are as slick and typical a pack as ever cavorted through a Louis Bromfield serial in Cosmopolitan, after the rain they seem sadly washed out and anticlimactic."—Frank S. Nugent, *The New York Times*

"As the doctor, Tyrone Power plays with skill and restraint. When he and Miss Loy are together on the screen, *The Rains Came* has considerable emotional power."—Howard Barnes, *The New York Herald Tribune*

The Real Glory

United Artists. 95 min. Directed by Henry Hathaway.

Cast: Gary Cooper, Andrea Leeds, David Niven, Reginald Owen, Broderick Crawford, Kay Johnson, Charles Waldron, Russell Hicks, Roy Gordon.

Following the Spanish-American War, doctor Cooper and soldier of fortune pals Niven and Crawford try to quell a Moro uprising in the Philippine Islands, as well as battle an outbreak of cholera.

The Return of Doctor X

Warner Bros. 62 min. Directed by Vincent Sherman.

Cast: Wayne Morris, Rosemary Lane, Humphrey Bogart, Dennis Morgan, John Litel, Lya Lys, Huntz Hall, Charles Wilson, Vera Lewis.

A futile attempt to capitalize on the success of Warners' earlier horror classic *Doctor X* (1932). Bogart had been arguing for better roles and more money, and casting him in this awful film as a smirking, pasty-faced vampire with a white streak through his hair was undoubtedly Jack Warner's way of punishing him. Although it is hard to believe, judging from pictures like this one, Bogie was only two years away from his film breakthrough (with performances in *The Maltese Falcon* and *High Sierra* in '41), when he could finally put these turkeys behind him and turn the tables on Mr. Warner.

The Roaring Twenties

A Warner Bros. Picture. Directed by Raoul Walsh and (uncredited) Anatole Litvak. Executive producer: Hal B. Wallis. Associate producer: Samuel Bischoff. Screenplay by Jerry Wald, Richard Macauley, and Robert Rossen. Story by Mark Hellinger. Photographed by Ernest Haller. Edited by Jack Killifer. Art direction by Max Parker. Music by Heinz Roemheld and Ray Heindorf. Costumes by Milo Anderson. Asst. director: Dick Mayberry. Makeup by Perc Westmore. Sound by Everett A. Brown. Dialogue director: Hugh Cummings. Special effects by Byron Haskin and Edwin DuPar. Running time: 104 minutes. Release date: October 28.

Songs: "My Melancholy Baby" by Ernie Burnett and George A. Norton; "I'm Just Wild About Harry" by Eubie Blake and Noble Sissle; "It Had to Be You" by Isham Jones and Gus Kahn; "In a Shanty in Old Shanty Town" by Jack Little, Joseph Young, and John Siras.

Cast: James Cagney *Eddie Bartlett;* Priscilla Lane *Jean Sherman;* Humphrey Bogart *George Hally;* Jeffrey Lynn *Lloyd Hart;* Gladys George *Panama Smith;* Frank McHugh *Danny Green;* Paul Kelly *Nick Brown;* Elizabeth Risdon *Mrs. Sherman;* Ed Keane *Pete Henderson;* Joseph Sawyer

Sgt. Pete Jones; Abner Biberman *Lefty;* George Humbert *Luigi the proprietor;* Clay Clement *Bramfield the broker;* Don Thaddeus Kerr *Bobby Hart;* Ray Cooke *Orderly;* Robert Dobson *Lieutenant;* John Harron *Soldier;* Vera Lewis *Mrs. Gray;* Murray Alper and Dick Wessel *Mechanics;* Joseph Crehan *Fletcher the foreman;* Norman Willis *Bootlegger;* Eddie Acuff, Milton Kibbee, and John Ridgely *Cab drivers;* Ann Codee *Salesgirl;* Jack Norton *Drunk;* Nat Carr *Policeman.*

> Raoul Walsh never spoke to the actors, and if he did, whatever he said was incomprehensible. — William Cagney[57]

Synopsis: *The Roaring Twenties* was Hollywood's first critical look back at the jazz decade (by men who lived through it), and the last of the great gangster films of the 1930s.

It begins during the final days of World War I, where three American soldiers, Eddie Bartlett (James Cagney), George Hally (Humphrey Bogart), and Lloyd Hart (Jeffrey Lynn), become friends in the European trenches. When the Armistice is signed, the trio part company and return home to resume their lives.

Eddie looks up an old pal, Danny Green (Frank McHugh), a cab driver, as well as a girl, Jean Sherman (Priscilla Lane), who had written him while he was in France but whom he never met. When he discovers that she is a schoolgirl still living at home with her mother and doing well in algebra — and that her letters were part of a school assignment — he politely excuses himself and returns home.

Next he returns to the garage where he worked as an auto mechanic before being drafted for service, but to his dismay he learns that his job has been filled and there are no current openings. Over the following weeks, he pounds the pavement looking for suitable employment but learns that employers are reluctant to hire a returning veteran. Danny offers him the use of his cab during the half of the day that he isn't using it, and Eddie has no choice but to accept.

When one of his fares asks him to deliver a package for him — which he doesn't know contains two bottles of whiskey — Eddie obliges without question. But when he hands the package over to Panama Smith (Gladys George), the police apprehend him and arrest him on violation of the Volstead Act. Both he and Panama are taken downtown.

Panama, considering him a "decent guy," bails him out of jail and takes him to a speakeasy, where he is introduced to the booming liquor industry. Before long, Eddie and Danny are stirring up their own "bathtub gin" and selling it as fine, imported liquor. When profits increase, he buys a fleet of cabs to serve as a front and transport the booze he is making. And when his business expands, he hires his old friend from the war, Lloyd Hart, as his attorney. Lloyd is very idealistic and doesn't like the profession Eddie has chosen; he advises him to get out of it and go straight. But Eddie has tried the other way, to no avail.

When he goes to a theatre to collect from a problematical customer, he meets Jean Sherman again, who is dancing in the chorus line. The three years since their first encounter have been kind to Jean. She is now a very beautiful young woman, and Eddie is hooked almost immediately.

They go out on a date and she confesses to him that she aspires to be a musical comedy star. To get her career started, he takes her to a prominent nightclub where Panama is working as the hostess and arranges an audition for the owner of the club, Pete Henderson (Ed Keane). Henderson can't use her, but Eddie forces him to hire her nevertheless, and pay her an exorbitant salary as well, which Eddie agrees to secretly reimburse him.

At her premiere the following week, Eddie stacks the house in her favor the way a spotted deck of cards is stacked for the dealer, and she is given a warm reception. Afterwards, in her dressing room, he asks her to marry him. Jean is very grateful for everything he has done for her and does not want to hurt him, but his love for her is not reciprocated. When she hedges, Eddie assumes it's because of his racket and vows to be completely legitimate in a few years' time, at which time they can be married.

On the business front, the activities of gangster Nick Brown (Paul Kelly) are cutting into Eddie's profits, so Eddie leads a crew of men disguised as Coast Guard patrolmen out to sea, where they hijack one of Brown's shipments. When the captain of the aforementioned vessel turns out to be Eddie's other old friend from the war, George Hally, the two men form an unlikely partnership (based on the premise that neither one trusts the other) and join their combined forces to battle Nick Brown.

They inform federal agents when Brown is running a liquor shipment, and when the agents confiscate the liquor, they break into a government warehouse and seize the contraband for themselves. During the break-in, George sadistically murders one of the security guards, Pete Jones (Joseph Sawyer), their old sergeant from the war.

When Lloyd hears the news report of the break-in and murder over the radio, he resigns as Eddie's lawyer, knowing it was George and Eddie who pulled the job. George doesn't want to let him off that easily. He thinks that Lloyd knows too much and will use what he knows to prosecute them, and therefore wants to knock him off. But Eddie stops him, assuring him that Lloyd will never take legal action against them.

Eddie tries to remedy the situation with Brown by dispatching Danny to arrange a truce with him, but Brown responds by murdering Danny and dumping his body on the street out in front of Panama's club. Eddie rounds up some of his boys and heads over to Nick Brown's restaurant. George, insulted by Eddie's condescending treatment of him and his diminishing role in the organization, seizes the opportunity to call Brown and tip him off. When they arrive at Brown's place, the gangsters are waiting to ambush them. However, in a shoot-out, it is Eddie who gains the upper hand and kills Brown. Then, suspecting but unable to prove that it was George who informed on him, Eddie dissolves their partnership.

George Hally (Humphrey Bogart, left) wants to knock off Lloyd Hart (Jeffrey Lynn, right), but Eddie Bartlett (James Cagney) intervenes in *The Roaring Twenties* (Warner Bros.).

Meanwhile, Lloyd and Jean are falling in love with each other and are taking every available opportunity to be alone together. When Eddie returns from Brown's place, Panama breaks the news to him gently, informing him that Jean has quit her job at the club and run off to marry Lloyd.

Eddie is emotionally devastated by the news, but pushes on bravely. The years pass, and when "Black Tuesday" hits, Eddie—a heavy investor in the stock market—is financially devastated by the crash. George buys his cab company out, leaving him just one taxi and telling him he's going to need it.

Eddie returns to hacking and, one day during the Christmas season, picks up Jean Sherman as a fare. She is married to Lloyd now and the mother of a small boy. When she brings him back to their house to visit, Eddie warns Lloyd not to proceed with his plan to prosecute George Hally.

The next morning, two of George's thugs show up at Jean's doorstep and threaten Lloyd's life. Panic-stricken, she searches desperately for Eddie, locating him finally at a hole-in-the-wall saloon where Panama is working as a singer. By this time, Eddie's choice of beverage has changed from homogenized milk to hard liquor, and when she finds him, he is properly soused. Jean pleads with him to speak to George and convince him to leave Lloyd alone, but Eddie refuses. He won't play the sap again, he tells her.

Famous final scene from *The Roaring Twenties* (Warner Bros.): Panama (Gladys George) and a policeman (Nat Carr) with the body of Eddie Bartlett (James Cagney), who used to be a big shot.

Despite his curt refusal, he does go to see George, leaving Panama waiting outside for him. At first, George is amused by Eddie's disheveled appearance, but listening to him plead Lloyd's case, he becomes convinced that Eddie would still do anything for Jean, including testify against him. So he instructs his boys to take Eddie for a ride. Eddie turns the tables on him, though, by disarming one of his boys and using his gun to kill George. There is a shoot-out with George's henchmen and, on the snow-covered street outside, Eddie is shot on the run. He continues running until slowly, finally, he collapses dead on the steps of a church. Panama arrives in time to write his epitaph for an inquiring cop. "This is Eddie Bartlett," she tells him, her voice choked with emotion. "He used to be a big shot."

Notes: Former newsman Mark Hellinger provided the story *(The World Goes On)*, budding director Don Siegel assembled all of the exciting montages, John Deering provided the stirring narration, Cagney and Bogart contributed the acting fireworks, Gladys George uttered the infamous last line — "He used to be a big shot" — as poignant a line as any in the genre, and Raoul Walsh tossed it all together to create one of the best gangster films of all time.

However, despite so many noteworthy collaborators, Hellinger managed to orchestrate the publicity into prominently linking his name with the picture, thereby ensuring that the movie became widely known, then and now, as *Mark Hellinger's The Roaring Twenties*. This was a source of deep resentment and unending derision on the Warner Bros. lot, especially when the film opened to surprisingly good box-office and laudatory reviews. There was even a heated confrontation between Hellinger and associate producer Sam Bischoff in the private studio dining room over who deserved more credit for its success; this confrontation nearly escalated into an exchange of blows.

Studio records reveal that no fewer than ten contract writers took a crack at Hellinger's story, and even then the script was said to have been so bad that Cagney, Bogart and McHugh ad-libbed many of their lines. Such prolific improvisation drove executive producer Hal Wallis crazy, and he wrote memo after memo to director Walsh protesting this policy.

And in the end, despite all of this, it was deservedly Raoul Walsh's name which appeared above the title. Walsh had worked at most of the major studios as a director after beginning his movie career as an actor in D.W. Griffith's classic silent film *Birth of a Nation* (1915). In 1939, he moved to Warner Bros., and *The Roaring Twenties* was his first assignment, replacing Anatole Litvak. It was at this studio that Walsh would make his most successful features, including a string of Errol Flynn epics.

Besides Jeffrey Lynn and Priscilla Lane, who do their best with bland, one-dimensional roles, the entire cast is excellent. Cagney and Bogart, in their third and final teaming, are especially good, one capping his reign of '30s gangsterdom and the other emerging as the principal antihero of the '40s. Gladys George, the last in a line of choices for the matronly role of Panama Smith that included Ann Sheridan, Lee Patrick and Glenda Farrell, gets the best line in the movie and makes the most of it.

The Roaring Twenties is presented in the semidocumentary style that was very popular at Warner Bros. during that time, and it borrows liberally from other gangster pictures of the era: Prohibition and the rackets from *Public Enemy*, year-by-year montage of '20s headlines, newsreels and song hits from *Three on a Match*, and a death scene on the steps of a church from *Little Caesar*. Nevertheless, it emerges as a highly original and effective gangster yarn and a fitting end to a genre that would not be revived for another ten years, when Walsh and Cagney would reteam for the definitive *White Heat*.

It is also interesting to note that Cagney's balletic, physically drawn-out death scene, though reminiscent of his gutter dance in *Public Enemy*, was actually inspired by his memory of a Frank Buck film in which the hunter killed a gorilla that died in a slow, amazed way. And Gladys George's line seems all the more profound when one realizes that the golden era of '30s gangster films officially ended with a dying Jimmy Cagney staggering across the steps of that church.

Reviews: "As though it were not already the most thoroughly cinematized decade of our history, the Warners are presenting *The Roaring Twenties* with the self-conscious air of an antiquarian preparing to translate a cuneiform record of lost civilization.

"If it all sounds familiar, Mr. Hellinger will remind you that it all really happened, as he so gratefully remembers. If it also seems to be good entertainment of its kind (and it is, barring the false dignity the Warners have attached to it), credit it to James Cagney in another of his assured portrayals of a criminal career man; to Gladys George, who has breathed poignance into the stock role of the night club hostess who calls her customers *chump;* to Raoul Walsh, who has kept his hectic story of the hectic years spinning." — Frank S. Nugent, *The New York Times*

". . . The picture, in addition to good writing and better than good directing, has — best of all — a cast that is about perfect. Actors so easily and so often typed as Humphrey Bogart, Frank McHugh, Joe Sawyer and Paul Kelly, shed their typiness and become individuals again. Priscilla Lane, whether it is impersonation or just being herself, is inconspicuously exactly right, just as Gladys George is more conspicuously just right as a sort of toned down, more sympathetic Texas Guinan. And Cagney. Once more, and never so successfully, he takes every line, every movement, every bit of business, and makes them so utterly an expression of Eddie Bartlett that they seem not something he learned or was told to do but a spontaneous creation of his own." — James Shelley Hamilton, *National Board of Review Magazine*

The Rose of Washington Square

Twentieth Century–Fox. 86 min. Directed by Gregory Ratoff.

Cast: Tyrone Power, Alice Faye, Al Jolson, William Frawley, Joyce Compton, Hobart Cavanaugh, Moroni Olsen, E.E. Clive, Louis Prima, Charles Wilson.

Faye is a singer who tries to keep her career going while also trying to keep incorrigible husband Power out of trouble. As she reaches the pinnacle of her success, singing "My Man" in the Ziegfeld Follies, he is being sentenced to five years in prison. With one new song by Mack Gordon and Harry Revel ("I Never Knew Heaven Could Speak") and a dozen old favorites, this was a lively and entertaining account of life in New York during the '20s. However, Fanny Brice thought the story was more than a little coincidental with her own and sued Fox for $75,000 for invasion of privacy. The two parties settled quietly out of court.

Rough Riders' Roundup

55 min. Directed by Joseph Kane.

Cast: Roy Rogers, Mary Hart, Raymond Hatton, Eddie Acuff, William Pawley.

Following the end of the Spanish American War, Roy and some of his

Rough Rider pals join the border patrol and fight a gang of outlaws who are holding up stages and express offices.

Rovin' Tumbleweeds

62 min. Directed by George Sherman.

Cast: Gene Autry, Smiley Burnette, Mary Carlisle, Douglass Dumbrille, William Farnum.

This one very easily could have been called *Mr. Autry Goes to Washington.* In it, a crooked politician is stalling a flood control bill in an attempt to line his own pockets. The common folk who are suffering because of this elect radio singer Gene to Congress, and he travels to Washington to fight for truth and justice. All that's missing here is the sore throat. (See *Mr. Smith Goes to Washington.*)

The Rules of the Game (La Regle du jeu)

La Nouvelle Edition Française. Directed by Jean Renoir. Produced by Claude Renoir. Screenplay by Jean Renoir and Carl Koch. Photographed by Jean Bachelet, Jean-Paul Alphen, and Alain Renoir. Edited by Marguerite Renoir and Marthe Huguet. Art direction by Eugene Lourie and Max Douy. Costumes by Coco Chanel. Music by Roger Desormieres and Joseph Kosma, from Mozart, Monsigny, and Saint-Saens. Assistant directors: Carl Koch, Andrew Zwoboda, and Henri Cartier-Bresson. Set decoration by Joseph de Bretagne. Makeup by Ralph. Technical adviser: Tony Corteggiani. Running time: 113 minutes. Release date: July 7.

Cast: Marcel Dalio *Robert, Marquis de la Chesnaye;* Nora Gregor *Christine de la Chesnaye;* Jean Renoir *Octave;* Roland Toutain *Andre Jurieux;* Mila Parely *Genevieve;* Paulette Dubost *Lisette;* Julien Carette *Marceau, the poacher;* Gaston Modot *Schumacher, the gamekeeper;* Pierre Magnier *the General;* Eddy Debray *Corneille, the majordomo;* Pierre Nay *Saint-Aubin;* Odette Talazac *Mme. de la Plante;* Richard Francoeur *La Bruyere;* Claire Gerard *Mme. de la Bruyere;* Anne Mayene *Jackie, Christine's niece;* Leon Larive *the cook;* Lise Elina *the radio reporter;* Nicholas Amato *the South American;* Tony Cortegianni *Berthelin;* Camille Francois *the radio announcer;* Andre Zwoboda *the engineer at Caudron;* Henri Cartier-Bresson *the English servant;* Jenny Helia *the kitchen servant.*

> During the shooting of the film, I was torn between my desire to make a comedy of it and the wish to tell a tragic story. The result of this ambivalence was the film as it is. — Jean Renoir[58]

Synopsis: *The Rules of the Game* is unequivocally the great filmmaker Jean Renoir's masterpiece and my own personal selection for the Best Film of 1939.

The story begins at La Bourget Airport, where Andre Jurieux (Roland Toutain) has just flown non-stop across the Atlantic in only 23 hours. It is twelve years after Charles Lindbergh's historic flight and, like "Lucky Lindy," Andre is instantly and unanimously proclaimed a national hero.

Among the vast crowd that rushes out to welcome and congratulate him on his achievement is his good friend Octave (played by Renoir himself), who finds Andre disappointed and hurt that the woman who inspired his heroic transatlantic flight, Christine de la Chesnaye (Nora Gregor), is not there to greet him.

Christine, in fact, is home listening to the radio broadcast of the event. She and her husband Robert (Marcel Dalio) are planning a trip with some guests to La Coliniere, their house in the country. Unbeknownst to Christine, Robert is having an affair with one of these guests, Genevieve (Mila Parley). Robert has become sated with the affair and wants to end it, but Genevieve is not of the same mind.

When Andre purposely smashes his car into the side of the road on the way back from the airport, Octave worries about the well-being of his friend. He goes to see Christine and Robert and persuades them to invite Andre to La Coliniere.

The gamekeeper at La Coliniere, Schumacher (Gaston Modot), is married to Christine's maid, Lisette (Paulette Dubost). Because they reside in separate towns and see each other only occasionally, Schumacher misses his wife very much. Lisette, on the other hand, would just as soon remain in the city with Christine and fool around with her numerous admirers.

When Schumacher nabs a poacher named Marceau (Julien Carette) on the grounds, he takes him back to Robert, who generously offers Marceau a job as one of his servants. Schumacher objects, but has little to say in his boss's decision. Marceau reports to the kitchen, where he immediately attracts the affections of Lisette.

Soon the guests begin to arrive, from out of a pouring rain. When Octave enters with Andre Jurieux, everyone congratulates the young aviator on his flight. The general (Pierre Magnier) tells Andre that he is part of a "vanishing race," to which the general surely belongs as well. But the main topic of discussion (among the servants as well as the guests) is Andre's rumored affair with Christine, which she openly addresses by explaining to everyone that her role was nothing more than that of friend and good listener to Andre while he was preparing for his journey.

The following morning, the guests all embark upon a massive hunt, slaughtering pheasants, rabbits, squirrels, and just about anything else they can find on the Marquis's grounds. While spotting for ducks, Christine instead spots her husband with Genevieve, kissing passionately in an open field. She is devastated.

Their rendezvous is actually the lovers' swan song, for they have mutually and amicably decided to terminate their liaison. While Genevieve is packing to leave the chateau, Christine takes the opportunity to question her, feigning that she's known about their affair all along and thereby eliciting all of the details from her. Christine convinces Genevieve to stay the remainder of the weekend, reasoning that if she's there to occupy Robert it will leave her freer to pursue her own extramarital activities.

The house party that is thrown that evening quickly goes awry, as the infidelities occurring upstairs, among the social class, and downstairs, among the working class, become violently entangled. Schumacher catches Marceau with his wife in the kitchen and swears that if he ever finds them together again, he will kill the poacher; Christine runs off with Saint-Aubin (Pierre Nay), and when Andre discovers the two alone together, he beats up Saint-Aubin and locks himself in the same room with Christine; when Robert finds Andre and Christine together, he impulsively punches the aviator in the face, and the two men engage in a brutal fistfight; meanwhile, Schumacher catches Marceau and Lisette together again and chases Marceau through the house with a pistol, while the guests dress with unconscious irony in skeleton costumes and cavort in a dance of death. Through it all, Renoir's camera moves through the chateau like a dispassionate observer, focusing ostensibly on whatever circumstances happen to pique his interest and curiosity.

Schumacher is finally subdued and both he and Marceau are relieved of their duties. Robert and Andre laugh about their blue-collar behavior and retire to the dining room to discuss the matter like refined, sophisticated gentlemen.

While they were alone together, Christine confessed to Andre that she loved him and wanted to run away with him. But instead of responding the way she hoped he would—taking her in his arms and whisking her away, like a hero—Andre insisted on talking to Robert first. When asked why, he replied, "Christine, there are still rules!" Confused and unsure, she takes a stroll in the moonlight with Octave, who enlightens her on modern heroes. "They can cross the Atlantic, but they can't cross the street," he tells her. The two walk down to the greenhouse and, in a careless moment, they plan to run away together. Octave returns to the chateau to get Christine's coat, where Lisette reminds him of his age and his dire financial condition. She convinces him that he could never make Christine happy, so Octave sends Andre back to the greenhouse to take his place.

Because she is wearing Lisette's hood, Schumacher has mistaken Christine for his wife and returned to the chateau as well, to retrieve his gun. When he sees Andre talking to Christine, he shoots and kills him, thinking he's running off to elope with his wife.

Robert calls the incident a "regrettable accident" and Andre Jurieux a "victim of fate," and the guests are all quick to rationalize it according to their own ethics. They believe that the murder was surely committed by Robert, who was justified in preventing the aviator from stealing his wife away from him.

In the amoral social world depicted in this film, the rules of the game

Schumacher (Gaston Modot) goes on a shooting rampage through the estate in an attempt to kill his philandering wife's latest paramour in *The Rules of the Game (La Regle du jeu)* (La Nouvelle Edition Française).

solely concern the shallow observance of appearances; any idea of living according to a stable form of morality has been lost.

Notes: When *The Rules of the Game* was first shown in Paris, in July of 1939, it caused a riot and attempts were made to burn down the cinema in which it was shown. In October of that year, even after some censorship, the government banned the film altogether, labeling it "morally unacceptable." The ban was lifted some months later, but reinforced when the Germans occupied Paris, and it remained in effect until the end of World War II. Though it was championed by a few discerning French critics, most found the film's mixture of drama, comedy, and farce unpalatable and chaotic, while others viewed it as a calculated attack on the haute bourgeoisie. Moreover, owing to the presence in the cast of the unmistakably Jewish actor, Dalio, and the Austrian refugee, Gregor, the film was attacked by both the anti–Semitic and the nationalist press.

In 1942, an Allied air raid destroyed the film's only negative. Thenceforward, it existed in only severely truncated and somewhat worn prints, and the film seemed doomed. In 1946, however, a French exhibitor discovered in a wine cellar a virgin print of the 85-minute version from which another negative could be struck. Five minutes were excised as substandard. From '46 on, *The Rules of the Game* went the rounds in three different versions—of 90, 85, and 80 minutes—on the basis of which it began to build its reputation as Renoir's masterpiece. In 1956, two French

enthusiasts (Jean Gaborit and Jacques Durand) approached Camille François, who was still in debt over the movie, and began to collate all of the
prints and negatives with a view to reestablishing the 90-minute version.
Their dedication led to the discovery of 200 tins of rushes, so it became
possible after a great deal of ingenuity and labor to recreate the original
100-minute version that had been released in July of '39, and finally, all but
one short scene of Renoir's original cut. (In the still-missing fragment, Octave attempts to persuade Jurieux of the pleasures of seducing maid-
servants rather than their mistresses.) Since its restoration, the picture has
repeatedly been voted one of the best films ever made, being placed at the
pinnacle of many international "Top Ten" lists of all time.

It is interesting to note that Renoir cast Nora Gregor in the lead role
of Christine—against the wishes of his collaborators and many of the cast
members—due to a chance encounter with her at a French theater. The
film's modest budget had already precluded the casting of his original
choice for the part, Simone Simon.

With *The Rules of the Game,* Jean Renoir (son of the great painter
Claude Renoir) was holding up a mirror to the decadent condition of
French society on the eve of World War II, and the French were conceivably outraged by what they saw, not so much out of effrontery as of fear
and identification.

Not long after filming was completed, Renoir fled his country and the
impending Nazi occupation and continued his filmmaking in America. In
1975, he was awarded an Honorary Oscar which recognized him as "a
genius who, with grace, responsibility and enviable devotion through silent
film, sound film, feature, documentary and television, has won the world's
admiration."

Saga of Death Valley

55 min. Directed by Joseph Kane.

Cast: Roy Rogers, George Hayes, Donald Barry, Doris Day, Frank M.
Thomas.

A gang of outlaws cuts off the water supply of local ranchers in an attempt to extort money from them, and Roy gets on the case. His leading
lady in this one, by the by, is not *that* Doris Day.

Second Fiddle

Fox. Directed by Sidney Lanfield.

Cast: Sonja Henie, Tyrone Power, Rudy Vallee, Edna May Oliver,
Mary Healy, Lyle Talbot, Alan Dinehart, Irving Bacon.

After a string of dramatic and heroic roles, Power was cast in this musical-comedy in an attempt by Darryl Zanuck to broaden the popularity of his fastest-rising young star. The strategy worked. In this clever and topical spoof of David O. Selznick's much-publicized search for an actress to play Scarlett O'Hara in his epic *Gone with the Wind,* Power is cast as the publicity chief for Consolidated Pictures and put in charge of a massive campaign for a film called *Girl of the North,* a project which has been delayed for two years until the right girl could be cast as Violet Jensen, the Southern belle. The film boasts several elaborate ice ballets designed to showcase the breathtaking Henie in action, a fine supporting cast and a score by Irving Berlin (six of his lesser-known tunes).

Son of Frankenstein

A Universal Picture. Produced and directed by Rowland V. Lee. Original Screenplay by Willis Cooper. Suggested by the story written in 1816 by Mary Wollstonecraft Shelley. Photographed by George Robinson. Edited by Ted Kent. Art direction by Jack Otterson. Art direction by Russell Gausman. Music by Frank Skinner. Musical director: Lionel Newman. Special effects by John P. Fulton. Costumes by Vera West. Makeup by Jack P. Pierce. Sound by Bernard B. Brown and William Hedgcock. Assistant director: Fred Frank. Running time: 94 minutes. Release date: January 13.

Cast: Basil Rathbone *Baron Wolf von Frankenstein;* Boris Karloff *The Monster;* Bela Lugosi *Ygor;* Lionel Atwill *Inspector Krogh;* Josephine Hutchinson *Elsa von Frankenstein;* Donnie Dunagan *Peter von Frankenstein;* Emma Dunn *Amelia;* Edgar Norton *Thomas Benson* Perry Ivins *Fritz;* Lawrence Grant *Burgomaster;* Lionel Belmore *Emil Lang;* Michael Mark *Ewald Neumuller;* Caroline Cook *Frau Neumuller;* Gustav von Seyffertitz *Councilor;* Edward Cassidy *Dr. Berger.*

> The reason I played the Monster only in the first three films was because I could (and I was right as it turned out) see the handwriting on the wall as to which way the stories were going . . . that they would go downhill. There was not much left in the character of the Monster to be developed; we had reached his limits. I saw that from here on he would become rather an oafish prop, so to speak, in the last act, or something like that, without any great stature, and I didn't see any point in going on.—Boris Karloff, on why he turned in his asphalter's boots after *Son of Frankenstein* was completed[59]

Synopsis: In 1931, James Whale's *Frankenstein* made Boris Karloff an international star. He reprised the role of the Monster four years later, in Whale's *The Bride of Frankenstein,* and—for the third and final time—in Rowland V. Lee's classic 1939 chiller, *Son of Frankenstein.*

It is set twenty-five years after the death of Dr. Frankenstein. His son, Baron Wolf von Frankenstein (Basil Rathbone), arrives in the village named after his family with his wife, Elsa (Josephine Hutchinson), and son, Peter (Donnie Dunagan), to start a new life. The villagers of Frankenstein—still living with the memory of his late father's murderous creation—give them a cold reception, and the Burgomaster (Lawrence Grant) presents Wolf with a box containing his father's papers.

When Frankenstein arrives at the ancestral castle which he was bequeathed in his father's will, he feels very much at home. He still considers his father an unrecognized genius, and he blames the horror of the Monster (Karloff) on an assistant who mistakenly gave it the brain of a psychopathic killer. He is dedicated to vindicating his father and proving his genius to the scientific world.

The wooden-armed Inspector Krogh (Lionel Atwill), whose military career was ruined when the Monster tore his arm off of his body, makes a friendly call to the castle, offering his help if ever Frankenstein is in danger. He also informs Wolf of the string of six unsolved murders, which have the villagers in a state of paranoia and fear.

The next morning, Wolf visits his father's watch-tower laboratory and, perusing through the roofless shambles, he is nearly killed by Ygor (Bela Lugosi). Ygor survived a hanging by the villagers, but has a broken neck to show for his experience, and has been creeping through the secret passageways of the castle ever since. When he learns that Frankenstein is a doctor, he takes him into one of these passageways, where Wolf discovers his father and grandfather buried. He also discovers the incapacitated body of the Monster. Ygor wants Frankenstein to revive the Monster, and—seeing the chance to finally complete his father's experiment—he agrees to try.

He rebuilds the laboratory, brings in newer and more sophisticated equipment and—with the aid of his longtime assistant, Thomas Benson (Edgar Norton)—brings the Monster back to life.

The six men who have died mysteriously were all members of Ygor's hanging party, and they were killed by the Monster at Ygor's behest. There are two men still left, and Ygor dispatches the Monster to dispose of them. At about the same time, Ygor overhears Benson talking about informing Inspector Krogh of the Monster, and Benson mysteriously disappears.

With the villagers in an uproar, Krogh arrives at the castle and puts Frankenstein under house arrest, for his own protection and safety more than a suspicion of guilt.

Peter tells Inspector Krogh about the false wall in his nursery, and he gives him a watch that "the giant" gave him, which turns out to be Thomas Benson's.

Frankenstein knows who is responsible for the recent slayings. He finds Ygor in the lab and shoots him dead. While he is gone, Krogh finds the secret passageway in Peter's nursery and discovers Benson's body inside.

Later, when the Monster finds his friend and—for all intents—master

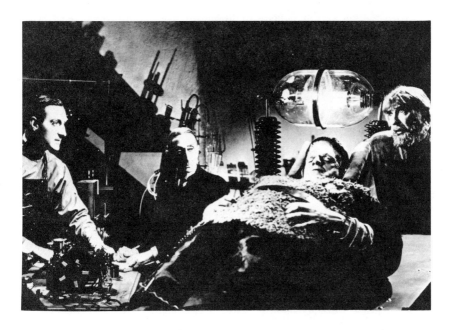

Basil Rathbone (far left) and Edgar Norton (second from left) work tirelessly to try and revive the Monster, Boris Karloff, while Bela Lugosi (right) looks on concernedly in *Son of Frankenstein* (Universal).

Ygor dead in the lab, he goes into an uncontrollable rage, smashing all of the doctor's equipment and tossing it into a pit of sulfuric acid. Then he kidnaps Peter from his nursery and, using the secret passageway, takes him back to the lab. Before he can do the boy any harm, though, Frankenstein swings across the lab on a rope and knocks the Monster backward into the bubbling pit of sulfur, destroying him once and for all.

Frankenstein turns the deed of the castle over to the village, bids them a fond farewell, and returns with his family to America aboard the train they arrived on.

Notes: Inspired by the successful reissue of *Frankenstein* and *Dracula* (1931) on a double bill, the new faction at Universal—who had taken the company over from the founding Laemmle family—mounted this lavish, expensive, and excellently played film. It turned out to be one of the best horror films ever made and successfully initiated the second "Golden Age" of that genre.

Because of the growing Nazi menace in Europe, Universal eliminated all Germanic references, changing the European locale in the plot to Hungary. After acquiring a print of the all-color British-made *The Mikado* (1939), the studio also decided to make *Son of Frankenstein* its first feature in Technicolor. However, when shooting began in October of 1938, it was discovered that Karloff's make-up did not photograph properly in color, so the film was shot in black-and-white.

The original screenplay was written by Willis Cooper, creator of the radio show *Lights Out.* During shooting, he was encouraged to write another *Frankenstein* sequel, to be called *After Frankenstein,* but that project was put aside and no more sequels emerged until *Ghost of Frankenstein* in 1942.

Reviews: "Artistically, *Son of Frankenstein* is a masterpiece in the demonstration of how production settings and effects can be made assets emphasizing literary melodrama. Histrionically, the picture is outstanding because of the manner in which Basil Rathbone, Boris Karloff, Bela Lugosi and Lionel Atwill ... sink their teeth into their roles."—*Motion Picture Herald*

"Rowland V. Lee has created an eerie atmosphere for the story and he has put into the working out of the plot enough horror to send the chills and shivers racing up and down the spectators' backs."—Kate Cameron, *The New York Daily News*

South of the Border

71 min. Directed by George Sherman.

Cast: Gene Autry, Smiley Burnette, June Storey, Lupita Tovar, Mary Lee.

This one, the last picture that Autry made in 1939, has only one thing going for it—the title song, which became a standard on two continents. Ironically, the tune was penned by a pair of Englishmen who never even saw America or Mexico before composing it. The storyline involves Gene and Smiley as government agents, trying to subdue a Mexican revolution.

Southward Ho

58 min. Directed by Joseph Kane.

Cast: Roy Rogers, Mary Hart, George Hayes, Wade Boteler, Arthur Loft.

Also set during the Civil War, this one has Roy and his new sidekick George "Gabby" Hayes—rustled by Republic from the Hopalong Cassidy series—traveling to Texas to take over a ranch that Gabby has inherited half-ownership of. The two former Confederate soldiers are dismayed to learn that the other half of the ranch is owned by an ex–Union officer with whom they tangled during the war. When it is later discovered that their old nemesis is the leader of a band of outlaws who have been plundering the area, Roy rallies the local citizens and does away with the whole bunch of 'em.

The Spy in Black

A London Films Production. Directed by Michael Powell. Produced by Irving Asher. Screenplay by Emeric Pressburger. Based on a story by J. Storer Clouston. Scenario by Roland Pertwee. Photographed by Bernard Browne. Edited by Hugh Stewart. Supervising film editor: William Hornbeck. Art direction by Frederick Pusey. Supervising art director: Vincent Korda. Sound by A.W. Watkins. Music by Miklos Rozsa. Musical direction by Muia Mathieson. Running time: 82 minutes.

Cast: Conrad Veidt *Captain Hardt;* Sebastian Shaw *Ashington;* Valerie Hobson *the Schoolmistress;* Marius Goring *Schuster;* June Duprez *Ann Burnett;* Athole Stewart *Reverend Hector Matthews;* Agnes Laughlin *Mrs. Matthews;* Helen Haye *Mrs. Sedley;* Cyril Raymond *Reverend John Harris;* Hay Petrie *Engineer;* Grant Sutherland *Bob Bratt;* Robert Rendel *Admiral;* Mary Morris *Chauffeuse;* George Summers *Captain Ratter;* Margaret Moffatt *Kate;* Kenneth Warrington *Commander Denis;* Torin Thatcher *Submarine officer;* Bernard Miles *Desk clerk.*

> Since talkies took over the movies, I had worked with some good writers, but I had never met anything like this. . . . He had stood Storer Clouston's plot on its head and completely restructured the film. — Michael Powell, on his first meeting with Emeric Pressburger[60]

Synopsis: Though overshadowed artistically by Carol Reed's *The Stars Look Down,* the British import called *The Spy in Black* (released in America as *U-Boat 29*) nevertheless remains one of the most taut and thrilling of all 1939 films, with enough plot twists to keep even mystery fans happy.

Set during World War I, it opens with German submarine commander Captain Hardt (Conrad Veidt) being dispatched to the coast of Scotland for an unspecified spying mission. Meanwhile, Ann Burnett (June Duprez), a girl who has been accepted to teach grade school in that coastal town, is abducted by female German agents and dropped off a high cliff into the sea below, to be replaced by a German spy who will serve as Captain Hardt's contact. Just as Ann's body hits the water, a British patrol boat inspecting the waters hears the sound and turns its lights toward it.

Captain Hardt makes it safely to the Scottish coastal town and locates the new "Ann Burnett" (Valerie Hobson) at her home. She greets him with their secret German password and shows him to his room in the house. Hardt is eager to learn what his assignment is, and Fraulein Teil (her real name) assures him that he will be given his orders the following morning.

The next day, Hardt is alarmed to see the entire British North Sea Fleet positioned outside his bedroom window. Teil tells him that his assignment is to sink all 15 ships in the fleet. The key to the operation is a disgraced British officer named Ashington (Sebastian Shaw), who lost his command of a destroyer due to alcoholism and still bears a grudge against the service.

He has been well-paid—with German money and Fraulein Teil's sexual favors—to provide Hardt with the top secret schedules and sailing times of the ships, which would make it possible for a group of German U-boats to sink the entire fleet.

On the eve of the North Sea Fleet's departure, Hardt and Teil prepare a departure of their own. Unbeknownst to them, however, a cleric named John Harris (Cyril Raymond) has arrived in their small village in search of his fiancée. Reverend Harris is engaged to marry Ann Burnett.

He encounters the local pastor, Hector Matthews (Athole Stewart), who directs him to Miss Burnett's home and invites him for dinner. Reverend Harris cordially accepts, continuing on his way. But when he bumbles into the lair of the German spies, he is taken prisoner and bound and gagged.

That night, Hardt and Ashington go off to a clandestine rendezvous with the German commander's sub. He gives his men the priceless information provided by Ashington and sends them off into the night to prepare their plan of attack (which includes 14 other U-boats). Hardt and Ashington return to the Scottish village to orchestrate their escape plans.

Captain Hardt has fallen in love with Teil, and that night he makes another in a series of advances, only to be rejected again. Afterwards, thinking she has locked him in his room, she steals away into the night to meet Ashington. From a safe distance behind, Hardt follows her. In the Scottish moonlight, he learns to his horror that Ashington is not a disgraced naval officer at all, but a British counter-spy named Blacklock, and Fraulein Teil is, in fact, Mrs. Blacklock. He realizes that the information he has been duped into providing them can be used to annihilate the fleet of German U-boats that his own orders have summoned from Germany.

Before moving in on Hardt, Blacklock escorts his wife to a nearby port and puts her on an outbound commercial freighter called the *St. Magnus*. Then, having provided for her safety, he goes back to deal with Hardt. When his men break into the German commander's room, though, they find only poor Reverend Harris, still bound and gagged, sans his clothing. Hardt manages to escape in the cleric's robe aboard the *St. Magnus*, which is also carrying a group of German POWs.

In the next scene, an irate Reverend Matthews is told why Reverend Harris was forced to miss their dinner engagement. It is in this scene that the audience learns how Ann Burnett survived the fall over the cliff, was rescued by the patrol boat and was able to provide them with enough information to make the switch in agents and sting Captain Hardt.

Meanwhile, aboard the *St. Magnus*, Hardt frees the German prisoners, overtakes command of the vessel and takes Mrs. Blacklock prisoner. He risks all of their lives by navigating the *St. Magnus* into a mine-filled stretch of ocean, in a desperate attempt to rescue his country's U-boats.

When the British navy realizes what has happened, Blacklock is dispatched to cut the *St. Magnus* off and, if necessary, sink it (even though he knows his wife is aboard it).

Passengers prepare to leave Conrad Veidt's sinking ship in *Spy in Black* **(London Films).**

Ironically, the *St. Magnus* is pummeled with shells from Hardt's own U-boat and destroyed. Before it sinks, though, Hardt gets all of the ship's passengers, crew and prisoners into lifeboats, and bids a fond farewell to Mrs. Blacklock. At the same time, the British navy arrives and blows the German U-boat out of the water.

The *St. Magnus* sinks, and Hardt — the proverbial captain — goes down with the ship.

Notes: *The Spy in Black* was the first collaboration between director Michael Powell and screenwriter Emeric Pressburger. The following year, they would make the film *Contraband* together, which would also star Conrad Veidt and Valerie Hobson. They would go on to produce such great films as *49th Parallel, The Life and Death of Colonel Blimp, Black Narcissus, A Matter of Life and Death,* and, of course, *The Red Shoes.*

Interestingly, Miss Hobson went on to marry John D. Profumo, the British Minister of War, who became embroiled in an international sex scandal in the 1960s that rocked England (and much of the world) to its core and forced Mr. Profumo to resign his post.

Look for Bernard Miles as a desk clerk in the film's opening scene.

Reviews: "The early arrival of a U-Boat on Broadway was only to be expected after the vague alarms recently sounded off Massachusetts, the Grand Banks and Alaska. And of course the logical base for such a charming little visitor (it answers to the name of *U-Boat 29*) was The Globe, where land, air and underwater marvels are continuously on view, even in peace time. What didn't necessarily follow but what fortunately does, is the fact that *U-Boat 29* is the most exciting spy melodrama since the advent of the Second World War. The British may not have the Bremen, but they still have Conrad Veidt."—B.R. Crisler, *The New York Times*

"Although made and finished in England before the war, this film is as timely and topical as tomorrow's headlines. That it also includes meritorious story, production and acting give it added value."—*Variety*

Stagecoach

A United Artists Picture. Directed by John Ford. Produced by Walter Wanger. Screenplay by Dudley Nichols. From the story "Stage to Lordsburg" by Ernest Haycox. Photographed by Bert Glennon. Edited by Dorothy Spencer and Walter Reynolds. Art direction by Alexander Toluboff. Costume design by Walter Plunkett. Set decorations by Wiard B. Ihnen. Assistant director: Wingate Smith. Special effects by Ray Binger. Editorial supervision by Otho Lovering. Music arranged by Boris Morros. Music by Richard Hageman, Franke Harling, John Leipold, Leo Shuken, and Louis Gruenberg, adapted from 17 folk tunes of the 1880s. Running time: 96 minutes. Release date: March 2.

Cast: John Wayne *Ringo Kid;* Claire Trevor *Dallas;* Thomas Mitchell *Doc Boone;* John Carradine *Hatfield;* Andy Devine *Bucky;* Donald Meek *Mr. Peacock;* George Bancroft *Curly Wilcox;* Louise Platt *Lucy Mallory;* Berton Churchill *Mr. Gatewood;* Tim Holt *Lt. Blanchard;* Francis Ford *Sgt. Billy Pickett;* Tom Tyler *Hank Plummer;* Chris-Pin Martin *Chris;* Elvira Rios *Yakima, Chris's wife;* Marga Daighton *Mrs. Pickett;* Kent Odell *Billy Pickett, Jr.;* Yakima Canutt *Chief Big Tree;* Harry Tenbrook *Telegraph operator;* Jack Pennick *Jerry, barman;* Paul McVey *Express agent;* Cornelius Keefe *Cpt. Whitney;* Florence Lake *Mrs. Nancy Whitney;* Louis Mason *Sheriff;* Brenda Fowler *Mrs. Gatewood;* Walter McGrail *Cpt. Sickel;* Joseph Rickson *Luke Plummer;* Vester Pegg *Ike Plummer;* William Hoffer *Sergeant;* Bryant Washburn *Cpt. Simmons;* Nora Cecil *Dr. Boone's housekeeper;* Helen Gibson, Dorothy Annleby *dancing girls;* Buddy Roosevelt, Bill Cody *ranchers;* Chief White Horse *Indian chief;* Duke Lee *Sheriff of Lordsburg;* Mary Kathleen Walker *Lucy's baby.*

> When I first got the story, I thought it was a mixture of *Grand Hotel, The Covered Wagon* and *The Iron Horse,* so I called it "The Grand Covered Iron Stagecoach."—Dudley Nichols[61]

Synopsis: On any list of the greatest directors of all time, John Ford would certainly have to be placed somewhere at the top. On any list of the greatest Westerns ever made, the same can be said of his 1939 classic, *Stagecoach.*

In the opening scene, we learn that the Indian warrior Geronimo has escaped from a reservation and is back on the warpath, terrorizing the American Southwest. From there, we go to Tonto, where a stage is boarding for Lordsburg. Preparing to travel on it this day are Doc Boone (Thomas Mitchell), a drunkard, philosopher, man of medicine and self-professed fatalist all rolled into one rather untidy bundle; Hatfield (John Carradine), a Confederate soldier turned cardsharp; Dallas (Claire Trevor), a lady of ill repute being run out of town by the self-righteous Women's League; Mrs. Lucy Mallory (Louise Platt), the pregnant wife of a cavalry lieutenant; Mr. Gatewood (Berton Churchill), a banker who has absconded with his bank's funds; Mr. Peacock (Donald Meek), a timid whiskey drummer who is constantly being mistaken for a clergyman; Bucky (Andy Devine), the skittish driver of the stage; Marshal Wilcox (George Bancroft) and his prisoner, whom we meet later, the Ringo Kid (John Wayne, in the role that made him a star). They are forewarned about the danger of marauding Apaches, but each one has an urgent reason for going to Lordsburg, so there are no ticket refunds. However, when they reach their first stop and discover that the army escort which was promised them is not there waiting, they decide to take a vote on whether to return to Tonto or continue on to Lordsburg. They vote almost unanimously to push forward, the lone dissenter being timid Mr. Peacock.

When they arrive at Apache Wells, their second stop, they learn once again there are no troops and that they must continue their journey through hostile Indian territory unescorted.

But when Mrs. Mallory suddenly goes into labor, they are faced with a more immediate emergency. As some of the men fill a shaky Doc Boone with hot coffee, Dallas takes charge of the situation, attending to Mrs. Mallory. When Doc Boone is sober enough to perform, he delivers a baby girl, with Dallas serving as his wet nurse. While the men celebrate the birth of the child, Mrs. Mallory sleeps while Dallas watches over and cares for her all night long.

By this time, a bond has formed between Dallas and Ringo, the two social misfits, due in part to the fact that their more "respectable" traveling companions have shunned them both. "I guess you can't break out of jail and into society in the same week," Ringo reasons. During a stroll they take that evening at the station, he asks her to marry him. And although they are very much in love with each other, there are many obstacles standing in the way of marital bliss. For one thing, she's a woman with a scarlet past, which he knows nothing about. "You're . . . the kind of girl a man wants to marry," Ringo tell her, awkwardly and naïvely, but from the heart. For another thing, he's on his way to Lordsburg for a showdown with the three Plummer brothers, who killed his father and brother. And even if he survives that, he still has a jail sentence to finish. So, nonplussed by his proposal, she tells him not to talk that way and runs off crying.

En route to Lordsburg (after an extra day of rest for Mrs. Mallory),

Left–right: John Wayne, Andy Devine, Claire Trevor, George Bancroft, Louise Platt, Tim Holt, John Carradine, Berton Churchill (in front of Carradine) and Francis Ford (in front of Holt) worry about a shaky Thomas Mitchell (right foreground) in *Stagecoach* (United Artists).

Peacock is suddenly hit in the shoulder with an Apache arrow, and the incessant bickering among the passengers comes to an abrupt halt. Their ultimate test is about to begin.

The scene which follows—the Indian attack—is one of pure cinematic wonder, and one which to this day cameramen are still studying. Indians fall two at a time, horses seem to be trampling over cameras, and then there is John Wayne's—well, actually veteran stuntman Yakima Canutt's—famous leap from the coach onto the team of unmanned horses. It is a truly amazing sequence which director Ford literally choreographs right down to the last bullet. When things look hopeless, Hatfield (with only one bullet left in his chamber) points his gun at the head of Lucy Mallory (who is kneeling in prayer) to save her from a fate worse than death. A gunshot is heard, the gun falls from his hand, and although the camera is focused on Lucy's face, we know that he has been hit. The next thing we hear is a bugle call, signifying the arrival of the cavalry, who chase the Apaches back up into the mountains as Ringo pulls the stage to a grinding halt.

When they ride into Lordsburg, Peacock is carried off for medical attention, Mrs. Mallory is taken off to be reunited with her husband, and Mr. Gatewood is summarily taken into custody by the local sheriff.

Before she is taken away, Lucy Mallory looks up at Dallas and says: "If there's ever anything I can do for—."

Pure cinematic wonder: The Indian attack in *Stagecoach* (United Artists).

"I know," Dallas acknowledges, rescuing her from an offer she can't conceivably honor.

Then Marshal Wilcox, feeling Ringo has earned it, gives the Kid his rifle and ten minutes to take care of business. Ringo removes from his hat three bullets he has been saving for the Plummer brothers, and walks off towards his rendezvous. Before he does, though, Dallas shows him exactly who she is.

Down the street, at the local saloon, someone arrives with the news that Ringo is in town and looking for the Plummer brothers. Hank Plummer (Tom Tyler) is sitting at one of the tables, playing poker, and prophetically enough he is holding aces and eights, the "dead-man's hand." He and his brothers go out into the street to face Ringo. From across town, Dallas can hear the gunfire. Back at the saloon, Hank Plummer walks inside, over to the bar and falls dead onto the floor.

Ringo, having settled his debt, returns to Dallas and they ride off together in a buckboard headed for his ranch in Mexico, to start a new life. As the buckboard races off into the night, Doc Boone christens them "saved from the blessings of civilization."

Notes: *Stagecoach* marked director John Ford's triumphant return to the Western after a 13-year hiatus. Since *Three Bad Men* in 1926, he had worked in a variety of genres and had earned a reputation as a hard-nosed craftsman. When he read Ernest Haycox's short story "Stage to Lordsburg" (clearly patterned after Guy de Maupassant's "Boule de Suif") in the April 1937 edition of *Colliers* magazine, he took it to United Artists as an idea for a movie he wanted to suggest. They agreed and suggested Gary Cooper and Marlene Dietrich for the lead roles, two top stars. But because of budget limitations, Ford instead cast Marion Michael Morrison, now calling himself John Wayne, as the Ringo Kid and Claire Trevor as Dallas. Morrison/Wayne made his motion picture debut in 1928 and since then had appeared in over sixty movies, most of them low-budget Westerns. His career was going nowhere, but by casting him in the part of Ringo, Ford made a star of John Wayne and set him on his path to screen immortality.

Stagecoach revolutionized the Hollywood Western. After the introduction of synchronized sound in the 1930s, Westerns were mostly "B" affairs. There were singing cowboys (Roy Rogers, Gene Autry), action heroes (Hopalong Cassidy, Lash LaRue), serials (The Lone Ranger, Johnny Mack Brown) and a parade of cheaply made quickies from the backlots of independent studios such as Republic, Monogram and Resolute. By 1939, Hollywood also had discovered rear-screen projection and put it to good use. Second units would head out for the sagebrush and record the proper outdoor scenery, which would then be unreeled to serve as a background for the soundstage-bound actors. Thus, most Westerns of that period tended to be "stagey."

Stagecoach bid a fond adieu to all that. Shooting on location for the first time in Monument Valley, with its broad panoramas of weathered plains, mesas, and rolling clouds, Ford creates a universe of natural order which deemphasizes the actions of the men who travel through it. He subsequently turned this magnificent landscape into a sort of private outdoor set that he would return to, time and time again, over the next quarter century.

But one must not overemphasize the technical aspects; it is the actions of the men who travel through this land that have made *Stagecoach* the enduring classic that it is. Dudley Nichols' screenplay, though overtly allegorical, exemplified the upbeat spirit of national optimism that emerged in the late '30s, while at the same time turning conventional mores upside down.

Using the format of the popular omnibus films of the '30s (*Grand Hotel, Shanghai Express, Lost Horizon, The Lady Vanishes,* and Ford-Nichols' 1934 collaboration, *The Lost Patrol*), where a colorful array of characters from different social strata are thrown together in dangerous or exotic circumstances which reveal each character's moral fiber, it tells a story of Balzacian scope and gusto that exalts the outcast over the "respectable" members of society. Indeed, in the two life-or-death instances during the journey — Lucy Mallory's delivery at Apache Wells and the Indian attack — it is the reprobates, the prostitute and the outlaw, who emerge as most notable and heroic, while the more respectable contingent display only greed, cowardice and petty self-importance. So by the conclusion, when Dallas and Ringo ride off together and Doc Boone — who serves as John Ford's voice throughout the film — christens them "saved from the blessings of civilization," we understand all too well what he means.

The ultimate compliment to this film, perhaps, is that Orson Welles over at RKO learned about photography and camera angles by watching it every night for a month, knowledge he put to good use in his first feature film, *Citizen Kane* (1941).

The film was nominated for seven Academy Awards, including Best Picture, but won only two: for Thomas Mitchell as Best Supporting Actor and for Best Musical Score. It was remade in 1966 under the same title.

Reviews: "Here . . . is a movie of the grand old school, a genuine rib-thumper and a beautiful sight to see. . . . [Ford] prefers the broadest canvas, the brightest colors, the wildest brush and the boldest possible strokes. He hews to the straight narrative line with the well-reasoned confidence of a man who has seen that narrative succeed before. He takes no shadings from his characters: either they play it straight or they don't play at all. He likes his language simple and he doesn't want too much of it. When his Redskins bite the dust, he expects to hear the thud and see the dirt spurt up. Above all, he likes to have things happen out in the open, where his camera can keep them in view. . . . His players have taken easily to their chores . . . but none so notably as its director. This is one stagecoach that's powered by a Ford."—Frank S. Nugent, *The New York Times*

"It is probably as enthralling a picture of the Old West as was ever brought to the screen. . . . The matchless team of Ford and Nichols . . . have the epic swing, the instinctive poetry of action, above all the technical mastery, that create the glamor of art and revivify once more the broken-down old horse opera. . . . *Stagecoach* is something for the true movie-lover to see more than once: once, perhaps, for the story, again and yet again for delight in how the story is told."—James Shelley Hamilton, *National Board of Review Magazine*

Stanley and Livingstone

Twentieth Century–Fox. 101 min. Directed by Henry King.

Cast: Spencer Tracy, Sir Cedric Hardwicke, Richard Greene, Nancy Kelly, Walter Brennan, Charles Coburn, Henry Hull, Henry Travers, Miles Mander.

After *Boys Town* (1938)—for which he had won his second consecutive Oscar—Spencer Tracy was hoping to begin work on *Northwest Passage,* but that monumental project had run into all sorts of problems. Though a team of writers were hard at work on developing the screen story, it was estimated that another six months would be needed before production could actually begin. In the meantime, Louis B. Mayer promised Tracy that he'd find the actor another project to keep him busy. And he did. Mayer loaned the actor out to Darryl Zanuck of Fox, a company that had been turning out some prestigious pictures of late. Zanuck wanted Tracy for the role of reporter Henry Stanley, and in return, he lent Mayer the services of his handsome new star Tyrone Power for the opulent MGM production of *Marie Antoinette* (1938). Tracy relished the opportunity to work with an actor he admired and respected as much as Sir Cedric Hardwicke—who had been cast in the role of the missionary lost in Africa—and the two worked well together. Tracy's performance was especially strong, and upon its release, many industry insiders were predicting he would win his third straight Oscar for it. When the list of Best Actor nominations for that year was announced, and Tracy's name wasn't even on it, many saw it as a sign that a great performance from Tracy was simply expected.

The Stars Look Down

A Grafton Film. Directed by Carol Reed. Produced by Isidore Goldsmith. Screenplay by J.B. Williams. From an adaptation by A.J. Cronin, based on his own novel. Photographed by Mutz Greenbaum and Henry Harris. Edited by Reginald Beck. Art direction by James Carter. Sceneries by J.B. Williams and A. Coppel. Production supervisor: Fred Zelnick. Assistant directors: Vincent Peamane and Hal Mason. Production manager: V.N. Dean. Sound by Norman Baines. Music by Hans May. Running time: 110 minutes.

Cast: Michael Redgrave *David Fenwick*; Margaret Lockwood *Jenny Sunley*; Emlyn Williams *Joe Gowlan*; Nancy Price *Martha Fenwick*; Edward Rigby *Bob Fenwick*; Allan Jeayes *Richard Barras*; Cecil Parker *Stanley Millington*; Milton Rosmer *Harry Nugent*; Olga Lindo *Mrs. Sunley*; Desmond Tester *Hughie Fenwick*; David Markham *Arthur Barras*; Frederick Burtwell *Heddon*; Edmund Willard *Ramage*.

> He [Carol Reed] had not yet acquired the technical virtuosity of his later style, but this straightforward film may just possibly be his best. — Pauline Kael[62]

Synopsis: The best British film made prior to 1940 was a film by a little-known director named Carol Reed. The film was *The Stars Look Down.*

It is set mostly in Sleescale, a mining town in Northern England. Bob Fenwick (Edward Rigby), a collier, learns that the mine of Scupper Flats is holding back a million tons of floodwater, making it a potential death trap. He leads all of the workers out on a strike, vowing not to return until the owner of the colliery, Richard Barras (Allan Jeayes), makes the necessary safety improvements.

Both of Bob's sons are very ambitious: David (Michael Redgrave) is studying for a scholarship to a college in Tynecastle, while Hughie (Desmond Tester), a gifted athlete, sees sports as his ticket out of the provincial mining town.

Out of work, the miners and their families are starving, and when a

The Stars Look Down (Grafton). *Top:* Allan Jeayes faces off with striking miners. *Bottom:* Miners are trapped after a cave-in.

local shopkeeper throws one of their own out of his store, they bombard the shop with rocks, smashing all of the windows. Then they break inside and steal all of the shopkeeper's meat. Bob tries to stop all of them, realizing that such actions will only hurt their cause and prolong their suffering, but they won't listen. When the police arrive, it is Bob who is caught inside the shop, along with another collier, and they are both taken into custody. The shopkeeper and his son accompany them down to the station, to file a complaint and press charges. Once they are all gone, a local young upstart named Joe Gowlan (Emlyn Williams) sneaks into the shop and steals all the money from the till. Then he runs to the outskirts of town and hops a train bound for Tynecastle.

Three months pass, and the strike has become a crippling one, killing the town of Sleescale. The miners have no alternative but to go back to work. David, who has earned his scholarship and wants to use his education to fight for the rights of the miners in Parliament, urges them to hold out, but to no avail. Barras has won this round. On the day that his father is released from jail, David leaves for the university in Tynecastle to win the war.

In Tynecastle, Joe has gone into business for himself as a bookmaker. One evening, while trying to brush off one of his girlfriends, Jenny Sunley (Margaret Lockwood), he spots his old friend David on the street and they decide to all go out and have a drink together. Over the course of the evening, Joe pushes Jenny off on David, and the two of them make a date for the following afternoon. Joe, meanwhile, sets his sights on winning a position in a prestigious company owned by Stanley Millington (Cecil Parker). A ruthless social climber, Joe is using Millington's wife—with whom he is having an affair—to get to her husband. He ultimately wins the position and leaves Jenny without as much as a goodbye.

Brokenhearted, Jenny runs off into David's arms. She riddles him with lies, telling him that she loves him and that when Joe found out about this, he left her in a state of hopelessness. David, who truly loves Jenny, assures her that he will marry her as soon as he earns his degree and gets his post. A prominent member of Parliament, Harry Nugent (Milton Rosmer), has offered to groom him for his seat as soon as he finishes college. But that would take a whole year, and Jenny isn't willing to wait that long. She seduces David and talks him into dropping out of school and taking a schoolmaster's position in Sleescale (which he already has enough credits for). They are married immediately and go back to David's hometown.

After living there only a short time, Jenny becomes a malcontent, constantly nagging her husband about every conceivable thing. She wants David to take her out at night, even though she knows that's the only time he has to study for his degree (a dream he hasn't given up entirely).

David is eventually fired from his post at the school and forced to accept the job of tutoring Mr. Barras's son, Arthur (David Markham), who couldn't care less about mathematics. While teaching the boy one night,

David sees Joe arrive with plans for selling drilling equipment to Mr. Barras for Scupper Flats, when the colliery is scheduled to be shut down soon due to hazardous working conditions. David is furious. He barges into Barras's office and threatens another crippling strike if he does not follow through with plans to close the mine. He tells them that he is leaving immediately for Tynecastle to solicit the aid of Harry Nugent and bring the matter before the union.

David does just that, and Nugent promises to do whatever he can to help, still fond of the young man despite the disappointment he has been. When David returns to Sleescale much later that night, he catches Joe leaving his house and his unfaithful wife, and he punches his unscrupulous former friend to the ground. Only then does David realize that Jenny has loved Joe all along, and that she has just used and manipulated him. He leaves his wife and goes before the union's board of directors, arguing vehemently for the closing of Scupper Flats. But when one member accuses him of protesting for personal reasons, pointing to the sordid love triangle and Joe Gowlan's financial interest in this deal, he is voted down unanimously.

His brother Hughie, meanwhile, has become a local football hero, and has been invited to play with the Tynecastle team on the following weekend. But on the same day, those million tons of floodwater come pouring into the mines at Scupper Flats, killing Hughie and his father, Bob Fenwick, among several others. The long-predicted disaster also claims the life of the man chiefly responsible for it, Richard Barras, who leads a relief column down into the mine and suffers a fatal stroke.

David gets his opportunity to go to Parliament and fight for the colliers, with the help of Nugent, who tells him: "The world's like a wheel. Your turn will come."

And so it does.

Notes: Carol Reed's career as a director began rather inauspiciously in 1935, with a little-remembered film called *It Happened in Paris*, which was co-written by a young John Huston. In 1938, the director had his first real success with *Bank Holiday* (which was released in America as *Three on a Weekend*). But not until a year later did he make the film that would earn him international acclaim and set him on the path that would lead, inevitably, to Hollywood: *The Stars Look Down*. The film was based on A.J. Cronin's novel and reteamed the young romantic leads of Hitchcock's *The Lady Vanishes* (1938), Michael Redgrave and Margaret Lockwood (who replaced Phyllis Calvert in the role of bad girl Jenny Sunley).

The film required an enormous budget that was quite rare in England at the time (save for the Alexander Korda epics). Isidore Goldsmith, an independent producer, managed to raise the necessary funds and the project went forward under the aegis of Grafton, a small production company.

The financing allowed for six days of shooting at a real coal mine, St. Helens Siddick Colliery at Washington in Cumberland, a coal-rich section of northeastern England. To add to the film's authentic look, the costumes used were purchased from real colliers. After location photography was wrapped, shooting resumed for six weeks at Twickenham Studios in London, where an elaborate mine-head was simulated. Finally, one more week of shooting was required at Shepperton Studios.

Due to intense pressure from Twentieth Century–Fox—which wanted its own coal-mining saga, *How Green Was My Valley* (1941), to have first crack at all box-office revenue available for this particular subject—*The Stars Look Down* did not reach American theatres until 1941. When it finally opened, it did so to mostly rave reviews, and Carol Reed—who would go on to make such classics as *The Third Man* (1949) and *Oliver* (1968)—finished a close second in the New York Film Critics balloting for the year's Best Director, which went to John Ford for *How Green Was My Valley*.

Reviews: "When there are reasons for anger, most films tread softly. Usually the producers count ten before speaking their minds. But now and again there comes along a film that seems to have been struck off at white heat, that surges with indignation, that says what it has to say with complete and undeviating honesty. *The Stars Look Down*, the English-made film which MGM has hesitatingly brought into the Criterion after holding it for many a long month, is such a work. . . . Directed with brilliant restraint by Carol Reed, faithfully performed in even the smallest role, it has caught the slow anguish of its coal-blackened people in a splendid and overwhelming film."—Theodore Strauss, *The New York Times*

"Surely one of the greatest pictures England has ever sent us."—Archer Winsten, *The New York Post*

The Story of Alexander Graham Bell

A Twentieth Century–Fox Film. Directed by Irving Cummings. Produced by Kenneth MacGowan. Screenplay by Lamar Trotti. Based on a story by Ray Harris. Photographed by Leon Shamroy. Edited by Walter Thompson. Art direction by Richard Day and Mark-Lee Kirk. Set decorations by Thomas Little. Costumes by Royer. Sound by Arthur von Kirbach and Roger Heman. Music by Louis Silvers. Running time: 97 minutes.

Cast: Don Ameche *Alexander Graham Bell;* Loretta Young *Mrs. Bell;* Henry Fonda *Thomas Watson;* Charles Coburn *Gardner Hubbard;* Gene Lockhart *Thomas Sanders;* Spring Byington *Mrs. Hubbard;* Sally Blane *Gertrude Hubbard;* Peggy Ann Garner *Grace Hubbard;* Georgiana Young *Berta Hubbard;* Bobs Watson *George Sanders;* Russell Hicks *Barrows;* Paul Stanton *Chauncey Smith;* Jonathan Hale *Western Union president;* Harry Davenport *Judge;* Beryl Mercer *Queen Victoria;* Elizabeth Patterson *Mrs. MacGregor;* Charles Trowbridge *George Pollard;* Jan Duggan *Mrs. Winthrop;* Claire DuBrey *Landlady;* Harry Tyler *Joe Eliot;* Ralph Remley *D'Arcy.*

Acting was not my whole life, as it was with some others. Hank Fonda, he comes to mind, he lived to act. It's kind of sad he had to wait so long to get the recognition he so craved. — Don Ameche[63]

Synopsis: Until Don Ameche was "rediscovered" in the 1980s, with performances in *Trading Places* and *Cocoon* (for which he won an Academy Award), the film he was always best known for — and kidded endlessly about — was *The Story of Alexander Graham Bell.*

It begins with the struggling would-be inventor eking out a living by teaching deaf-mute children. He comes to the attention of a prominent citizen, Gardner Hubbard (Charles Coburn), who hires him to instruct his deaf daughter, Mabel (Loretta Young). She turns out to be a beautiful young woman, and the two fall in love very quickly. Mabel convinces her father to finance Bell's ongoing experiments with a multiple telegraph system. The inventor becomes obsessed with the idea of transmitting human sound through wire, and he hires a young electrician named Tom Watson (Henry Fonda) to assist him.

Bell asks Mabel to marry him and she happily accepts, but her father is outraged, as much by the young man's experiment failures as by his proposal. Bell is discouraged as well by his own lack of progress and he decides to devote his life to teaching, hopeful that he can earn a substantial enough living for Mr. Hubbard to give his consent to marrying his daughter. He tells Mabel his plans by writing the words on the back of a piece of paper on which he has sketched his designs for the telephone. But Mabel refuses to let him quit, so he and Watson struggle on in their attic workshop.

One day, Bell pours sulfuric acid into the transmitter and accidentally spills some on his leg. In pain, he cries out: "Mr. Watson, come here, I want you!"

In another room, Watson is startled to hear the words coming over the equipment. "It talked!" he shouts with a mixture of joy and disbelief.

Thus, in 1876, the telephone was born. However, it was not hailed immediately as one of the world's greatest inventions. Bell has to travel all the way to England and convince Queen Victoria (Beryl Mercer) herself of the importance of his revolutionary device before the Western world really takes notice.

Bell and Mabel are married at last, with Mr. Hubbard's blessing; Mabel becomes pregnant with their first child; and everything seems wonderful until Western Union charges that they invented the telephone before Bell did. He is taken to court, and his case looks grim due to lack of proof. But when Mabel shows up with the message he wrote her on the dated set of telephone designs, the day is saved, and Alexander Graham Bell claims his rightful place in history.

Notes: For a long time after the release of *The Story of Alexander Graham Bell,* leading man Don Ameche was known to many as the man who invented the telephone. People around the country even began to call the

Don Ameche (foreground) and Henry Fonda work and dream together in *The Story of Alexander Graham Bell* (Twentieth Century–Fox).

telephone by the monicker "the Ameche" in his honor. It was a joke that never seemed to get too old to tell, and one that hounded Ameche throughout his career . . . until he finally earned respect and recognition in 1985 for break-dancing in *Cocoon*, that is.

Loretta Young was an unknown actress who had done little more than stand around in Twentieth Century–Fox pictures looking pretty. She was looking for a role that would challenge her as an actress. When she was cast as Alexander Graham Bell's deaf-mute wife, she was thrilled and elated. However, her euphoria was somewhat curbed when Zanuck informed her that she would be playing Mrs. Bell as a woman whose only handicap would be deafness, and that spoken dialogue was inclusive in the role. She made one more picture for the studio after *The Story of Alexander Graham Bell* before quitting and going out on her own.

Although he was coming off the very hot *Jesse James*, Henry Fonda was regarded by the studio—and by Zanuck, particularly—as a limited actor relegated to supporting roles. His part in this film is nothing more than comedy relief. That was all about to change, however, with a call asking him to report to the office of John Ford.

In his review of the film for the *New York Times*, critic Frank S. Nugent (who obviously felt that Tyrone Power was being cast in far too many Twentieth Century–Fox productions) wrote acerbically: "If only because it has omitted Tyrone Power, Twentieth Century–Fox's *The Story of Alexander Graham Bell* (at the Roxy) must be considered one of that company's more sober and meritorious contributions to the historical drama." Well, both Fox and the Roxy were outraged that Nugent would assail an actor who wasn't even in the movie, and they both boycotted the *New York Times* for nearly a full year. The *Times* lost approximately $50,000 in advertising revenue because of this review.

Reviews: ". . . Don Ameche has done rather well, script and all considered, with the role of the founder of the wrong-number industry, and Director Irving Cummings has dealt piously, sincerely and (we trust) faithfully with the dramatic facts which came to his hands. The film may be slow, but it is honestly made. It is interesting even when it is not exciting and, although it probably will not create the dramatic splash *Suez* and *Jesse James* did, it is far the better picture." — Frank S. Nugent, *The New York Times*

"Seldom have the bitter struggles and meager joys of a great man been intermingled with such cumulative and forceful effect. . . . Behind the eloquence of a film that never loses momentum is the splendid playing of Don Ameche, who must have caught some of Bell's genius to interpret him so admirably. . . . If one were inclined to find fault, one might reason that the comedy contrast of Thomas Watson, who is a loyal but unimaginative soul, is a bit too finely drawn. However, one would have to admit that these strains of levity, furnished by the increasingly capable Henry Fonda, are welcome safety valves when the situations are most tense." — Robert W. Dana, *The New York Herald Tribune*

The Story of the Last Chrysanthemum (Zangiku Monogatari)

A Shochiku Production. Directed by Kenji Mizoguchi. Screenplay by Yoshikata Yoda. Based upon an original idea by Shofu Miramatsu. Photographed by Shigeto Miki. Art direction by Hiroshi Mizutani. Music by Senji Ito. Running time: 142 minutes.

Cast: Shotaro Hanayagi *Kikunosuke Onoue;* Kakuko Mori *Otoku;* Gonjuro Kawarazaki *Kikugoro Onoue;* Kokichi Takada *Fukusuke Nakamura;* Eiju Dayu *Ryotaro Kawanami;* Benkei Shiganoya *Genshun Anma;* Kisho Hanayagi *Tamisaburo Onoue.*

> The shinpa tragedy, one can say, makes a grand display of the ego or will of a woman who endures her fate in tears. — Tadao Sato[64]

Synopsis: Kenji Mizoguchi's *The Story of the Last Chrysanthemum* depicted the tragedy of a woman's life in the feudalistic world of Kabuki. It explored beautifully the director's favorite theme, which was the situation of woman: her suffering, her love and her power of saving man, often by great personal sacrifice.

The story begins as a kabuki performance in Meiji Tokyo is coming to an end. Afterwards, back in the dressing room, the actors and stagehands are uniformly perturbed that their production was spoiled by the performance of one inept actor—the young Kikunosuke (Shotaro Hanayagi)—simply because he is the adopted son of their troupe's leader, the peerless Kikugoro (Gonjuro Kawarazaki).

At a party later, Kikunosuke can sense the animosity towards him, so he returns home early and finds himself alone with one of his family's maids, Otoku (Kakuko Mori). During a stroll they take to quiet his baby brother, she speaks candidly to the naïve but well-meaning Kikunosuke about his inferior work and of the troupe's discontent over his special treatment and the nepotism that is poisoning their work.

Kikunosuke can't help falling in love with the forthright yet gentle Otoku, and he declares his love over a watermelon they share. However, when his parents return to find the two of them alone together and practically exchanging vows, Otoku is summarily dismissed.

Barred from seeing her, Kikunosuke does eventually succeed in letting her know that he is leaving Tokyo for Osaka, where he hopes to find work in a theater run by a renegade uncle.

One year later, the two are reunited in Osaka and married. Their blissful domestic life inspires Kikunosuke to work harder at his craft and study diligently. All is going ostensibly well until his uncle dies and he finds himself out of work. Kikunosuke joins a traveling theater troupe, vowing to perfect his trade and return triumphant.

Some more years pass. The troupe is a sorry bunch of actors who, at one point, are released early from their contract in favor of a circus featuring female wrestlers. Their miserable shortcomings force them to get by in just-as-miserable living conditions, and that abject poverty ultimately causes Otoku to fall seriously ill.

When she learns that the Tokyo troupe is scheduled to perform in nearby Nagoya, she secretly goes to see them and begs Kikugoro to give his son a chance to act with them. He agrees, but only on the condition that she relinquish all claims to him. She does so, and Kikunosuke is hired.

The production is an overwhelming success, due mostly to the majestic performance of Kikunosuke. While he acts, Otoku prays beneath the stage for him. Afterwards, as the audience is saluting her husband with a thunderous ovation, she slips away quietly.

Kikunosuke is asked to return to Tokyo with the troupe and prepares to leave immediately. Otoku sends him off, telling him she'll meet him at the train station. But when she doesn't show up, Kikugoro hands his son the farewell note she was forced to write.

Kikunosuke travels back to Tokyo, where he is celebrated by his family. He is chosen by his father to head the great boat parade that opens their troupe's visit to Osaka. However, just as the parade is beginning, he gets word that his wife's illness has reached its final stages. He rushes to her bedside, where she confesses why she left him waiting at the train station. His father, however, has finally accepted their marriage, and he tells her the good news. Otoku is proud and happy to call him "husband," and she sends him back to the parade. Amid all of the music, fireworks and cheers of the crowd, she passes away. In the leading boat, Kikunosuke stares serenely out before him.

Notes: Kenji Mizoguchi was an art student and actor who learned later in life that he had an extraordinary gift for directing films. The critical success of two 1936 projects—*Naniwa ereji (Osaka Elegy)* and *Gion no shimai (Sisters of the Gion)*—earned him a reputation as Japan's leading director around the time that that country was entering its war campaigns. However, both of these films had been financial failures and had angered the government with their gritty, all-too-realistic, contemporary subject matter. After another impressive effort, *Aienkyo (The Straits of Love and Hate)* in '37, Mizoguchi capitulated to pressure and made a militarist film in Manchuria called *Roei no uta (The Song of the Camp)*, which was released a year later. He loathed the project but did not feel he had a choice in the matter, especially after his politically radical younger brother died under mysterious circumstances.

On the strength of his reputation, the Shochiku studios offered him a free hand in choosing the subject matter for his next venture. Suggesting a piece on the bunraku puppet theater (which Mizoguchi ultimately would make in 1940), they encouraged him to choose any actor whom he might like to direct, and Shotaro Hanayagi—the most famous actor on the shinpa (popular melodrama) stage—was approached.

He agreed on the condition that he be allowed to choose the story material. The filmmakers consented and Hanayagi chose *The Story of the Last Chrysanthemum*. The studio couldn't have been more pleased with the actor's selection, since at that very moment the work was playing to enthusiastic audiences on the Japanese stage. It also pleased Mizoguchi, since the plot cut straight to the heart of his obsessions and artistic sensibilities.

The apolitical director would shoot two more pictures focusing on the innocent Meiji era (1868–1921)—his favorite period in Japanese history—after completing *Story*. But it was his majestic work on that project which incontrovertibly led to his being chosen to shoot the immense, government-sponsored *Genroku chushingura (The 47 Ronin)*, which occupied him all during World War II.

The Story of Vernon and Irene Castle

An RKO Picture. Directed by H.C. Potter. Produced by George Haight. Screenplay by Richard Sherman. Based on the stories "My Husband" and "My Memories of Vernon Castle," by Irene Castle. Adapted by Oscar Hammerstein II and Dorothy Yost. Photographed by Robert de Grasse. Edited by William Hamilton. Art direction by Van Nest Polglase. Set decorations by Darrell Silvera. Ginger Rogers' costumes designed by Irene Castle. Dance director: Hermes Pan. Wardrobe and ensembles by William Plunkett. Music director: Victor Baravalle. Orchestrations by Roy Webb and Robert Russell Bennett. Montage by Douglas Travers. Sound by Richard Van Hessen. Assistant director: Argyle Nelson. Technical adviser: Irene Castle. Running time: 93 minutes.

Cast: Fred Astaire *Vernon Castle;* Ginger Rogers *Irene Castle;* Edna May Oliver *Maggie Sutton;* Walter Brennan *Walter Ash;* Lew Fields *Himself;* Etienne Giradot *Papa Aubel;* Rolfe Sedan *Emile Aubel;* Janet Beecher *Mrs. Foote;* Robert Strange *Dr. Foote;* Leonid Kinskey *Artist;* Clarence Derwent *Papa Louis;* Victor Varconi *Grand Duke;* Frances Mercer *Claire Ford;* Donald MacBride *Hotel manager;* Douglas Walton *Student pilot;* Sonny Lamont *Charlie the tap dancer.*

> I'm sure the studio would rather I had been dead. They even waited two years for me to kick off, I suspect, after I had sold them the story. But when they found that I was indestructible, they went ahead and made it. — Irene Castle[65]

Synopsis/Notes: As I said in the introduction to this book, 1939 was a year for endings as well as beginnings, and the saddest ending of all, perhaps, was the release of *The Story of Vernon and Irene Castle,* for it marked the end of a wonderful series of RKO musicals starring Fred Astaire and Ginger Rogers.

The movie tells the true story of Vernon and Irene Castle, a famous dancing team in the early part of this century who were single-handedly responsible for the phenomenal growth of ballroom dancing in the United States. They toured the continent extensively, appeared on Broadway together, conducted dance studios, performed at their own night spots, and introduced and popularized such ballroom innovations as the Maxixe, the Turkey Trot, the Castle Walk and the Tango. As if all that weren't enough, Irene was a trend-setter in fashion and hair style as well.

The two met in the summer of 1910, while Vernon was appearing in a Broadway musical with Lew Fields at a beach in New Rochelle. They fell in love and were married soon after. Irene convinced her husband to give up his second-banana comedy role and pursue a career in dancing, and the team of Vernon and Irene Castle was born. They went to Paris— accompanied by Irene's faithful servant, Walter—where they first gained attention and acclaim dancing in a Parisian nightclub. Their fame sky-rocketed until, before long, they were international stars. When World War I erupted, Vernon enlisted in the Royal Air Corps and saw service in France. Ironically, following a series of perilous missions against the Germans, he was killed in a routine flight exercise when, in an effort to avoid

The Castles (Fred Astaire and Ginger Rogers) dance their way across America in
***The Story of Vernon and Irene Castle* (RKO).**

a student-piloted plane, he deliberately crashed his plane and was killed instantly. All of this was true and all of it was dramatized in the film, with Astaire as Vernon Castle, Rogers as Irene, Lew Fields as himself, and Walter Brennan as Irene's servant, Walter.

Irene Castle was offered the role of her own mother, but turned it down; the idea struck her as unnatural. The studio got Janet Beecher to play the part instead. Miss Castle remained behind the scenes, where she worked as the film's technical adviser, as well as having approval over cast, direction, script and costumes. She was not, however, allowed any say over the choice of Ginger Rogers to play her in the movie—but she did not conceal her disapproval, either.

All of the songs sung and danced to in the picture were period songs from the early part of the century, except for one new ballad, "Only When You're in My Arms" (which detracted from the film's otherwise strong historical accuracy with its distinct, unmistakably late-thirties sound and flavor). The song's lyricist, Bert Kalmar, was later portrayed by Fred Astaire in the movie *Three Little Words* (1950).

Lew Fields — the famous "Dutch" comic with whom Vernon appeared in five Broadway musicals — played himself in the movie. Fields was also the father of Dorothy Fields, who was the lyricist for two earlier Astaire pictures, *Roberta* (1935) and *Swing Time* (1936).

Astaire and Rogers were reunited one last time ten years later in the MGM musical *The Barkleys of Broadway.*

Reviews: "To say that Fred Astaire and Ginger Rogers are well fitted to fill the Castles' dancing slippers is an understatement. Astaire and Rogers symbolize their era just as completely as the Castles symbolized theirs." — *Time*

"Rogers and Astaire brilliantly recreate the famous couple's inspired contributions to the dance world. The result is not only a refreshing musical but a haunting screen biography." — *Newsweek*

They Made Me a Criminal

A Warner Bros.–First National Picture. Directed by Busby Berkeley. Produced by Jack L. Warner and Hal B. Wallis. Associate producer: Benjamin Glazer. Screenplay by Sig Herzig. Based on a novel by Bertram Millhauser and Beulah Marie Dix. Photographed by James Wong Howe. Edited by Jack Killifer. Art direction by Anton Grot. Gowns by Milo Anderson. Sound by Oliver S. Garretson. Assistant director: Russ Saunders. Music by Max Steiner. Musical director: Leo F. Forbstein. Running time: 92 minutes.

Cast: John Garfield *Johnnie Bradfield;* Claude Rains *Detective Phelan;* Ann Sheridan *Goldie;* May Robson *Grandma;* Gloria Dickson *Peggy;* Billy Halop *Tommy;* Bobby Jordan *Angel;* Leo Gorcey *Spit;* Huntz Hall *Dippy;* Gabriel Dell *T.B.;* Bernard Punsley *Milt;* Robert Gleckler *Doc Ward;* John Ridgely *Magee;* Barbara Pepper *Budgie;* William Davidson *Ennis;* Ward Bond *Lenihan;* Robert Strange *Malvin;* Louis Jean Heydt *Smith;* Frank Riggi *Rutchek;* Cliff Clark *Manager;* Dick Wessel *Collucci;* Raymond Brown *Sheriff;* Sam Hayes *Fight announcer.*

> It was so hot, we had to stop shooting by noontime, and there were times when the heat was so intense it melted the film in the camera. — Director Busby Berkeley, on the filming conditions of *They Made Me a Criminal*[66]

Synopsis: After making an impressive feature film debut as a disillusioned piano player in the 1938 soap *Four Daughters,* John Garfield officially became a bankable star the following year with the release of his second movie, *They Made Me a Criminal.* He plays tough southpaw Johnnie Bradfield, who in the film's opening sequence wins the lightweight boxing championship. In his dressing room after the fight, Johnnie meets Detective Phelan (Claude Rains), who was demoted to morgue duty years ago when he convicted a man of murder and sent him to the electric chair, only to have the man later proven innocent. Phelan is embittered but hopeful of someday redeeming himself. He helps Johnnie out by strapping on the fighter's wristwatch for him, all the while telling him how every boxer in the world can be identified by his stance, each having one as unique and individual as his own set of fingerprints.

Later that night, while celebrating his victory with his manager, Doc Ward (Robert Gleckler), and some other people, Johnnie gets into an altercation with a reporter (John Ridgely), who learns about the boxer's double life and threatens to print the story in his column. Johnnie passes out, and while he is unconscious, Doc smashes a bottle over the reporter's skull, inadvertently killing him. Panic-stricken, Doc steals Johnnie's wallet, his watch and his girl (Ann Sheridan) and makes a desperate run for the border. En route, he and the girl are both killed in a high-speed auto crash while trying to elude the police.

When Johnnie awakens from his drunken stupor, he is astonished to read about his own death in the morning newspaper. Since his watch was on Doc Ward's wrist, the burned corpse was identified as Johnnie Bradfield's and the case was closed.

However, when Phelan learns that the wristwatch was found on the victim's left hand and buckled in the third hole, he is convinced that Johnnie is still alive and that the corpse belongs to someone else. He distinctly remembers putting the watch on Johnnie's right hand and buckling it in the first hole. He wants the case to be reopened and requests to be assigned to it. His superiors in the department laugh at this request, but Phelan is determined to find Johnnie and, after a decade on morgue detail, finally regains his status as an inspector.

Johnnie, meanwhile, leaves New York for good and takes the name "Jack Dorney," hopping freight trains, bedding down in cheap motels, working wherever possible. After several aimless months of drifting, exhausted and hungry, he passes out on Rancho Rafferty in Arizona, a home for juvenile delinquents from New York's tough East Side. The ranch is inhabited by Grandma (May Robson) and an attractive young woman named Peggy (Gloria Dickson), who run the place, and a bunch of kids from reform school (The Dead End Kids), who are there to regenerate.

When Johnnie regains consciousness, he is pleasantly surprised to find Peggy nursing him back to health. He wastes no time in making a pass at her, but is quickly rejected.

He takes a job picking berries on the farm and becomes very friendly with the kids, but gains no ground with Peggy. He learns that she and

John Garfield shows the Dead End Kids a few of his boxing moves in *They Made Me a Criminal* (Warner Bros.–First National).

Grandma have been footing the bill themselves for the farm ever since Reverend Rafferty—who originally sponsored the program—died over a year ago, but the bills have become overwhelming. The kids want to open a gas station, since there isn't one for many miles in any direction from Rancho Rafferty, but acquiring the two thousand dollars it would take to open such a place is another matter.

One day, Johnnie and some of the kids go swimming in an irrigation tank. As soon as they are in, though, a nearby farmer begins irrigating his land, thereby draining the enormous tank. Before they realize it, none of them can reach the top of the tank, yet it is still too full for them to stop swimming. Caught between a rock and a hard place, and with some of the kids tiring, Johnnie swims to the bottom of the tank and locates a valve which slowly but surely drains the water out, saving all of their lives.

When they return home very late, they try a phony story on Peggy that doesn't take. Convinced from day one that Johnnie was nothing but trouble, she blames him and orders him off the ranch.

While he is packing to leave, though, one of the kids tells Peggy what really happened. She apologizes and asks Johnnie to stay. He agrees and makes another pass at her. This time, she doesn't stop him.

They decide to drive into town together, where Johnnie sees an advertisement announcing the world tour of a European boxer named Gaspar Rutchek (Frank Riggi), alias "the Wild Bull." The ad offers $500 for every round that any challenger can stay in the ring with Rutchek when he makes a stop at nearby Legion Stadium.

Seeing a chance to earn enough money for the gas station, Johnnie goes to sign up. When the promoter (Ward Bond) tells him he's too small, Johnnie slugs him to the ground, convincing him to change his mind and add Johnnie to the boxing card (which includes two other challengers).

While training for the bout, he learns to his chagrin that one of the kids took his picture without his knowledge and won a photography contest with it. The picture ends up in a local paper and, when Phelan sees it, he is convinced that the subject in the photograph is not Jack Dorney at all, but Johnnie Bradfield. He leaves immediately for Arizona.

On the night of the fight, Johnnie discovers that Phelan has ringside tickets for the bout and is snooping around asking if Jack Dorney is a southpaw. Johnnie tells Grandma, Peggy and the kids that he can't fight after all, and he blames it on a bad heart. However, they have already heard the results of his physical and know that he is in perfect condition.

He packs his belongings and prepares to leave the ranch, but he doesn't quite make it. The ties that bind have bound him and he decides to fight after all, hoping to fool Phelan by changing his boxing stance and fighting from the right side.

The two other challengers are beaten quickly and convincingly by Rutchek, and Johnnie enters the ring as the third and final opponent. "Hey, Johnnie!" Phelan calls out from ringside, but Johnnie doesn't fall for it.

Not using his normal fighting style, Johnnie is beaten to a pulp by Rutchek for more than three rounds. In the fourth, he is knocked down hard, and Phelan yells that he's not fooling him at all and he knows his real identity. With nothing to lose, Johnnie gets back up fighting southpaw and unloads on Rutchek. In the next round, Johnnie is knocked out, but not before earning enough money for the gas station.

At the train station, Phelan releases Johnnie and returns to New York alone. He knows that the fighter is innocent, and he does not want to be responsible for another innocent man being executed. Johnnie returns to Peggy and the kids, to live the rest of his life, happily, as Jack Dorney.

Notes: *They Made Me a Criminal* was a remake of the 1933 Warners hit *The Life of Jimmy Dolan*, which starred Douglas Fairbanks, Jr., and featured John Wayne in a bit part. Like its predecessor, *Criminal* became a commercial success by combining elements of *Boys Town* (1938) with elements of the fight melodrama.

In his last assignment for Warner Bros., Busby Berkeley was assigned to direct. The project was a far cry from the series of musical extravaganzas which had become synonymous with his name, but nevertheless he did a fine job, bringing out the qualities in John Garfield which would soon make him one of the studio's top stars and an antihero for all time.

Berkeley shot the picture on location in Palm Desert, California, during the summer of 1938, withstanding heat so intense it cut their workdays drastically short and an uprising of gnats so bothersome that the entire crew (actors excluded, of course) had to wear protective nets.

The film was photographed by the great Chinese cinematographer James Wong Howe, who would go on to lens several other Garfield pictures, including the 1947 classic *Body and Soul.*

Reviews: "If you repeat the title of the new picture *They Made Me a Criminal*—you can almost fancy you hear the voice of John Garfield accusing the Warner Brothers. . . . So now they've made John Garfield a criminal, and since Mr. Garfield is young, resilient and no end talented, he is making the best of what, after all, is not such a bad situation. In spite of veteran scene-stealers like May Robson and the Dead End Kids (give the boys another year to polish their routines and they can bill themselves as the Six Stooges) it is always Mr. Garfield who carries the show along. . . . It's an elderly plot, all right, but Mr. Garfield is young; he will live it down."—B.R. Crisler, *The New York Times*

"Garfield and the kids and the gal, the director and those who worried the script into shape—and even Claude Rains as the broken but hopeful flatfoot—these people manage to salvage enough truth out of it to make most of the business convincing and pleasant."—Otis Ferguson, *The New Republic*

Tower of London

A Universal Picture. Produced and directed by Rowland V. Lee. Screenplay by Robert N. Lee. Photographed by George Robinson. Edited by Edward Curtiss. Art direction by Jack Otterson. Set decoration by Russell Gausman. Musical director: Charles Previn. Orchestrations by Frank Skinner. Make-up by Jack P. Pierce. Costumes by Vera West. Technical advisors: Major G.O.T. Bagley and Gerald Grove. Sound by Bernard B. Brown and William Hedgcock. Running time: 92 minutes. Release date: November 17.

Cast: Basil Rathbone *Richard III;* Boris Karloff *Mord;* Barbara O'Neil *Queen Elyzabeth;* Ian Hunter *Edward IV;* Vincent Price *Duke of Clarence;* Nan Grey *Lady Alice Barton;* John Sutton *John Wyatt;* Leo G. Carroll *Lord Hastings;* Miles Mander *Henry VI;* Lionel Belmore *Beacon;* Rose Hobart *Anne Neville;* Ralph Forbes *Henry Tudor;* Frances Robinson *Isobel;* Ernest Cossart *Tom Clink;* G.P. Huntley *Prince of Wales;* John Rodion *De Vere;* Ronald Sinclair *Prince Edward;* Donnie Dunagan *Prince Richard.*

> It was a pleasure to know such a charming man and a constant wonder that this fearful ogre in pictures should be so addicted to . . . cricket!—Ian Hunter on costar Boris Karloff[67]

Synopsis: Hoping to repeat the success of *Son of Frankenstein,* Universal reunited producer-director Rowland V. Lee with stars Basil Rathbone and Boris Karloff (as well as a number of the technical people) for the lively fifteenth-century melodrama *Tower of London.*

The story begins in 1471, as King Henry VI (Miles Mander) is deposed by his nephew, who proclaims himself King Edward IV (Ian Hunter). The old king's son, the Prince of Wales (G.P. Huntley), flees and begins to assemble an army to fight Henry.

In an effort to raise funds to supplement his own army and power, Edward orders his brother, Richard III (Rathbone)—the infamous crook-backed Duke of Gloucester—to marry an elderly duchess and claim her dowry. Richard refuses, for he is still in love with Anne Neville (Rose Hobart), who has married the Prince of Wales with the aid of Richard's other brother, the Duke of Clarence (Vincent Price). Instead, Richard suggests John Wyatt (John Sutton), the queen's cousin, as a suitable mate for the duchess. But when Edward commands Wyatt to consent, the young man refuses. He is waiting to marry Lady Alice Barton (Nan Grey). The king—whose axiom is "marry your enemies and behead your friends"—imprisons Wyatt. But to appease his wife, Queen Elyzabeth (Barbara O'Neil), Edward banishes him to France instead of having him executed.

When news arrives that the Prince of Wales has landed with his army to rescue his father, Richard is elated. He leads an army into battle, taking along the senseless King Henry, and they crush the invading army in deadly hand-to-hand combat. The prince himself is outdueled by Richard in a swordfight.

Henry somehow manages to survive the battle, but is murdered afterward by Richard's henchman, the evil, club-footed executioner, Mord (Boris Karloff). Anne Neville goes into hiding, disguised as a serving wench, but is spotted by one of Mord's spies, arrested, and taken to the tower, where she is told that only the Duke of Gloucester can save her. Helpless, she agrees to marry Richard.

Threatened with the loss of a sizeable portion of his own inheritance, the Duke of Clarence conspires against the king. Richard learns of this plot and has Clarence arrested and taken to the tower. There, Richard challenges his brother to a wine-drinking contest, with the whole of the Warwick estates going to the winner. Clarence, who is much better acquainted with the grape, readily accepts the challenge. Predictably, he wins the contest, but when he passes out in its aftermath, Richard and Mord drown him in a vat of wine. Once sixth in line for the throne, Richard is getting closer and closer to his ultimate goal.

More than a decade passes and the story picks up in 1483, with King Edward IV on his deathbed. His last acts as king are to pardon John Wyatt and make Richard the Protector of England, to look after Henry's two young sons, Prince Edward (Ronald Sinclair) and Prince Richard (Donnie Dunagan). After his father's death, Prince Edward is groomed for the throne.

Richard orders Mord to murder the two boys and finally makes his ascension to king. The queen retaliates by having Wyatt steal the royal

Tower of London (Universal). *Top:* The two armies prepare to do battle. The rain machines left cardboard armor and helmets so soggy that battle scenes had to be reshot. *Bottom:* Mord (Boris Karloff, right) and Richard III (Basil Rathbone, center) prepare to murder the Duke of Clarence (Vincent Price).

treasure, to be used in raising an army for another exiled rebel, Henry Tudor (Ralph Forbes). Wyatt is captured, but not before hiding the treasure.

Wyatt is taken to the tower, where Mord goes to work on him with all the tools of his diabolical trade. Wyatt endures the torture, refusing to divulge the location of the treasure.

A chimney sweeper loyal to the queen, Tom Clink (Ernest Cossart), sneaks Anne Neville—disguised as a sweep's boy—into Richard's compound. She finds her way into Wyatt's cell, leaves him a file to cut through his chains and a rope hanging in the chimney. He escapes and they set sail for France with the treasure, where Henry Tudor awaits.

They return with an army and defeat the English opposition, killing Richard and Mord in battle. Wyatt is made an earl and marries Alice Barton.

Notes: The success of *Son of Frankenstein* spawned this effective chiller, which contains menacing performances by Basil Rathbone and a bald, club-footed Boris Karloff.

With the exception of a brief speech recited by John Barrymore in the 1929 revue *Show of Shows*, Rathbone was the first actor to play Richard III in a talking motion picture. Unlike future Richards Laurence Olivier and Vincent Price (who would play the part in United Artists' 1962 remake of *Tower of London*), Rathbone did not portray him as a grotesque hunchback, but rather as a handsome and deceptively charming character, stricken with only a slight deformity.

Besides using many cast and crew members from *Son of Frankenstein*, this film also repeated the Monster theme music for Karloff. The cast included Rathbone's son, who had a brief fling in films, appearing under the name of John Rodion.

During location shooting of battle scenes in Tarzana, California, the cardboard armor and helmets worn by the extras became hopelessly soggy after the rain machines were turned on. Inevitably, the scenes had to be reshot. Some of the standing sets from the picture wound up in the serial *Flash Gordon Conquers the Universe* and in *Horror Island*.

Reviews: "*Tower of London* is as sinister as Basil Rathbone, Boris Karloff and the rest of Universal's horror department can make it.... Although the picture is not without its weaknesses, lack of thrills is not one of them. Neither is the casting.... Rathbone and Karloff ... are savage enough to please the most bloodthirsty...."—Dorothy Masters, *The New York Daily News*

"...As a horror picture, it's one of the most broadly etched, but still so strong it may provide disturbing nightmares as aftermath.... Rathbone provides a most vivid portrayal.... Karloff is familiar.... Rowland Lee has directed deftly, neatly mixing his dramatic ingredients for suspenseful values."—*Variety*

Twenty-One Days

London Films, England. 75 min. Directed by Basil Dean.

Cast: Vivien Leigh, Laurence Olivier, Leslie Banks, Francis L. Sullivan, Hay Petrie, Esme Percy, Robert Newton, Victor Rietti, Morris Harvey.

This Alexander Korda production was actually filmed in 1937 but not released until two years later (and then only to capitalize on the newfound fame of its two stars). Olivier plays the brother of an eminent barrister who falls in love with Leigh and accidentally kills her rejected husband. When an innocent man is blamed, Olivier wants to turn himself in, but the accused man dies of a heart attack while in custody and the two lovers are free to go off together. Graham Greene, who adapted the screenplay, wrote of his own movie in *The Spectator:* "I wish I could tell the extraordinary story that lies behind this shelved and resurrected picture, a story involving a theme song, and a bottle of whiskey, and camels in Wales. . . . Meanwhile, let one guilty man, at any rate, stand in the dock, swearing never to do it again." That story might have been better than the film itself. But, although it wasn't one of the most memorable releases of the year, there was one off-screen incident which occurred near the end of shooting that no one present would likely soon forget. The final scene called for the lovers to take a trip down the Thames River, from Tower Bridge to the Southend. On the boat, a group of the cast and crew members were conversing together while waiting for the shot to be set up. The discussion soon turned to MGM's unprecedented search for an actress to play Scarlett O'Hara in the film version of Margaret Mitchell's best-seller *Gone with the Wind.* Bette Davis, Paulette Goddard, Barbara Stanwyck and Miriam Hopkins were just a few of the names suggested by various members of the group. When talk turned to who would play Rhett Butler in the film, someone suggested Olivier, but he just laughed the idea off. Other actors mentioned included Errol Flynn, Robert Taylor and Gary Cooper. Miss Leigh, who had remained silent throughout the conversation (and who had done relatively little in movies up to this time), then declared boldly that although "Larry" would not be Rhett Butler, she herself would be Scarlett.

Union Pacific

A Paramount Picture. Produced and directed by Cecil B. DeMille. Executive producer: William LeBaron. Associate producer: William Pine. Scenarists: Walter DeLeon, C. Gardner Sullivan, and Jesse Lasky, Jr. Adaptation by Jack Cunningham. Based on the novel *Trouble Shooter,* by Ernest Haycox. Photographed by Victor Milner. Edited by Anne Bauchens. Art direction by Hans Dreier and Roland Anderson. Set decorations by A.E. Freudeman. Sound by Harry Lindgren and John Cope. Musical score by

George Antheil, Sigmund Krumgold, and John Leipold. Conducted by Irvin Talbot. Costumes by Natalie Visart. Special effects by Gordon Jennings and Loren L. Ryder. Location director: Arthur Rosson. Assistant directors: Charles Barton and Edward Salvin. Dialogue director: Edwin Maxwell. Technical adviser: Lucius Beebe. Running time: 130 minutes. Release date: April 28.

Cast: Barbara Stanwyck *Mollie Monahan;* Joel McCrea *Jeff Butler;* Akim Tamiroff *Fiesta;* Robert Preston *Dick Allen;* Lynne Overman *Leach Overmile;* Brian Donlevy *Sid Campeau;* Robert Barrat *Duke Ring;* Anthony Quinn *Cordray;* Stanley Ridges *Casement;* Henry Kolker *Asa M. Barrows;* Francis McDonald *Grenville M. Dodge;* Willard Robertson *Oakes Ames;* Harold Goodwin *E.E. Calvin;* Evelyn Keyes *Mrs. Calvin;* Richard Lane *Sam Reed;* William Haade *Dusky Claxton;* Regis Toomey *Paddy O'Rourke;* J.M. Kerrigan *Monahan;* Fuzzy Knight *Cookie;* Harry Woods *Al Brett;* Lon Chaney, Jr. *Dollarhide;* Joseph Crehan *Ulysses S. Grant;* Julia Faye *Mame;* Sheila Darcy *Rose;* Joseph Sawyer *Shamus.*

> She is fearless and has more guts than most men. — Joel McCrea on Barbara Stanwyck[68]

> I have never worked with an actress who was more cooperative, less temperamental, and a better workman, to use my term of highest compliment, than Barbara Stanwyck. — Cecil B. DeMille[69]

Synopsis: Cecil B. DeMille's contribution to this year of epics was, of all things, a Western; but it's a brawling, two-fisted, action-packed Western. It is the story of the Union Pacific Railway, which was destined to link two oceans and open up the West.

The story begins in Washington, where President Ulysses S. Grant (Joseph Crehan) — in an unwontedly sober moment — approves the challenge of creating a transcontinental railroad. Before long, the Union Pacific is chugging across the plains, engineered by Irish immigrant Monahan (J.M. Kerrigan), with his spunky daughter Mollie (Barbara Stanwyck) serving as the tracklayers' postmistress and her father's inspiration, and protected by troubleshooter Jeff Butler (Joel McCrea) and his two saddle pals, Fiesta (Akim Takiroff) and Leach Overmile (Lynne Overman).

Their rival is the Central Pacific Railroad, which is represented by financier Asa M. Barrows (Henry Kolker). One of his cronies, the evil Sid Campeau (Brian Donlevy), is riding in one of the Union Pacific's coaches, trying to distract the railroad employees with booze and women. His right-hand man is a gambler named Dick Allen (Robert Preston), an old army buddy of Jeff's. Although the two fought together in the Civil War, they suddenly find themselves on opposite sides, as well as rivals in the wooing of Mollie Monahan.

It is not long before the two sides clash. Campeau dispatches Allen to

Union Pacific (Paramount). *Top:* An unwelcome guest arrives through the back door as Robert Preston, Barbara Stanwyck and Joel McCrea fight off Indians from a wrecked train. *Bottom:* The cavalry arrives just in time to subdue the Indian attack.

steal the railroad payroll. Mollie persuades Allen to return it and, in the course of her pleading, becomes his bride (although she really loves Jeff). Jeff, meanwhile, retaliates against Campeau by leading the railroad men into town and destroying his saloon. Campeau, in turn, vows bloody vengeance.

When Jeff, Mollie and Allen board the train, they encounter a new enemy: Indians. The savages overturn a water tank and—in the film's most impressive sequence—derail the train. After the wreck, the Indians begin to slaughter the train passengers, while engaging in hijinks with the ladies' undergarments. They are only moments away from victimizing Mollie when a train carrying United States Army troops arrives to rout the savages.

Allen flees after reconciling with Jeff. On the historic day at Promontory Point, when the railroads meet and the golden spike is to be driven, Jeff, Mollie and Allen all show up for the inauguration. Campeau shows up as well, planning to murder Jeff. Learning of the scheme, Allen searches his former boss out and is shot in cold blood by him. Jeff arrives just in time to hear his dying friend's last words: "I've drawn the black deuce."

Campeau, meanwhile, is taking aim at Jeff's back, preparing to squeeze the trigger. Before he can get a shot off, though, Fiesta and Leach arrive on the scene and blast him to a deserved end.

Jeff returns to the ceremony, and Mollie asks him where Allen is. Jeff—who is undoubtedly fated to wed the widow—replies: "He'll be waiting for us, Mollie, at the end of the track."

The spike is driven, the crowd roars, the scene switches to a roaring diesel train while "Stars and Stripes Forever" plays, and *Union Pacific* races to its triumphant finish.

Notes: Cecil B. DeMille, overworked and recovering from a prostate operation, directed much of this film from a stretcher. Arthur Rosson and James Hogan, meanwhile, supervised some of the location work, which was shot in Iron Springs, Utah, and Canoga Park, California (the spot chosen to represent historic Promontory Point).

DeMille's first choice for the role of Mollie was Jean Arthur. When she was unavailable, he turned to an actress whom he respected and admired greatly, Barbara Stanwyck. They had worked many times on the DeMille-produced "Lux Radio Theatre," and Miss Stanwyck did not let him down.

Anthony Quinn, who at the time was DeMille's son-in-law, appeared as a gambler in a role he considered "embarrassingly small." And Barbara Stanwyck's brother was one of the extras on the film.

Incidentally, the golden spike used in the film was the actual one used at Promontory Point. DeMille had it exhumed from the vault of San Francisco's Wells Fargo Bank for use in the picture.

Union Pacific was nominated for Best Special Effects, but lost to the earthquake and flood created in *The Rains Came*.

Reviews: "Cecil B. DeMille's *Union Pacific* is like a rough-and-tumble heavyweight slug fest—exciting, thrilling, gory and cumbersome. . . . The

The historic driving of the golden spike in *Union Pacific* (Paramount). The golden spike used here is the genuine article, borrowed from the vault of the Wells Fargo Bank.

cast is a good one. Barbara Stanwyck is excellent as Molly, Joel McCrea is first-rate as Jeff, Robert Preston does an outstanding job as Dick Allen. . . . Here's a western at its most spectacular."—William Boehnel, *The New York World-Telegram*

"Cecil B. DeMille has made a fine, big, boisterous film in *Union Pacific*. . . ."—Kate Cameron, *The New York Daily News*

Wall Street Cowboy

66 min. Directed by Joseph Kane.

Cast: Roy Rogers, George Hayes, Raymond Hatton, Ann Baldwin, Pierre Watkin.

When a Wall Street syndicate learns that Roy's ranch is rich in a precious metallic element called molybdenum (used in the mining of steel), they summarily try to foreclose. It's a move they regret by film's end.

We Are Not Alone

Warner Bros. 112 min. Directed by Edmund Goulding.

Cast: Paul Muni, Jane Bryan, Flora Robson, Raymond Severn, Una

O'Connor, Henry Daniell, Montagu Love, James Stephenson, Stanley Logan, Cecil Kellaway, Alan Napier, Eily Malyon.

This excellent film tells the tragic story of Muni's love for governess Bryan and the accidental death of his wife, played by Robson, being blamed on the two and resulting in their being sent to the gallows. Actress Dolly Haass was initially cast by Warners as the governess, but a personality conflict with Muni caused her to be fired from the project and replaced by studio contract player Jane Bryan. Because of Muni's personal dislike for romantic roles, he was inclined to turn this film down, but his wife, Bella, convinced him to reconsider. First, though, the actor insisted that James Hilton—who wrote the book on which the movie was based—be hired to rewrite the script. After reading the novelist's new draft, Muni commented: "That's the difference between chicken shit and chicken salad." This was the actor's tenth and final film for Warner Bros., and although it received excellent notices, it bombed at the box office.

When Tomorrow Comes

RKO. 90 min. Directed by John M. Stahl.

Cast: Irene Dunne, Charles Boyer, Barbara O'Neil, Nydia Westman, Onslow Stevens.

The stars of *Love Affair* were quickly reunited in an effort to capitalize on their screen chemistry and broad audience appeal, but this was no *Love Affair*. It's a standard soap opera—written by, of all people, author James M. Cain (who wrote the books *Double Indemnity* and *The Postman Always Rings Twice*, among others)—with married man Boyer falling in love with Dunne. The film was remade in 1957 and again in 1968, both times as *Interlude*.

The Wizard of Oz

A Metro-Goldwyn-Mayer Picture. Directed by Victor Fleming and (uncredited) Richard Thorpe and King Vidor. Produced by Mervyn LeRoy. Associate producer: Arthur Freed. Screenplay by Noel Langley, Florence Ryerson and Edgar Allan Woolf. Based on the book by L. Frank Baum. Photographed in Technicolor by Harold Rosson. (Opening and closing sequences in sepia.) Edited by Blanche Sewell. Art direction by Cedric Gibbons and William A. Horning. Set decoration by Edwin B. Willis. Special effects by Arnold Gillespie. Costumes by Adrian. Music by Harold Arlen. Lyrics by E.Y. Harburg. Musical adaptation by Herbert Stothart. Musical numbers staged by Bobby Connolly. Character make-ups created by Jack Dawn. Sound by Douglas Shearer. Running time: 100 minutes. Release date: August 17.

Songs: "Over the Rainbow," "Munchkinland," "Follow the Yellow Brick Road," "If I Only Had a Brain," "We're Off to See the Wizard," "Merry Old Land of Oz," "Laugh a Day Away," "If I Were King," "Courage," "Ding, Dong, the Witch Is Dead," "If I Only Had a Heart," "Optimistic Voices," and "The Jitterbug" (cut from the film following the first public preview).

Cast: Judy Garland *Dorothy;* Frank Morgan *Professor Marvel/The Wizard;* Ray Bolger *Hunk/Scarecrow;* Bert Lahr *Zeke/Cowardly Lion;* Jack Haley *Hickory/Tin Woodman;* Billie Burke *Glinda;* Margaret Hamilton *Miss Gulch/Wicked Witch;* Charles Grapewin *Uncle Henry;* Clara Blandick *Auntie Em;* Pat Walshe *Nikko;* and Toto.

> There's no place like home.... Everybody has a heart. Everybody has a brain. Everybody has a soul. —Ray Bolger[70]

Synopsis: Ageless and timeless, *The Wizard of Oz* seems destined to stand forever as the undisputed king of the musical fantasy genre, as well as the most popular movie ever shown on television.

The film opens, not in fantasy, but in the stark reality of sepia-toned Kansas, where young Dorothy (Judy Garland) dreams of a better place far beyond the skies in the song "Over the Rainbow." Her biggest concern, at the moment, is the well-being of her cairn terrier Toto, who has incurred the wrath of the evil Miss Gulch (Margaret Hamilton) by feeding on her garden vegetables. When Miss Gulch arrives at Dorothy's farm with a sheriff's order authorizing her to impound the animal, Dorothy's guardians, Auntie Em (Clara Blandick) and Uncle Henry (Charles Grapewin), are forced to comply. Miss Gulch puts little Toto in a basket and whisks him away on her bicycle, but the dog escapes and scurries back home to Dorothy. Realizing that Miss Gulch will return, Dorothy decides to run away from home and take Toto with her. She doesn't get far, though, before meeting the irascible Professor Marvel (Frank Morgan), who gazes into his crystal ball and—using a picture he finds of Dorothy with her aunt, as well as a bit of conjecture—convinces the young runaway to return home to the people who love her.

En route back to her farm, Dorothy and Toto are caught in a Kansas twister, a cyclone that transports them from the real to the fantastic; from the drab existence of life on a small Kansas farm to the wonderful and magical (and bright Technicolor) land of Oz.

"Toto, I have a feeling we're not in Kansas any more," she says as they cross the imaginary borderline. "We must be over the rainbow!" Indeed she was, and she had taken the rest of us along with her.

Dorothy's house (which has served as the vehicle of passage for her and Toto) has landed on the Wicked Witch of the East, killing her. The Good Witch of the North, Glinda (Billie Burke), appears from the sky and the tiny munchkins (played by the Singer Midgets) who populate this foreign land appear from the ground. They rejoice in song and pageantry that the

The Wizard of Oz (MGM). *Top:* Judy Garland makes a stop in Munchkinland and meets Glinda, the Good Witch of the North (Billie Burke), before setting off on the Yellow Brick Road to the wonderful land of Oz. *Bottom:* Judy Garland, Ray Bolger, Bert Lahr and Jack Haley prepare to enter The Haunted Forest.

Wicked Witch is dead, declaring the day a national holiday and proclaiming Dorothy their heroine. The grandiloquent proceedings are disrupted, however, by the sudden arrival of the Wicked Witch of the West (whom the audience recognizes as Miss Gulch), sister of the recently deceased. She demands her sister's powerful ruby slippers, which have been magically transported onto Dorothy's feet and cannot be removed. The Wicked Witch of the West vanishes, in a puff of smoke, but not before threatening to settle with Dorothy at a later time.

Dorothy's only desire, despite the wonders of Oz, is to find her way back to Kansas. Glinda tells her about the powerful and mysterious Wizard of Oz, who resides in the Emerald City, and suggests that only he can help her. When Dorothy asks how to get to the Emerald City, she is instructed to "follow the Yellow Brick Road," which she does. She is escorted to the border of Munchkinland, and sets off on her own from there to find the Wizard of Oz.

She travels a ways before coming to a division in the road, where she stops and ponders which path to choose. It is here that she meets the first of her three traveling companions, the Scarecrow (Ray Bolger), whom she helps down off of his perch. Sadly, the Scarecrow can't even scare a crow, because he has no brain. Dorothy suggests that perhaps the Wizard of Oz would grant him a brain and, claiming that he'd face a box of matches for the cause of acquiring one, he takes her arm and accompanies her on her journey to the Emerald City.

After an encounter with some plucky apple trees, Dorothy discovers a Tin Woodman (Jack Haley), where he has been rusted in the same position for over a year. She finds his oil can nearby and uses it generously on him, freeing his tin nerves and allowing him to walk, talk and move. When he tells her that his tinsmith forgot to give him a heart, they in turn tell him about the Wizard of Oz, and the Tin Man joins them in hopes that the Wizard will rectify the tinsmith's error. They waltz off merrily together down the Yellow Brick Road.

Later, in a dark and forbidding forest, Dorothy encounters her third and final traveling companion, the Cowardly Lion (Bert Lahr). At first, the Lion acts and speaks courageously, scaring Dorothy's two new friends, as well as her dog Toto, but when Dorothy reprimands him with a slap, the Lion breaks down and cries. He confesses to them that he lacks courage, and is indeed a Cowardly Lion . . . he even scares himself sometimes. They take him along with them, assuring him that the Wizard will be able to grant him courage and thereby reinstate him as the true "king of the jungle."

The Wicked Witch tries to stop them by using a field of poppies to put them to sleep, but Good Witch Glinda counters with an unseasonal snowfall, reawakening them and sending them on to the Emerald City.

When they are given an audience with the great and mighty Wizard of Oz (a giant concoction of smoke, fire, and intermittent explosions, with a deep, resonant voice that echoes through the halls of his palace), he tells them that he will grant all of their wishes, but first they must bring him the broomstick of the Wicked Witch. Disappointed, they leave the Emerald City.

Meanwhile, the Wicked Witch—still determined to get those ruby slippers—dispatches a horde of flying monkeys with the deadliest expressions imaginable to kidnap Dorothy and Toto and bring them back to her castle. When they accomplish this, the Witch tries to get the slippers off of Dorothy's feet, but soon realizes that they cannot be removed until Dorothy is dead. The Witch turns an hourglass over and tells the young girl that its sand represents all the time she has left to live.

Toto escapes, and while the grains of sand filter through the vessel, he locates the Scarecrow, Tin Woodman, and Cowardly Lion and leads them back to the castle. Once there, they jump a few of the castle guards and borrow their uniforms, then slip inside with the rest of the regiment. They manage to find Dorothy, but before they can all escape, the Wicked Witch catches them. She sets the Scarecrow on fire, and when Dorothy extinguishes the flame with water, some of it accidentally hits the Wicked Witch, causing her to slowly melt away while crying out: "What a world! What a world!"

The Witch's subjects—like the munchkins—rejoice at her death and hail Dorothy. When their heroine asks for the Witch's broom, they gratefully surrender it to her.

She and her companions ecstatically take the broom back to the Emerald City and present it to the Wizard, but when they ask him to hold up to his end of the bargain, he tells them to come back the next day. They refuse, demanding he fulfill the vow he made to them and grant their wishes. While they argue, Toto runs over and pulls the curtain on the mighty, omniscient, omnipotent Wizard of Oz, exposing for what he truly is, a mere mortal (Frank Morgan). A "humbug," as Dorothy describes him.

Nevertheless, he turns out to be a wise humbug, and a resourceful one, too. He convinces them that they already possess the wisdom, compassion, and courage which each has been respectively seeking—qualities which have already been revealed to us in their brave and clever and love-inspired rescue of Dorothy.

He gives the Scarecrow a diploma and makes him a "Doctor of Thinkology," and instantly he is spewing geometric principles with the accuracy of a mathematician; he gives the Cowardly Lion a medal and makes him an honorary member of the "Legion of Courage," and instantly he is prepared to take on the world; finally, he gives the Tin Woodman a testimonial (complete with ticking heart) and reminds him that "a heart is not judged by how much you love, but by how much you are loved by others."

As for Dorothy, the Wizard says that he's leaving shortly for Kansas in his hot air balloon and agrees to take her along with him. However, when Toto runs off in pursuit of a Siamese cat, Dorothy runs off in pursuit of him and the Wizard leaves without her.

Glinda arrives shortly thereafter, telling Dorothy that she's always had the power to go back to Kansas. All she has to do is click the heels of her ruby slippers together and repeat the magic words: "There's no place like home."

Dorothy obeys, and soon awakes back in sepia-toned Kansas, from what was apparently all a dream. She is surrounded by concerned neighbors Zeke, Hunk, and Hickory, whom she recognizes as her three friends from Oz, and Professor Marvel, whom she recognizes as the Wizard. Her Uncle Henry and Auntie Em are there as well. When they explain to her that she was hurt in the twister and has been sleeping the whole time, she insists that there is such a place as Oz and that she has been there. In any case, she is thrilled to be home, in her room, with her family and friends and dog Toto, and she never ever wants to leave again.

"Oh, Auntie Em," she gushes. "There's no place like home!"

Notes: MGM, inspired by the success of Walt Disney's *Snow White and the Seven Dwarfs* (1938), struck gold with this wonderful musical adaptation of a classic children's story. In between the sepia shots of Kansas, their art and special effects departments had a field day creating all of the magical, Technicolor wonders of Oz.

The Wizard of Oz, however, was not an original film idea in 1939. L. Frank Baum, author of the phenomenally popular children's book, published in 1900, as well as thirteen other volumes in the *Oz* series, had formed his own movie company in 1914 and produced three five-reel *Oz* films based on his stories. Even before that, there had been a number of one-reel *Oz* movies, as well as a musical extravaganza on the Broadway stage. Two silent-screen versions were also produced: one from Polyscope Productions in 1910 and another from the Larry Semon Company in 1925 (which featured Oliver Hardy as a corpulent Tin Woodman).

Beset by distribution problems, Baum's Oz Film Manufacturing Company soon collapsed, and its facilities were sold to Universal Pictures. In 1934, Samuel Goldwyn purchased the screen rights to the *Oz* stories for $40,000 and planned to turn them into a vehicle for Eddie Cantor. But when that project failed to materialize, Goldwyn sold the rights to MGM for $75,000. The resulting film, perhaps more than any other of its time, was representative of the Hollywood studio system at its best.

Norman Taurog, who had a reputation for coaxing mature performances out of often immature actors, was originally penciled-in to direct the one version of *The Wizard of Oz* that would survive long after all of the others had been forgotten. But when shooting began on October 12, 1938, it was Richard Thorpe (who had just directed Robert Montgomery's riveting performance in *Night Must Fall*, 1937) who was at the helm. Less than two weeks later, Thorpe was fired and sent off to Palm Springs by studio public relations director Howard Strickland, to avoid embarrassing questions from the press. Next up to bat was George Cukor, whose approach to the assignment was cavalier at best. "I was brought up on

Tennyson," Cukor noted haughtily. Three days later, he was gone. Finally, producer Mervyn LeRoy managed to talk "the man's man" director Victor Fleming into taking over. According to friends, Fleming accepted only to please his little daughter.

Fleming did a splendid job, pacing the film extremely well (especially when you consider that forty of its hundred minutes' screening time is devoted to song). He must also be commended for his sensitive handling of the touching relationship between Dorothy and her three friends; it is a tender kinship that becomes neither romantic nor maudlin.

The screenplay (by Noel Langley, Florence Ryerson, and Edgar Allen Woolf) cleverly combines elements of Baum's book with imaginative and amusing innovations such as the Wicked Witch skywriting "Surrender Dorothy!" as she rides through the air on her broom, and the Horse of a Different Color, which carries Dorothy and her friends through the streets of the Emerald City.

Also worth mentioning is the splendid artwork of scenic and costume designers and make-up artists, all of which served to enhance the spectacular special effects (without which no fantasy film would be complete) of Munchkinland, the Emerald City, and the merry old land of Oz.

But, above all, *The Wizard of Oz* owes its place in film history to its cast and its musical score. Ironically enough, these are the two areas in which the studio and LeRoy encountered the most problems in putting the whole thing together.

When MGM couldn't acquire Shirley Temple from Twentieth Century–Fox—Zanuck and Mayer were feuding—they instead cast 16-year-old Judy Garland. Judy was too old for the part, and too well-developed, also; her breasts had to be strapped down. Besides that, she didn't even remotely resemble the drawings of the Dorothy character in Baum's book. Still, she proved to have just the right quality of vulnerable sincerity for the part, and it made her a major star.

One of MGM's top favorites had his heart set on playing the Wizard—Wallace Beery. He coveted the part to impress his little adopted daughter, Carol Ann. However, Beery had reached the point in his career at Metro where his crass behavior and rudeness had relegated him to strictly "B" pictures. The studio wanted W.C. Fields for the role, and offered him $75,000 to do it. That wasn't enough for Mr. Fields—he wanted $100,000 and was busy preparing the script for *You Can't Cheat an Honest Man,* anyway—so he passed. Next they offered it to Ed Wynn, fresh from his triumph in *Hooray for What!",* but Wynn thought the part was too small and turned it down. Finally, Frank Morgan was cast (he also played the Doorman of Emerald City, the Carriage Driver, and the Guard of Oz's palace), and he went into movie history with the role.

Ray Bolger had his eye on the part of the Scarecrow and was heartbroken when it as given to Buddy Ebsen. Bolger was cast as the Tin Woodman. Even as the two actors were being fitted for their respective costumes,

Bolger was pleading with LeRoy for a switch in roles, and eventually he succeeded. Ebsen good-naturedly accepted the switch, but soon regretted it. The aluminum dust they used in the Tin Woodman's costume coated his lungs and nearly killed him. Buddy Ebsen went to the hospital, and Jack Haley went to Oz.

Bert Lahr was a Broadway favorite who had worked with Bolger in the 1934 revue *Life Begins at 8:40,* a Harburg-Arlen credit. He had never clicked in films, but in the role of the Cowardly Lion, Lahr found the perfect movie vehicle for himself—although, as Frank Morgan warned him on the set one day, making a hit as an animal might not necessarily help his career.

Edna May Oliver was the original front-office choice for the part of the Wicked Witch of the West, but she was busy working on John Ford's *Drums Along the Mohawk* at the time (for which she would be nominated for a Best Supporting Actress Oscar). Another contender was Gale Sondergaard, who had won the first Oscar for that category in 1936, for her performance in *Anthony Adverse.* Margaret Hamilton eventually won out, and reprised the role in a number of stage productions over the ensuing decades. Though the other actors suffered miserably in their costumes and heavy makeup, perhaps none suffered as miserably as Miss Hamilton did. The fiery special effect when she disappeared from Munchkinland burned the skin off her right hand, singed her right eyebrow and lashes, and scalded her chin, nose, and forehead. Not long afterward, she understandably refused to mount a "flying broomstick," which she was assured was safe; the subsequent explosion sent her stand-in, Betty Danko, to the hospital for eleven days (the Witch's hat and wig were found days later in the soundstage rafters).

But most troublesome, perhaps, were the 124 midgets assembled by Leo Singer of "Singer's Midgets" to play the Munchkins. According to Hugh Fordin in his book *The World of Entertainment,* they were "an unholy assemblage of pimps, hookers and gamblers" who infested the MGM lot and the community at large, propositioning the stars, chasing the showgirls, and causing general pandemonium. They also provided the cast and crew with outrageous anecdotes and stories that become a part of Hollywood folklore.

Despite all of the changes, *The Wizard of Oz* remains one of the few perfectly cast films ever made. In fact, few members of the cast would ever again find roles so perfectly tailored for their respective talents as those they found in this production. This holds especially true for Ray Bolger, Jack Haley, and Bert Lahr as the three marvelous personifications of human frailty: the Scarecrow with no brain, the defenseless Tin Woodman, and the Cowardly Lion.

The musical score—with songs by Harold Arlen and E.Y. Harburg—is one of the best of any movie musical. Each song either advances the suspenseful plot or explains the motivations of one of the intriguing characters. The background music uses many of the themes of the songs, along with small recurring motifs that symbolize each character. The arrangements make use of audible effects which are just as important as the visual ones: The voices are speeded up or slowed down while the orchestral instruments sound normal. And the enormous talents of the song-and-dance performers add a great deal of effectiveness to all of the musical material.

Of all the songs, though, none evokes Baum's theme of belief more than the one that Dorothy sings while still in her native Kansas. Dreaming of something lovelier than the endless expanse of Midwestern plains, she looks up and sings, "Somewhere, over the rainbow. . . ." The song was an irresistible magnet for sentimentalists and romantics who, like Dorothy and her friends, were willing to believe, and it became the lifelong trademark of Judy Garland.

However, "Over the Rainbow" (which was added almost as an afterthought) was ordered by studio executives to be cut from the film after its first public preview (along with another number, "The Jitterbug," which *was* cut). Fortunately, saner heads prevailed, and "Over the Rainbow" went on to win the Academy Award for Best Song of that year.

Several weeks before production was completed, Victor Fleming left to work on *Gone with the Wind*. He was replaced by King Vidor, who directed all of the Kansas sequences, including the "Over the Rainbow" scene.

Another noteworthy contribution to the film was that of Arthur Freed. Freed was a successful songwriter who wanted to be a producer and was given his chance as assistant to Mervyn LeRoy on *The Wizard of Oz*. His unerring judgment of talent and his knack for surrounding himself with talented people proved invaluable to LeRoy. Having earned his stripes, Freed went on to produce some of Hollywood's greatest musicals, including *Meet Me in St. Louis* (1944), *Easter Parade* (1948), *On the Town* (1949), *Annie Get Your Gun* (1950), *Singin' in the Rain* (1952), *The Band Wagon* (1953), and the Best Picture of 1951, *An American in Paris*.

The Wizard of Oz, though almost unanimously lauded by critics upon its initial release and generally enjoyed by movie audiences, did not become a consistent money-maker until its theatrical revival in 1948. In fact, in its first 20 years of theatrical engagements, it grossed a mere $4 million in domestic rentals. But with its first television broadcast in 1956, it found a new and even wider audience, and since then has become a major annual event for the medium enjoyed by children and adults alike.

It was nominated for Best Picture but lost out to *Gone with the Wind*. It did win for Best Song (as mentioned) and for Herbert Stothart's score. Judy Garland was awarded a miniature statuette, as well, for her oustanding juvenile work that year.

The film was remade in 1978 with an all-black cast and a Motown score entitled *The Wiz*, which was also a hit Broadway play, and as an Australian film called *Oz*. There was an animated sequel made in 1974 called *Journey Back to Oz*, which featured the voice of Liza Minelli and Margaret Hamilton, and a live-action sequel in 1985 called *Return to Oz*.

Reviews: "*The Wizard of Oz* was intended to hit the same audience as *Snow White*, and won't fail for lack of trying. It has dwarfs, music, Technicolor, freak characters, and Judy Garland. It can't be expected to have a sense of humor as well—and as for the light touch of fantasy, it weighs like a pound of fruitcake soaking wet. Children will not object to it, especially as it is a thing of many interesting gadgets; but it will be delightful for children mostly to their mothers, and any kid tall enough to reach up to a ticket window will be found at the Tarzan film down the street. The story of course has some lovely and wild ideas—men of straw and tin, a cowardly lion, a wizard who isn't a very good wizard—but the picture doesn't know what to do with them, except to be painfully literal and elaborate about everything—Cecil B. DeMille and the Seven Thousand Dwarfs by Actual Count."—Otis Ferguson, *The New Republic*

"By courtesy of the wizards of Hollywood, *The Wizard of Oz* reached the Capitol's screen yesterday as a delightful piece of wonder-working which had the youngsters' eyes shining and brought a quietly amused gleam to the wiser ones of the older. Not since Disney's *Snow White* has anything quite so fantastic succeeded half so well. . . . It is so well intentioned, so genial and so gay that any reviewer who would look down his nose at the film-making should be spanked and sent off, supperless, to bed."—Frank S. Nugent, *The New York Times*

The Women

A Metro-Goldwyn-Mayer Picture. Directed by George Cukor. Produced by Hunt Stromberg. Screenplay by Anita Loos, Jane Murfin, and (uncredited) Donald Ogden Stewart and F. Scott Fitzgerald. Based on the play by Clare Boothe. Photographed by Oliver T. Marsh and Joseph Ruttenberg. Edited by Robert J. Kern. Art direction by Cedric Gibbons and Wade B. Rubottom. Set decoration by Edwin B. Willis. Gowns and Technicolor fashion show by Adrian. Music by Edward Ward. Sound by Douglas Shearer. Running time: 132 minutes. Release date: September 1.

Cast: Norma Shearer *Mary Haines;* Joan Crawford *Crystal Allen;* Rosalind Russell *Sylvia Fowler;* Mary Bowland *Countess De Lave;* Paulette Goddard *Miriam Aarons;* Joan Fontaine *Peggy Day;* Lucile Watson *Mrs. Morehead;* Phyllis Povah *Edith Potter;* Florence Nash *Nancy Blake;* Virginia Weidler *Little Mary;* Ruth Hussey *Miss Watts;* Muriel Hutchison *Jane;* Margaret Dumont *Mrs. Wagstaff;* Dennie Moore *Olga;* Mary Cecil *Maggie;* Marjorie Main *Lucy;* Esther Dale *Ingrid;* Hedda Hopper *Dolly De Peyster;* Priscilla Lawson *Hairdresser;* Ann Morriss *Exercise instructor;* Mary Beth Hughes *Miss Trimmerback;* Virginia Grey *Pat;* Cora Witherspoon *Mrs. Van Adams;* Theresa Harris *Olive;* Vera Vague *Receptionist;* Judith Allen *Model;* Aileen Pringle *Saleslady.*

Synopsis: A long-running stage hit in 1936, *The Women* continued

Gossip rules in *The Women* (MGM). Just ask these ladies (left–right): Extra, Paulette Goddard, Mary Bowland, Norma Shearer, Joan Fontaine and extra.

Irving Thalberg's tradition of glossy high society comedies at MGM, a format which remained formidable long after Thalberg himself had passed away.

In the clever and original opening sequence, the main players are all identified by members of the animal kingdom chosen to represent their respective characters. Mary Haines (Norma Shearer) is the defenseless fawn; Crystal Allen (Joan Crawford) is the predatory leopardess; and Sylvia Fowler (Rosalind Russell) is the unlucky black cat.

The plot begins to unwind in a dizzying run through Sydney's Salon, a favorite hangout and gossip factory of the gender in question, that sets the tone for this bitchy, fast-paced, gossip-filled movie. The camera eventually settles on Sylvia, who is receiving a juicy piece of information about one of her closest friends, Mary Haines. The manicurist, Olga (Dennie Moore), is telling her that Mary's beloved husband, Stephen, is cheating on her with a common salesgirl over at Black's [sic] Fifth Avenue. This bit of news clearly makes Sylvia's getting out of bed that morning worthwhile. She wastes no time in getting to a telephone—the favorite instrument of the Park Avenue matrons—and spreading the word, all in the good name of protecting Mary.

Over at the Haines residence, everything appears to be sunshine and roses. The home is luxurious, complete with servants and grounds for horseback riding. Dinner is being carefully planned, and Mary and her daughter, Little Mary (Virginia Weidler), are busy packing for a family trip.

Stephen is apparently at work and nowhere to be found. In fact, there isn't a single male to be found anywhere in the picture (pets included). But, perhaps because they are a major topic of discussion, they seem to be omnipresent.

As Mary flips wistfully through a bunch of old photographs taken during her honeymoon and over a romantic two-day period when she and Stephen were snowbound in a cabin, she reminisces fondly about these events, revealing to us that she is a woman deeply in love with her husband and completely devoted to him.

However, Sylvia is continually hinting that Stephen has a "beautiful blonde" on the side, and Stephen is continually calling up to say he has to work late and missing their engagements. At Sylvia's suggestion, Mary makes an appointment with Sylvia's manicurist, during which time Olga — unaware of who her client is — blabs the "Stephen Haines story" to her. Mary is shocked and moved to tears.

While Mary's mother (Lucile Watson) consoles her daughter, Mary's friends march off to face the "other woman," salesgirl Crystal Allen. Before the girls arrive, Stephen calls her at the shop to try and cancel their dinner engagement for that evening so he can be with his wife. Crystal's wheedling response, keeping her tone impulsive and desperate while expressions, movements and asides expose the methodical calculation of her plan, is a tour-de-force for Crawford and ranks with Luise Rainer's famous telephone scene in *The Great Ziegfeld* (1936), for which she won an Oscar. Her entire performance, in fact, is one of delightful bitchiness, permeated with a sense of sexual availability that helps to understand her appeal over the wan Mary Haines. When the girls finally do arrive, it is a Mexican standoff, with both sides exchanging unpleasantries.

At a fashion show later — where this black-and-white movie comes magically to life in bright Technicolor while the patterns of MGM's star costume designer Adrian are modeled — Crystal shows up unexpectedly and begins to toss around money she can't possibly make as a salesgirl, using Stephen Haines's name as a reference. This leads to a confrontation with Mary in one of the fitting rooms, where Mary, indicating a playsuit Crystal has chosen, tells her: "Take my advice and don't wear that. Stephen hates anything so obvious." "If Stephen dislikes anything I'm wearing," Crystal snaps back, "I take it off." Mary retreats, her breeding and manners no match for the unsympathetic, tough-as-nails girl of the streets.

When one of Mary's friends "inadvertently" recounts the story to a news-hungry columnist, the paper's headline the following day reads "WIFE K.O.'s LOVE THIEF" in big bold type.

The scandal leads inevitably to divorce proceedings and, on the train to Reno, Mary meets two other women in the same predicament: the empty-headed but ever-hopeful Countess De Lave (Mary Bowland), who believes that her first husband, a Jew, was complimenting her when he called her a *schlemiel* in his will, and Miriam Aarons (Paulette Goddard, who would much rather have been playing Scarlett O'Hara at the time), a hard-boiled gold digger. They make a toast to Reno, which to them symbolizes freedom the way the Statue of Liberty does for boatloads of immigrants.

All the would-be divorcees spend their required six-week separations at a ranch run by a woman named Lucy (Marjorie Main, better known to film audiences as "Ma Kettle"). There, the Countess enters into an affair with one of the cowhands, Buck Winston, whom she hopes to make a singing star. Mary's girlfriend Peggy (Joan Fontaine) learns that she is pregnant and decides to return home to her husband after they reconcile over the phone. Mary, lonesome and unsure about her actions, grows only more despondent when she is notified, after her divorce is finalized, that Stephen has married Crystal. Sylvia shows up unexpectedly and soon discovers that Miriam Aarons is the girl her husband has left her for. A fight breaks out between the two, and when Mary intervenes, Sylvia disowns her as a friend.

Eighteen months pass. Back in the city, Crystal is making Stephen's life miserable and having an affair with Buck Winston, a radio singing star by now and married to the Countess De Lave. When Little Mary informs her inconsolable mother of Stephen's despondence, Mary springs into action. But this is a new, revitalized Mary. She has claws! She cajoles the scoop of Crystal's affair out of Sylvia and passes it on to a columnist (played by real life columnist Hedda Hopper), thereby winning Stephen back for good and sending Crystal back to the sales counter.

"What about pride?" Mary is quizzed.

"Pride!" she bellows. "That's something a woman in love can't afford!"

She bursts out the door and down the staircase that leads to Stephen's waiting arms.

Notes: Years before she was the politically active wife of *Time* maverick Henry Luce, Clare Boothe enjoyed a lucrative career as editor of *Vanity Fair* magazine, syndicated columnist and playwright. She was the author of two enormously successful Broadway plays, *The Women* and *Kiss the Boys Goodbye.* The former ran for 666 performances at the Ethel Barrymore Theatre in New York. The play was reportedly inspired by virulent gossip overheard by Boothe at a nightclub ladies' room. It employed a large, all-female cast (some 140 women reputedly) to dissect the lives of several Park Avenue matrons, whose days are filled with beauty parlor appointments, bridge and incessant bitchery involving one another's marital woes.

At least nine scenarists worked on adapting the difficult and (for Hollywood) excessively outspoken play, including at one point the failing writer F. Scott Fitzgerald, who was assigned, with Donald Ogden Stewart, to work on it but whose material was never used. The allocation of sole credit to Anita Loos and Jane Murfin suggests that consistency to the all-girl image of the project may have dictated removal of all other names. And although some of Boothe's best lines were cut to pacify the censors, the script still sparkles with witty and sometimes incisive dialogue, enhanced by a perfectly chosen cast.

For these ladies, MGM's reigning movie queens of the thirties, *The Women* would be their last great fling before being dispersed in the harsher forties. Norma Shearer, the widow of Irving Thalberg, worked very little after its completion; Joan Crawford later abandoned her vixen image to join Warner Bros. and revitalize her career with *Mildred Pierce* in 1945; while both Rosalind Russell and Joan Fontaine went on to starring roles because of their appeal in *The Women* and the strength of its success.

Director George Cukor—fresh from the set of *Gone with the Wind*, where he was replaced by Victor Fleming because Clark Gable considered him a "women's director"—had a blast directing them all.

One of 1939's biggest financial successes, *The Women* is one of those rare films that, fifty years after its release, still rings with truth and emotion while still being just as entertaining.

It was remade with a far inferior cast in the far inferior movie *The Opposite Sex* (1956).

Reviews: "The tonic effect of Metro-Goldwyn-Mayer's film of Clare Boothe's *The Women* is so marvelous we believe every studio in Hollywood should make at least one thoroughly nasty picture a year. The saccharine is too much with us: going and coming to syrupy movies we lose our sense of balance. Happily, Miss Boothe hasn't. She has dipped her pen in venom and written a comedy that would turn a litmus paper pink. Metro, without alkalizing it too much, has fed it to a company of actresses who normally are so sweet that butter (as the man says) wouldn't melt in their mouths. And, instead of gasping and clutching at their throats, the women—bless 'em—have downed it without blinking, have gone on a glorious cat-clawing rampage and have turned in one of the merriest pictures of the season."—Frank S. Nugent, *The New York Times*

"I think probably the movies have made something more solid out of *The Women* than the stage play did. The picture runs two hours and a quarter which is inexcusable in itself, and features Norma Shearer in some of the most incessant weeping and renunciation since Ann Harding—which may not be inexcusable but it's no fun for me. It is a holiday from Hays all right; there is more wicked wit than Hollywood has been allowed since *The Front Page*."—Otis Ferguson, *The New Republic*

A Working Family (Hataraku Ikka)

A Toho (Tokyo) Prod., Japan. Directed by Mikio Naruse.

Cast: Musei Tokugawa, Kyoko Honma, Akira Ubukata, Kaoru Ito, Seikichi Minami, Sumie Tsubaki, Den Ohinata.

This is the compelling story of a printer's family—eleven people in all, living under one roof—and how their combined earnings are just enough to get the family by. Because a loss of any of the incomes would devastate the family, the elder sons are not able to go off and make their own place in the world, causing conflict between them and their father. The film was based on the novel by Sunao Tokunaga, who himself rose from the ranks of labor, and is another shining example of the fine year that Japanese cinema was enjoying in '39.

Wuthering Heights

A United Artists Release of a Samuel Goldwyn Production. Directed by William Wyler. Screenplay by Ben Hecht and Charles MacArthur. Based on the novel by Emily Brontë. Photographed by Gregg Toland. Edited by Daniel Mandell. Art direction by James Basevi. Set decoration by Julia Heron. Costumes by Omar Kiam. Music by Alfred Newman. Sound by Paul Neal. Asst. director: Walter Mayo. Special character makeup by Blagoe Stephanoff. Running time: 104 minutes. Release date: April 13.

Cast: Merle Oberon *Catherine Earnshaw;* Laurence Olivier *Heathcliff;* David Niven *Edgar Linton;* Flora Robson *Ellen Dean;* Donald Crisp *Dr. Kenneth;* Hugh Williams *Hindley Earnshaw;* Geraldine Fitzgerald *Isabella Linton;* Leo G. Carroll *Joseph;* Cecil Humphreys *Judge Linton;* Miles Mander *Mr. Lockwood;* Sarita Wooten *Cathy as a child;* Rex Downing *Heathcliff as a child;* Douglas Scott *Hindley as a child;* Romaine Callender *Robert;* Cecil Kellaway *Earnshaw.*

I made *Wuthering Heights.* Wyler only directed it. — Samuel Goldwyn[71]

Synopsis: Emily Brontë's tragic tale of ill-fated love and vengeance was brought vividly to life in one of the greatest love stories ever made, the oft-filmed but never-improved-upon 1939 version of *Wuthering Heights.*

As the story begins, a stranger wanders into the estate of Wuthering Heights from the throes of a heavy snowstorm. It is here that we first meet the head of the household, the brooding, tormented Heathcliff (Laurence Olivier). He is unjustly hostile to the stranger, but grudgingly offers him a room to sleep in for the night (after nearly banishing him to the servants' quarters).

When the stranger is escorted to the room, he hears a woman's voice calling in the wind: "Heathcliff! Heathcliff!" He goes to the window and instinctively sticks his hands outside, only to feel it clutched by an icy grasp. He screams for help and Heathcliff runs upstairs to his room. When the man tells him what has happened, Heathcliff goes running off recklessly into the stormy night, in a half-crazed search for his long lost love, Catherine (Merle Oberon).

Sitting near the fireplace with the stranger, the housekeeper (Flora Robson) begins to recount the tragic story of passion, vengeance, and death that has plagued this dark, desolate house, and it is through her narration that the story is told.

She goes back forty years, to a time when Wuthering Heights was owned by Catherine's father, Mr. Earnshaw (Cecil Kellaway), a kind and generous man. One day, he returns from a business trip in Liverpool carrying an orphaned gypsy boy whom he has named Heathcliff. Cathy likes the boy almost immediately, but her brother Hindley (Hugh Williams) does not. Unlike his father, Hindley is cruel and selfish, and he despises Heathcliff, constantly referring to him as "a gypsy beggar" and "scum."

When Mr. Earnshaw dies, it is Hindley who inherits Wuthering Heights, and his first order of business is to make Heathcliff a stable boy and kick him out of the main house.

The years pass and Hindley only becomes more evil, still referring to Heathcliff as "gypsy beggar" when ordering him about. Unbeknownst to him, though, Heathcliff and Catherine are spending a great deal of time together alone out on the moors. Their childhood fondness has blossomed into passionate adult love. But when Heathcliff asks her to run away with him, she refuses. Catherine yearns for wealth and social position and will not forfeit her dreams to live the life of a gypsy.

One day, while riding together on The Grange, property owned by the wealthy Linton Family, they hear the sounds of a formal dance being held in the main house and sneak over to a window to get a closer look. As they watch the stately gentlemen in tuxedos and the beautiful women in evening gowns waltzing together, they fantasize about what it will be like when they are part of that well-heeled crowd. On the way out, Cathy trips and falls, and the Linton guard dogs attack them viciously. Cathy's leg is hurt badly, and Edgar Linton (David Niven, one of Goldwyn's contract players), recognizing her, rushes to her aid, carries her gallantly into the house and attends to her leg. Heathcliff is summarily dismissed.

Catherine spends several weeks with the Lintons while her leg heals, living the lifestyle she so fervently hopes for, and when she finally returns to Wuthering Heights, she is a changed woman — superficially, at least — wearing borrowed finery. She is torn between the uncontrollable passion she feels for Heathcliff and her social aspirations, which become more tangible when Edgar Linton begins courting her.

She ends up scorning Heathcliff, and he runs away, leaving Wuthering Heights for good it seems. Catherine marries Edgar, and their life together over the next few years is tranquilly pleasant.

Then one day, Heathcliff returns from America, a gentleman now with his own fortune. He uses some of his money to buy up the gambling debts and liquor bills of his old nemesis and half brother Hindley, who over the years has become a bitter, pathetic drunkard. He also uses Edgar's sister, Isabella (Geraldine Fitzgerald), as a pawn in his ruthless game, marrying her against her brother's (and Catherine's) wishes. Although Isabella loves Heathcliff deeply, her life with him at Wuthering Heights is one of loneliness and despair. He neglects her and treats her with contemptuous cruelty. "Why are your eyes so hollow?" he demands to know.

Wuthering Heights (United Artists). *Top:* Edgar Linton (David Niven) and Cathy (Merle Oberon) are married. *Bottom:* Before she dies, Heathcliff (Laurence Olivier) carries Cathy to the window so she can look out upon the moors one last time.

We learn through a visit from Dr. Kenneth (Donald Crisp) that Catherine has taken gravely ill and has but a short time left to live. Heathcliff runs off to be with her. When he gets to the Linton estate, he forces himself inside and rushes up to Catherine's bedside.

In this, the film's most memorable scene, the lovers are reunited, embracing and kissing the way they did when they were younger. Fulfilling her last request, Heathcliff carries her to the window so she can look out over the moors one final time. Catherine dies in his arms, as Edgar and Dr. Kenneth arrive. All three men pray over the body, but Heathcliff's is a personal plea for Catherine's spirit to haunt and torment him for the rest of his days, just so he can always be with her.

Heathcliff is killed chasing Catherine's beckoning call out on the stormy moors, and in the final shot, we see the lovers reunited again, this time in heaven, walking off into the clouds.

Notes: Emily Brontë's classic novel *Wuthering Heights* (published in 1847 under the pseudonym of Ellis Bell, to disguise the fact that its author was a woman), her only book, went on to become a perennial nineteenth-century best-seller and a lucrative subject for twentieth-century moviemaking. There was a 1920 British adaptation; Luis Buñuel's 1953 translation, *Abismos de Pasión*; and a 1970 British remake starring the future James Bond, Timothy Dalton. But for many, there is only one *Wuthering Heights:* the haunting, black-and-white 1939 version starring Laurence Olivier and Merle Oberon. Scenarists Ben Hecht and Charles MacArthur limited their screenplay to only the first seventeen chapters of Miss Brontë's book, but the resulting film was a rousing success with moviegoers as well as critics.

Director William Wyler, from the inception of this project, insisted on casting the British stage actor Laurence Olivier in the role of Heathcliff. But convincing his boss, as well as the actor himself, to accept turned out to be quite problematical (and something he conceivably regretted at times during the shooting of the film).

Olivier liked the screenplay, but he had not been happy in either of his two previous Hollywood outings, and had serious misgivings about ever attempting a third. When he was informed that Merle Oberon had been cast as Catherine (in lieu of Vivien Leigh, whom he would marry the following year; she was offered but rejected the supporting role of Isabella), those misgivings were only intensified. He turned down the role.

Wyler tested several other actors, among them Douglas Fairbanks, Jr., and Robert Newton, but each new screen test only convinced him further that Olivier was the only actor who could play Heathcliff. He asked him to reconsider, but Olivier was adamant.

It was at this point that Vivien Leigh interceded, reasoning with her husband-to-be that it was not wise for them to continue turning down offers simply on the grounds that there were not leading roles for both of them in the project. She convinced him to reconsider, and he signed a contract with Samuel Goldwyn to play the part.

Miss Leigh didn't do too badly as a result of this decision. During an impulsive visit with Olivier in Hollywood, she met producer David O. Selznick, who had her tested for the part of Scarlett O'Hara in *Gone with the Wind* and subsequently cast her in the most coveted role in Hollywood. So although Olivier and Leigh weren't able to work on the same picture together, they were at least able to work in Hollywood at the same time, in roles that would launch both of their careers.

But *Wuthering Heights* did more for Laurence Olivier than just launch his budding acting career. The film—and director Wyler, in particular—made him realize the power and the potential of the medium, and it was instrumental in his later involvement with the Shakespearean productions which would earn him the title of the greatest actor of his generation. "It was Wyler who gave me the simplest thought," Olivier said. "If you do it right, you can do anything. And if he hadn't said that, I think I wouldn't have done *Henry V* five years later."[72]

His first days on the set, however, were a nightmare. He missed Leigh and his home in London, both of whom he had left behind for his three-month tenure. And his battles on the set with costar Oberon are now legendary in Hollywood. There were disagreements with Goldwyn as well, and even with Wyler, who had done everything to get him signed to the movie. Although Goldwyn would later single this film out as his personal favorite of all his productions, he often spoke of it with aggravation at the time of shooting as "a doubtful picture." Eventually, however, the volatile personalities stopped clashing, tempers cooled and relationships actually became amiable.

When filming was completed, Goldwyn ordered Wyler to reshoot the ending, saying he didn't want it to end with a shot of a dead man. He wanted to see the lovers reunited in heaven. Wyler refused, but Goldwyn had somebody else lens the shot—a double exposure of Olivier's stunt double and a girl walking on the clouds.

Wuthering Heights won the New York Film Critics' vote for Best Picture, beating out even *Gone with the Wind*. Olivier was nominated for an Academy Award for Best Actor, but lost—not to Clark Gable, as he had expected, but to fellow Englishman Robert Donat of "Mr. Chips" fame. The film also earned nominations for Best Picture, Director, Screenplay, Supporting Actress (Fitzgerald), and Musical Score, but the only contributor to take home an Oscar that evening was the brilliant cinematographer Gregg Toland (two years later he would shoot *Citizen Kane* for Welles), whose moody, atmospheric expressionism was carefully worked out between himself and Wyler to maintain a certain distance from reality.

Reviews: ". . . A very faithful adaptation, written reverently and well, which goes straight to the heart of the book. . . . And it has been brilliantly played. Laurence Olivier's Heathcliff is the man. He was Heathcliff's broad lowering brow, his scowl, the churlishness, the wild tenderness, the bearing, speech and manner of the demon-possessed . . . and Merle Oberon . . .

has matched the brilliance of his characterization with hers. She has perfectly caught the restless, changeling spirit of the Brontë heroine. . . . And . . . Mr. Goldwyn has provided a flawless supporting cast.

"William Wyler has directed it magnificently, surcharging even his lighter scenes with an atmosphere of suspense and foreboding, keeping his horror-shadowed narrative moving at a steadily accelerating pace, building absorbingly to its tragic climax. It is, unquestionably, one of the most distinguished pictures of the year, one of the finest ever produced by Mr. Goldwyn, and one you should decide to see."—Frank S. Nugent, *The New York Times*

"The best [picture] that Mr. Goldwyn has ever made. . . . It has dramatic grip and emotional power to catch and hold any intelligence that looks to the screen for something besides laughter. . . . The picture isn't without minor, if negligible, faults. The musical score is particularly unfortunate, syrupy and banal. . . . The very ending, of ghosts moving hand-in-hand through the show up to the crag that represented the only moments of happiness in their mortal lives, is trite and unimaginative. Some such ending is necessary—Emily Brontë herself had it—but it should have been much better. Inspiration faltered at the final moment."—James Shelley Hamilton, *National Board of Review Magazine*

You Can't Cheat an Honest Man

A Universal Picture. Directed by George Marshall and (uncredited) Eddie Cline. Produced by Lester Cowan. Screenplay by George Marion, Jr., Richard Mack and Everett Freeman. Original story by Charles Bogle (W.C. Fields). Photographed by Milton Krasner. Edited by Otto Ludwig. Art direction by Jack Otterson. Music by Charles Previn. Asst. director: Vernon Keays. Associate art director: Charles H. Clarke. Gowns by Vera West. Set decorations by R.A. Gausman. Sound by Bernard B. Brown and Robert Pritchard. Running time: 76 minutes. Release date: February 17.

Cast: W.C. Fields *Larson E. Whipsnade;* Edgar Bergen *Himself;* Charlie McCarthy *Himself;* Mortimer Snerd *Himself;* Constance Moore *Vicky Whipsnade;* Mary Forbes *Mrs. Bel-Goodie;* Thurston Hall *Mr. Bel-Goodie;* Princess Baba *Princess Baba;* John Arledge *Phineas Whipsnade;* Charles Coleman *Butler;* Edward Brophy *Corbett;* Arthur Hohl *Burr;* Blacaman *Blacaman;* Eddie "Rochester" Anderson *Cheerful;* Grady Sutton *Chester;* Ferris Taylor *Deputy Sheriff;* James Bush *Roger Bel-Goodie;* Ivan Lebedeff *Ronnie.*

> Bill Fields never made me laugh. He was one of the meanest men I ever knew.—George Marshall[73]

Synopsis: W.C. Fields was notorious for his disdain of children and animals, but he certainly had nothing against dummies. In *You Can't Cheat* *an Honest Man,* Fields and Charlie McCarthy reprise their ever-popular radio feud, exchanging rapid-fire one-liners in a snappy battle of wits. This film is one of Fields' classics, and therefore a classic of the genre.

He plays Larson E. Whipsnade, a charlatan who runs an indebted circus (complete with the world's smallest giant and tallest midget) that must inevitably flee the law in every county in which it plays. In fact, when we first meet him, Whipsnade is just making it past the border of one county and safely out of jurisdiction of the pursuing authorities. The law is his enemy from the outside; from within it is Edgar Bergen and his aforementioned accomplice, Charlie McCarthy, whose contract makes it impossible for Whipsnade to fire them. It does not, however, prevent him from throwing helpless Charlie into a den of lions or a pit of crocodiles. Such deeds — combined with the fact that Larson E. never pays his employees — lead Bergen and McCarthy to quit the circus.

Just as they are making this decision, Whipsnade's daughter Victoria (Constance Moore) enters, inquiring about her father's whereabouts. Bergen is infatuated with the lovely Vicky and asks her out on a date. She nervously accepts, and Bergen eagerly nixes his plans of leaving. He placates Charlie by telling him that Vicky has a younger sister. Vicky eventually locates her father (just as he is eluding one of his many creditors) and learns of his financial bind. She has been courted by a pompous but wealthy man, Roger Bel-Goodie (James Bush), who very much wants to marry her. Filled with empathy for her father's plight, she reluctantly agrees. Her brother, Phineas (John Arledge), whose only concern is his own social advancement, is elated to hear the news, and so is her father. A date is set and the marriage is planned to be held at the Bel-Goodie mansion.

Meanwhile, Vicky and Edgar are falling in love, meeting every day at the circus's hot-air balloon. When her wedding day arrives, though, she leaves for the Bel-Goodie estate and sends her father off to talk with Edgar and Charlie. He promises to break the news to them gently and compassionately. Then he grabs a knife and a block of wood and heads for the balloon.

While conversing with the two (but saying nothing of the impending marriage), Whipsnade cuts away at the tether of the balloon with his knife whenever the duo aren't watching. Soon, they are airborne. Larson races back to his trailer, attends to some business, and dresses for the evening's affair. He puts his empty-headed assistant Chester (Grady Sutton) in charge, then leaves for the wedding.

Meanwhile, up in the air, Edgar and Charlie decide they would be better off parachuting from the balloon, and when they do, they land in the back seat of Vicky's car! Her vision impaired by the parachute, Vicky veers off of the road and smashes into a policeman's car. The three are arrested and taken to jail.

When the judge finally arrives, he allows Vicky to go free, so she will not be late for her wedding. This is the first Edgar has heard of her

W.C. Fields (right foreground) wreaks his inimitable kind of havoc on a ritzy society party in *You Can't Cheat an Honest Man* (Universal).

engagement. Although he is shocked and hurt by the information, he keeps a stiff upper lip and wishes her well. Later, when he is released, he takes a bike and pedals down the road with Charlie on his back.

When Whipsnade arrives at the Bel-Goodie mansion, all soon goes afoul, as he engages in a hilarious ping-pong game and manages to insult nearly everyone at the party. He also causes the fainthearted Mrs. Bel-Goodie (Mary Forbes) to pass out several times, by telling what he considers an innocent snake story.

When Vicky finally shows up, Roger admonishes her for her tardiness and her father. She, in turn, shoots back: "Why don't you get off the trapeze and get down to the sawdust where you belong!"

The marriage is called off, Vicky is reunited with Edgar, and Larson E. Whipsnade, in the end, is pedaling, hard and fast.

Notes: In 1936, Universal had changed its approach to filmmaking for the sake of survival. Carl Laemmle, Jr., had just left, and with him went the prestige films he had made which were bankrupting the studio. They returned to strictly "B" movie-making, low-budget affairs with no big stars (except for the fast-rising young Deanna Durbin). Gradually, Universal developed its own modest stars for the program musicals, comedies, westerns and serials that had always done very well for them. So by 1938, they could afford to take a chance on W.C. Fields, and they did.

And a chance it was, for Fields' career, though not at its nadir, was certainly in need of a boost. He had been absent from the screen for two years due to an illness exacerbated by his penchant for alcohol. The only thing that had kept him in the public consciousness at all were his frequent appearances on Edgar Bergen's hugely successful radio show, where he traded barbs with Charlie McCarthy. *You Can't Cheat an Honest Man* was a comeback vehicle of sorts for Fields, and it led directly to *My Little Chickadee* (1940), *The Bank Dick* (1940), and *Never Give a Sucker an Even Break* (1941), three of his finest films.

The embryo for this movie was a story called "Grease Paint," a script which had been written for Fields in 1933 by H.M. Walker, but which for some reason he had rejected. Several years later, after leaving Paramount to begin anew with Universal, Fields reconsidered the material and decided to add plot elements from his silent movie, *Two Flaming Youths* (1927). He freely altered the two old scripts as the spirit moved him, adding new scenes and comic bits along the way. When he was finished, he had a truly original screen story (for which he was credited under one of his favorite aliases, "Charles Bogle") that he called *You Can't Cheat an Honest Man*. The title certainly befitted Fields' image of himself, as a man of integrity surrounded by cheats and charlatans who tried to get the best of him: vaudeville theatre managers who refused to pay him; Ziegfeld, who put Ed Wynn under Fields' pool table to try and steal laughs; Paramount, who had promised him artistic freedom and left him on the editing room floor; and a wife who stole his son.

Problems arose soon after shooting began. For one thing, Fields and director George Marshall hated each other. The fighting between the two became so bad that Universal finally had to assign Eddie Cline to direct all of Fields' scenes. Cline had worked with Fields in 1932, on the classic *Million Dollar Legs*. And after *Honest Man*, he would direct the comedian's three subsequent films.

Fields also had a couple of run-ins with his old pal Bergen. Jules Stein headed the Music Corporation of America (eventually MCA would buy Universal) and they represented Bergen at the time. Because he was such a radio sensation, MCA felt that Bergen should be allowed to choose his own director and be assured a certain amount of screen time. Fields complained strongly about these demands and threatened to work instead for MGM on *The Wizard of Oz* (he had been offered the role of the Wizard). Universal, fearful of losing their temperamental star, quickly worked out a settlement between the two parties.

The second encounter between the two was of a much lighter nature. Apparently, every night after shooting, Fields would rewrite all of the pages slated for the following day. Then, the next morning, he would conduct a cast meeting, during which everyone was expected to pay close attention and stay awake. One morning, when Edgar Bergen closed Charlie McCarthy's eyelids, Fields kicked the dummy out of the room for falling asleep and banned him from all future meetings.

The fighting over this film did not end in 1939, either. Four years later, when Fields used the snake story on a radio show, a man named Harry Yadkoe sued him for plagiarism. He claimed that he had written the story, sent it to Fields, and never received a reply. Fields countered that Yadkoe was so "feeble-minded," he never bothered writing back. Because he hadn't replied, the decision went to the plaintiff, and when Fields was leaving the courtroom, he commented to the press that he had been seeing snakes all night long and, as a result of it, had a terrible hangover.

Reviews: ". . . A drab, labored and generally misguided comedy. Considering that he wrote it himself . . . Mr. Fields seems singularly ignorant of the qualities that have endeared him to his millions. . . .

"Whipsnade is not the Fields we have known. We want no part of him. He is something created by the radio, the result of nagging and being nagged by a pert ventriloquist's dummy.

"Charlie . . . has all the best of the picture. . . . The Fields sequences, on the other hand, have a mutilated look. Several of them are quite pointless; others, after a promising beginning, trail off into bored slap-stick. It was all most disappointing." — Frank S. Nugent, *The New York Times*

Young Mr. Lincoln

A Cosmopolitan–Twentieth Century–Fox Film. Directed by John Ford. Executive producer: Darryl F. Zanuck. Associate producer: Kenneth Macgowan. Screenplay by Lamar Trotti. Based on the life of Abraham Lincoln. Photographed by Bert Glennon and Arthur Miller. Edited by Walter Thompson. Art direction by Richard Day and Mark-Lee Kirk. Set decorations by Thomas Little. Music by Alfred Newman. Musical director: Louis Silvers. Costumes by Royer. Sound by Eugene Grossman and Roger Heman. Sound effects editor: Robert Parrish. Running time: 101 minutes. Release date: June 9.

Cast: Henry Fonda *Abraham Lincoln;* Alice Brady *Abigail Clay;* Marjorie Weaver *Mary Todd;* Dorris Bowdon *Carrie Sue Clay;* Eddie Collins *Efe Turner;* Pauline Moore *Ann Rutledge;* Arleen Whelan *Sarah Clay;* Richard Cromwell *Matt Clay;* Ward Bond *John Palmer Cass;* Donald Meek *John Felder;* Spencer Charters *Judge Herbert A. Bell;* Eddie Quillan *Adam Clay;* Milburn Stone *Stephen Douglas;* Cliff Clark *Sheriff Billings;* Robert Lowery *Juror;* Charles Tannen *Ninian Edwards;* Francis Ford *Sam Boone;* Fred Kohler, Jr. *Scrub White;* Kay Linaker *Mrs. Edwards;* Russell Simpson *Woolridge;* Charles Halton *Hawthorne;* Edwin Maxwell *John T. Stuart;* Robert Homans *Mr. Clay;* Jack Kelly *Matt Clay (as a child);* Dickie Jones *Adam Clay (as a child);* Harry Tyler *Hairdresser;* Louis Mason *Court clerk;* Jack Pennick *Big Buck;* Steven Randall *Juror.*

> I had never met anyone remotely like him. Pappy was full of bullshit, but it was a delightful sort of bullshit. — Henry Fonda on John "Pappy" Ford[74]

Synopsis: This is one of the truly great films of 1939, as beautiful and lyrical and inspirational now as it must surely have been fifty years ago and most certainly will still be fifty years from now.

It opens in New Salem, Illinois. The year is 1832 and young Abe Lincoln (Henry Fonda) is running for the state legislature. He is also studying law from a book he acquired in a business transaction with the Clay family, poor settlers traveling through New Salem to Springfield. Abe takes the principles in the law book fervently to heart.

In another early scene, we see him walking along a lakeside with Ann Rutledge (Pauline Moore), and it is obvious that the two are falling in love with each other. That winter, we watch as he takes some hand-picked flowers to her grave, located near the same lakeside where they once walked and talked and dreamed together.

The film picks up again in 1837, as Abe is riding a mule into Springfield to practice law. There, he sets up a practice with his friend, John T. Stuart (Edwin Maxwell). Unlike young Abe, Stuart has political ambitions. While he is off campaigning for the Senate—against another lawyer, Stephen Douglas (Milburn Stone)—Abe handles the bulk of their caseload, which consists mostly of minor disputes and domestic quarrels.

At an Independence Day parade, he is introduced to Mary Todd (Marjorie Weaver). While there, Abe participates in many of the day's activities, judging pies, winning a log-splitting contest and helping his team win a tug-of-war by tying his end of the rope to a wagon and having the wagon pull away. As the opposing team is dragged into a mud pile, the crowd of spectators gathered to watch the contest bursts into uncontrolled laughter.

Later that night, during a fistfight in the woods between Matt Clay (Richard Cromwell) and bully Scrub White (Fred Kohler, Jr.)—being refereed by Matt's brother Adam (Eddie Quillan)—Scrub pulls a gun. There is a struggle between the three men, witnessed by the two boys' mother, Abigail Clay (Alice Brady). A gun goes off. Scrub's friend, J. Palmer Cass (Ward Bond), comes running onto the scene. Scrub is lying on the ground, mortally wounded by a knife.

"Murder!" Cass cries out, his words echoing throughout the countryside.

Sheriff Billings (Cliff Clark) arrives on the scene next, along with many of the curious townspeople. When he asks the brothers who the guilty party is, both of them claim culpability. Their mother—the sole eyewitness—refuses to say which one did it, so both boys are taken into custody.

A drunken mob gathers, thirsty for the blood of the Clay brothers. They go off towards the jailhouse, seeking to administer frontier justice. Abe—who has been nothing more than a casual observer up to this point—tells Mrs. Clay that they must hurry to the jail.

"Who are you?" she demands to know.

"I'm their lawyer, ma'am," he replies comfortingly.

The vigilante mob storms the jailhouse, using a log to try and smash

Young Mr. Lincoln (**Cosmopolitan–Twentieth Century–Fox**). *Top:* Henry Fonda as Lincoln. *Bottom:* Lincoln fights off a vigilante mob.

the front door in. Before they can unhinge it, though, Abe arrives and steps up in front of them. Using his wit, his wisdom and, finally, his great capacity for reason, he shames the crowd into dispersing and seeking their vengeance through the legal system.

Abe receives a letter from Mary Todd, requesting his presence at a social function. At the supper party, Mary gets tired of waiting for the shy and physically graceless young lawyer to ask her to dance, so she boldly asks him. He obliges her, and afterwards they take a walk out onto the terrace together.

Amidst a great deal of excitement and anticipation by the denizens of Springfield, the Clay murder trial begins. After wading through a litany of prospective jurors, twelve men are finally selected and the testimonies commence.

When Mrs. Clay is called to the stand, prosecuting attorney John Felder (Donald Meek) offers her the life of her innocent son for the name of the guilty one. She refuses. He reminds her that, according to state law, she can be charged as an accomplice and punished with a jail sentence if she does not cooperate. Still, she refuses. Lincoln, who is more cognizant of the difference between what's "right" and what's "wrong" than he is of the letter of the law, pleads with Judge Herbert A. Bell (Spencer Charters) for mercy on behalf of the old woman. Before the judge rules, Felder withdraws the question and excuses her.

Cass drops a bomb on the proceedings when he takes the stand and claims to have also witnessed the incident, from a hundred yards away and by the light of the full moon. He names Matt Clay as the murderer, and the courtroom erupts. The state prosecutor rests his case, and Judge Bell calls for a recess until the following day.

That night, the judge visits Abe in his office and offers him the aid of the formidable Stephen Douglas — even if only in an advisory capacity — but Abe decides to continue the fight on his own. The judge also asks him to change his clients' plea, promising leniency for Adam, but again Abe refuses. He will not break his word to Mrs. Clay.

The next morning, he cross-examines Palmer Cass, who reiterates his story. As he is leaving the witness stand, Abe asks him why he killed Scrub White. Cass is visibly shaken by this query. Abe pulls out the Farmer's Almanac and shows him that there was only a quarter-moon on the night in question, and that it set a full forty minutes before the murder occurred, so he couldn't have seen anything. Abe goes on to recapitulate the events of that fateful Fourth of July evening: the fight Scrub and Cass had earlier in the day, how Scrub was still alive when Cass arrived on the scene, and how Cass used his knife to kill Scrub, then blamed it on Matt Clay.

Under intense pressure from Abe, Cass breaks down and confesses to the crime. The Clay brothers (each one having thought the other one did it) and Mrs. Clay (having seen the knife in Matt's hand after the fact and assuming that he did it) are all shocked.

After the trial, Mary Todd congratulates Lincoln on his victory. And Stephen Douglas promises never to underestimate the shrewd backwoods lawyer again.

"Well, Steve, I don't reckon either of us better underrate each other from here in," Lincoln replies wisely.

He steps out of the courtroom to a tremendous ovation from the people of Springfield.

In the film's final scene, we watch Abraham Lincoln walk over the hill, with thunder crashing in the sky, and into the annals of history. The last shot is of the Lincoln Memorial, with "Glory, Glory Hallelujah!" playing over it.

Notes: When this project was first proposed to Darryl Zanuck, he promptly turned it down, claiming that the subject had been done to death. In the previous couple of years, two Broadway plays had covered Lincoln's early years: *Prologue to Glory* and Robert Sherwood's Pulitzer Prize–winning *Abe Lincoln in Illinois*. But when he read the Lamar Trotti script—which was too good to be discarded so casually—Zanuck changed his mind and gave the project a green light.

For the part of Lincoln, they chose a relatively unknown actor by the name of Henry Fonda, not only because of the resemblance he bore to the sixteenth president, but also because Fonda was an avid Lincoln buff. They immediately sent him a copy of the script, which Fonda just as immediately returned. "Lincoln's too big a man," he reasoned. "Not only too big in history, but too big in everyone's heart and affections. I'm not ready for a part like that."[75]

But Zanuck and Trotti kept after him until the actor finally relented, agreeing to make a test for the part. When it was screened, a few days later, Fonda was even more adamant. "No way," he said. "I am not going to play Abraham Lincoln!"[76]

By this time, though, John "Pappy" Ford had been assigned to direct the film, having just finished his duties on *Stagecoach*. He called Fonda into his office and proceeded to assault the mild-mannered, soft-spoken young actor with a barrage of his usual four-letter words, forcing him to see the character for what he was (not yet a great and revered leader of our nation, but a backwoods lawyer who rode a mule because he couldn't afford a horse). He literally shamed Fonda into playing the part.

Fonda had the appropriate height (he was 6'1") and lankiness to play Lincoln, but the makeup artists at Fox provided him with a false nose, a mole, the illusion of deeply set eyes and a protruding brow. He also wore lifts, for extra leverage. These additional features made his resemblance to the young Abraham Lincoln uncanny.

Ford deliberately shot the film with a slow and leisurely pace, despite the fact that Zanuck was constantly calling for more action. Realizing that he would be assigned to another project as soon as shooting on *Young Mr. Lincoln* was completed—and that Zanuck would be free then to make his own changes—Ford did everything he possibly could to "lock the film in."

He printed only one take of each scene, and burned the negatives of any others. He also "camera cut" by surrounding those scenes with built-in dissolves (done by stopping down the camera and thereby eliminating the light). When Zanuck finally got his hands on it, there was little he could do.

Robert Parrish, who was the movie's sound effects editor, claimed that when Ford was finished shooting, there was so little film remaining that it was virtually impossible to alter the final product. "We just cut the slates off and spliced it together," he said.[77]

Lamar Trotti's script was based in part on a trial he had covered as a young newspaper reporter, in which two brothers were being tried for a murder that one of them had committed. The only eyewitness to the crime was the boys' mother, who refused to name which one of them did it. They were both found guilty and subsequently hanged.

Young Mr. Lincoln marked the first collaboration between director John Ford and actor Henry Fonda. Although they never became great friends (the way, for instance, Ford and "Duke" Wayne did), they respected each other enormously and always welcomed the opportunity to work together. Fonda's subsequent association with Ford—after *Lincoln,* they would go on to make *Drums Along the Mohawk* and *The Grapes of Wrath* consecutively, as well as five more pictures over the course of their respective careers—changed Fonda's career, making him not only a star, but a great actor as well.

Young Mr. Lincoln was nominated for an Oscar for Trotti's original story. Though overlooked commercially and artistically in 1939, it is now considered by many film scholars and historians a cinematic masterpiece, and its legion of admirers continues to grow.

Reviews: "Henry Fonda's characterization is one of those once-in-a-blue-moon things: a crossroads meeting of nature, art and a smart casting director. Nature gave Mr. Fonda long legs and arms, a strong and honest face and a slow smile; the make-up man added a new nose bridge, the lank brown hair, the frock coat and stove-pipe hat (the beard hadn't begun to sprout in those days) and the trace of a mole. Mr. Fonda supplied the rest— the warmth and kindness, the pleasant modesty, the courage, resolution, tenderness, shrewdness and wit that Lincoln, even young Mr. Lincoln, must have possessed. His performance kindles the film, makes it a moving unity, at once gentle and quizically comic."—Frank S. Nugent, *The New York Times*

"*Young Mr. Lincoln* very sensibly confines itself to what is implied in its title. . . . It is deceptively simple, so few things seem to happen and yet so much is shown. Not the ribald Lincoln, not the rough-and-tumble Lincoln, not the Lincoln in love (what a complicated thing *The Loves of Abraham Lincoln* would be if some one had the temerity to try it!) nor the Lincoln who was such a superb actor when he got going before an audience. But, plain and moving, the Lincoln who became America's symbol for the man of the people, the Lincoln whose humanity was his greatest quality.

Which is the essential and most important thing."—James Shelley Hamilton, *National Board of Review Magazine*

Zaza

Paramount. 83 min. Directed by George Cukor.

Cast: Claudette Colbert, Herbert Marshall, Bert Lahr, Helen Westley, Constance Collier, Ann Todd, Genevieve Tobin, Walter Catlett, Rex Evans.

This remake of a 1923 Gloria Swanson silent cast Colbert as a music hall singer who has an affair with married aristocrat Marshall. The film was a box-office dud, which director Cukor blamed on censorship cuts by the Hays Office. To help Colbert inject more professional expressiveness into the film's period songs, the director hired Fanny Brice to tutor her. Miss Brice advised her pupil: "You know, kid, when you sing a ballad you'll find it a comfort to touch your own flesh."[78] Based on the play by Pierre Berton and Charles Simon, the original David Belasco stage production of *Zaza* made a star of Mrs. Leslie Carter.

The Movie Series of 1939

Not all of the films released in 1939 went on to become classics. In fact, some of them weren't even very good (as some of the following titles would serve to indicate). But the movie series were a major source of revenue for the studios, in some cases even saving companies from bankruptcy. In the immortal words of Louis B. Mayer: "Any good [Andy] Hardy picture made $500,000 more than *Ninotchka* made."[79]

It all started during the Depression, when double-billing had become standard practice and studios were scrambling to meet their quota agreements with exhibitors. The cheapest and easiest way for them to do that was to create a basic property which — if it captured the imagination of the public — could be churned out again and again in the guise of a series.

What follows is a look at the movie series that were running in 1939, along with the various series installments which were released that year. They include some of the most popular movie series of all time — Andy Hardy, Charlie Chan, Sherlock Holmes — as well as some others which have long since been forgotten.

Andy Hardy

In 1937, MGM made an unpretentious domestic comedy called *A Family Affair,* which was based on the 1928 Broadway play *Skidding* by Aurania Rouveyrol. It was a pleasant though by no means extraordinary black-and-white programmer which dealt with the normal, everyday trials and tribulations of the Hardy family: Judge James Hardy (Lionel Barrymore), his wife (Spring Byington), Aunt Millie (Sara Haden), and the three Hardy children (Mickey Rooney, Julie Haydon, and Cecelia Parker).

It was not intended to be the beginning of a movie series, but when audiences responded so overwhelmingly to it, Louis B. Mayer promptly decided to make it just that. The series began officially in 1938, with *You're Only Young Once.* Lewis Stone took over the role of Judge Hardy, Fay Holden the role of his wife, and Ann Rutherford was cast as Polly, Andy's girlfriend. Sara Haden, Cecilia Parker and, of course, Mickey Rooney as wholesome, all–American Andy Hardy all retained their original roles. The

Andy Hardy (Mickey Rooney) and his dad (Lewis Stone) discuss Andy's plans for the future, which include dropping out of school and marrying his drama teacher, in *Andy Hardy Gets Spring Fever* (MGM).

series was set in the small Midwestern town of Carvel, a sort of Anytown, U.S.A.

Over the next two decades, fifteen more "Hardy Family" segments were made, grossing over $25 million for MGM. Most of the installments were directed by George B. Seitz, and the series served as a launching pad for such future stars as Judy Garland, Lana Turner, Kathryn Grayson, Donna Reed and Esther Williams.

Testament to the great appeal of this series was the special Oscar given to MGM "for its achievement in representing the American Way of Life."

The Hardys Ride High. 80 min. Directed by George B. Seitz. **Cast:** Lewis Stone, Mickey Rooney, Cecilia Parker, Fay Holden, Ann Rutherford, Sara Haden, Virginia Grey, Marsha Hunt, William T. Orr. The Hardys inherit a large fortune and take possession of a palatial mansion. The plot is constructed around how the family adapts to its new social status.

Andy Hardy Gets Spring Fever. 85 min. Directed by W.S. Van Dyke II. **Cast:** Lewis Stone, Mickey Rooney, Cecilia Parker, Fay Holden, Ann Rutherford, Sara Haden, Addison Richards. Andy falls in love with his high school drama teacher, writes a play and performs the lead role in it. In the end, as usual, it is the judge's wisdom—along with cooperation from the teacher—which brings Andy back down to earth. In between, he suffers all the agonies of first love.

Judge Hardy and Son. 87 min. Directed by George B. Seitz. **Cast:**

Lewis Stone, Mickey Rooney, Cecilia Parker, Fay Holden, Ann Rutherford, Sara Haden, June Preisser, Maria Ouspenskaya, Henry Hull, Martha O'Driscoll. This one centers on the judge's attempts to help an elderly couple in dire financial straits. In the midst of his family's involvement with the couple, Mrs. Hardy is stricken with pneumonia. By the conclusion, the Hardys have emerged with a whole new perspective on life.

Blondie

Chic Young's long-running comic strip "Blondie" — a natural for movie seriesdom — was finally started up as a series by Columbia Studios in 1938. By 1950, the studio had churned out 28 episodes, all of them filmed in black-and-white, and all of which centered around the harried lives of scatter-brained Dagwood Bumstead (Arthur Lake), his more sensible wife, Blondie (Penny Singleton), their two children, Baby Dumpling (Larry Simms) and Cookie (who would not be introduced until 1942, when Blondie gave birth to her in "Blondie's Blessed Event"), and the smartest member of the whole family, their dog Daisy. Other regulars included Jonathan Hale as Dagwood's boss, Mr. Dithers (in later installments, Jerome Cowan would play his new boss, Mr. Radcliffe), and Irving Bacon as the family's mailman, whom Dagwood almost always ran over in his last-second rushes to the office.

Like "The Honeymooners" television show of the fifties, the essence of this series was that the typical American male was a boob and buffoon at heart. Because of his overinflated ego and delusions of grandeur, Dagwood was continually mucking things up, and only through the love, patience, and understanding of a good wife like Blondie could he get his life back into any semblance of sanity and order.

A number of future stars popped up in the Blondie series, including Glenn Ford ("Blondie Plays Cupid"), Rita Hayworth ("Blondie on a Budget"), Larry Parks and Janet Blair ("Blondie Goes to College"), and several others.

Blondie Meets the Boss. 58 min. Directed by Frank Strayer. **Cast:** Penny Singleton, Arthur Lake, Larry Simms, Dorothy Moore, Jonathan Hale, Stanley Brown, Inez Courtney, Don Beddoe. The title says it all.

Blondie Takes a Vacation. 61 min. Directed by Frank Strayer. **Cast:** Penny Singleton, Arthur Lake, Larry Simms, Danny Mummert, Donald Meek, Elizabeth Dunne, Robert Wilcox, Irving Bacon. This one finds the Bumsteads at a resort, helping out the owner.

Blondie Brings Up Baby. 67 min. Directed by Frank Strayer. **Cast:** Penny Singleton, Arthur Lake, Larry Simms, Danny Mummert, Jonathan Hale, Fay Helm, Peggy Ann Garner, Helen Jerome Eddy, Irving Bacon. Baby Dumpling starts his school career.

Bulldog Drummond

Hugh "Bulldog" Drummond, an ex–British army officer constantly on the prowl for new adventures, was created in 1919 by "Sapper" (Herman Cyril McNeile). He was the subject of several silent films, and in 1929 — with the advent of talking pictures — was played perfectly by Ronald Colman in *Bulldog Drummond* and again later in *Bulldog Drummond Strikes Back*.

In 1937, the movie series was born, with John Howard in the title role, and it ran for fourteen years. The Paramount-produced series featured John Barrymore as Inspector Neilson of Scotland Yard, Reginald Denny as Drummond's constant companion Algy, E.E. Clive as the butler Tenny, and a healthy variety of love interests. The various villains included J. Carrol Naish, Anthony Quinn, George Zucco, and Eduardo Ciannelli.

Towards the end of the series, Tom Conway, Ron Randell and Walter Pidgeon all took turns playing Drummond, but by that time the popularity of the character was drying up.

Arrest Bulldog Drummond. 57 min. Directed by James Hogan. **Cast:** John Howard, Heather Angel, H.B. Warner, George Zucco, E.E. Clive, Reginald Denny, John Sutton. Drummond is en route to his bachelor dinner again (after several unsuccessful tries), while patient bride-to-be Phyllis pleads with him not to get involved in any more murder cases. But, of course, he does. This one involves a man who calls himself "The Earl of Destiny" and has devised a gadget that can detonate explosives anywhere within a half mile range.

Bulldog Drummond's Secret Police. 56 min. Directed by James Hogan. **Cast:** John Howard, Heather Angel, H.B. Warner, Reginald Denny, Leo G. Carroll, Elizabeth Patterson. When old Professor Downie is murdered in the North Wing of Drummond Towers, Phyllis is once again left waiting at the altar. The story revolves around the recovery of a royal treasure in the basement of the towers during the reign of Charles I.

Bulldog Drummond's Bride. 55 min. Directed by James Hogan. **Cast:** John Howard, Heather Angel, H.B. Warner, Reginald Denny, Elizabeth Patterson, Eduardo Ciannelli. At last, Drummond and Phyllis are married. After the ceremony, Drummond tosses a grenade at Ciannelli, blowing him to bits, and recovers the loot he has stolen from the Southern Midland Bank.

Charlie Chan

Earl Derr Biggers's famous Chinese sleuth, Charlie Chan, was first introduced to the reading public in a serialized version of the 1925 novel *The House Without a Key*. After a couple of silent films featuring the Oriental detective were made — as well as a sound film in 1929 called *Behind the Curtain*, which starred Warner Baxter and featured Chan (played by English actor E.L. Park) as a nominal character — the movie series officially began

Sidney Toler as Earl Derr Biggers's infamous proverb-spouting sleuth in *Charlie Chan at Treasure Island* (Twentieth Century–Fox).

with *Charlie Chan Carries On* (1931). Swedish actor Warner Oland played the sleuth and continued playing him (in 16 more episodes) until his death in 1938. Scotch-descended character actor Sidney Toler took over and successfully carried on the role until his own death in 1947. By that time, Monogram Pictures had picked up the property from Twentieth Century–Fox, and they replaced Toler with film and television character actor Roland Winters, who was completely unsuited for the part. He played Chan in six dismal entries, until the series ended (mercifully, by then) in 1949.

The bitter end to this movie series does not, however, detract from the freshness and fun of all the early episodes which featured Oland and many of those which featured Toler. The detective's bickering with sons #1 and

#2 (Keye Luke and Sen Yung, respectively) and his little pearls of wisdom ("Insignificant molehill sometimes more important than conspicuous mountain," etc.) are still as witty and entertaining as ever.

Charlie Chan in Reno. 70 min. Directed by Norman Foster. **Cast:** Sidney Toler, Ricardo Cortez, Phyllis Brooks, Slim Summerville, Kane Richmond, Robert Lowery, Morgan Conway, Sen Yung. A divorcée has been murdered, and you-know-who is on the case, along with the standard room full of suspects.

Charlie Chan in City of Darkness. 75 min. Directed by Herbert I. Leeds. **Cast:** Sidney Toler, Lynn Bari, Richard Clarke, Pedro de Cordoba, Douglass Dumbrille, Leo G. Carroll, Lon Chaney, Jr. Murder during a blackout, spies, and a heinous plot to smuggle arms to America's foreign enemies. Chan wraps it all up in the end.

Charlie Chan at Treasure Island. 75 min. Directed by Norman Foster. **Cast:** Sidney Toler, Cesar Romero, Pauline Moore, Douglass Dumbrille, Billie Seward, Louis Jean Heydt, Charles Halton. This is one of the best installments of the entire series. A man is found dead on a plane as it lands in San Francisco. The clues lead Charlie and son Jimmy to the great fair at Treasure Island.

Dr. Christian

In 1935, a Canadian man named Dionne gained international fame when he fathered quintuplets. Twentieth Century–Fox decided to make a film based on this extraordinary event, and distinguished Danish actor Jean Hersholt was signed to play the attending physician, Allan Dafoe. (Will Rogers had been initially signed for the part, but was killed that same year in a plane crash.) A trio of pictures involving Dr. Dafoe and the quintuplets appeared over the next few years, and the box-office success of these films convinced Hersholt and executives at RKO that a popular series could be made on the career of a country doctor.

Because the rights to Dr. Dafoe's life were not available, a new character was created, humanitarian and perennial optimist "Dr. Christian." The name was chosen partly because it was Scandinavian and justified Hersholt's accent, and also because Hans Christian Andersen was the actor's favorite author.

Hersholt played him in six modestly budgeted, black-and-white feature films produced by RKO, beginning with *Meet Dr. Christian* in 1939. The series centered around the beloved physician, his practice in River's End, Minnesota, and his humanitarian efforts.

Hersholt, it should be noted, was himself a great humanitarian. He founded the Motion Picture Relief Fund, served as president of the Academy of Motion Picture Arts and Sciences, and was awarded three Academy Awards for his various philanthropic works.

Meet Dr. Christian. 63 min. Directed by Bernard Vorhaus. **Cast:** Jean Hersholt, Dorothy Lovett, Robert Baldwin, Enid Bennett, Paul Harvey, Marcia Mae Jones, Jackie Moran. The opening entry in the series focuses on the good doctor's attempts to get the town a new hospital. He also performs an incredibly complicated operation brilliantly, without the advantage of proper equipment.

Dr. Kildare

On the opposite side of the medical spectrum was sophisticated, big-city physician James Kildare. Based on a Max Brand work, Dr. Kildare first appeared in a 1938 gangster melodrama from Paramount called *Interns Can't Take Money,* which featured Joel McCrea in the title role. Later that same year, MGM acquired the property, restructured the format to insert all the necessary ingredients for a successful movie series, replaced McCrea with contract player Lew Ayres, and began production on what evolved into a fifteen-film, black-and-white series that ran for almost a decade.

Ayres played Dr. Kildare for the first nine installments of the series. He was followed by Philip Dorn, Van Johnson, and James Craig. The stories were set at Blair General Hospital and featured the dominating presence of Lionel Barrymore as gruff but lovable Dr. Leonard Gillespie.

Other regulars included Nurse Mary Lamont (Laraine Day), Kildare's girlfriend; Molly Bird (Alma Kruger), the unaccostable Superintendent of Nurses; Dr. Walter Carew (Walter Kingsford), head of the hospital; Miss Parker (Nell Craig), the floor nurse; Sally (Marie Blake), the switchboard operator; Joe Wayman (Nat Pendleton), the ambulance driver—in later entries, Hobart Genet (Rags Ragland)—and the orderly, Vernon Briggs (Red Skelton). Samuel S. Hinds and Emma Dunn played Kildare's parents.

The series was stacked with appearances by various MGM starlets, such as Lana Turner, Ava Gardner, and Marilyn Maxwell.

Calling Dr. Kildare. 86 min. Directed by Harold S. Bucquet. **Cast:** Lew Ayres, Lionel Barrymore, Laraine Day, Lana Turner, Lynne Carver, Nat Pendleton. Dr. Gillespie transfers Kildare to the downtown outpatient department, to gain some much-needed practical experience. Things get complicated when he helps a gangster who's been shot, becomes involved with gun moll Turner, and finds himself a police suspect.

The Secret of Dr. Kildare. 84 min. Directed by Harold Bucquet. **Cast:** Lew Ayres, Lionel Barrymore, Laraine Day, Lionel Atwill, Helen Gilbert, Sara Haden. This one finds Gillespie pushing himself beyond his own strength and endurance while trying to find a cure for pneumonia. He eventually collapses from exhaustion and Kildare takes over for him, while also supervising the treatment of a traumatic shock victim.

Mr. Moto

Having achieved success with its first Oriental detective series *(Charlie Chan)*, Twentieth Century–Fox began another one in 1937, based on John P. Marquand's books about the ubiquitous Japanese sleuth Mr. Moto. Over a period of two years, the studio produced eight entries starring Peter Lorre in the title role. However, with anti–Japanese sentiments escalating in America, the character died off quickly, while his Chinese counterpart prospered through the war years and beyond.

Mr. Moto's Last Warning. 71 min. Directed by Norman Foster. **Cast:** Peter Lorre, Ricardo Cortez, Virginia Field, John Carradine, George Sanders. Moto foils a plot to blow up the French fleet at the entrance to the Suez Canal, which would disrupt Franco-British diplomatic relations.

Mr. Moto in Danger Island. 63 min. Directed by Herbert I. Leeds. **Cast:** Peter Lorre, Jean Hersholt, Amanda Duff, Warren Hymer, Richard Lane, Leon Ames. Moto is summoned to Puerto Rico (Danger Island) to investigate diamond smuggling down there and finds himself in one predicament after another. Somehow, he manages to survive every one of them.

Mr. Moto Takes a Vacation. 68 min. Directed by Norman Foster. **Cast:** Peter Lorre, Joseph Schildkraut, Lionel Atwill, Virginia Field, John King, Iva Stewart. Actually, he's guarding the priceless Queen of Sheba's crown while pretending to be on vacation.

Nancy Drew

This very short-lived Warner Bros. series, based on the popular novels by Carolyn Keene, featured Bonita Granville as the dogged and ebullient Nancy. The four entries in the series were all written by Kenneth Ganet and directed by William Clemens. The series began in 1938 with *Nancy Drew, Detective* and continued through 1939 with the mysteries *Nancy Drew, Trouble Shooter, Nancy Drew and the Hidden Staircase,* and *Nancy Drew, Reporter,* all of which were released within a few months of each other. They all had Nancy coming to the aid of senior citizens.

The Saint

Leslie Charteris' sophisticated sleuth Simon Templar first appeared in print in the late 1920s, but did not attract Hollywood's interest until 1938, when RKO produced *The Saint in New York.* Louis Hayward was cast as the gallant half crook, half detective, and was immediately followed in the role by George Sanders, who took over for five episodes. The British then acquired rights to the property and made two installments with Hugh Sinclair as Templar, one of which was released by RKO and the other of which

Republic Pictures picked up for distribution. In 1954, RKO released a final entry in the series, which returned Louis Hayward to the role he had originated on the screen.

During the 1960s, Roger Moore had his first big success playing Simon Templar on the television series "The Saint."

The Saint Strikes Back. 64 min. Directed by John Farrow. **Cast:** George Sanders, Wendy Barrie, Jonathan Hale, Jerome Cowan, Neil Hamilton, Barry Fitzgerald. Set in San Francisco, this one involves the daughter of a former police detective who died in disgrace. She has formed an underworld gang to avenge his death. For comedy relief, Barry Fitzgerald shows up as good-hearted safecracker "Zipper" Dyson.

The Saint in London. 72 min. Directed by John Paddy Carstairs. **Cast:** George Sanders, Sally Gray, David Burns, Gordon McLeod, Henry Oscar, Ralph Truman. Templar returns to England following a sojourn in the United States and takes on a counterfeiting ring.

Sherlock Holmes

The Adventures of Sherlock Holmes. 85 min. Directed by Alfred L. Werker. **Cast:** Basil Rathbone, Nigel Bruce, Ida Lupino, Alan Marshal, Terry Kilburn, George Zucco, E.E. Clive, Mary Gordon. The incredible success of *The Hound of the Baskervilles* (see in alphabetical sequence in "The Movies of 1939") prompted Darryl F. Zanuck to hurry this remake of William Gillette's stage play *Sherlock Holmes* into production, to serve as the second installment in what was now a bona fide movie series. It was easily the best of the lot, detailing the plot of archnemesis Professor Moriarty (George Zucco, as much the quintessential Moriarty as Rathbone was the quintessential Holmes) to steal the crown jewels. Whereas future episodes of this enormously popular series would show the Baker Street detective fighting crime all over the modern world, this one was beautifully and atmospherically set in author Conan Doyle's original setting, foggy and mysterious London. Two years later, the series would resume, but never again would it capture the flavor and essence of Holmes as marvelously as the first two installments of the series did (particularly "Adventures").

Tarzan

Edgar Rice Burroughs, an ex-miner and businessman turned writer, wrote his first Tarzan story in 1912. It appeared in the October issue of *All-Story Magazine*. The story was novelized in 1914 and published by A.C. McClurg. Burroughs went on to write 26 Tarzan books, creating one of the most enduring figures in popular fiction (not to mention movie seriesdom).

The series began in 1932 with *Tarzan, the Ape Man*, which starred former Olympic champion Johnny Weissmuller as lord of the jungle. Maureen O'Sullivan (Mia Farrow's mother) played Jane.

Weissmuller swung, swam, and trumpeted his patented jungle call through fourteen installments (easily the best ones of the series) before hanging up his trunks. He was followed by a host of other actors (among them, Buster Crabbe, Gordon Scott, and Jock Mahoney) who took turns as Tarzan, but none who ever bettered him in the role. Weissmuller is as much Tarzan as Basil Rathbone is Sherlock Holmes and Sean Connery is James Bond.

Tarzan Finds a Son! 90 min. Directed by Richard Thorpe. **Cast:** Johnny Weissmuller, Maureen O'Sullivan, John Sheffield, Ian Hunter, Henry Stephenson, Laraine Day. This episode introduced "Boy" to the series. He arrived, not via the stork, but in a plane that crashed in Tarzan's jungle.

The Thin Man

With screwball comedies and dime-store detective novels at the peak of their popularity in the '30s and '40s, MGM had the brilliant idea to combine both formats and, in so doing, created one of the best movie series of all time, *The Thin Man* series. Between 1934 and 1946, the studio produced six of these pictures, all of which starred William Powell and Myrna Loy as millionaire detective couple Nick and Nora Charles, and all of which featured their adorable dog, Asta (played by Asta and, in later installments, Asta, Jr.). Perhaps no movie series ever captured the heart or the mood of the nation as accurately—or as wittily—as this one did.

Another Thin Man. 102 min. Directed by W.S. Van Dyke II. **Cast:** William Powell, Myrna Loy, C. Aubrey Smith, Otto Kruger, Nat Pendleton, Tom Neal, and Asta. The third entry in this delightful series has the couple arriving—along with eight-month-old Nick, Jr.—at a Victorian estate, for a weekend of scotch, soda, and murder.

William Powell and Myrna Loy try to entertain junior in *Another Thin Man* (MGM).

Appendix A:
The Academy Awards
Ceremony of 1939

Feb. 29, 1940, 8:30 p.m.
In the Coconut Grove of the Ambassador Hotel

Your Host:
Bob Hope

Presenters

Scientific and Technical Awards
Film Editing
Sound Recording
Cinematography
Art Direction
Special Effects .... Darryl F. Zanuck
Music Awards.............................. Gene Buck
Short Subjects .... Bob Hope
Special Award to Judy Garland .... Mickey Rooney
Best Director .... Mervyn LeRoy
Writing Awards .... Sinclair Lewis
Best Picture .... Y. Frank Freeman
Special Awards to Jean Hersholt, Ralph
    Morgan, Ralph Block and Conrad Nagel .... Basil O'Connor
Irving Thalberg Award...................... Dr. Ernest Martin Hopkins
Commemorative Award to Douglas Fairbanks ..... Walter Wanger
Supporting Actor
Supporting Actress .... Fay Bainter
Best Actor
Best Actress .... Spencer Tracy

Awards are nice, but I'd much rather have a job.—Jane Darwell[80]

There was little mystery or suspense surrounding the Academy Awards ceremony of 1939. Bob Hope, in his first year as emcee of the banquet, opened the proceedings by quipping: "What a wonderful thing, this benefit for David O. Selznick."[81] And later, when Paramount executive Y. Frank Freeman stepped up to the podium to present the Oscar for Best Picture, he said, "The only reason I was called upon to give this honor is because I have a Southern accent."[82]

273

As expected, *Gone with the Wind* swept the awards, winning a record eight of them, the most until *Ben-Hur* came along in 1958. It had been nominated for a record thirteen. The lone upset was the nod to Robert Donat, the Englishman with the unforgettably beautiful voice, for Best Actor, over favorite Clark Gable. Gable was very disheartened over his loss, and told his wife so on their way home later that evening. "Don't worry, baby, we'll take one home next year," she consoled him. "No," he replied, "this was it. This was my last chance. I'll never win one of those things again." "I don't mean you, you self-centered son of a bitch!" Carole Lombard screamed back at him. "I mean *me!*"[83]

Some firsts that evening:

This was the first Academy Awards ceremony to be captured on film.

GWTW became the first film ever to win an Oscar for color photography.

Sidney Howard, winner of the Best Screenplay statuette, had been run over by a tractor on his Massachusetts farm, thus becoming the first posthumous winner.

And Hattie McDaniel received the greatest ovation of the evening when she became the first black performer to win an Academy Award, for her performance as Mammy in *GWTW*. Black groups had condemned Miss McDaniel for playing what they considered to be a Negro stereotype and demanded she refuse the Oscar. But such accusations were ridiculous; Mammy was one of the smartest and strongest characters in the whole movie, and audiences understood completely when Rhett said that Mammy was one of the few people whose respect he'd like to have.

Miss McDaniel stepped up to the podium, decked out in gardenias, and gave an eloquent and heartfelt speech, saying she hoped that she would be a credit to her race as well as to the film industry. She then burst into tears and walked off stage.

Olivia de Havilland, nominated in the same category, rushed over from the Selznick table to congratulate her, then rushed to the kitchen and burst into tears herself.

Oddly enough, however, during the entire ceremony—while *GWTW* swept through the Academy like Sherman through the South—one name was never mentioned: that of Margaret Mitchell, the woman who wrote the novel that started it all.

That's Hollywood.

The Awards

Best Picture:	*Gone with the Wind*, Selznick, MGM. Produced by David O. Selznick.
Other Nominees:	*Dark Victory*, Warner Bros. Produced by David Lewis.
	Goodbye Mr. Chips, MGM (British). Produced by Victor Saville.
	Love Affair, RKO Radio. Produced by Leo McCarey.
	Mr. Smith Goes to Washington, Columbia. Produced by Frank Capra.
	Ninotchka, MGM. Produced by Sidney Franklin.
	Of Mice and Men, Roach, UA. Produced by Lewis Milestone.
	Stagecoach, Wanger, UA. Produced by Walter Wanger.
	The Wizard of Oz, MGM. Produced by Mervyn LeRoy.

Wuthering Heights, Goldwyn, UA. Produced by Samuel Goldwyn.

Best Actor: Robert Donat in *Goodbye Mr. Chips* (MGM) (British).

Other Nominees: Clark Gable in *Gone with the Wind* (Selznick, MGM).
Laurence Olivier in *Wuthering Heights* (Goldwyn, UA).
Mickey Rooney in *Babes in Arms* (MGM).
James Stewart in *Mr. Smith Goes to Washington* (Columbia).

Best Actress: Vivien Leigh in *Gone with the Wind* (Selznick, MGM).

Other Nominees: Bette Davis in *Dark Victory* (Warner Bros.).
Irene Dunne in *Love Affair* (RKO Radio).
Greta Garbo in *Ninotchka* (MGM).
Greer Garson in *Goodbye Mr. Chips* (MGM) (British).

Supporting Actor: Thomas Mitchell in *Stagecoach* (Wanger, UA).
Other Nominees: Brian Aherne in *Juarez* (Warner Bros.).
Harry Carey in *Mr. Smith Goes to Washington* (Columbia).
Brian Donlevy in *Beau Geste* (Paramount).
Claude Rains in *Mr. Smith Goes to Washington* (Columbia).

Supporting Actress: Hattie McDaniel in *Gone with the Wind* (Selznick, MGM).

Other Nominees: Olivia de Havilland in *Gone with the Wind* (Selznick, MGM).
Geraldine Fitzgerald in *Wuthering Heights* (Goldwyn, UA).
Edna May Oliver in *Drums Along the Mohawk* (Twentieth Century–Fox).
Maria Ouspenskaya in *Love Affair* (RKO Radio).

Director: Victor Fleming for *Gone with the Wind* (Selznick, MGM).

Other Nominees: Frank Capra for *Mr. Smith Goes to Washington* (Columbia).
John Ford for *Stagecoach* (Wanger, UA).
Sam Wood for *Goodbye Mr. Chips* (MGM) (British).
William Wyler for *Wuthering Heights* (Goldwyn, UA).

Original Story: *Mr. Smith Goes to Washington,* Columbia. Lewis R. Foster.

Other Nominees: *Bachelor Mother,* RKO Radio. Felix Jackson.
Love Affair, RKO Radio. Mildred Cram and Leo McCarey.

Ninotchka, MGM. Melchior Lengyel.
Young Mr. Lincoln, Twentieth Century–Fox. Lamar Trotti.

Screenplay:

Gone with the Wind, Selznick, MGM. Sidney Howard.

Other Nominees:

Goodbye Mr. Chips, MGM (British). Eric Maschwitz, R.C. Sherriff and Claudine West.

Mr. Smith Goes to Washington, Columbia. Sidney Buchman.

Ninotchka, MGM. Charles Brackett, Walter Reisch and Billy Wilder.

Wuthering Heights, Goldwyn, UA. Ben Hecht and Charles MacArthur.

**Cinematography
(BLACK AND WHITE)**

Wuthering Heights, Goldwyn, UA. Gregg Toland.

Other Nominees:

First Love, Universal. Joseph Valentine.

The Great Victor Herbert, Paramount. Victor Milner.

Gunga Din, RKO Radio. Joseph H. August.

Intermezzo: A Love Story, Selznick, UA. Gregg Toland.

Juarez, Warner Bros. Tony Gaudio.

Lady of the Tropics, MGM. Norbert Brodine.

Only Angels Have Wings, Columbia. Joseph Walker.

The Rains Came, Twentieth Century–Fox. Arthur Miller.

Stagecoach, Wanger, UA. Bert Glennon.

Cinematography (COLOR)

Gone with the Wind, Selznick, MGM. Ernest Haller and Ray Rennahan.

Other Nominees:

Drums Along the Mohawk, Twentieth Century–Fox. Ray Rennahan and Bert Glennon.

Four Feathers, Denham, UA. Georges Perinal and Osmond Borradaile.

The Mikado, Universal. William V. Skall.

The Private Lives of Elizabeth and Essex, Warner Bros. Sol Polito and W. Howard Greene.

The Wizard of Oz, MGM. Hal Rosson.

Interior Decoration:

Gone with the Wind, Selznick, MGM. Lyle Wheeler.

Other Nominees:

Beau Geste, Paramount. Hans Dreier and Robert Odell.

Captain Fury, Roach, UA. Charles D. Hall.

First Love, Universal. Jack Otterson and Martin Obzina.

Love Affair, RKO Radio. Van Nest Polglase and Al Herman.

Man of Conquest, Republic. John Victor Mackay.

Mr. Smith Goes to Washington, Columbia. Lionel Banks.

The Private Lives of Elizabeth and Essex, Warner Bros. Anton Grot.

The Rains Came, Twentieth Century–Fox. William Darling and George Dudley.

Stagecoach, Wanger, UA. Alexander Toluboff.

The Wizard of Oz, MGM. Cedric Gibbons and William A. Horning.

Wuthering Heights, Goldwyn, UA. James Basevi.

Sound Recording: *When Tomorrow Comes,* Universal. Bernard B. Brown.

Other Nominees: *Balalaika,* MGM. Douglas Shearer.

Gone with the Wind, Selznick, MGM. Thomas T. Moulton.

Goodbye Mr. Chips, MGM (British). A.W. Watkins.

The Great Victor Herbert, Paramount. Loren Ryder.

The Hunchback of Notre Dame, RKO Radio. John Aalberg.

Man of Conquest, Republic. C.L. Lootens.

Mr. Smith Goes to Washington, Columbia. John Livadary.

Of Mice and Men, Roach, MGM. Elmer Raguse.

The Private Lives of Elizabeth and Essex, Warner Bros. Nathan Levinson.

The Rains Came, Twentieth Century–Fox. E.H. Hansen.

Song: "Over the Rainbow" (*The Wizard of Oz,* MGM); Music by Harold Arlen. Lyrics by E.Y. Harburg.

Other Nominees: "Faithful Forever" (*Gulliver's Travels,* Paramount); Music by Ralph Rainger. Lyrics by Leo Robin.

"I Poured My Heart into a Song" (*Second Fiddle,* Twentieth Century–Fox); Music and lyrics by Irving Berlin.

"Wishing" (*Love Affair,* RKO Radio); Music and lyrics by Buddy De Sylva.

Score: *Stagecoach,* Walter Wanger, UA. Richard Hageman, Frank Harling, John Leipold and Leo Shuken.

Other Nominees: *Babes in Arms,* MGM. Roger Edens and George E. Stoll.

First Love, Universal. Charles Previn.

The Great Victor Herbert, Paramount. Phil Boutelje and Arthur Lange.

The Hunchback of Notre Dame, RKO Radio. Alfred Newman.

Intermezzo: A Love Story, Selznick, UA. Lou Forbes.

Mr. Smith Goes to Washington, Columbia. Dimitri Tiomkin.

Of Mice and Men, Roach, UA. Aaron Copland.
The Private Lives of Elizabeth and Essex, Warner Bros. Erich Wolfgang Korngold.
She Married a Cop, Republic. Cy Feurer.
Swanee River, Twentieth Century–Fox. Louis Silvers.
They Shall Have Music, Goldwyn, UA. Alfred Newman.
Way Down South, Lesser, RKO Radio. Victor Young.

Original Score: *The Wizard of Oz,* MGM. Herbert Stothart.
Other Nominees: *Dark Victory,* Warner Bros. Max Steiner.
Eternally Yours, Walter Wanger, UA. Werner Janssen.
Golden Boy, Columbia. Victor Young.
Gone with the Wind, Selznick, MGM. Max Steiner.
Gulliver's Travels, Paramount. Victor Young.
The Man in the Iron Mask, Small, UA. Lud Gluskin and Lucien Moraweck.
Man of Conquest, Republic. Victor Young.
Nurse Edith Cavell, RKO Radio. Anthony Collins.
Of Mice and Men, Roach, UA. Aaron Copland.
The Rains Came, Twentieth Century–Fox. Alfred Newman.
Wuthering Heights, Goldwyn, UA. Alfred Newman.

Film Editing: *Gone with the Wind,* Selznick, MGM. Hal C. Kern and James E. Newcom.
Other Nominees: *Goodbye Mr. Chips,* MGM (British). Charles Frend.
Mr. Smith Goes to Washington, Columbia. Gene Havlick and Al Clark.
The Rains Came, Twentieth Century–Fox. Barbara McLean.
Stagecoach, Wanger, UA. Otho Lovering and Dorothy Spencer.

Special Effects: *The Rains Came,* Twentieth Century–Fox. Photographic: E.H. Hansen. Sound: Fred Sersen.
Other Nominees: *Gone with the Wind,* Selznick, MGM. Photographic: John R. Cosgrove. Sound: Fred Albin and Arthur Johns.
Only Angels Have Wings, Columbia. Photographic: Roy Davidson. Sound: Edwin C. Hahn.
The Private Lives of Elizabeth and Essex, Warner Bros. Photographic: Byron Haskin. Sound: Nathan Levinson.
Topper Takes a Trip, Roach, UA. Roy Seawright.
Union Pacific, Paramount. Photographic: Farciot Edouart and Gordon Jennings. Sound: Loren Ryder.
The Wizard of Oz, MGM. Photographic: A. Arnold Gillespie. Sound: Douglas Shearer.

Short Subjects

Cartoon:	*The Ugly Duckling*, Walt Disney, RKO Radio.
Other Nominees:	*Detouring America*, Warner Bros.
	Peace on Earth, MGM.
	The Pointer, Walt Disney, RKO Radio.
One-Reel:	*Busy Little Bears*, Paramount (Paragraphics).
Other Nominees:	*Information Please*, RKO Radio.
	Prophet Without Honor, MGM (Miniatures).
	Sword Fishing, Warner Bros. (Vitaphone Varieties).
Two-Reel:	*Sons of Liberty*, Warner Bros. (Historical Featurette).
Other Nominees:	*Drunk Driving*, MGM (Crime Doesn't Pay).
	Five Times Five, RKO Radio. (Special).

The Irving G. Thalberg Memorial Award

David O. Selznick.

Special Awards

Douglas Fairbanks (Commemorative Award)—recognizing the unique and outstanding contribution of Douglas Fairbanks, first president of the Academy, to the international development of the motion picture (statuette).

The Motion Picture Relief Fund—acknowledging the outstanding services to the industry during the past year of the Motion Picture Relief Fund and its progressive leadership. Presented to Jean Hersholt, President; Ralph Morgan, Chairman of the Executive Committee; Ralph Block, First Vice-President; Conrad Nagel (plaques).

Judy Garland for her oustanding performance as a screen juvenile during the past year (miniature statuette).

William Cameron Menzies for outstanding achievement in the use of color for the enhancement of dramatic mood in the production of *Gone with the Wind* (plaque).

The Technicolor Company for its contributions in successfully bringing three-color feature production to the screen (statuette).

Appendix B:
The Irving Theatre
(An Epitaph)

Back in 1939, one of the staples of small town American life was the local movie house. In my own hometown of Carbondale, Pennsylvania, that was the Irving Theatre.

For many years, the Irving's schedule was the same each week: Sunday, Monday and Tuesday were the big days, during which a top "A" release would be showcased; on Wednesday and Thursday, a second picture was shown; and on Friday and Saturday, the third and final picture of the week could be seen. All movies featured different combinations of cartoons, newsreels and shorts along with them. Only on occasion (when a picture did extraordinarily well) would it run for four days, which back then was an eternity for moviegoers. During 1939, only four movies stayed that long at the Irving: *Jesse James, Babes in Arms, Mr. Smith Goes to Washington,* and *Hollywood Cavalcade.* Also worth noting is the fact that, through the years, the really big Hollywood blockbusters (*Giant, The Ten Commandments, The Sound of Music,* etc.) always took at least two whole years to make it to Carbondale. *Gone with the Wind,* for instance, didn't arrive until 1941.

Film rentals varied, costing the theater anywhere from around fifty dollars (for something like the James Stewart–Claudette Colbert vehicle *It's a Wonderful World*) to nearly a thousand dollars (for something like *Jesse James*).

What did they get for their money?

Well, *It's a Wonderful World* played for two days—June 7 and 8—along with a 21-minute short from Vitaphone called *Sons of Liberty* and a 10-minute newsreel from Paramount. Rental for all three came to $87.03. The Irving's box-office receipts for those two days came to $230.76. *Jesse James* played on February 5, 6, 7, and 8, along with a couple of ten-minute newsreels. The rental for all three came to $983.26. The Irving's four-day take: $2,739.70.

Considering labor and advertising costs and other expenses were very low in those days, you can pretty much figure out what kind of an annual profit the Irving—and hundreds of small theaters like it around the country—made back then.

However, with the collapse of the studio system and the emergence of television, many of the small neighborhood theaters across the country fell on hard times and were forced to shut down. The Irving Theatre, sadly, was one of the casualties. On July 27, 1973, it closed its doors and never reopened them for business. Movies just weren't what they used to be, and when quality and quantity fell off drastically,

280

The Irving Theatre in its heyday (February 13, 1944). A reissue from 1939, *The Oklahoma Kid,* **is the feature attraction on this evening.**

so too did business. The last film to play there was an abysmal thing called *The Tomb of the Blind Dead,* a tragic end to an illustrious history. Ironically, it played for eight whole days.

The Irving's glory days had long since passed. So, too, had Hollywood's.

· Notes

1. Groucho Marx, *Groucho and Me* (New York: Random House, 1959).
2. Arthur Marx, *Groucho* (Victor Gollancz, 1954).
3. Mason Wiley and Damien Bona, *Inside Oscar: The Unofficial History of the Academy Awards* (New York: Ballantine, 1986).
4. Anne Edwards, *Judy Garland* (New York: Simon & Schuster, 1974).
5. David Niven, *The Moon's a Balloon* (New York: Putnam, 1972).
6. Frank Thompson, *William A. Wellman* (Metuchen, N.J.: Scarecrow, 1983).
7. Bob Hope and Bob Thomas, *The Road to Hollywood: My 40-Year Love Affair with the Movies* (Garden City, N.Y.: Doubleday, 1977).
8. William R. Meyer, *Warner Brothers Directors* (New York: Arlington House, 1978).
9. Wiley and Bona.
10. James Reid Paris, *The Great French Films* (Secaucus, N.J.: Citadel, 1983).
11. Leslie Halliwell, *Halliwell's Filmgoer's Companion* (New York: Scribner, 1965).
12. Errol Flynn, *My Wicked, Wicked Ways* (New York: Putnam, 1959).
13. Andrew Sinclair, *John Ford* (New York: Dial, 1979).
14. James Brough, *The Fabulous Fondas* (New York: McKay, 1973).
15. Lewis Yablonsky, *George Raft* (New York: McGraw-Hill, 1974).
16. Randy Skretvedt, *Laurel and Hardy: the Magic Behind the Movies* (Moonstone, 1987).
17. Will Holtzman, *William Holden: Pyramid Illustrated History of the Movies* (Pyramid, 1976).
18. Holtzman.
19. Wiley and Bona.
20. James Robert Parish and Gregory Mank, *The Best of MGM: The Golden Years (1928–59)* (New York: Arlington House, 1981).
21. Parish and Mank.
22. Parish and Mank.
23. Parish and Mank.
24. Parish and Mank.
25. Both quotes from Kenneth Barrow, *Mr. Chips: The Life of Robert Donat* (New York: Methuen, 1985).
26. Parish and Mank.
27. Leslie Cabarga, *The Fleischer Story* (Nostalgia, 1976).
28. Screenwriter William Goldman, whose favorite film of all time is *Gunga Din*, used this same scene in his script *Butch Cassidy and the Sundance Kid*. "If you're going to steal," Goldman wrote in his book *Adventures in the Screen Trade*, "steal from the masters."

283

29. Pamela Trescott, *Cary Grant: His Movies and His Life* (Washington: Acropolis, 1987).

30. Trescott.

31. Tony Thomas, *The Films of Ronald Reagan* (Secaucus, N.J.: Citadel, 1980).

32. Thomas.

33. Robert W. Pohle, Jr., and Douglas Itart, *Sherlock Holmes on the Screen: The Motion Picture Adventures of the World's Most Popular Detective* (San Diego: Barnes, 1977).

34. Charles Higham, *Charles Laughton: An Intimate Biography* (Garden City, N.Y.: Doubleday, 1976).

35. Higham.

36. Joseph Henry Steele, *Ingrid Bergman: An Intimate Portrait* (New York: McKay, 1959).

37. Robert A. Harris and Michael S. Lasky, *The Films of Alfred Hitchcock* (Secaucus, N.J.: Citadel, 1976).

38. Frank N. Magill, ed., *Magill's Survey of Cinema (First Series)* (Englewood Cliffs, N.J.: Salem Press, 1980).

39. Frank N. Magill, ed., *Magill's Survey of Cinema (Second Series)* (Englewood Cliffs, N.J.: Salem Press, 1980).

40. Michael B. Druxman, *Paul Muni: His Life and His Films* (San Diego, Barnes, 1974).

41. Lawrence J. Quirk, *The Films of Robert Taylor* (Secaucus, N.J.: Citadel, 1975).

42. Thompson.

43. Shirley Temple Black, *Child Star* (New York: McGraw-Hill, 1988).

44. Larry Swindell, *Charles Boyer: The Reluctant Lover* (Garden City, N.Y.: Doubleday, 1983).

45. James Curtis, *James Whale* (Metuchen, N.J.: Scarecrow, 1982).

46. Denis Gifford, *Karloff: The Man, the Monsters, the Movies* (Curtis, 1973).

47. Pauline Kael, *5,001 Nights at the Movies* (New York: Holt, Rinehart & Winston, 1982).

48. James Kotsilibas-Davis, *The Barrymores: The Royal Family in Hollywood* (New York: Crown, 1981).

49. *The New York Times,* October 20, 1939.

50. Halliwell.

51. Elaine Steinbeck and Robert Wallsten, eds., *John Steinbeck: A Life in Letters* (New York: Viking, 1975).

52. Jerry Vermilye, *Bette Davis: Pyramid Illustrated History of the Movies* (Pyramid, 1973).

53. Trescott.

54. Trescott.

55. Flynn.

56. James Kotsilibas-Davis and Myrna Loy, *Myrna Loy: Being and Becoming* (New York: Knopf, 1987).

57. Patrick McGilligan, *Cagney: The Actor as Auteur* (San Diego: Barnes, 1975).

58. Jean Renoir, *My Life and My Films* (New York: Atheneum, 1974).

59. Gifford.

60. Michael Powell, *A Life in Movies* (Heinemann, 1986).

61. *The National Board of Review Magazine,* March 1939.

62. Pauline Kael, *Kiss Kiss Bang Bang* (Boston: Little, Brown, 1965).

63. Wiley and Bona.

64. Tadao Sato, *Mizoguchi Kenji no Sekai (The World of Kenji Mizoguchi)* (Tokyo, 1982).

65. Stanley Green and Burt Goldblatt, *Starring Fred Astaire* (New York: Dodd, Mead, 1973).

66. James N. Beaver, Jr., *John Garfield: His Life and Films* (San Diego: Barnes, 1978).

67. Peter Underwood, *Karloff: The Life of Boris Karloff* (Drake, 1972).

68. Ella Smith, *Starring Miss Barbara Stanwyck* (New York: Crown, 1974).

69. Smith.

70. Parish and Mank.

71. Halliwell.

72. Margaret Morley, *The Films of Laurence Olivier* (Secaucus, N.J.: Citadel, 1977).

73. Ronald J. Fields, *W.C. Fields: A Life on Film* (New York: St. Martin's, 1974).

74. Dan Ford, *Pappy: The Life of John Ford* (Englewood Cliffs, N.J.: Prentice Hall, 1979).

75. Michael Kerbel, *Henry Fonda: Pyramid Illustrated History of the Movies* (Pyramid, 1975).

76. Norm Goldstein, *Henry Fonda* (New York: Associated Press/Holt, Rinehart & Winston, 1982).

77. Ford.

78. Lawrence J. Quirk, *Claudette Colbert* (New York: Crown, 1985).

79. Otto Friedrich, *City of Nets: A Portrait of Hollywood in the 1940's* (New York: Harper & Row, 1986).

80. Wiley and Bona.

81. Wiley and Bona.

82. Wiley and Bona.

83. Wiley and Bona.

Index

287